VICTIMS, CRIME & SOCIETY

Sara Miller McCune founded SAGE Publishing in 1965 to support the dissemination of usable knowledge and educate a global community. SAGE publishes more than 1000 journals and over 800 new books each year, spanning a wide range of subject areas. Our growing selection of library products includes archives, data, case studies and video. SAGE remains majority owned by our founder and after her lifetime will become owned by a charitable trust that secures the company's continued independence.

Los Angeles | London | New Delhi | Singapore | Washington DC | Melbourne

VICTIMS, CRIME & SOCIETY

An Introduction

Pamela Davies, Peter Francis and Chris Greer

SECOND EDITION

Los Angeles | London | New Delhi
Singapore | Washington DC | Melbourne

Los Angeles | London | New Delhi
Singapore | Washington DC | Melbourne

SAGE Publications Ltd
1 Oliver's Yard
55 City Road
London EC1Y 1SP

SAGE Publications Inc.
2455 Teller Road
Thousand Oaks, California 91320

SAGE Publications India Pvt Ltd
B 1/I 1 Mohan Cooperative Industrial Area
Mathura Road
New Delhi 110 044

SAGE Publications Asia-Pacific Pte Ltd
3 Church Street
#10-04 Samsung Hub
Singapore 049483

Editor: Natalie Aguilera
Editorial assistant: Delayna Spencer
Production editor: Sarah Cooke
Marketing manager: Sally Ransom
Cover design: Francis Kenney
Typeset by: C&M Digitals (P) Ltd, Chennai, India

First published 2007
This second edition published 2017

Library of Congress Control Number: 2016957760

British Library Cataloguing in Publication data

A catalogue record for this book is available from the British Library

ISBN 978–1–44625–590–2
ISBN 978–1–44625–591–9 (pbk)

CONTENTS

DETAILED CONTENTS

LIST OF FIGURES AND TABLES

FIGURES

TABLES

NOTES ON CONTRIBUTORS

Hazel Croall has retired from her post of Professor in Criminology at Glasgow Caledonian University but retains an interest in several areas of criminology and criminal justice.

Pamela Davies is Associate Professor in Criminology in the Department of Social Sciences at Northumbria University.

Peter Francis is Professor in Criminology and Deputy Vice-Chancellor at Northumbria University.

Barry Godfrey is Professor in Social Justice at the University of Liverpool.

Chris Greer is Professor in Criminology and Head of Department of Sociology, City, University of London.

Matthew Hall is Professor in Law and Criminal Justice, and Director of Research, School of Law, University of Lincoln.

Murray Lee is Professor in Criminology at Sydney Law School, University of Sydney.

Michael Salter is Senior Lecturer in the Department of Sociology, Criminology & Anthroplogy, Western Sydney University.

Stephen Tomsen is Professor in Criminology and member of the Institute for Culture and Society at Western Sydney University.

Sandra Walklate is Professor and Eleanor Rathbone Chair in Sociology, School of Law and Social Justice, University of Liverpool conjoint with Professor of Criminology, Monash University and Editor in Chief of the British Journal of Criminology.

Colin Webster is Professor in Criminology in the School of Social Sciences, Leeds Beckett University.

ACKNOWLEDGEMENTS

We would like to extend our thanks to a number of people who have contributed to the production of this book. First, we would like to thank our esteemed contributors who turned around copy quickly and who then waited patiently for the three of us to bring together the contents in a coherent and structured way. With each edition we have approached academics to contribute whose work we have admired and this book has been no different. We are humbled that everyone we asked to contribute not only said yes, but took the task on with enthusiasm and produced chapters that are not only easily accessible, but also wonderfully engaging for the reader. Second, we would like to say a huge thank you to Natalie Aguilera and Delayna Spencer of SAGE who waited patiently for the final manuscript to land on their desk, and who offered constructive feedback on early drafts and effective support throughout. We look forward to continuing our long and successful relationship with you and SAGE. We would also like to note our thanks to Solveig Gardner Servian of Polar Publishing who delivered an excellent copy-editing service. Finally, but certainly not least, we would like to thank Gillian Howie of Northumbria University for her professional support in the administration of the book, liaising with contributors, SAGE and Polar, and doing so with good humour and willing endeavour at all times.

Pamela, Peter, Chris

1 VICTIMS, CRIME AND SOCIETY: AN INTRODUCTION

Pamela Davies, Peter Francis and Chris Greer

This is a book about victims of crime, survivors of abuse, the consequences of social harm, the nature of victimhood and the extent and impact of victimisation. It is a book concerned with the study of victims and victimisation, and is written from a critical perspective that seeks to: challenge taken-for-granted assumptions about the study of victimology; question key concepts and approaches to thinking about victims and survivors; critique ways of understanding the nature and extent of victimisation; and provide an alternative reading of many conventional approaches to responding to victims' needs and experiences. It is a book that provides students of criminology, criminal justice and victimology with an all-encompassing, in-depth critical analysis of the relationship between victims, crime and society. We hope it will become essential reading for anyone interested in understanding the social, political, economic and cultural context of victims in society, historically, contemporaneously and globally.

Throughout its chapters the book addresses a number of critical questions including: Who are the victims of crime? How did the study of victims emerge? What is the nature, extent and impact of victimisation? What are the core perspectives that shape victimological thinking? How do media constructions influence our understanding of crime victims and victimisation? What is the relationship between social relations, politics, globalisation, the economy and structure and agency in generating, exacerbating and/or obfuscating forms of victimisation? What are the factors that drive unequal experiences of victimisation across social groups, geographical locations, jurisdictions and historical periods? How can victimisation be managed, prevented and/or responded to?

Having studied and taught victimology for many years, it is our contention that these questions not only animate students' curiosity, and thus their criminological imagination, they also underpin important societal questions about the precise nature of crime, victimisation, harm and injustice in contemporary society. The study of victims and victimisation has converged with the discipline of criminology for many decades now. It is our view that over the next few decades victimology will become more contested as it continues to challenge at the heart of the study of crime and its control. Victimology has the potential to shape debates that affect the future landscape of victimisation and the ability and willingness of the state and its agencies to provide for victims of crime. Moreover, it has the capacity to challenge criminology to transform itself into a progressive social democratic discipline willing and able to provide a social blueprint for understanding and intervention. In order to explore those questions detailed above, and to bring alive what is after all a fast-moving (and exciting) area of academic study, the book is structured around three key central organising themes.

The first key organising theme is the relationship between theory, method and practice in making sense of victimhood and victimisation. It is here that we are interested in: the nature of media representation about victims and victimisation; the conceptual and theoretical approaches underpinning the study of victims and victimisation; the social construction of victimhood; the ways in which evidence about the nature, extent and impact of victimisation is uncovered and understood; and in the way in which victimological ideas, assumptions and approaches have developed and impacted on policy and practice over time and place, historically, internationally and globally.

The second key organising theme concerns the nature of criminal victimisation in relation to the intersecting and overlapping social divisions of class, race, age, religion, sexuality and gender. Beneath this rubric, the book explores: the unequal distribution of criminal victimisation; the patterning and nature of risk; the experiences of crime victims as groups and individuals; and the social, political and criminal justice response to both crime victims and criminal victimisation. It foregrounds how social divisions provide a useful starting point for understanding the complex and dynamic nature of criminal victimisation in society.

The third key organising theme explores the frequent tensions between social divisions, criminal victimisation and state policy and practice. Across the chapters of this book contributors explore the interconnections between theory, method and practice, all informing what to do about victimisation. It is important that this thematic is cross-cutting across all chapters in that a key message that runs throughout the book is that any dislocation between theory, research and intervention will invariably be unable to deliver evidence-based, theoretically informed, targeted and effective intervention capable of addressing the needs and rights of those identified as victims and survivors.

Specifically, chapters within this book critically examine and evaluate:

- the key conceptual, theoretical, methodological and empirical approaches that are important for understanding criminal victimisation in contemporary society;
- the core models of victimological thinking and their impact on policy and practice;
- the importance of media representation for understanding social divisions, inequality and criminal victimisation;
- the political, cultural, global and social context of criminal victimisation and public and 'official' responses;

- the role of social divisions – class, race and ethnicity, age, gender, sexuality, religion – in the unequal distribution, patterning and experiences of criminal victimisation;
- the various political, governmental and policy responses to crime victims and criminal victimisation and the role of the voluntary and community sectors in supporting victims of crime.

Our aim in the rest of this introductory chapter is to map out the key organising themes of the book, identify various 'golden threads' that run throughout its pages and, in so doing, introduce, contextualise and interconnect the various chapters that follow.

First, we introduce the importance of media analysis to an understanding of victims, crime and society. Second, we outline the various social research methods that have been used to uncover the nature, extent and impact of criminal victimisation. Third, we present the relationship between the study of victims, victimisation and justice – *victimology*, and the study of crime, criminalisation and crime control – *criminology,* and outline the key models of victimology. Fourth, we articulate the concept of social divisions as social categories, discuss their constructed nature and examine the connectedness between social divisions, inequality and victimisation. Fifth, we discuss political and policy responses to victimisation. Finally, we conclude this chapter by introducing the various pedagogic features that we have used throughout the book. Under each section we offer a brief summary of each thread, and offer further reading and 'pause for review' study questions.

MEDIA REPRESENTATIONS OF VICTIMS OF CRIME

The problem of crime is a 'socially constructed' problem. The same can be said of victimisation and social harm. Try telling the victim of a violent assault that their pain is 'socially constructed' and they are likely to give you short shrift. We are not proposing that criminal victimisation has no external reality, or that this reality is unknowable in any meaningful, empirical way. What we mean is that since most of us have limited first-hand experience of serious criminal victimisation, we are reliant on other sources of information for much of our knowledge about it. Few of these sources are more important than the media. Media representations contribute to shaping what the issues of crime, criminal victimisation and social harm 'mean' to people. They help to socially construct these issues by presenting particular 'views of reality'. There is no necessary connection, however, between what is constructed in the media and what is happening 'in the real world'. The issues of crime, victimisation and social harm, then, are highly mediatised. On this basis, it is our contention that any comprehensive critical exploration of crime victims, victimisation and wider social harm must engage with media constructions and (mis) representation.

As Stanley Cohen (1972) noted decades ago, while the media may not necessarily tell us what to think, they can be remarkably effective in shaping what we think about.

They are of fundamental importance to those who would promote a particular view of crime victims and victimisation, or seek to challenge or change existing views. They are a key site of contestation on which policy makers seek to legitimise and secure popular consent for new measures affecting victims of crime. Groups espousing competing values, interests and beliefs struggle to secure 'ownership' – and with it, political power – of a plurality of contested victim-related issues and debates across media forums.

In the digital age, where communications technologies occupy a central and increasingly important role in most people's lives, understanding complex social issues like crime and victimisation, control and social order requires engaging with media. As one of us has argued elsewhere (Greer, 2013: 143):

> The rapid and relentless development of information technologies over the past 100 years has shaped the modern era, transforming the relations between space, time and identity. Where once 'news' used to travel by ship, it now hurtles across the globe at light speed and is available 24 hours-a-day at the push of a button. Where once cultures used to be more or less distinguishable in national or geographical terms, they now mix, intermingle and converge in a constant global exchange of information. Where once a sense of community and belonging was derived primarily from established identities and local traditions, it may now also be found, and lost, in a virtual world of shared values, meanings and interpretations. In short, media are not only inseparable from contemporary social life; they are, for many, its defining characteristic.

In common with many countries, the UK is experiencing a proliferation of scandal, activated in the news media, relating to serious instances of criminal victimisation. Predatory sexual abuse within British institutions, in particular, has attracted unprecedented media attention following the death of the celebrity entertainer, presenter and charity campaigner Sir Jimmy Savile (Greer and McLaughlin, 2013, 2016). In October 2012, almost a year after his death, an ITV documentary examining claims of sexual abuse against him culminated in a joint report by the NSPCC and the Metropolitan Police, *Giving Victims a Voice* (Gray and Watt, 2013), which reported that 450 people had made complaints against Savile, with the period of alleged abuse stretching from 1955 to 2009. Some 214 criminal offences were recorded, with 34 rapes having been reported across 28 police forces. Savile was never charged during his lifetime (see Chapter 3).

New Zealand also has a chequered history in respect of scandals involving victimisations of the vulnerable. As Jordan (2015) points out, police responses to rape victims have ranged from the inadequate and inappropriate to the predatory and sexually abusive, including the recent uncovering of a series of rapes against young women perpetrated by serving police officers during the 1980s. Few women dared report their abuse in the climate of the time, and those who did, Jordan argues (2015), were met with the police code of silence. It took approximately 20 years before details of these crimes became public. While news media focus on the most newsworthy cases, due to their particular combination of 'news values' and victims' and/or parents' determination to keep the stories alive in the public eye, the vast majority of sexual victimisation remains unreported and invisible.

These examples briefly illustrate the importance of media representations in raising the visibility and the public and political salience of sexual violence against children and adults.

Yet one need only skim the chapter headings and index pages of the vast majority of victimology books to realise that consideration of media representations scarcely feature. This, for us, represents an important gap in the literature, and in this book we seek to contribute to filling that gap. It is not our contention that the reality of crime, inasmuch as it can be known empirically or experientially, is of secondary significance to what people *believe to be* the reality of crime. On the contrary, we are keen to point out that criminal victimisation tends to be disproportionately concentrated among some of the most vulnerable and marginalised sections of society. For these groups the pains of victimisation are experienced not only most often, but also most acutely. What we would insist, however, is that popular and political (mis)understanding of the nature, extent, distribution and experiences of criminal victimisation, of the risks of being victimised, of the measures that might be taken to reduce victimisation, and of victims' needs and victims' rights are, to a significant extent, shaped by the media.

PAUSE FOR REVIEW

How do media influence what the issues of crime, criminal victimisation and social harm 'mean' to people?

To what extent have media representations of victimisation and victims of crime more generally remained under-researched?

RESEARCHING VICTIMS AND VICTIMISATION

To read more about media representation and victims of crime see:

Greer, C. and Reiner, R. (2012) 'Media made criminality: the representation of crime in the mass media', in M. Maguire, R. Morgan and R. Reiner (eds), *The Oxford Handbook of Criminology* (3rd edn). Oxford: Oxford University Press.

The second golden thread connecting the chapters in this book concerns the methodologies, tools and techniques used to find out about victims, crime and victimisation. The recognition that official recorded criminal statistics may tell us more about the organisational processes involved in their collation and collection than about actual levels of crime has motivated criminologists and victimologists to seek out alternative sources of information about crime and criminal victimisation (Maguire, 2002). Today, two broad approaches to researching and uncovering victimisation can be identified: counting and measuring using quantitative survey methodologies, and observing, reading and listening through various qualitative approaches, alongside archival research, investigative journalism and campaigning. Each are discussed briefly below.

Since the crime survey was first developed in the US in the late 1960s, it has seemingly become the new orthodoxy (Maguire, 2012) in terms of research on victims and victimisation. Certainly the direct questioning of the victim of crime is central to the victimological enterprise, some of the features of which are generic to social surveys whereas others are specific responses to the problems of studying victimisation (Davies et al., 2003, 2011). With the growth in political and academic interest in crime victims during the 1960s and 1970s in the US and the 1980s in the UK, and the enormous impact of feminist research and methodologies, the victimisation survey began to emerge as an alternative source of information about victims of crime and criminal victimisation (Goodey, 2005). The US National Crime and Victimisation Survey (NCVS) established in 1973 is the longest running such national survey. The first British Crime Survey was conducted in 1982 following an experimental survey in London by Sparks et al. (1977), and within the UK similar surveys have been carried out in Scotland covering the Highlands and Islands on an annual basis since 2008 and in Northern Ireland since 2005. Today victim surveys are carried out in many countries across the globe, albeit in jurisdictions that have different historical and socio-legal traditions where surveys are based on different degrees of comparability in terms of the types of victimisation covered. Surveys are carried out in amongst other countries, Australia, Canada, Finland, France, Germany, the Netherlands, Sweden and New Zealand. In terms of methodological development, the Dutch, British and Swiss crime survey models have been especially influential in the European context.

Surveys are also conducted on different scales. National and city samples, though based on representative samples of the population and statistically significant – meaning they are representative and findings are generalisable – are relatively small, whereas the International Crime Victims Survey (ICVS) is a unique survey of the experience of being victimised in that it is standardised and far-reaching. The aim of the ICVS is to produce estimates of victimisation that can be used for international comparison. It has been carried out six times over the period 1989–2010, moving from computer-assisted telephone interviewing towards self-completion via the web. The sixth ICVS took place in 2009 in six countries – Canada, Denmark, Germany, the Netherlands, Sweden and the UK (Hoyle, 2012) – though in total it has been conducted in more than 80 countries. The survey provides a measure of common crimes to which the general public is exposed, including relatively minor offences such as petty theft as well as more serious crimes such as car thefts, sexual assaults or threats/assaults. For the crime types it covers, the survey asks about incidents that accord with legal definitions of common offences, using colloquial language.

As with other crime surveys, the ICVS largely ignores victimisation by complex crimes on collective populations, such as corruption or organised crime, thus limiting some comparisons of rates between countries (van Dijk, 2015). Furthermore, the comparatively small samples sizes preclude estimation of less prevalent crimes such as rapes or aggravated assaults. However, as van Kesteren et al. (2014) have highlighted by dwelling on four important areas of analysis, there are valuable ways in which victimologists can capitalise on the comparative nature of the ICVS. They particularly draw out the capacity the ICVS produces to look at victimisation experience at the level of both individuals and countries. First, they look at the level of crime in different countries according to the ICVS, compared to the picture from police figures where they point towards some distinct differences. The second focus concerns what ICVS measures of trends in crime show relative to trends in police figures. The third focus is on victims reporting crime to the police and their level of satisfaction with the police response, as well as the provision of and need for specialised victim assistance, underlining the importance of the ICVS as an instrument to monitor the implementation of international standards on victims' rights, and to benchmark national victim policies. Their fourth focus is on attitudes towards crime and criminal justice, looking in particular at similarities and differences across country populations. One feature is a multi-level analysis of the social correlates of public attitudes towards punishment, in particular differentiating between victims and non-victims.

In making the case for survey-based comparative measures of crime, van Dijk has argued that stand-alone national victimisation surveys, with their varying methodologies and questionnaires, cannot reliably be used for cross-national comparisons (see Box 1.1).

BOX 1.1 THE CASE FOR SURVEY-BASED COMPARATIVE MEASURES OF CRIME

As regards the unreliability of national victimisation surveys for cross-national comparisons, van Dijk argues:

> This is especially true for older versions of such surveys, modelled after the National Crime Victimization Survey (NCVS) of the USA, which try to mimic their country's official statistics of police-recorded crimes. Victimization surveys in the European tradition use less legalistic definitions of the public's experiences of crime and are therefore more conducive to international standardization. When such surveys are standardized to cover the common ground of crime in multiple jurisdictions, as is the case in the International Crime Victims Survey, they can provide comparable data on the level and trends of crime of individual nations at relatively modest costs. In addition, such surveys can provide comparative data on crime reporting by victims, on satisfaction with responses from police and other agencies, as well as on public attitudes towards safety and criminal justice. (van Dijk, 2015: 437)

The purpose of surveys can differ too. Crime surveys have been carried out with the intention of uncovering crime and victimisation in the context of business and retailing. The Commercial Victimisation Survey (CVS) is an example of a large scale survey that examines the extent of crime against businesses in England and Wales. The first CVS dates back to 1994, more than ten years after the first British Crime Survey. Also conducted in 2002, it has been an annual survey since 2012. Each year a selection of industry sectors is included in the sample. The 2014 CVS focused on premises in three industry sectors:

agriculture, forestry and fishing; wholesale and retail trade; and accommodation and food services activities.

Another large-scale survey is the Retail Crime Survey (RCS). This is undertaken by the British Retail Consortium, which maintains that crime remains a persistent problem for businesses whether in the form of theft, violence against shop staff or cyber-based threats (BRC, 2016). Since the early 1990s it has been conducted on an annual basis and provides for detailed reports on each major type of retail crime with a separate reporting for the small and medium enterprise (SME) sector for each type of crime. The findings from this survey report on the cost of theft, fraud and cyber-crime to the retail sector with information on 'insider' employee thefts and frauds as well as customer thefts, burglary, robbery, criminal damage, and violence against staff. Similar questionnaires to the first International Crime Business Survey (see below) were used in Australia, Estonia and South Africa in 1994, 1997 and 1998 respectively. National surveys on the retail sector took place in Australia in 1999, south-western Finland in 1994–95 and between 1995 and 1999 in St. Petersburg, Latvia and Lithuania to address the issue of the security of foreign businesses (Alvazzi Del Frate, 2004).

The first International Commercial Crime Survey (ICCS) was carried out in 1994 when eight countries participated. Six years later in 2000 an International Crime Business Survey (ICBS) was conducted in nine central-eastern European capital cities (Alvazzi Del Frate, 2004). Despite attempts to obtain a standardised and comparable approach to all of the surveys and use of a standard questionnaire in all countries, alongside a standard mode of interviewing, important differences remained in the approach to sampling, translation of questions into different national languages, interview lengths and response rates, which make comparisons of both international crime victimisation and international commercial and business victimisation problematic.

Surveying victims has become one of the most flexible and rewarding research methodologies, facilitating the generation of details about the circumstances of the offence, relationships between victims, and victims' experiences of the various criminal justice agencies. Davies et al. (2011) (See also Davies and Francis, 2017) demonstrate how the refinement and development of the crime victimisation survey in the US and Europe has made it universally known that police recorded crimes form only a small part of the total volume of crime, and have helped provide insights into victims' experiences, perceptions and worries of crime and of the criminal justice system. In a variety of ways, surveys of victims have been concerned with differing dimensions of victimisation. They help capture data about trends, victims' experiences, static risks (gender, age, social class and race), dynamic risks (risks that are amenable to change) and impacts of victimisation. These include reasons for: under-reporting and under-recording; the correlates of victimisation; the risk of victimisation; the fear of crime and its relationship to the probability of victimisation; the experience of crime from the viewpoint of victims; and the treatment of victims in the criminal justice system.

Whatever the purpose, size, focus and nature of survey used, however, they are not without criticism. These criticisms range from the simple, such as they can often assume a level of literacy and/or understanding amongst the sample population that may not be available, to the more complex. In particular, they have been criticised for not being able to get behind the mere appearance of things. Less visible harms are much more difficult to capture by survey method. Harms arising from mass pollution for example, that affect large populations, are difficult to capture, and measures of crimes such as fraud are not adequately captured.

Moreover, victimisation surveys are unable to situate and contextualise victimisation with the everyday lives and routine activities that each of us engages in. They are unable to situate our experiences of crime and victimisation within socio-economic, cultural and political contexts. In addition, surveys can often reflect the agenda and priorities of those carrying out the research or consultation rather than the participants involved as subjects. Victim surveys are closely tied to the confines of the criminological and victimological enterprises. Therefore, such surveys are often viewed as inappropriate to questions raised by forms of thinking which view such enterprises as constraining and instead seek to add a critical edge by locating victimisation in wider structural issues.

As a consequence, some victimologists have looked beyond the victimisation survey to more qualitative methods of research and inquiry, involving forms of observing and listening through ethnographic interaction. Indeed, many have heeded the clarion call for triangulation to pick and mix and match different methods for different areas of research. Sandra Walklate (2003: 41), for example, has suggested that exploration of the complexity of human interaction through time and space demands a research agenda which goes beyond the victimisation survey. Similarly, Roger Matthews (2010) has identified the need to use a mixed method approach in acknowledgement that the method must fit the question and the context within which it is being asked. The kind of framework supported by Walklate and Matthews is one that locates victimisation within a socio-economic, global, cultural and political context and which examines the processes that go on behind people's backs which contribute to the victims (and the crimes) we see as opposed to those we do not see. For Walklate research may involve comparison, triangulation of method and longitudinal studies.

Alongside a call for a mixed method approach to doing victimological research (Davies and Francis, 2017), much knowledge about injustice and forms of victimisation has been developed through archival explorations, historiography, investigative journalism and campaigning. Whilst the former can involve very clear rules and forms of engagement in the use of historical documents to uncover the nature and form of victimisation in specific periods of time, the latter are more loosely applied and sometimes opportunistic, if no less compelling in terms of the information that they provide in terms of our understanding of victims and victimisation. Class, race, age and gender all play their part in locating victimisation in wider structural issues as do personal histories, habits and behaviours.

Throughout the book, each chapter explores the ways in which victims of crime are rendered visible through documenting and cataloguing their experiences either by counting and measuring and/or observing and listening. They examine how victimisation is uncovered and how unreported victimisation remains an issue as they trace the development of the ways in which the socially divided nature of victimisation is increasingly appreciated and understood.

What are the main strengths and weaknesses of the crime survey method in uncovering victims' experiences of crime and victimisation?

What methods fall under the broad heading of 'ethnographic approaches', and how do they contribute to the study of victims and victimisation?

PAUSE FOR REVIEW

VICTIMOLOGICAL THEORY AND CONTEXT

To read more about researching and investigating victims and victimisation see:

Deakin, J. and Spencer, J. (2011) 'Sensitive survey research: an oxymoron?', in P. Davies, P. Francis and V. Jupp (eds), *Doing Criminological Research* (2nd edn). London: Sage.

van Kesteren, J., van Dijk, J. and Mayhew, P. (2014) 'The international crime victims surveys: a retrospective', *International Review of Victimology*, 20(1): 49–69.

The third thread situates and locates the study of victims and victimisation within a theoretical and political context – one that is broadly critical in aim and approach. It is informed by the importance of delivering social justice.

Victimology – the study of victims of crime – emerged in the 1940s, and is now an established if contested disciplinary enterprise (Fattah, 1992; Goodey, 2005; Walklate, 2007). It has influenced the discipline of criminology and the social sciences more broadly, and has, as will be seen in later sections, made an important contribution to developments in criminal justice, crime prevention and restorative justice, to conflict resolution and mediation. Certainly debates about victim's needs and rights are now fundamental to policy and practice surrounding crime and its control as a consequence of the contribution made by victimology and victimologists.

Victimology can be viewed as catholic in its incorporation of people and ideas (Rock, 2010). For some it is an established academic discipline, while at the very least, an important and substantial sub-discipline of criminology for others (Walklate, 2007). Without doubt there are today striking similarities between victimology and criminology (Karmen, 2016). The study of victims and victimisation underpins much criminological work, and many victimological perspectives draw from a broad criminological heritage. Moreover, victimology does not have a single viewpoint but is made up of a variety of often competing perspectives reflecting various historic, political, disciplinary and personal standpoints, but unlike criminology, victimology's disciplinary historical narrative is much shorter, its content more focused and its influence within the wider social science disciplines less well developed. It shares many conceptual, theoretical and methodological ideas and perspectives, tools and techniques with criminology yet at the same time, many victimologists continue to map out a separate narrative for victimology, boasting of its own association, academic journals, networks, annual conferences and academic champions.

Victimology ensures that the victim of crime, victimisation, and more recently those identified as experiencing social harm (Hillyard et al., 2004, 2005), as well as survivors of abuse and injustices, receive much-needed academic and scholarly attention, and simultaneously, exposure to policy makers, practitioners and ultimately, state officials. Simply put, victimology has provided an opportunity to uncover, to expose and to address the needs and rights of those less heard, and this remains the case today, especially given the role of the state and its agencies, as well as corporations, big business and organisations as victimisers, often unwilling to either acknowledge their own wrongdoing, and/or that of others.

As noted above, the historical narrative of victimology is much shorter than that of criminology. Whilst the origins of criminology as a philosophy of criminal justice can be dated to the 18th century Enlightenment and as a science of the criminal to the late 19th century, victimology's evolution is more recent (Walklate, 2003). Victimology emerged in the mid-20th century and has matured only in the last 45 or so years (see Chapter 5). It must also be remembered that as recently as the late-1960s, criminology offered little or no in depth analysis of the victim. Even within studies of criminal justice, the victim remained until recently a forgotten 'actor' in the analysis and exposure of the machinery and delivery of justice. The early pioneers of the study of victims of crime were academic European lawyers and human scientists, many of whom worked on the fringes of law, criminology and psychiatry (Rock, 2010; Walklate et al., 2011). And whilst Fattah (1992) notes that the term 'victimology' was first used by Wertham in 1949, most commentators ascribe the title of 'founder' of victimology to von Hentig (Walklate, 2007; Spalek, 2006; Rock, 2010). It was von Hentig who noted in 1940 the potential that an understanding of 'victim' attributes, motives and experiences could contribute to furthering the investigation of crime and its control.

Numerous attempts have been made to categorise and describe the core theoretical perspectives in victimology. Walklate (2007) and Spalek (2006), for example, list positivist, radical, feminist and critical victimologies, whilst Karmen (2016) identifies three perspectives: conservative, liberal and radical-critical. Often commentators attempt to show how each perspective has its own disciplinary history, framework and academic reference points, offers its own understanding of the type and nature of victimisation and the problem of crime, and articulates a specific viewpoint on the response of the state to victims of crime and the role of the charitable and voluntary sector in providing support to victims of crime. Often these same commentators fail to discuss the interconnections between each and with criminology, as well as their relative influence. For the purpose of this book we favour the view that two basic models of victimology can be identified. The history of victimology is one of competition between these two models or ways of thinking about victims and victimisation.

The first model is an extension of the scientific victimology that emerged with von Hentig during the mid-20th century, and is often referred to as 'positivist', administrative or 'conservative' victimology. It is a model that predominates much academic and political thinking, defines victims predominantly through legal means and whose perspectives variously utilize concepts of 'risk', 'precipitation', 'proneness' and 'lifestyle' to explain crime victimisation. This model views most forms of criminal victimisation as an interaction between victim and offender and seeks to understand the role victims might play in their own victimisation as part of that interactive process. The second model is a product of social and political change and is associated with the radical and critical social sciences that developed in the 1960s, in direct opposition to positivist thinking. It is a model concerned with the politics of victimisation, and comprises perspectives that offer analyses informed by concepts of power, gender, dominance and control. It is a model predominantly interested in the processes through which victims and victimisation are constructed, reconstructed, sustained, maintained or denied, and includes 'radical', 'feminist' and 'critical' victimologies.

Neither of the two broad models is aligned to a specific political ideology. Both models comprise various perspectives, ideas and commentaries, and there are many contradictions and contradistinctions within each model. Each model adheres to certain 'domain' assumptions about the problem of crime and victimisation (Walklate, 2007), and these form the basis upon which contemporary victimological debate has developed and matured. Significantly, these models differ as to how each conceptualises the term 'victim'. As students of criminology and criminal justice, you will be acutely aware that not all activities which are harmful are criminalised, and thus those victimised may not acquire the term 'victim'. Others who do experience crime may still fail to acquire the label 'victim', and the chapters in this volume address how and why this is the case. Finally, some individuals who acquire the term 'victim' may not define themselves as such, and may wish to reject the label and the implications that may arise from its application. Christie (1986) gave claim to the notion of the 'ideal' victim, against which all others are measured, whilst Carrabine et al. (2004: 115) refer to 'hierarchies of victimization' whereby 'some victims enjoy a higher status in the crime discourse, and their experiences of victimization are taken more seriously than others'.

The term 'victim' is to a large extent defined along disciplinary and political lines. Conservative or positive victimologies, for example, usually work with a legal definition of crime, and thus maintain a legalistic conception of the crime victim. In contrast, radical and critical victimologies look to deconstruct the term and its use. Some prefer to use the term 'survivor'. Others, in acknowledgement of the limitations of the term 'crime', refer to 'victims of social harm' in order to better reflect the broader aspects of social and political victimisation that arise as a result of the troubles of everyday life.

It is our view that much that can be found under the umbrella headings of positivist and conservative victimology is flawed as a consequence of its conceptual naivety, theoretical limitations, methodological positivism and interventionist focus (Francis, 2016). Our preference is for those victimologies that draw upon radical and critical ideas in that they focus attention towards: the interconnections between structure and agency; the impact that social, political, global and economic conditions have on crime and victimisation; an analysis of the nature and form of late modern predatory capitalism and its impact on crime and victimisation; the role of the state and its agencies; and the role that corporations and big businesses have on the social construction of crime. It is our view that such victimologies contribute significantly to understanding the interrelationships between inequality, vulnerability and victimisation in time and place.

As noted already, the contributors to this volume are concerned not only to explore and explain the nature and extent of criminal and non-criminal victimisation in contemporary society, but also to understand the unequal distribution and experience of that victimisation through reference to social division and inequality. Inequality is understood as being a necessary by-product of the current political-economic and social-cultural arrangements of late modern society. Crime, victimisation, social division and inequality all simultaneously derive from and feed into wider structures of inclusion and exclusion, power and subordination, containment and control. As such, they are defining features of the contemporary social and criminal justice landscape.

Radical and critical criminology has a long and varied history within the criminological academy. Partly in response to the atheoretical, ahistorical, situationally oriented approaches of the conservative administrative criminologies resulting from the Home Office 'what works' mantra of the 1980s, critical criminology has undergone something of a recent resurgence. One of its central aims is to reinforce and tighten the links between criminology and its theoretical and political moorings, at a time when administrative criminology risks casting it adrift from both. Whilst conservative/administrative criminologists pay at best secondary attention to the causes of crime, radical and critical criminologists consider an appreciation of aetiology to be fundamental, not least because many of the sources of criminal behaviour, and thus criminal victimisation, can be found in the political and economic structures of late capitalist societies. Whilst administrative criminologists retain a narrow definition of crime – in many ways reflecting tabloid representations of street violence, burglary, car theft and vandalism – critical criminologists are keen to convey that much suffering through criminal victimisation results from the activities of the powerful. Corporate and white-collar offending, state crimes, deaths in custody, everyday experiences of racial and sexual violence and prejudice, and social exclusion can all be understood in terms of political and economic power and the unequal distribution of social justice in society.

Thus, a critical approach is shared across each of the contributions in this volume. Whether discussing race, religion, age, gender, sexuality, class or media constructions of these social categories and their connection to images of crime and victimisation, analysis is informed by an appreciation of the political economy of crime and criminal victimisation and a desire to highlight victimisation caused by the powerful as a pressing and ongoing concern.

What are the similarities and differences between victimology and criminology?

What are the overarching models and specific perspectives in victimology and what are their key concepts, assumptions and approaches?

PAUSE FOR REVIEW

SOCIAL CATEGORIES, INEQUALITY AND VICTIMISATION

To read more about victimology, theory and context see:

Mawby, R.I. and Walklate, S. (1994) *Critical Victimology: International Perspectives*. London: Sage.

Walklate, S. (2007) *Imagining the Victim of Crime*. Buckingham: Open University Press.

Everyday social existence involves the definition and continual reassessment of 'who we are'. An important part of defining 'who we are' is determining who we are not. Our sense of 'self' and our construction of 'who we are' is defined, to a significant extent, in contradistinction to conceptions of the 'other'. Notions of 'self' and 'other' can be isolated and highly individualised or shared and deeply embedded in culture. Sometimes they are institutionalised and become custom or law. Sometimes they remain marginal, and are considered quirky or eccentric. Sometimes their expression provokes censure and approbation. What is crucial is that constructions of 'self' and 'other' are intimately connected to the power relations that permeate the social and cultural world. We all live in a set of patterned and structured relations of unequal status and power – political, cultural or economic, for example. These relations can both free up and constrain our everyday lives. Having more money opens up certain opportunities which remain closed to those who have less. Having power and influence may open doors which would otherwise remain shut. These relations of power which help to shape our everyday experiences are bounded by social divisions.

Social divisions are social categories. Such categories can include race and ethnicity, gender, age, class, sexuality, disability, and mental health. Social categories are not static, but rather dynamic and change over time, space and place. As Best (2005: 324) states, 'Social categories are not simply given, they have to be established and maintained and the process through which they appear is known as *social division*.' They are situated historically, culturally, economically and politically. Cultural and economic transformations over the last few decades, such as deindustrialisation and globalisation, have each impacted upon the nature of social division. Best, for example, discusses how the concept of globalisation has 'racialised our notions of citizenship, and led us to question the validity of the nation state as a political entity' (2005: 2). In one sense, social divisions are arbitrary.

Yet they are also enduring. For Best, the most enduring social divisions are those we believe are rooted in nature. In this sense, the most enduring social divisions portray continuity. Being young and working class, for example, continues to represent disadvantage, marginalisation and exclusion.

In 2007 we were acutely conscious of the problems relating to structuring that book according to what may appear, superficially at least, to be distinct and separate structural variables. We acknowledged that the intersectionalities of class-race-age-gender or multiple inequalities variously combine 'as intersecting, interlocking and contingent' (Daly, 1997: 33). We have now stretched the content of this book to include dimensions of religion and sexuality. We could have stretched the content further, to be even more comprehensive including chapters on mental health and disability, and we discussed this as editors and authors. We may have been more inclusive in these respects were it not for the fact that in relation to crime victims and criminal victimisation, these areas, as in 2007, remain under-researched.

The social categories upon which this book primarily focuses – class, race and ethnicity, religion, age, gender, sexuality – happen also to be the major social inequalities in our society. To be poor, to be black, to be young, to be female and/or to experience a particular sexuality or enjoy a particular religious belief simultaneously represents different distinct social categories with combined significance and relation to relative disadvantage, exclusion, marginalisation and powerlessness. We do not all start life equally. We come into it as unequal individuals. Advantage and disadvantage are therefore with us from the start, and the nature and impact of these social structural inequalities persist and change over time, place and space. Moreover, inequality is situated across and within generations. Our experiences in childhood may well affect our experiences later in life, and these will often affect our children's experiences as well. Who we fall in love with is often constrained by inequalities. And, importantly for this book, our experiences, fears, vulnerabilities and perceptions of crime and victimisation are experienced through social divisions of inequality.

Whereas social divisions remain one of the driving themes of the book as a whole, individual chapters are connected by an assessment of social inequality, risk, vulnerability and victimisation. Since the mid-1990s, reported and recorded rates of crime and victimisation have fallen across many countries including the US, Canada, England and Wales. Figure 1.1 provides detail of the reported and recorded crime and victimisation for England and Wales.

In England and Wales (Allen, 2016):

- Reported rates of victimisation rose steadily reaching a peak in 1995, before dropping markedly until 2005, and since this time the underlying trend has been downwards, albeit with fluctuation in year.
- In the year ending March 2016, there were 6.3 million incidents of crime experienced by adults aged 16 or over, 6 per cent fewer than the previous year.
- In 2016 it was estimated that around 15 per cent of adults aged over 16 were a victim of crime in the preceding year (around 7 million residents of England and Wales).

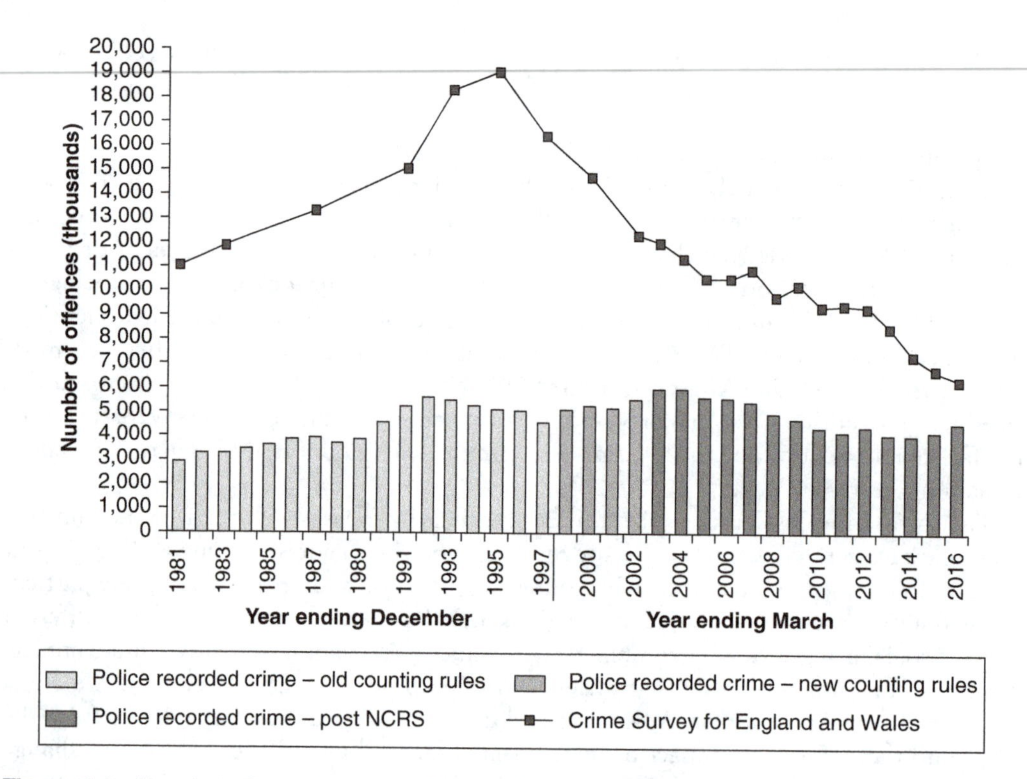

Figure 1.1 Trends in Crime Survey for England and Wales and police recorded crime, year ending December 1981 to year ending March 2016 (Allan, 2016)

- Recorded crime also showed a similar upward and downward trajectory, reaching a peak in 1992, before falling until 1997. From this date there have been variations and fluctuations as a result of police counting rule changes in 1998 and 2002, before a reduction in police recorded crime from 2004 to 2014, with the increase post-2014 being attributed to the quality of police recording rather than actual increases in crime rates.
- While the figure exposes many crimes and victim experiences, they exclude many serious but low-volume offences including homicide, and sexual offences as well as crime against children.
- The likelihood of being a victim of crime has fallen from around 40 in every 100 adults in 1995, to around 23 in 100 in 2006, to around 15 in every 100 adults in 2016.

In 2016, Crime Survey for England and Wales (CSEW) (Allan, 2016) included fraud and computer misuse for the first time, and it shows an estimated 5.8 million fraud and computer misuse offences (3.8 million fraud and 2 million computer misuse) experienced by adults in the 12 months prior to interview. It must also be noted that the CSEW estimates of victimisation amongst children aged 10–15 are not directly comparable with the main survey reported above. In the year 2015/16, the CSEW estimated that around 13 in 100 children aged 10–15 were victims of at least one crime. A total of 844,000 crimes were experienced by children, of which 49 per cent were categorised as violent crimes (418,000) whilst most of the remainder were thefts of personal property (274,000).

There have been a number of attempts to understand the reasons for the reduction in crime and victimisation in England and Wales, and also further afield, although there remains much debate as to the significance and clarity of argument around the studies. For some, more and better use of security by individuals and organisations is the single biggest factor associated with the crime drop (Farrell, 2013). While there is some merit in this thesis, it is too empiricist in its approach and fails to adequately assess the impact of other notable variables including demographic change, globalisation, economic prosperity, incarceration, and amongst other variables, the lag associated with the extension of credit linked to housing and mortgages (Lynch, 2013).

A central contention of this book, as with its predecessor, is that criminal victimisation is felt most often and most acutely by the most marginalised and powerless sections of society. At the same time, prevailing definitions of victim and victimisation – in terms of who can or cannot legitimately claim victim status, who is or is not deserving of social support or media attention – does much to reify dominant white, male, middle-class, heterosexual discourses on crime and control. They reinforce rather than challenge existing structures of power. In so doing, they help to maintain the social, political and economic conditions under which much victimisation takes place. It is within this critical framework, sensitised in particular to the issues of inequality, social justice and inclusion and exclusion, that all the contributions in this book are located. For these reasons, this book – as was the 2007 edition – is a political book. As Currie (2010: 118) has noted, the aim of a critical criminology is:

> taking crime seriously; recognising that it disproportionally afflicts the most vulnerable; understanding its roots in the economic disadvantages; social deviants and cultural distortions characteristic of (but not limited to) predatory capitalism, insisting that those conditions are modifiable by concerted social action, and acknowledging the usefulness of some smaller scale interventions that stand the test of evidence – while rejecting as counter-productive and unjust the massive expansion of repression as a response to crime.

Indeed, it is important to note that the figures and surveys reported on above:

- confirm findings from previous surveys that suggest there are fairly high rates of under-reporting and under-recording of crime and victimisation to the police, and that rates of both are contingent on a range of interrelated factors such as offence type, victim characteristics (young, old, black, white, male, female, straight, gay), previous experiences and, among other factors, perception of the police response.
- mask variation in people's risk and vulnerability to crime and victimisation. The CSEW has since its inception (and before that the British Crime Survey) provided evidence that crime and victimisation are unevenly distributed across and between groups of individuals based upon their ethnicity, gender, age, class, lifestyle, relationships and so on.

- continue to indicate that geographic patterns and concentrations of offences vary by crime type. Variations differ across regions, in urban and rural areas, and between most employment-deprived and least unemployment-deprived areas.
- are unable to uncover the impact that crime and victimisation have on individuals. After all, the impact that victimisation has upon an individual is again dependent upon a range of factors, many of which are, to use Daly's phrase, intersecting, interlocking and contingent.

The differential risk rates associated with specific categories of social division are considered in detail across the different chapters in this book. Here we want to stress that these categories should not be viewed as static and separate but as interconnecting and closely related. Hope and Chester (2011), for example, drawing on extensive analysis of the British Crime Survey and the social distribution of household property crime in England and Wales, highlight that substantial inequality exists in the distribution of household crime, specifically its concentration in a small proportion of the population and types of residential areas, and that the distribution of crime victimisation is related to the distribution of socio-economic inequality, with the risk of victimisation highest amongst the poorer residents of high-risk areas with high levels of social deprivation.

Similarly, examining data drawn from the BCS alongside socio-economic data, Dixon et al. (2006) highlight three specific findings in relation to income, victimisation and concern. These are:

- Richer households are more likely to be victims of some crimes, such as vehicle crime and criminal damage.
- Poorer households are more likely to be victims of serious intrusive crime such as burglary, mugging and domestic violence.
- Poorer households are much more likely to report being very worried about specific types of crime and feeling unsafe when walking alone after dark. Importantly, the difference in concern is greater than the difference in victimisation.

The broad finding is that that those people most likely to be victimised by crime and to experience social harm in England and Wales are often the most marginalised social groups living in the poorest areas (Zedner, 2002). Vulnerability to crime, risk and fear of crime are exacerbated by social, economic and political exclusion. Dixon et al. provide similar findings for ethnicity, age and gender. There are also interesting points to be noted in relation to age and gender. Young people, for example, are often the most likely to be criminally victimised, and risk of victimisation declines with age. But gender also affects the risk and vulnerability of younger and older people. And so on.

However, while the crime survey can offer insights into inequality, vulnerability and victimisation, this method of analysis also has its problems (Hope, 2007). Tim Hope (2015) has noted that what we might know about inequality, crime and victimisation is constrained by changes in the way in which crime surveys are sampled and delivered in England and Wales:

> One of the most significant changes that happened almost by stealth was that the BCS/EWCS ceased to be a crime survey and became a police performance survey instead. Earlier BCS samples had been weighted to over-select inner-city (socially deprived) areas in order to ensure there were enough victims to study. Nevertheless, during the Blair administration the sampling design was changed so that 'inner city' (high crime) areas were under-sampled, while suburban and rural (low crime) areas were over-sampled, ostensibly in order to provide sufficient 'customer' representation in every police force area (Hope, 2015: no page number).

Not only did this result in a huge sample size, but clearly it also inflated the number of non-victims in the sample (and may well have reduced the count of crime accordingly). At the same time, living in a socially deprived area ceased to be a 'risk factor' for crime victimisation, even though it had previously been the main predictor not only of victimisation risk but also of repeat victimisation (something that the government had once tried to do something about). In short, who knows how many more chronic victims are now being overlooked?

PAUSE FOR REVIEW

Why is the concept of power important in understanding social divisions and social categories?

What are the key elements associated with the likelihood of being victimised and how do these differ by crime and type of social harm?

POLITICAL AND POLICY APPROACHES TO VICTIMS OF CRIME

To read more about social categories, inequality and victimisation see:

Croall, H. (2011) *Crime and Society in Britain* (2nd edn). Harlow: Pearson.

Hope, T. (2015) 'We need a different crime survey', *Centre for Crime and Justice Studies*, May 2015. Available at www.crimeandjustice.org.uk/resources/we-need-different-crime-survey (accessed 12.9.16).

The fifth key thread that interconnects the chapters in this book is that of political and policy responses to victims of crime. Victims of crime that often appear in the public arena usually do so because they have made contact with the police (or the criminal justice system as witnesses). The criminal justice system relies on victims and witnesses in a number of ways, including reporting crimes and furnishing the police with information to build evidence for a court case to prosecute an offender. These individuals are already a selective category of crime victim and a socially divided group. They have become separated from other victims of crime and social harm because they have become part of the political and policy process, and thus, in relative terms, what we might call 'visible victims'. These are the people whose victimisation has come to official notice. Their experiences are officially known about and they may qualify for assistance and support. Where public policy and practice for victims is concerned, they might be considered the lucky ones.

However, even at this stage this may not be the case. For example, they may experience secondary victimisation. Secondary victimisation occurs at the hands of criminal justice system staff or anyone else responding to an offence. It results from the insensitive treatment of victims of crime – often inadvertently – by the criminal justice system or by friends and acquaintances. For example, a young person may find their account of an alleged criminal assault being tested by police officers or social workers to the extent that they feel their truthfulness is being questioned.

One of the major developments arising from a recognition of the importance of victims as witnesses is Witness Service support. Between 1989 and 2015 Victim Support delivered a Witness Service, piloted first in selected Crown Courts then extended to all criminal courts in England and Wales by 2003. It provided emotional support and practical help for prosecution and defence witnesses as well as their family and friends (Wolhuter et al., 2009), with the aim of making the experience of being in court less daunting and confusing. As part of this, they arranged pre-trial courtroom tours, supported witnesses during the trial, and provided witnesses with private waiting areas in court. While scholars of the criminal justice system have spent time thinking about the identity of a victim, witnesses have largely been ignored (Cook and Davies, 2016). The extent to which evolving support and provisions have been introduced to meet the wants and needs of a generic victim has been the topic of critical scrutiny. Several have concluded that developments ostensibly in support of the victim can be seen rather differently, not as primarily in the interests of victims and witnesses but as efficiency measures designed to improve the smooth running of the criminal justice system and to build evidence for the successful prosecution in court of an offender, and to please the voting public (Duggan and Heap, 2014).

Very few victims of crime seek help and public support and assistance of their own accord. For the vast majority of victims who become users of services provided by the criminal justice system or supportive provisions funded by the government, few will seek help spontaneously. Most will take up the offer of practical assistance and emotional support after having been referred by the police. For enormous numbers of people who are socially harmed or criminally victimised it is more difficult for them to access services, and some are even excluded from making use of some schemes because they have not come into the public arena of the criminal justice system or managed to make their victimisation visible.

Landmark dates in the development of victim support and services in England and Wales are detailed in Table 1.1. Many changes have been introduced, particularly since 1990, aimed at 're-balancing' the system in favour of victims (and, by implication, at the expense of offenders) and, it is now almost sixty years since Steven Schafer (1968) described the crime victim as the Cinderella of the criminal justice system. Since Schafer described the victim in this way, criminal justice policies across the globe have been mobilised to bring

Table 1.1 Landmark dates in the development of victim support policy

Date	Action
1964	Criminal Injuries Compensation Board (CICB) set up to administer the Criminal Injuries Compensation Scheme (CICS) for victims of violent crime
1972	First UK women's refuge set up for victims of domestic violence in Chiswick, London
1974	First Victim Support project set up in Bristol, England
1976	First UK rape crisis centre opened, London, England
1981	Creation of British Crime Survey
1982	First British Crime Survey Roger Graef's TV documentary on the treatment of women reporting rape
1985	UN declaration of the basic principles of justice for victims of crime and abuse of power
1986	Childline established The Islington Crime Survey
1987	First Domestic Violence Unit established in London (Tottenham) First Home Office funding for Victim Support
1989	Victim Support launch the first Victim/Witness in Court pilot
1990	Home Office Victim's Charter published
1991	Launch of the Citizen's Charter Crown Court Witness Service introduced
1993	James Bulger murdered Stephen Lawrence murdered
1996	Home Office Victims Charter revised 2nd edition 'One Stop Shops' and 'Victim Statements' piloted
1998	Crime and Disorder Act – reparation for victims of young offenders
1999	Youth Justice and Criminal Evidence Act – vulnerable witness provision Publication of the Macpherson report into the Stephen Lawrence investigation Witness Service in Magistrates Courts introduced
2001	Victim Personal Statements (VPS) introduced
2002	Home Office Victims Charter revised 3rd edition
2003	'Securing the attendance of witnesses in court', consultation paper Victim Support provides a Witness Service in all criminal courts
2004	Domestic Violence, Crime and Victims Act Victims Fund – to develop services for victims of sexual offending Establishment of the Victims Advisory Panel – giving victims a greater voice in policy making
2005	'Rebuilding Lives: Supporting Victims' Green Paper – victim support to prioritise practical and emotional help, as well as financial compensation *The Code of Practice for Victims of Crime* published
2006	Code of Practice for Victims of Crime – creation of statutory obligations on the Criminal Justice System to provide minimum standard of service to victims Recruitment of a Commissioner for Victims and Witnesses
2007	The Witness Charter published
2008	Criminal Evidence (Witness Anonymous) Act

(Continued)

Table 1.1 (Continued)

Date	Action
2009	Sarah Payne appointed first Victims' Champion
2010	Louise Casey appointed as first Victims' Commissioner Jonathan Djanogly MP appointed Victims Minister
2012	Hillsborough Independent Panel releases its findings detailing numerous failings of authorities on the day of the 1989 football tragedy.
2013	A revised *Code of Practice for Victims of Crime* published *The Witness Charter: Standards of Care for Witnesses in the Criminal Justice System* published Victims' Right to RevietMinistry of Justice publishes 2010 to 2015 government policy: victims of crime
2014	Independent inquiry into child sexual abuse announced Domestic Violence Disclosure Scheme - Clare's Law
2015	Revised *Code of Practice for Victims of Crime* published
2016	The Inquest into the Hillsborough football disaster delivers its verdict that 96 football fans were unlawfully killed.

the victim centre stage with policies increasingly framed in terms of the needs and rights of the victim, and justified in their name. Victims' 'rights' debates are increasingly central to developments in different criminal justice systems (Davies, 2015). However, the 'rights' of the victim in penal procedure in common law countries such as England and Wales, Australia, Canada, New Zealand and most of the US are largely limited to that of witness for the prosecution, though changes have recently seen the granting of participatory rights for crime victims as part of a concerted endeavour to bring the victim to the forefront.

Certain time periods can be identified with specific social groups achieving victimological recognition. The re-emergence of the feminist movement was enormously influential in the development of services for victims of rape, sexual assault and domestic violence in the 1970s and well into the 1980s in both the US and UK. In England and Wales, Victim Support (VS) emerged in the 1970s and spread throughout the UK. In doing so it became established as the national victims' service, offering support for victims of most types of crime becoming an increasingly professionalised example of community-based support. Since the 1990s, a proliferation of different victimagogic activities have occurred, blurring the boundaries of whether help and assistance is public, private or voluntary and whether it is offered as of right. In England and Wales, developments in the 1990s were especially significant in changing the political and policy landscape for victims. This decade produced the Stephen Lawrence Inquiry, which acknowledged police institutional racism and inadequacies surrounding public policies associated with black people, crime, victimisation and criminal justice. This decade also ushered in the Victim's Charter (1990). That Charter's full title was: *The Victim's Charter: A Statement of the Rights for Victims of Crime*. It claimed to set out for the first time the rights and entitlements of victims of crime. The revised version, published six years later (1996), tellingly had a different sub-title: *The Victim's Charter: A Statement of Service Standards for Victims of Crime*, a more realistic reflection of actual content. The 1990s also witnessed the rediscovery of popular punitiveness towards young offenders, which an emerging youth victimology has since been heavily critical of (Francis, 2007).

The *Code of Practice for Victims of Crime* (2013) was probably one of the most significant victim related publications emanating from the Ministry of Justice during the 2000s. This Victims' Code is perhaps best summarised as the 21st-century version of The Victim's Charter. The Code is a 78-page document comprising 19 entitlements for victims of crime. The first of these suggests victims of crime are entitled to a needs assessment. The last is about making a complaint. Together the words 'entitled' and 'entitlements' appear 201 times and these words are used alongside the less frequently used words 'duties' and 'duty' – 29 references. Common phrases are 'putting victims first' and 'vulnerable victims'.

If we take this document as indicative of the current state of victim oriented policy, rights-based vocabularies remain noticeably absent. Minimum standards covering 14 different service providers are listed as being covered by the code. It would seem that victims of crime continue to occupy a position defined by their need rather than by any notion of rights. This mirrors the conclusion arrived at 20 years ago by Rob Mawby, who was then commenting upon the ethos of Victim Support, The Victim's Charter and Criminal Injuries Compensation (Mawby and Walklate, 1994). So, has anything changed?

From the above discussion it can be surmised that there have been numerous developments involving the victim of crime in state and charitable/voluntary sector policy and practice over the past four decades. Indeed, criminal justice policies in respect of victims have gathered increasing momentum. Many have had a positive impact, especially in terms of changing the status of the victim in the criminal justice system. Some measures have significantly improved victims' experiences in connection with helping achieve criminal justice whilst other developments over the last 40 years or so have been helpful in meeting the needs of victims in the short, medium and longer term.

Whilst there have been positive gains for some crime victims in England and Wales, there have also been some stalemate predicaments and even losses. In terms of stalemates, despite an array of victim-oriented activities and measures there continues to be a lack of any coherent victims' policy and victims continue to occupy a position defined by their need rather than by a notion of rights. Another stalemate situation is that victims' 'lived experiences' of criminal justice and its agencies – namely the police, courts and prosecution process – continue to be less positive than hoped. For example, much literature details the fragile nature of police – victim relations, especially when the victim represents a marginalised and oppressed group or individual – such as ethnic minorities, women, children and young people and those from vulnerable groups and thus protected categories according hate crime legislation. And finally in terms of losses, some victims continue to be further traumatised and victimised by inappropriate treatment from public sector services including the criminal justice system and other official bodies and authorities. Victimologically, excluded citizens and consumers of services, are those that fall short of the socially acceptable stereotype of the 'ideal victim'. There continues to be forgotten, lost or neglected victims whose wants and needs are unmet in part due to policies dominated by assumptions about deserving and undeserving victims and legacies attributable to positivist traditions that dominate both cultural discourse and policy developments.

In more recent austerity years, as all manner of services have contracted, the place of Victim Support as the core agency in England and Wales supporting victims of crime entered a period where its future became uncertain. The growing influence of Police and Crime Commissioners (PCCs) and a major review of services has already resulted in the loss of the Victim Support contract for the Witness Service.

Victim policy and legislations in England and Wales and elsewhere are increasingly impacted upon by international organisations and institutions. However distinctive a country's criminal justice system, political and policy developments are to a greater or lesser extent likely to be influenced in their operation by globalisation and global processes. International influence is most overtly felt through the work of transnational organisations like the European Union and the United Nations, as well as the operation of institutions like the International Criminal Court and the European Court of Justice. In Europe, the notion of rights is traditionally less engrained and this is especially the case in the UK, where there is no written constitution. Consequently, European nations were slower to refer to victims having rights in official policy documents than was generally the case in North America. Indeed, this is a relatively recent development, following the proliferation of rights language in a 2001 EU Framework Decision on the standing of victims in criminal proceedings (2001/220) and, before that, the introduction of the European Convention on Human Rights in 1950 (Hall, 2016). The impact of Brexit, and the UK's vote to leave Europe in 2016, on victim policy has yet to be seen.

Many of the various contributions to this volume consider the nature and impact of the political and the policy response to victims mostly in the context of England and Wales, but comparisons with other jurisdictions are also used. Hall, in Chapter 6, offers a particularly global perspective. In doing so they ask a number of questions:

- How appropriate are the various state responses to victimisation, victims and witnesses?
- What has been the political and policy response to specific victims of crime?
- How do victims of different types of criminal victimisation experience criminal justice systems and processes?

In addition, there are numerous sections within the various chapters in this book that specifically address questions about anti-social experiences, unfairness and bias, injustice and inequality, discrimination and prejudice as pertaining to criminal justice systems generally or to different components of systems (i.e. the police, the courts, the CPS, the magistracy and judiciary, the prison and probation services). Thus there are several key victimological concerns and debates that repeatedly occur in reviewing the relationship between victims, victim policy, criminal justice and the major social divisions. This provokes discussions that focus upon the absence of appropriate public policy and practices directed towards those who have been criminally victimised or socially harmed and which might aid their recovery. Other discussions focus upon the victim's representation or lack of representation and even neglect in criminal justice policy and practice. Another angle to many of the contributions concerns how public and criminal justice policy and practice can actually result in social harm and criminal victimisation. Many chapters in the volume effectively examine the ways in which people experience victimisation as a result of criminal justice policy and practice and as a result of wider measures aimed at reducing crime and/or improving quality of life and well-being – the unintended consequences of poorly researched and implemented victim related initiatives. Additionally, several of the chapters highlight recent developments in the provision of mediation and restorative justice programmes as such philosophies have variously penetrated the broader spectrum of criminal justice policy and practice generally.

PAUSE FOR REVIEW

Since the 1960s, what has been the focus in each decade in the development of victim policies and services?

What are the key challenges and opportunities in developing victim policies and services?

READING VICTIMS, CRIME AND SOCIETY

To read more about political and policy approaches to victims of crime see:

Duggan, M. and Heap, V. (2014) *Administrating Victimisation: The Politics of Anti-Social Behaviour and Hate Crime Policy*. Basingstoke: Palgrave Macmillan.

Hall, M. (2010) *Victims and Policy Making: A Comparative Perspective*. Cullompton: Willan.

Victims, Crime and Society: An Introduction 2e represents a single point of reference and a comprehensive resource. It encompasses the intersecting and overlocking socio-economic, comparative, theoretical and historical dimensions to the study of victims in society. It is replete with pedagogic features that make it attractive to students and to those involved in delivering innovation in teaching and learning.

To ensure consistency across all chapters in terms of the presentation of theory, research, policy and practice, and to secure a thorough review of all aspects of the academic and scholarly research literature, we have been keen to identify a common format or component listing for each chapter that helps reading and understanding. Where relevant, each chapter includes:

- A critical review of the theoretical and research literature on the area of study.
- An assessment of the development of any policy and legislative responses.
- A discussion on key developments/issues in the area of study.
- A discussion on any future research directions.
- A concise summary.

In addition, each of the chapters provide:

- Key terms highlighted in the text and referenced in the Glossary at the end of the book.
- 'Pause for review' questions for reflection and discussion.
- Suggestions for further reading.

In structuring each chapter in this way, we have been particularly keen to balance the authors' expertise in particular substantive areas with the needs of the reader new to the discipline of victimology and the study of victimisation and victims of crime. In doing so, we think that the format strengthens the student-centred nature of the book and allows for cross-referencing to be made within and between chapters.

Chapters 1 to 6 introduce victim constructs, representations, concepts and definitions in historical, global, theoretical and research contexts. These contributions are essential components of the study of victims in society. They help introduce, what in our estimation are, the fundamental aspects of the study of victims in society. Chapters 7 to 13 explore the nature of criminal victimisation in relation to the intersecting and overlapping social divisions of class, race, religion, age, gender, sexuality. They allow us to apply the fundamental conceptualisations of the study of victims of crime to people's lived experiences. This part of the book also sets the scene for, and explores, the frequent tensions between social divisions, criminal victimisation, and state policy and practice.

The detailed structure of the book is:

1. Victims, Crime and Society: An Introduction – Pamela Davies, Peter Francis and Chris Greer
2. Defining Victims and Victimisation – Sandra Walklate
3. News Media, Victims and Crime – Chris Greer
4. Historical Perspectives in Victimology – Barry Godfrey
5. Theoretical Perspectives in Victimology – Peter Francis
6. Global Perspectives in Victimology – Matthew Hall
7. Fear, Vulnerability and Victimisation – Murray Lee
8. Gender, Victims and Crime – Pamela Davies
9. Older People, Victims and Crime – Matthew Hall
10. Socio-Economic Inequalities, Victims and Crime –Hazel Croall
11. Race, Religion, Victims and Crime – Colin Webster
12. Sexuality, Victims and Crime – Stephen Tomsen and Michael Salter
13. Victims of the Powerful – Hazel Croall

REFERENCES

Allan, J. (2016) *Crime Outcomes in England and Wales: Year Ending March 2016*, Statistical Bulletin. London: ONS.

Alvazzi Del Frate, A. (2004) 'The international crime business survey: findings from nine central-eastern European cities', *European Journal on Criminal Policy and Research*, 10(2): 137–61.

Best, S. (2005) *Understanding Social Divisions*. London: Sage.

BRC (2016) *BRC Retail Crime Survey 2015*. London: British Retail Consortium. Available at www.businesscrime.org.uk/assets/files/BRC-2015-Crime-Survey.pdf (accessed 5.10.16).

Carrabine, E., Iganski, P., Lee, M., Plummer, K. and South, N. (2004) *Criminology: A Sociological Introduction*. London: Routledge.

Christie, N. (1986) 'The ideal victim', in E. Fattah (ed.), *From Crime Policy to Victim Policy*. London: Macmillan. pp. 17–30.

Cohen, S. (1972) *Folk Devils and Moral Panics*. London: MacGibbon and Kee.

Cook, I.R. and Davies, P. (2016) 'Supporting victims and witnesses', in J. Harding, P. Davies and G. Mair (eds), *An Introduction to Criminal Justice*. London: Sage.

Currie, E. (2010) 'Plain left realism: an appreciation, and some thoughts for the future', *Crime, Law and Social Change*, 54(2): 11–124.

Daly, K. (1997) 'Different ways of conceptualising sex/gender in feminist theory and their implications for criminology', *Theoretical Criminology*, 1(1): 25–51.

Davies, P. (2015) 'Victims: continuing to carry the burden of justice', *British Society of Criminology Newsletter*, 76(Summer).

Davies, P. and Francis, P. (eds) (2017) *Doing Criminological Research* (3rd edn). London: Sage.

Davies, P., Francis, P. and Jupp, V. (eds) (2003) *Victimisation Theory, Research and Policy*. Basingstoke: Palgrave.

Davies, P., Francis, P. and Jupp, V. (eds) (2011) *Doing Criminological Research* (2nd edn). London: Sage.

Dixon, M., Reed, H., Rogers, B. and Stone, L. (2006) *Crime Share: The Unequal Impact of Crime*. London: Institute for Public Policy Research.

Duggan, M. and Heap, V. (2014) *Administrating Victimisation: The Politics of Anti-Social Behaviour and Hate Crime Policy*. Basingstoke: Palgrave Macmillan.

Farrell, G. (2013) 'Five tests for a theory of the crime drop', *Journal of Crime Science: An Interdisciplinary Journal*, 2(5): 1–8.

Fattah, E. (ed.) (1992) *Towards a Critical Victimology*. Basingstoke: Palgrave Macmillan.

Francis, P. (2016) 'Positivist victimology', in K. Corteen, S. Morley, P. Taylor and J. Turner (eds), *A Companion to Crime, Harm and Victimisation*. Bristol: Policy Press.

Francis, P. (2007) Young People, Crime and Society in P. Davies, P. Francis and C. Greer (eds) *Victims, Crime and Society*. London: Sage.

Goodey, J. (2005) *Victims and Victimology: Research, Policy and Practice*. London: Longman.

Gray, D. and Watt, P. (2013) *Giving Victims a Voice: Joint Report into Sexual Allegations Made against Jimmy Savile*. London: MPS/NSPCC.

Greer, C. (2013) 'Crime and media: understanding the connections', in C. Hale, K. Hayward, A. Wahidin and E. Wincup (eds), *Criminology* (3rd edn). London: Oxford University Press. pp.143–63.

Greer, C. and McLaughlin, E. (2013) 'The Sir Jimmy Savile scandal: child sexual abuse and institutional denial at the BBC', *Crime, Media and Culture: An International Journal*, 9(3): 243–63.

Greer, C. and McLaughlin, E. (2016) 'Theorizing institutional scandal and the regulatory state', *Theoretical Criminology*, doi: 10.1177/1362480616645648.

Hall, M. (2016) 'Globalisation and international criminal justice', in J. Harding, P. Davies and G. Mair (eds), *An Introduction to Criminal Justice*. London: Sage.

Hillyard, P., Pantazis, C., Tombs, S. and Gordon, D. (eds) (2004) *Beyond Criminology: Taking Harm Seriously*. London: Pluto Press.

Hillyard, P., Pantazis, C., Tombs, S., Gordon, D. and Dorling, D. (2005) *Criminal Obsessions: Why Harm Matters More Than Crime* (Monograph). Sheffield: Crime and Society Foundation.

Home Office (1990) *The Victims Charter: A Statement of Rights for Victims of Crime*. London: Home Office.

Home Office (1996) *Victim's Charter: A Statement of Service Standards for Victims of Crime*. London: Home Office.

Hope, T. (2007) 'The distribution of household property crime victmisation: insights from the British Crime Survey', in M. Hough and M. Maxfield (eds), *Surveying Crime in the 21st Century: Commemorating the 25th Anniversary of the British Crime Survey*, Crime Prevention Studies Vol. 22. Cullompton: Willan Press.

Hope, T. (2015) 'We need a different crime survey', *Centre for Crime and Justice Studies*, May 2015. Available at www.crimeandjustice.org.uk/resources/we-need-different-crime-survey (accessed 12.9.16).

Hope, T. and Chester, H. (2011) 'Social inequality and the distribution of crime victimisation in England and Wales', paper presented to the Welsh Centre for Crime and Social Justice, 11–12 May.

Hoyle, C. (2012) 'Victims, the criminal process, and restorative justice', in M. Maguire, R. Morgan and R. Reiner (eds), *The Oxford Handbook of Criminology* (5th edn). Oxford: Oxford University press.

Jordan, J. (2015) 'Justice for rape victims? The spirit may sound willing, but the flesh remains weak', in D. Wilson and S. Ross (eds), *Crime, Victims and Policy: International Contexts, Local Experiences*. Basingstoke: Palgrave Macmillan. pp.84–106.

Karmen, A. (2016) *Crime Victims: An Introduction to Victimology* (9th edn). Andover: Cengage Learning.

Lynch, M. (2013) 'Reexamining political economy and crime and explaining the crime drop', *Journal of Crime and Justice*, 36(2): 248–62.

Maguire, M. (2012) 'Criminal statistics and the construction of crime', in M. Maguire, R. Morgan and R. Reiner (eds), *The Oxford Handbook of Criminology* (5th edn). Oxford: Clarendon Press.

Matthews, R. (2010) 'Realist criminology revisited', in E. McLaughlin and T. Newburn (eds), *The Sage Handbook of Criminological Theory*. London: Sage.

Mawby, R. and Walklate, S. (1994) *Critical Victimology*.London: Sage.

Ministry of Justice (2013) *Code of Practice for Victims of Crime*. London: Ministry of Justice.
Rock, P. (2010) 'Approaches to victims and victimisation', in E. McLaughlin and T. Newburn (eds), *The Sage Handbook of Criminological Theory*. London: Sage.
Schafer, S. (1968) *The Victim and His Criminal: A Study in Functional Responsibility*. New York: Random House.
Spalek, B. (2006) *Crime Victims: Theory Policy and Practice*. London: Palgrave.
Sparks, R., Genn, H. and Dodd, D. (1977) *Surveying Victims*. Chichester: Wiley.
van Dijk, J. (2015) 'The case for survey-based comparative measures of crime', *European Journal of Criminology*, 12(4): 437–45.
van Kesteren, J., van Dijk, J. and Mayhew, P. (2014) 'The international crime victims surveys: a retrospective', *International Review of Victimology*, 20(1): 49–69.
Walklate, S. (2003) 'Can there be a feminist victimology?', in P. Davies, P. Francis, and V. Jupp (eds), *Victimisation Theory, Research and Policy*. Basingstoke: Palgrave.
Walklate, S. (2007) *Imagining the Victim of* Crime. Buckingham: Open University Press.
Walklate, S., Mythen, G. and McGarry, R. (2011) 'Witnessing Wootton-Bassett: an exploration in cultural victimology', *Crime, Media and Society*, 7(2): 149–65.
Wolhuter, L., Olley, N. and Denham, D. (2009) *Victimology: Victimisation and Victims' Rights*. London: Routledge-Cavendish.
Zedner, L. (2002) 'Victims', in M. Maguire, R. Morgan and R. Reiner (eds), *The Oxford Handbook of Criminology* (3rd edn). Oxford: Clarendon Press.

2 DEFINING VICTIMS AND VICTIMISATION

Sandra Walklate

The purpose of this chapter is to encourage critical thinking around what the concepts of victim and victimisation mean. In order to do so this chapter will consider why being a victim is problematic, what the features associated in acquiring the label of victim are, and what the assumptions associated with this label are. In so doing it will introduce the concepts of ideal victim, hierarchies of victimisation, vulnerability to victimisation, primary, secondary and indirect victimisation. We shall then go on to consider two ways in which the concept of victimisation has been understood: as an interactional process and as a pattern of experiences. This discussion introduces the concept of repeat victimisation. In thinking about repeat victimisation the case will be made for the importance of appreciating the role of different theoretical perspectives in victimology in understanding the terms 'victim' and 'victimisation'. But first, why is being a victim so problematic?

> To imagine a life of momentary impulse, of short-term action, devoid of sustainable routines, a life without habits, is to imagine indeed a mindless existence. (Sennett, 1998: 44)

> The majority of criminal victimisation, at least in Britain, remains:
>
> - Home grown (by and against citizens, as opposed to being by non-citizens);
> - Conventional (burglary and petty theft, as opposed to international drug smuggling);
> - Local (occurring locally rather than globally).
>
> (Goodey, 2005: 229)

WHY IS BEING A VICTIM (OF CRIME) A PROBLEM?

In my own early work for a victim support scheme in Liverpool in 1983, I interviewed an elderly lady extremely distressed by the theft of her son's watch. (For the purposes of this chapter I shall call her Doris – not her real name). It transpired that her son, who lived with her, had died in his forties from cancer, and her coping mechanisms for managing this had been to organise her time in such a way so that she spent less time in the house on her own; one day shopping, one day in the library, one day at the luncheon club, and so on. The burglary including the theft of her son's watch not only challenged her way of managing to live alone, it also added further pain to the loss of her son through the theft of his watch – the one possession she had left to cherish. As the quote from Sennett above captures, life for Doris had become 'mindless' insofar as her routines and habits had been taken away from her; first by the bereavement, second by the burglary. Her coping routine had been taken away. She chose to stay at home to prevent a further invasion of her privacy but in doing so was faced with her other loss, that of her son. Her suffering was private. It was a mere happenstance that she shared it with me. Her experiences were mundane, routine, ordinary and local as suggested by Goodey (2005) on the previous page.

As early research showed (Maguire and Bennett, 1982), people's ability to cope with criminal victimisation is often exacerbated when they are also dealing with other events of significance in their lives, and this was certainly the case for Doris. After talking with her I returned to the victim support scheme office, some three hours later having abandoned the purpose of my interview, and suggested that someone might want to lend a further helping hand to her. However, her story has stayed with me ever since. The point of relaying it here is to offer a flavour of some of the key ingredients associated with being victimised.

Doris' story epitomises the ordinary nature of much criminal victimisation for many people: coming home to find that your house has been burgled, having your wallet or purse taken surreptitiously while you were out shopping, theft of your property whilst at work, or perhaps a more personally violent experience, being the victim of an assault (sexual or otherwise). Much of this criminal victimisation is, as Goodey (2005) quite rightly points out, local. By that she means that when it comes to burglary, offenders often live within the same neighbourhood as their victim; when it comes to domestic thefts or pick-pocketing, it is likely that the offenders are at a minimum members of the victim's wider community (unless, of course, you happen to be abroad at the time) and in the case of assault is more than likely to be someone you know. Thus much criminal victimisation is intra-class and intra-ethnic: the crimes of the streets. If we take this idea just a little further and think about other kinds of criminal victimisations that are routine, mundane, ordinary and local, like for example family violence (taken here to include child abuse, elder abuse and all forms of 'domestic' violence), then we can clearly see that people's experiences of criminal victimisation are also intra-personal; that is, they more often than not involve others who are not only known to them but also close family members: the crimes behind closed doors.

As many academics and practitioners will be quick to point out, the intra-class, intra-ethnic, intra-personal routine, mundane and ordinary nature of criminal victimisation is not the complete picture. It is also the case that much criminal activity that has an impact on us all goes on 'behind our backs'. These 'crimes of the suites' are less readily recognised as criminal, but they nevertheless constitute an important layer in unpacking some of the problems with 'becoming a victim' that we are concerned with here. If we add to that the contemporary dynamic associated with the 'crimes of terrorism', we have a much fuller picture of the less routine, less mundane, less ordinary and possibly less local nature of the possibilities of 'becoming a victim'. All of which only serve to add to Sennett's (1998) observation with which this chapter began: the importance to human beings of sustainable routines. Criminal victimisation, whatever form it takes, disrupts, distorts or even dismantles such routines. At the same time, the foregoing discussion also puts to the front of our minds the extent to which the term 'victim' is contested (a victim of what, from whom, with what impact) and as a consequence defining the term itself can be problematic.

WHY IS BEING A VICTIM SO PROBLEMATIC?

Defining the term 'victim'

Early victimological theorists were concerned to develop ways of thinking about the victim that would enable the victim to be differentiated from the non-victim. In other words, they were clearly suggesting that there is a normal person and that when the victim is measured against them, the victim somehow falls short. As a result early victimological work produced 'victim typologies'. Von Hentig's (1948) typology worked with a notion of 'victim proneness'. He argued that there were some people, by virtue of their socio-economic characteristics, who were much more likely to be victims (in this case of crime) than other people. These he identified as being women, children, the elderly, the mentally subnormal and so on (he had 13 categories in all). This suggests that von Hentig thought the normal person against whom the victim was to be measured was the white, heterosexual male. Mendelsohn (1956) adopted a more legalistic framework in developing his typology. His underlying concept was the notion of 'victim culpability'. Using this concept he developed a six-fold typology from the victim who could be shown to be completely innocent, to the victim who started as a perpetrator and during the course of an incident ends as the victim. Embedded here is a legal understanding of what counts as a reasonable course of action under particular circumstances, and in this respect his understanding of 'reasonable' also equates with that which the white, heterosexual male would consider to be reasonable. In different ways this early work reflects the historic foundational focus of victimology with differentiation: what makes victims different from non-victims. As we shall see, this pre-occupation is an ongoing issue in defining who the victim is (see Table 2.1).

Spalek (2006: 9) points to four different definitions of 'victim' in the *Oxford English Dictionary*, all of which are quite specific. Commonly this term is used to refer to someone who has suffered a misfortune through no fault of his/her own and as Dignan (2005) and Furedi (2013) have indicated, as a term it has only recently become commonly used and intertwined with crime. Indeed, in the criminal justice system talking of 'victims' is highly problematic given that in that context it is more usual to refer to 'complainants'. In the legal context the terms 'victim' and 'offender' are deemed inappropriate since to

Table 2.1 Typologies of victimisation compared

von Hentig's typology of victim proneness	Mendelsohn's typology of victim culpability
Young people, females, the elderly	The completely innocent
The mentally defective, 'dull' normals, the depressed	Those with 'minor' guilt
Immigrants, members of minority groups	Those as guilty as the offender
The acquisitive, the wanton, the lonely and heartbroken	Those more guilty than the offender
The tormentor, the 'fighting victim'	Those who are the most guilty

use them potentially assigns guilt and/or innocence in a process yet to be determined. So in law, the term 'victim' is inappropriate. However, there are other difficulties with the term, historically for feminists in particular.

When the word 'victim' is gendered, as in French for example, it becomes inextricably linked with being female. Feminists object to this since it implies that the passivity and powerlessness that are also linked with the term 'victim' become, by implication, associated with being female. Consequently those working within the feminist movement prefer to talk of **survivors** rather than victims, as this term suggests a more active and positive image of women (see Figure 2.1). The implied either/or of either being a victim or being a survivor is in itself somewhat problematic, since any individual's response to the experience of crime can be hugely variable. However, the tension that exists with either being labelled a victim or a survivor is also problematic, since both labels fail to capture the processes of victimisation. For example, it is possible that an individual at different points in time in relation to different events could be an active victim, a passive victim, an active survivor, a passive survivor and all the experiential possibilities in between. From this point of view the term 'victim' does seem quite sterile.

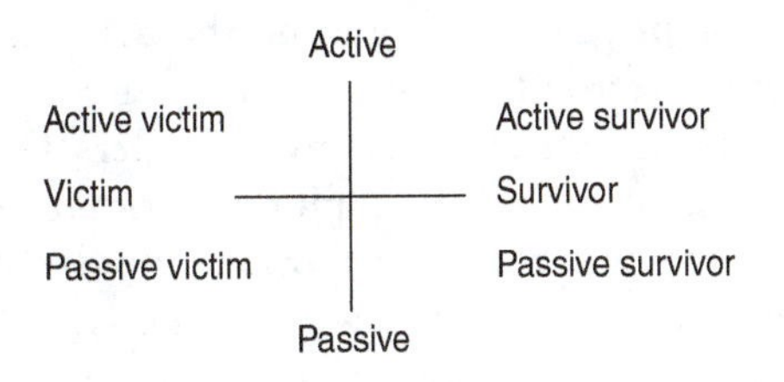

Figure 2.1 A possible relationship between victim and survivor

PAUSE FOR REVIEW

What kind of person would you put in each of the categories identified in Figure 2.1?

So for analytical purposes it is probably more helpful to think of the victim/survivor dichotomy as capturing opposite ends of a continuum. Moreover, it is also important to add to this discussion the observations made by Furedi (1997) and Cole (2007) on the cultural endorsement of **victimhood.** For them being a victim (of crime) carries with it culturally constructed values and meanings that render individual responses to their misfortunes more or less acceptable. Indeed, both of these writers suggest that the cult of victimhood is so prevalent contemporarily that it has become almost a defining characteristic of citizenship, of belonging to society. This shift in orientation is clearly evident in contemporary criminal justice policy and practice (as will be illustrated in the chapters that follow) and elides victimhood with citizenship commented on by Young (1996) some time ago.

- So, what the term 'victim 'means is neither simple nor straightforward: it is subject to debate.
- If we add to this the recognition some people acquire the victim label quite readily and others do not, then the picture of who is considered to be a victim and what the term actually means becomes quite messy.
- Historically it has been a highly gendered concept.

WHO ACQUIRES THE LABEL 'VICTIM'?

The process in which an individual acquires the label of victim reflects social pre-occupations with what Christie (1986) called the **ideal victim.** For Christie (1986) the 'ideal victim' is the victim of the Little Red Riding Hood fairy tale: a young, innocent female, out doing good deeds, who is attacked by an unknown stranger. This ideal stereotype results in some people being viewed as **deserving victims**; that is, acquiring the victim label very readily and easily. It includes those people who could not be held responsible for what has happened to them, like Doris referred to above. Others can be labelled **undeserving victims** and may never acquire the victim label. Many offenders find themselves in this latter category. Indeed, the power of such stereotyping contributes to the assumption that victims are 'good' and offenders are 'bad' as well as having the effect that it is very difficult to consider the extent to which offenders might also be victims. This distinction between deserving and undeserving victims prompted Carrabine et al. (2004: 117) to talk of a **hierarchy of victimisation.** At the bottom of this hierarchy would be the homeless, the street prostitute, the drug addict – indeed, all those categories of people for whom it is presumed that they expose themselves to victimisation and as a consequence making a claim to the label and status of 'victim' very difficult for them. Of course as this volume illustrates, the shape and form of these labels can change over time: some groups and/or individuals acquire victim status and others lose it, adding another layer to the difficulties in defining the term 'victim'. Box 2.1 considers who can be a victim.

BOX 2.1 WHO CAN BE A VICTIM?

Consider the claim of historical child sexual abuse made in the Autumn of 2012. Steven Messham, a man who had been in care in North Wales, made the claim that he had been sexually abused while he was in care. During the process of making this claim, Lord McAlpine was named as his abuser. Lord McAlpine's name as the abuser was distributed by Sally Bercow on Twitter. Lord McAlpine was subsequently found to have been falsely accused. He accepted an apology from Steven Messham but subsequently won compensation for damages through the courts from Sally Bercow.

PAUSE FOR REVIEW

From the example in Box 2.1 think about:

- Who was the victim?
- Who is the victim?
- Does the fact that it was a man claiming historic child sexual abuse raise any questions to be thought about?
- What questions does 'historic child abuse' raise for understanding the definition of the victim?
- What is the role of the wider cultural context in which this particular incident came to the attention of the media?
- What role does the media (in all its forms) play in constructing victims?
- What role does the media (in all its forms) play in creating victims?
- How do the notions of ideal victim, deserving/undeserving victim, and the hierarchy of victimisation help us to make sense of this particular example and the public response to it?

The example in Box 2.1 draws attention to the following features associated in acquiring the label of victim:

- acquiring the status of a victim is something that has to be achieved;
- it involves a process starting with the individual recognising that they have been victimised (not as obvious as it may seem);

- it involves claiming the label of victim;
- it can involve embracing a victim identity;
- being recognised in social or policy terms as a victim and responded to accordingly is neither simple nor straightforward.

Neither Doris nor Messham possessed all the characteristics of an 'ideal' victim but these examples taken together remind us that underpinning the hierarchy of victimisation are also presumptions about who is and who is not **vulnerable** to victimisation.

VULNERABILITY AND VICTIMISATION

The concept of vulnerability has rarely been explored in its own right (Green, 2007). However, Green (2007) has pointed out that vulnerability to crime, risk from crime and harm as a result of crime have become intimate bedfellows. Criminal victimisation survey data measures vulnerability by identifying who is at the most risk from crime and putting that up against the data on whom crime has the most impact. It is then presumed that the relationship between these two variables provides data on who are most vulnerable victims. Green (2007) calls this the 'axis of vulnerability' (see Figure 2.2).

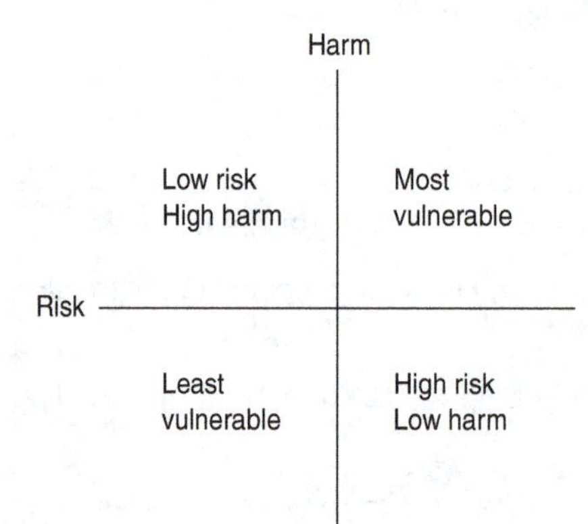

Figure 2.2 Axis of vulnerability (taken from Green, 2007: 92)

For Green (2007), every individual could be placed on this axis in terms of his or her vulnerability. In this diagrammatic representation it is easy to situate what has been gleaned from criminal victimisation survey data in relation to the risk from and harm done by crime. In this schema the elderly female would find herself in the low risk, high harm quadrant; the young, ethnic minority male would be in the high risk, low harm quadrant, with the least vulnerable likely to be the affluent, middle-class male and the most vulnerable likely to be the poor, single-parent household.

PAUSE FOR REVIEW

Think about the 'axis of vulnerability':

- What are the problems in linking definitions of being a victim with definitions of vulnerability in this way?
- What does linking victims and vulnerability in this way mean for offenders?
- What does this kind of link imply for people's coping strategies?

The patterns of victimisation, when linked with images of vulnerability, mirror the thinking that assumes an individual is either a victim or they are an offender. So not only are some groups of people more readily identified as victims than others (qua Christie's 1986 construction of the ideal victim), some people are more readily identified as vulnerable to victimisation than others. The story of Doris epitomises the classic image of who is seen to be vulnerable both emotionally and socio-economically: not only was Doris seen to have inherent vulnerabilities because of her sex and age, she also reflected structural vulnerabilities as she lived in a high crime area on a state pension. So, especially in terms of victim support and service delivery, it might also be useful to think of a hierarchy of vulnerability alongside a hierarchy of victimisation; who is thought of as vulnerable and why; and to map the similarities and differences between these two hierarchies and how they may change over time. Such a mapping exercise might also encourage some analytical thinking about why it is that some victims get more attention than others. (For a fuller discussion of the relationship between victimisation, fear and vulnerability, see Chapter 7.)

The links between being recognised as a victim and being vulnerable to victimisation encourages us to think about how being defined as a victim is frequently seen through the lens of the kind of impact that crime has on people. So in addition to understanding the nature of vulnerability, being identified as a victim is also related, in terms of impact, to whether or not an individual is considered to be a primary victim, a secondary victim or an indirect victim. These features of victimisation add further dimensions to our understanding of who is considered to be a victim.

PRIMARY VICTIMISATION

Primary victimisation refers to the direct impact that crime has on a victim. This can range from the financial loss associated with goods stolen, to time taken off work to sort out the aftermath of a burglary, to physical injury as a result of an assault, to the post-traumatic stress syndrome reported by some victims of rape. Drawing on a wide range of studies, the direct effects of victimisation are listed by Hall and Shapland (2007: 3–4) as follows:

- Shock, and a loss of trust/faith in society.
- Guilt often associated with feelings of anger and/or fear.
- Physical injury; minor to severe.
- Financial losses.
- Psychological; fear, anger, depression.
- Social, including changes to lifestyle.
- Consequential effects: perceptions of the likelihood of future victimisation.

Such wide-ranging consequences from self-blame, or indeed to what Spalek (2006) refers to as 'spirit injury', to more simply understood lifestyle changes, to physical, emotional and/or financial impacts, or indeed some combination of all of these, are features of the variable responses that individuals have subsequent to criminal victimisation. For example, Dixon et al. (2006: 21) reported that in 2002–3 some 180,000 people moved home as a result of their experiences of crime, with 32,000 people changing jobs for the same reason. Indeed, if the total cost of criminal victimisation was factored into this discussion in terms of insurance, health service cost and so on, these authors estimate that this would have amounted to £36.2 billion each year (based on 2002–3 figures). So whilst criminal victimisation takes its toll on individuals, it also takes its toll on the wider economy and the processes of service delivery invoked as a consequence. These kinds of measurable costs are multiplied for some individuals by the feelings of stress, shock, fear, difficulty in sleeping reported by victims of a wide range of different kinds of crime from burglary, to rape, to acts of violence like terrorism. As Maguire and Bennett (1982) reported some time ago this kind of impact, while difficult to predict, is likely to affect individuals who are also going through some other traumatic event in their lives like a divorce or bereavement (as was Doris discussed earlier). Moreover, Hall and Shapland (2007: 23) report in their review of what is known about the impact of crime, 'For more serious/violence offences, psychological, social and physical (injury) effects can be long lasting, whereas financial effects and loss of property are almost always short-term'. For example, the longer lasting effects of post traumatic stress syndrome that can result from the direct experience of criminal victimisation, or more indirectly as a result of being a witness to traumatic events, are well documented in the psychiatric literature. These kinds of responses to criminal victimisation can have an effect on immediate relationships too (see Hodgson, 2005).

Of course, much of this preceding discussion draws on findings of studies that have taken a rather conventional and limited understanding of what might be included as criminal victimisation. However, Spalek and King's (2007) study of the impact of the collapse of Farepak on its victims resonates with all those features of primary victimisation listed by Hall and Shapland (2007). When writ large of course, for example through an appreciation of the impact of the continued use of white asbestos in poorer countries (Tombs and Whyte, 2006), the direct impact of crime, whilst hugely variable on an individual level, is also structured by socio-economic variables (see also Whyte, 2007).

To summarize, the direct impact of criminal victimisation can be hugely variable at an individual level. How individuals respond to this kind of experience will be a reflection of their own coping mechanisms, the nature of their persona, their personal relationships and for some, the kind of support that they receive. All of which clearly have some associated structural dimensions. However, what might be an exceptional experience for an individual is more often than not an ordinary, mundane and routine experience for the criminal justice system. That exceptional experience for the individual can be made better or worse by how they are treated by the criminal justice system. This is what is referred to as **secondary victimisation.**

SECONDARY VICTIMISATION

Research has indicated that individuals who are involved in the criminal justice process as either victims or witnesses frequently feel let down by that process from not being kept informed of what was happening in their case, to being treated unsympathetically by the professionals working in the criminal justice process, to not being believed when they are giving their evidence (see inter alia Walklate, 2007). However, it is in the space between how victims/complainants/witnesses might like to be treated and some of their reported experiences in how they are actually treated that practices that perpetuate the distinction between deserving and undeserving victims occur. Indeed, the current policy desire to 'redefine justice', to borrow a title from a report produced in 2009 by Sara Payne, the Victims' Champion, is concerned to address these practices and to better meet the needs of victims and witnesses. Some of the suggested changes are relatively non-contentious, but others are more difficult to address since they are rooted in the principles of the adversarial system of justice.

Whilst the problems associated with the giving of evidence within the system of justice in the UK have largely been highlighted in relation to allegation of rape, the experience of feeling challenged, undermined and accused of not 'telling the truth' is not solely confined to the complainant of rape. People as complainants/witnesses across a whole range of different crime categories, and sometimes even professional witnesses, can feel intimidated by the legal process in general and this aspect of the process in particular. Recognition of this reminds us of the tensions between the popular/policy or academic use of the term 'victim' and the legal use of the term 'complainant' referred to earlier.

INDIRECT VICTIMISATION

Indirect victimisation draws attention to experiences, like for example those involving murder, in which the families of both the murderer and the murder victim can feel victimised by their experiences of the criminal justice process. These more indirect experiences can manifest themselves in relation to feelings of bereavement, to maybe being under suspicion themselves for what has happened, through to just not being able to make sense of what has happened (see Rock, 1998; Cowdry, 2007). As Howarth and Rock (2000: 70) observe:

> Unlike many other traumatised people they can resort to no resolution of confusion. They cannot distance themselves from the other and align themselves morally in a newly polarised world. On the contrary they are stuck between the offender whom they may not have renounced and his victim for whom they may well feel compassion.

Spalek (2006) argues that thinking more deeply about the diversity of the crime experience might result in a more finely tuned understanding of indirect victimisation. She introduces the notion of 'spirit injury' and suggests that 'embedded within the notion is an assertion of the interconnected self, so that common and recurrent experiences of racist and sexist abuse amounts to a brutalisation of an individual's self-identity and their dignity' (p. 88). She goes on to suggest that thinking in this way allows an understanding of not only the impact of victimisation on the individual but on the wider audience who might be indirectly victimised as a result of their shared 'subject position'.

The idea of a shared indirect victimisation as a result of crime has some resonance with not only appreciating the importance of cultural and ethnic difference (which Spalek's concept is designed to include) but also taps into other shared experiences of crime. Returning to the earlier example of the impact of cases like murder, it is without doubt that the wider impact of the activities of Ian Brady and Myra Hindley in the 1960s and the burial of their victims on Saddleworth Moor in Greater Manchester that capture some of the potential impact on the local community there (see Box 2.2).

BOX 2.2 IAN BRADY AND MYRA HINDLEY

Ian Brady and Myra Hindley were convicted of the murder of five children between July 1963 and October 1965. These became designated as the 'moors murders' since three of the victims were buried on Saddleworth Moor, Greater Manchester, with one grave not being discovered until 1987. Myra Hindley, whom the media suggested was 'evil personified' died in prison in 2002, aged 60. Brady was declared insane in 1985 and is currently confined in a high security hospital.

In a similar way the activities of Harold Shipman in Hyde, Cheshire do too (see Box 2.3).

BOX 2.3 HAROLD SHIPMAN

Harold Shipman was a general medical practitioner in Hyde, a suburb of Greater Manchester, England. In January 2000 he was convicted of the murder of 15 of his patients, though it is clear that the inquiry that was set up to investigate how that could have happened believed that they had evidence that he had murdered somewhere in the region of 200 patients throughout his medical career. By far the majority of his victims were elderly females. He was found dead in his prison cell, having committed suicide, in January 2004, never having admitted to the acts of which he had been found guilty.

Historically, following on from the Ruxton murders in Lancashire, there was a public house named after the murderer who lived in that locality. Other communities have become associated with similar events like, for example, Dunblane in Scotland and Columbine in North America (the latter having had a film made about the events that took place there). So communities can be both diminished and enhanced as a result of such indirect victimisation.

This discussion of indirect victimisation also enables us to revisit the victimising potential of events, like the bombings in London in July 2005 (see inter alia Tulloch, 2006) and their impact both on eye witnesses and the wider local community, but also the media coverage of potentially highly impactive events. As Valier (2004) has observed, such coverage is intended to excavate our feelings, to put us by the side of the victim; for us to share in their suffering. At this point we are returned to the cultural dimensions of understanding who the victim might be and how that might be defined reflected in the work of Furedi (1997) and Cole (2007).

In reviewing some of the problems in becoming a victim, Strobl (2010: 6) suggests that there are four possibilities in the construction of victimhood:

- *The actual victim*: A person regards himself/herself as a victim and is also regarded as a victim by relevant others.
- *The nonvictim*: A person does not regard himself/herself as a victim and is not regarded as a victim by relevant others.
- *The rejected victim*: A person regards himself/herself as a victim but is not regarded as a victim by relevant others.
- *The designated victim*: A person does not regard himself/herself as a victim but is regarded as a victim by relevant others.

Consider these possibilities in the construction of victimhood in the light of the preceding discussion and think about the following questions:

- What impact might each of these possibilities have on the individual who is so categorised?
- What impact might each of these possibilities have on those close to the individual so categorised?
- Are there some people who would fit more readily into one or other of these categories?
- Is it possible to measure all of these possibilities? If so, how would you do it?

Your answers to all of the questions above might depend upon how you have understood and defined victimisation.

DEFINING VICTIMISATION

The concept of victimisation can be used in at least two different ways. The first focuses attention on the *process* of interaction that takes place, that results in one party being assigned as the victim. This has two dimensions to it. In the first instance, understanding what actually happens that results in the victimisation of one of the parties concerned. In the second instance, understanding how what actually happened resulted in the acquisition by the person victimised acquiring the status of victim. The interactional processes associated with who acquires, and who fails to acquire victim status, and the impact that these processes have on an individual's identity is relatively under-explored. Moreover, Rock (2002) has observed that appreciation of victimisation as an interactional process also requires that we appreciate when and how people define themselves as having been a victim, what does it mean when this has been recognised and what significance is attached to it, and when do these processes become problematic. Put simply, when do the processes of victimisation result in an individual embracing a victim identity? All of these questions constitute an important part of understanding the circumstances in which some people acquire victim status and others do not but become particularly acute when the process of victimisation is a result of intimate relationships either within the family or within an individual's neighbourhood.

The second usage of the concept of victimisation draws our attention to the ways in which becoming a victim of crime is not evenly distributed in society. In this context victimisation is used to refer to the patterning of criminal victimisation structured by age, class, sex and ethnicity. Criminal victimisation survey data consistently reveals that younger people are much more likely to be victimised than older people; the economically marginal and those lower down the social hierarchy are much more likely to be victimised than those higher up the social hierarchy; people from ethnic minorities are much more likely to be victimised than others; and in the context of street crime, men are much more likely to be victimised than women (see Chapters 9 to 15). When the picture of victimisation is framed in this way it becomes clear that the young, economically marginal male who belongs to an ethnic minority group is much more likely to be victimised, especially in the street, that any other category of victim. Yet it is also the case that they are the least likely to be viewed as vulnerable to such victimisation and most likely to be seen as the perpetrators of such victimisation.

Thus the patterning of victimisation when linked with images of vulnerability mirrors thinking that assumes either an individual is a victim or they are an offender – despite the fact that the empirical patterning of victimisation would suggest that young, economically marginal males from ethnic minority groups belong to both categories; that is, they offend and victimise each other. All of these features are particularly acute when the patterning of criminal victimisations points to **repeat victimisation.**

Tseloni and Pease (2003: 196) state that 'Victimisation is a good, arguably the best readily available, predictor of future victimization'. This assumes that it is possible to differentiate victims from non-victims. Hope (2007) points out that this is a very difficult starting point when the data on which it is based (criminal victimisation survey data) does not provide information on what the characteristics of a non-victim are. Genn (1988) offers a different starting point to this phenomenon. She suggested that multiple victimisations 'are just a part of life'. Hazel Genn was a member of the research team that conducted the pilot study for the first British Crime Survey (see Box 2.4).

BOX 2.4 HAZEL GENN – THE BRITISH CRIME SURVEY

Becoming interested in what appeared to be examples of 'victim-proneness' in one geographical area, I visited one particular block on a council estate over a number of months, tape-recorded interviews with several families, their neighbours and friends, and eventually moved in for a short period with the woman who had suffered the greatest number of victimisations in our survey. The views which I formed after this period of intensive observation have a substantial bearing not simply on the experiences of multiple victims but on the limitations of victim surveys as they are currently designed … What also became apparent was the fact that events reported to us in the survey were not regarded as particularly remarkable. They were just part of life. (Genn, 1988: 92–3)

The quote in Box 2.4 relates to one woman's experience of criminal victimisation, some of which she probably identified as criminal victimisation and others she did not. However, for the purposes this discussion the key phrase is: 'They were just part of life'. This emphasises lifestyle, not as a series of discreet, measurable incidents or events, but as a process. Lifestyle as a process cannot be captured by survey methodology as conceived by positivist victimology, as the quote from Genn clearly implies. It demands a different way of thinking about and exploring what 'just part of life' means for people. It is the case, of course, that much feminist inspired work has always been committed to different ways of thinking about the routine nature of women's lives and has always been committed to challenging accepted knowledge(s) about everyday life.

Genn's (1988) analysis of living with a multiple-victimised woman in what she called 'Bleak House' could have been drawn from a whole range of studies which have been concerned to document the nature of many women's routine lives. Largely located within feminist analyses, that literature refuses to adopt an individualised event-oriented approach to women's experiences, including their experiences of criminal victimisation. From this position there is no presumption of the non-victim status. This work prefers to locate an understanding of women's experiences of crime (and violence in particular) within the reality of women's routine lives in relation to men that they know. Put more simply, this latter approach privileges processes over events. So if it is the *processes* underpinning 'domestic' violence (as in Genn's comment; they are just part of life), bullying and racial attacks (see e.g. the work of Hesse et al., 1992; Bowling, 1998) which are the 'normal' case of victimisation, it is the 'one-off' victimising event that is abnormal. The 'one-off' needs to be explained. In other words, some sections of society feel the impact of criminal victimisation not only repeatedly but also *routinely*. If this is the case, then the targeting of repeat victims, predicated as it is on the notion that these are somehow different from other forms of victimisation, is misplaced.

Understanding the distinction between victimisation as a one-off event or as part of routine daily life has important implications for not only how we understand the nature of repeat victimisation in the context of 'domestic' violence or racial harassment, but also how we understand the nature of criminal victimisation more generally. In other words it points to the importance of *theory*. So how victimisation is defined is related to which theoretical perspective within victimology is being privileged. The discussion above has drawn upon two competing theoretical perspectives available to victimology to make sense of repeat victimisation: positivist victimology and a feminist approach. The relevance of theory in making sense of victimisation is discussed more fully in Chapter 6. At this juncture it is sufficient to be aware that there are problems in making sense of criminal victimisation when the perpetrator and victim are known to each other.

PAUSE FOR REVIEW

You might like to reflect at this point on what kinds of questions the phenomenon of repeat victimisation raises for:

- The distinction between deserving and undeserving victims.
- The concept of the ideal victim.
- The notion of a hierarchy of victimisation.
- What other kinds of crime might be considered 'domestic' and/or 'interpersonal'?
- The problems in recognising the victim in these kinds of crimes.

SUMMARY

This chapter has demonstrated that the concepts of victim and victimisation are not only highly contested, but also the process whereby an individual may or may not be recognised as a victim and be responded to as such is neither simple nor straightforward. In making this case this chapter has considered the importance of the continued presence of distinctions between the deserving and the undeserving victim, and the concept of the ideal victim all of which fuel a hierarchy of victimisation. It is important to note, however, that this hierarchy is not static. It can and does change over time, through time and works differently in different cultural settings. A good example of how such changes occur is reflected in the discussion proffered by McGarry and Walklate (2011) on soldiers as victims: two words that would have certainly seemed like a contradiction in terms when victimology as a discipline first made its presence felt but are perhaps not such uncomfortable bedfellows contemporarily. Thus it is important to remember that, as Quinney (1972: 314) once observed, 'our conceptions of victims and victimisation are optional, discretionary and are by no means innately given'. Thus victims are brought into being, not by some innate characteristics that they may or may not possess (as the early victimologists were concerned to explore) but by social processes, and it is within those social processes that the experiences that people have may or may not be recognised as victimisation.

FURTHER READING

Spalek, B. (2006) *Crime Victims: Theory, Policy and Practice*. Basingstoke: Palgrave Macmillan.

This offers a very useful discussion of the different definitional issues associated with these terms and brings to that discussion a nuanced understanding of the ethnic and masculinist limitations embedded in these terms.

Cole, A. (2007) *The Cult of True Victimhood*. Stanford, CA: Stanford University Press.

Furedi, F. (2013) *Moral Crusades in an Age of Mistrust: The Jimmy Savile Scandal*. Basingstoke: Palgrave Macmillan.

Both these books are accessible and thought provoking reads on what the term 'victim' actually means and what value can be assigned to it.

McGarry, R. and Walklate, S. (2015) *Victims: Trauma, Testimony, Justice*. Abingdon: Routledge.

This book offers a full exploration of the impact of criminal victimisation on both individuals and collectivities and provides a provocative intervention in terms of the relationship between culture and victimology.

REFERENCES

Bowling, B. (1998) *Violent Racism, Victimisation, Policing and Social Context*. Oxford: Clarendon.

Carrabine, E., Iganski, P., Lee, M., Plummer, K. and South, N. (2004) *Criminology: A Sociological Introduction*. London: Routledge.

Christie, N. (1986) 'The ideal victim', in E.A. Fattah (ed.), *From Crime Policy to Victim Policy*. London: Macmillan.

Cole, A. (2007) *The Cult of True Victimhood*. Stanford, MA: Stanford University Press.
Cowdry, R. (2007) *Families Shamed*. Cullompton: Willan.
Dignan, J. (2005) *Understanding Victims and Restorative Justice*. Maidenhead: Open University Press.
Dixon, M., Reed, H., Rogers, B. and Stone, L. (2006) *CrimeShare: The Unequal Impact of Crime*. London: IPPR.
Furedi, F. (1997) *Culture of Fear: Risk Taking and the Morality of Low Expectation*. London: Continuum.
Furedi, F. (2013) *Moral Crusades in an Age of Mistrust: The Jimmy Savile Scandal*. London: Palgrave-MacMillan.
Genn, H. (1988) 'Multiple victimisation', in M. Maguire and J. Pointing (eds), *Victims of Crime: A New Deal?* Milton Keynes: Open University Press.
Goodey, J. (2005) *Victims and Victimology*. London: Longmans.
Green, S. (2007) 'Crime, victimisation and vulnerability', in S. Walklate (ed.), *Handbook of Victims and Victimology*. Cullompton: Willan.
Hall, M. and Shapland, J. (2007) 'What do we know about the effects of crime on victims?', *International Review of Victimology*, 14: 175–217.
Hesse, B., Rai, D.K., Bennett, C. and McGilchrist, P. (1992) *Beneath the Surface: Racial Harassment*. Aldershot: Avebury.
Hodgson, C. (2005) 'Angry or what? Experiences of being a victim of crime', *British Journal of Community Justice*, 3(3): 50–61.
Hope, T. (2007) 'Theory and method: the social epidemiology of crime victims', in S. Walklate (ed.), *Handbook of Victims and Victimology*. Cullompton: Willan.
Howarth, G. and Rock, P. (2000) 'Aftermath and the construction of victimisation: "the other victim of crime"', *Howard Journal of Criminal Justice*, 39: 58–78.
Maguire, M. and Bennett, T. (1982) *Burglary in a Dwelling*. London: Heinemann.
McGarry, R. and Walklate, S. (2011) 'The soldier as victim: peering through the looking glass', *British Journal of Criminology*, 51(6): 900–917.
McGarry, R. and Walklate, S. (2015) *Victims: Trauma, Testimony, Justice*. London: Routledge.
Mendelsohn, B. (1956) 'A new branch of bio-psychological science: la victimology', *Revue Internationale de Criminologie et de Police Technique*, 2.
Payne, S. (2009) *Redefining Justice: Addressing the Individual Needs of Victims and Witnesses*. London: Ministry of Justice.
Quinney, R. (1972) 'Who is the victim?', *Criminology*, November: 309–239.
Rock, P. (1998) *After Homicide*. Oxford: Clarendon.
Rock, P. (2002) 'On becoming a victim', in C. Hoyle and R. Young (eds), *New Visions of Crime Victims*. Oxford: Hart.
Sennett, R. (1998) *The Corrosion of Character*. New York: Norton.
Spalek, B. (2006) *Crime Victims: Theory, Policy and Practice*. London: Palgrave.
Spalek, B. and King, S. (2007) *Farepak Victims Speak Out*. London: Centre for Crime and Justice Studies.
Strobl, R. (2010) 'Becoming a victim', in S.G. Shoham, P. Knepper and M. Kett (eds), *International Handbook of Victimology*. Boca Raton, FL: CRC Press.

Tombs, S. and Whyte, D. (2006) 'Risk and work', in G. Mythen and S. Walklate (eds), *Beyond the Risk Society: Critical Reflections on Risk and Human Security*. Maidenhead: Open University Press.

Tseloni, A. and Pease, K. (2003) 'Repeat victimisation: boosts or flags?', *British Journal of Criminology*, 43(1): 196–212.

Tulloch, J. (2006) *One Day in July*. London: Little Brown.

Valier, C. (2004) *Crime and Punishment in Contemporary Culture*. London: Routledge.

von Hentig, H. (1948) *The Criminal and His Victim*. New Haven, CT: Yale University Press.

Walklate, S. (2007) *Imagining the Victim of Crime*. Maidenhead: Open University Press.

Whyte, D. (2007) 'Victims of corporate crime', in S. Walklate (ed.), *Handbook of Victims and Victimology*. Cullompton: Willan.

Young, A. (1996) *Imagining Crime*. London: Sage.

3 NEWS MEDIA, VICTIMS AND CRIME

Chris Greer

Chapters 1 and 2 offered an overview of the emergence and development of victimology, and outlined some of the conceptual, practical and political problems associated with notions of 'victim' and 'victimhood'. Not least, the determination of who may legitimately claim victim status is influenced profoundly by social divisions including, class, race, ethnicity, gender, age and sexuality, and as such remains a matter of debate. Such debates are framed and inflected, to a significant extent, in the news media. This chapter, then, explores how the status of victim, and different acts and processes of criminal victimisation, are defined and constructed in the news media.

Research evidence has repeatedly confirmed that, across news and entertainment formats, media focus overwhelmingly on the most serious examples of violent, interpersonal offending (Marsh, 1991; Reiner et al., 2000). By contrast, lower-level property offences that make up the significant majority of recorded crime, and white-collar and corporate offences that place a major social and financial burden on society, have tended to receive less attention (Hillyard et al., 2004; Machin and Mayr, 2013; Whyte, 2015). Levi (2009) argues that the low visibility of corporate crime has been maintained by 'the "softly, softly" approach of the enforcement agencies, media averse to the genuine risk of libel suits, and governments and public almost superstitiously afraid of meddling with the market.' He also notes, however, that when corporate crimes become 'embodied in visible and known persons', media outcry can follow, not least because 'society is seen to be changing and becoming less moral' (ibid.). Yet these visible and known persons tend to be offenders. The victims of corporate crime remain mostly invisible. It is still the victims of violent, frequently fatal interpersonal crime that receive the greatest media attention. And even here, research evidence makes abundantly clear that news constructions are highly selective and unrepresentative, tending to focus on particular types of victims suffering particular types of victimisation by particular types of offender (Greer and Reiner, 2012; Gekoski et al., 2012).

Critically exploring news media constructions of crime victims is important because, over the past few decades, victims have taken on an unprecedented significance in media and criminal justice discourses, in the development of crime policy and in the popular imagination (Maguire and Pointing, 1988; Rock, 2004). Indeed, as Reiner and colleagues noted, the foregrounding of crime victims is one of the most significant qualitative changes in media constructions of crime and control since the Second World War (Reiner et al., 2000). This chapter is structured as follows. First, it takes a critical look at how social divisions shape the news media construction of crime victims and criminal victimisation, with a particular focus on 'ideal victims'. Second, it examines the newsworthiness of crime victims and explores how changes in the news environment have affected the reporting of criminal victimisation 'as news'. Third, it considers the growing significance and impact of institutional failure in victim-centred crime stories. Fourth, it identifies gaps in the existing research literature, raises some questions for further reflection, and suggests potentially fruitful areas for future research and investigation.

NEWS MEDIA CONSTRUCTIONS OF 'IDEAL', PRIMARY AND INDIRECT VICTIMS

Media interest in crime victims is at its greatest when they can be portrayed as 'ideal'. Christie (1986: 18) describes the **'ideal victim'** as 'a person or category of individuals who – when hit by crime – most readily are given the complete and legitimate status of being a victim.' This group includes those who are perceived as vulnerable, defenceless, innocent and worthy of sympathy and compassion. Elderly women and young children, it is suggested, are typical 'ideal victims', whereas young men, the homeless, those with drug problems, and others existing on the margins of society may find it much more difficult to achieve legitimate victim status, still less secure a conviction in court. In this sense, there exists a **'hierarchy of victimisation'**, reflected and reinforced in media and official discourses. At one extreme, those who acquire the status of 'ideal victim' may attract massive levels of media attention, generate collective mourning across the globe, drive significant change to social and criminal justice policy and practice, and even transform how society views itself. At the other extreme, those crime victims who never acquire legitimate victim status or, worse still, are perceived as 'undeserving victims' may receive little if any media attention, and pass virtually unnoticed in the wider social world (Greer, 2004; Peelo, 2006; Smolej, 2010). Examples spanning the past three decades can illustrate these dynamics in action.

In the summer of 2002, two 10-year-old girls, Holly Wells and Jessica Chapman, went missing from their home in Soham. Their disappearance attracted international media attention and precipitated the biggest ever manhunt in Britain. In 1996, two boys of similar age, Patrick Warren and David Spencer, went missing from their homes. Their disappearance failed to register much outside the local press. Shortly after 13-year-old Milly Dowler went missing in 2002, the body of a teenage girl was recovered from a disused cement works near Tilbury docks. Amidst press speculation that it was another missing teenager, Danielle Jones, who had disappeared almost a year earlier, the body was identified as that of 14-year-old Hannah Williams. Yet it was Milly's story that continued to dominate the headlines. Hannah received only a few sentences on the inside pages.

How might this media selectivity be understood? The answer lies, at least partly, in dominant conceptions of legitimate and ideal victims. Holly and Jessica were archetypal 'ideal victims'. They were young, bright, photogenic girls from stable and loving middle-class family backgrounds, and each had an exemplary school record. David and Patrick were working-class, they were boys, and they had been brought up on a rough West-Midlands council estate. They had been in trouble at school and one of them, David, had been caught shoplifting. While Holly and Jessica captured the hearts and minds of a nation, Patrick and David did not attract the same media or public interest, and few ever knew about their disappearance. Like Holly and Jessica, Milly Dowler epitomised the notion of an 'ideal victim'. By contrast, Hannah Williams was working-class, raised by a single mother on a low income, and had run away before. Her background denied her 'deserving' victim status and, eclipsed by Milly's ongoing story, Hannah was forgotten almost immediately. Hannah Williams' murder generated just over 60 articles in the British national press, mostly after her body was found. In its first two weeks alone the hunt for Holly and Jessica produced nearly 900 (Fracassini, 2002).

The attribution or otherwise of ideal or legitimate victim status and related levels of media interest are clearly influenced by demographic characteristics. The cases of missing and murdered children discussed above indicate that both 'class' – or perhaps better, a middle-class notion of 'respectability' – and gender can be defining factors. Race, too, can be central. In 1993 black teenager Stephen Lawrence was fatally stabbed in a racist attack. At first the police assumed that because the victim was a young, black male the murder must have been gang-related (Cottle, 2004; McLaughlin and Murji, 2001). It was not until later that Stephen was recognised and reported as a legitimate victim worthy of national media attention. Partly because of his race and partly because of his gender, legitimate victim status was not automatic as it was for Holly, Jessica and Milly, but needed to be won. The murder of white London solicitor Tom ap Rhys Price in 2006 received 6,061 words in the national press, while the murder of Asian London cement merchant Balbir Matharu, killed on the same day, received only 1,385 (Gibson and Dodd, 2006). For some, including the then Commissioner of the London Metropolitan Police, Sir Ian Blair (now Lord Blair of Boughton), the explanation was sad but simple: the British news media are institutionally racist in how they report murder. He further questioned news media selectivity by asking why the disappearance of Holly Wells and Jessica Chapman received so much attention:

> If you look at the murders in Soham, almost nobody can understand why that dreadful story became the biggest story in Britain. Let's be absolutely straight. It was a dreadful crime, nobody is suggesting anything else. But there are dreadful crimes which do not become the greatest story in Britain. Soham did for that August [2002] period become the greatest story (quoted in Steele, 2006: 6).

There was some limited media debate regarding the merits of the Commissioner's allegation of news media racism. Overwhelmingly, though, the media response was hostile. Outraged newspaper editors reproduced high-profile coverage of black and Asian murder

Daily Mail

FRIDAY, FEBRUARY 14, 1997

NEWSPAPER OF THE YEAR 35p

WIN UP TO £50,000 INSTANT CASH EXTRA

TODAY'S AMOUNT: PAGE 69

Jonathan Cainer: How you can find your Valentine

SEE PAGES 50-52

MURDERERS

The Mail accuses these men of killing. If we are wrong, let them sue us

Gary Dobson | Neil Acourt | Jamie Acourt | Luke Knight | David Norris

THE Daily Mail today takes the unprecedented step of naming five young men as murderers.

They may not have been convicted in a court of law, but police are sure that David Norris, Neil Acourt, Jamie Acourt, Gary Dobson and Luke Knight are the white youths who killed black teenager Stephen Lawrence.

We are naming them because, despite a criminal case, a private prosecution and an inquest, there has still been no justice for Stephen, who was stabbed to death in a racist attack almost four years ago.

One or more of the five may have a valid defence to the charge which has been repeatedly levelled against them. So far they have steadfastly refused every opportunity to offer such a defence.

Four have refused to give any alibi for that night in April 1993. One initially offered an alibi, but it did not stand up when police checked it out.

This week the five refused to answer any questions at the inquest on Stephen, citing their legal right of privilege not to say anything which might incriminate them.

The Lawrence case threatens to damage race relations and the reputation of British justice.

If these men are innocent they now have every opportunity to clear their names in a legal action against the Daily Mail. They would have to give evidence and a jury in possession of all the facts would finally be able to decide.

Yesterday the jury at Southwark Coroner's Court had little doubt of one thing. It took only 30 minutes to decide unanimously that the 18-year-old A-level student was unlawfully killed, the victim of 'a completely unprovoked racist attack by five white youths'.

The criminal cases against Norris, 20, Neil Acourt, 21, Jamie Acourt, 19, Dobson, 21, and Knight, 20, failed because of a lack of evidence. But if they thought they had got away with the killing they

COMMENT: Page 8

Turn to Page 6, Col. 2

INSIDE: Andrew Alexander 12, Femail 19, Diary 39, Friday First 42-48, Letters 53, TV 54-56, Coffee Break 67-69, City 70-72, Sport 73-80

Figure 3.1 *Daily Mail* headline naming the alleged killers of Stephen Lawrence

victims – including Stephen Lawrence – as 'proof' that they were not racist. The conservative *Daily Mail*, known for its 'traditionally reactionary stance on race issues in Britain' (McLaughlin and Murji, 2001: 377), reprinted its infamous front page which risked legal action by sensationally naming and picturing the alleged killers of Stephen Lawrence beneath the headline 'Murderers: The Mail accuses these men of killing. If we are wrong, let them sue us!' (see Figure 3.1).

But the heaviest criticism was directed at Sir Ian Blair for his Soham comment. Eclipsing the comparatively marginal discussion of racism in the press, Blair was castigated across a succession of front pages for daring to question the newsworthiness of ideal victims Holly Wells and Jessica Chapman. The following morning he made an unreserved 'on air' apology on BBC Radio 4 for any offence his comments might have caused the murdered girls' families (Blair, 2009). The Soham intervention was the tipping point in a relentless **trial by media** that coalesced with a hostile political environment to make the position of the Commissioner – considered too liberal by the UK conservative press and the newly elected Conservative Mayor of London – untenable (Greer and McLaughlin, 2011). In 2011, Sir Ian Blair became the first Metropolitan Police Commissioner to resign before the end of his term since Sir Charles Warren in 1888 – also in the midst of trial by media – who stepped down for failing to catch Jack the Ripper. Calling the press 'institutionally racist' was an irritation for journalists, who quickly rebutted the claim. Questioning the newsworthiness of 'ideal victims' Holly and Jessica was unforgivable, and the press went on the attack.

Sir Ian Blair's successor, Sir Paul Stephenson, became the second Met Commissioner since 1888 to resign before term, as a result of the phone hacking scandal of 2011. The symbolic and political power of 'ideal victims' was pivotal here too. The phone hacking story broke in 2007 with revelations that journalists at the Sunday tabloid *News of the World* had worked with private investigators to hack the phones of the royal family, politicians and celebrities. The story became a full-blown scandal when the *Guardian* (Davies, 2011) reported that journalists' hacking activities had extended to ordinary members of the public, and crime victims – including victims of the 7 July 2005 London Bombings and 'ideal victim' Milly Dowler. It was alleged that journalists had hacked Milly Dowler's phone in 2002, before her body was found, eavesdropped on voicemail messages left by her family and deleted messages from her phone. Deleting messages created space for new ones, giving the family – who never stopped calling – false hope that Milly was still alive, and hampering the police investigation by destroying potential evidence.[1] Public outcry and the legal repercussions of the phone hacking scandal were so damaging that in 2011 the *News of the World*'s owner, Rupert Murdoch, closed the 168-year-old newspaper and the UK Government established the Leveson Inquiry (2012) to investigate the 'culture, practices and ethics of the press and, in particular, the relationship of the press with the public, police and politicians'. The Metropolitan Police Service was implicated in the scandal for failing properly to investigate allegations of hacking, for the possible involvement of police officers in facilitation and cover-up, for not informing victims whose phones had been hacked, and for misleading the public and Parliament about the scale of phone hacking. When it was revealed that the Met had hired the former executive editor of the disgraced *News of the World* as an advisor, allegations of institutional corruption and cover-up forced Sir Paul Stephenson's resignation (Greer and McLaughlin, 2012a).

Ideal victims are **primary victims**: those harmed directly and immediately as participants in the criminal event. Most cases of criminal victimisation also feature **indirect victims**: the

[1] Evidence subsequently brought to court confirmed the hacking and the parents' experience of 'false-hope', but cast doubt on the source of the message deletions, suggesting they were more likely to be automatic than deliberate (https://www.theguardian.com/uk-news/2014/jun/26/phone-hacking-trial-milly-dowler-voicemail).

families, friends and relatives of primary victims, those who may be distressed by witnessing serious crimes, and the wider community (Howarth and Rock, 2000; see also Chapter 2). The legitimacy of primary crime victims is attributed, or denied, on the basis of that victim's characteristics, the wider socio-economic context in which they live and their degree of separation from the offender. As we have seen, ideal victim status is the news media's most emphatic expression of victim legitimacy. Since only a tiny minority of crime victims ever achieve ideal victim status, it tends once attributed to be robust and remain stable over time. The news media construction of indirect victims is altogether more unpredictable. Their status as worthy of news media support and public sympathy is established, or denied, through the closeness of their association with the primary victim, their personal and demographic characteristics, and crucially their willingness and ability to engage with the news media. The news media construction of indirect victims can change dramatically with the twists and turns of a developing news story.

Three-year-old Madeleine McCann disappeared on 3 May 2007 from a holiday apartment in Portugal, while her parents, Kate and Gerry McCann, were having dinner with friends approximately 120 metres away. The case received unprecedented global media attention. Across rolling 24/7 news coverage and social media, Madeleine was constructed as the archetypal 'ideal victim' (see Figure 3.2). In stark contrast, her parents, at first universally supported by a sympathetic press as the indirect victims of a terrible crime against their daughter, quickly became the targets for sustained and defamatory **trial by media** (Greer and McLaughlin, 2012b). These white, mediagenic, middle-class doctors proactively engaged with journalists to try and maximise the news visibility of the case and manage the news agenda. For a period, the strategy worked. Unlike in the UK, however, there is no culture of open dialogue between the Portuguese police and the news media, so when the investigation failed to produce a breakthrough and the 'facts' of the case dried up, the news void needed to be filled. Madeleine's parents went from managing the news agenda to becoming the news agenda. Their news construction shifted from *indirect victims* of Madeleine's abduction to *primary suspects* in her abduction and murder. After months of media speculation based on unofficial sources, police leaks, rumour and gossip, the McCanns' trial by media reached its height in January 2008 when a flood of front-page newspaper stories insinuated that Kate and Gerry McCann were responsible for their daughter's death, had disposed of her body, and had conspired to cover up their actions by deliberately diverting police attention from evidence that would expose their guilt (for Statement in Open Court see Carter-Ruck, 2008). In an attempt to reclaim both the news agenda and their status as legitimate victims, the McCanns took legal action against those newspapers for publishing 'utterly false and defamatory allegations' (ibid.). Realising there was little chance of winning a High Court battle, several newspapers published unprecedented front-page apologies and contributed substantial sums to the parents' 'Find Madeleine' fund. Others settled by private agreement. Once again, the McCanns were constructed in the UK press as indirect victims of their daughter's still-unresolved abduction, and now also as primary victims of news media defamation. In 2016 Madeleine was still missing. While dwindling UK news coverage remains overwhelmingly supportive, the McCanns are still subjected to an array of internet and social media attacks which they appear powerless to prevent.

Figure 3.2 Find Madeleine poster

These cases illustrate the complexity of what it is to be a 'victim' in the news. They demonstrate how demographic characteristics like class, ethnicity, gender and age can at times determine news media interest in a fairly straightforward manner, but can also cut across each other and interact with other variables in nuanced and unpredictable ways that do much to invalidate blanket claims that 'the press' or, still worse, 'the media' are institutionally prejudiced. The influence of victim demographics needs to be considered within the wider context of the news production process, the influence of social media, the other elements of the case in question, and the prevailing cultural and political environment at that time. In order to unravel this complexity a little further, it is helpful to explore the concept of newsworthiness.

Stop now and try to think of some well-known victims of crime.

How would you describe these victims?

Other than their victimisation, do they share anything in common?

What do your findings tell you about news media representations of crime and criminal victimisation?

PAUSE FOR REVIEW

NEWSWORTHINESS, CRIME AND CRIMINAL VICTIMISATION

There exists an extensive literature on the various factors that make events attractive – or 'newsworthy' – to journalists (Chibnall, 1977; Hall et al., 1978; Katz, 1987; Greer, 2012; Jewkes, 2015). Newsworthiness is shaped by **news values** – those criteria that determine which events come within the horizon of media visibility, and to what extent, and which do not. Since the first sociological statement of news values by Galtung and Ruge in 1965, numerous commentators have offered their own interpretation of the key determinants of newsworthiness. Most accounts agree on certain criteria, which can be thought of as core or fundamental news values, including: drama, novelty, titillation, simplification and conservative ideology. With specific reference to crime news, most accounts also highlight the importance of violence. The observation made by Hall et al. (1978: 68) four decades ago still holds today:

> One special point about crime as news is the special status of *violence* as a news value. Any crime can be lifted into news visibility if violence becomes associated with it ... Violence represents a basic violation of the person; the greatest personal crime is 'murder' ... Violence is also the ultimate crime against property, and against the State. It thus represents a fundamental rupture in the social order.

Despite enduring similarities between accounts, it is important to recognise that news values are also culturally specific in that they reflect the historical and social moment in which they are situated. As media and society change, so too can the criteria that influence the selection and production of events as news. The 'celebritization' of society has rendered just about anything related to 'celebrity culture' newsworthy (Driessens, 2013). Celebrity crime is especially so. The 'sexualisation' of society has also affected the news (Duschinsky, 2013). With the breaking down of many sexual taboos in recent decades, sex and violence are presented more frequently and graphically across all media forms, including crime news (Greer and Jewkes, 2005; Reiner et al., 2000).

At the same time, specific criminal incidents can have a lasting influence on crime reporting. The racist murder of Stephen Lawrence, and evidence of institutional racism in the police (mis)handling of the case (Macpherson, 1999), intensified interest in race and racism and their connection to 'crime and victimisation', 'law and order', 'policing and criminal justice' (Cottle, 2005; McLaughlin and Murji, 2001; see also Chapter 11). The sexually-motivated abduction and murder of 8-year-old Sarah Payne in the summer of 2000 by a convicted paedophile crystallised fears around the image of the predatory child sex offender and fuelled debate on 'risk and dangerousness', 'punishment and rehabilitation', 'surveillance and control' and the suitability of public notification regarding sex offenders in the community (Silverman and Wilson, 2002). And the scandalous revelation in 2012 that television icon and national treasure Sir Jimmy Savile had for decades exploited his BBC celebrity status to sexually abuse children and young people in Britain's public institutions led to a flood of fresh accusations of abuse against television celebrities, public figures and institutions across the UK (Greer and McLaughlin, 2013, 2016). In the wake of these cases, further incidents of child violence, racist violence, predatory sexual violence and institutional violence are rendered more newsworthy still because they can be reported in relation to the paradigmatic incident at that time, which in turn can be revisited, reactivated and recreated across corporate and social media for a mass audience. Thus, while violence endures as a core news value, its newsworthiness can be intensified considerably when focused through the lenses of celebrity, childhood, sex and race, institutional corruption and cover-up, among others – categories that are not in themselves new, but which have gained increased and lasting media currency due to wider social change and/or specific, high-profile crimes.

NEWSWORTHINESS, CRIME VICTIMS AND THE VISUAL

Until recently, accounts of crime newsworthiness have paid insufficient attention to the importance of the **visual** (Brown and Carrabine, 2017). The rapid development of communication technologies has changed the terrain on which crime news is produced. Today, crime stories are selected and 'produced' as *media events* on the basis of their visual (how they can be portrayed in images) as well as their lexical-verbal (how they can be portrayed in words) potential. Of course, television stations are primarily concerned with producing an appealing visual product, but press representations too – in their print and, especially, their online formats – have become increasingly driven by visuals, incorporating: photographs of victims, offenders, or loved ones; diagrams and interactive digital maps of a route taken, a geographical area, or a crime scene; graphic illustrations of crime rates, prison populations, and police numbers; satirical cartoons lampooning bungling criminal justice professionals; the list goes on. These visual elements of the news product depict immediately, dramatically, and often in full colour what it may take several paragraphs to say in words. As one British reporter explained, 'A tabloid journalist often thinks about collects first (photographs) and interviews second, because the picture is paramount to the amount of space your story gets in the paper' (cited in Gekoski et al., 2012: 1218). If the visual has always played an important part in the manufacture of crime news (Hall, 1973), today it has become a universally defining characteristic.

Where victims of crime are concerned, the potential to visualise a case can have a direct impact on its perceived newsworthiness. Gekoski et al. (2012: 1220; see also Chermak, 1995) interviewed a number of British newspaper journalists about crime news production, one of whom said:

> What is important is the co-operation the victim's family and friends give the press. If they close the door and refuse to speak to the press, then it makes their job more difficult and they may not be able to glean the necessary information required to make it a good story. However if they decide to hold press conferences, give out photographs of the victim, and talk on their door steps about the victim, then it will make the job of the journalist easier, and therefore increase the space it is given in the newspaper article.

Indeed, the press conference has become integral, both to the police investigation and the news reporting of murder cases. Today it is *expected* that indirect victims – most often the primary victims' loved ones – will express their emotions and share their pain and suffering with media audiences, at once horrified and fascinated by the spectacle unfolding before them. As well as increasing the likelihood of public co-operation in a murder investigation, police are also aware that 'emotional displays of this kind make a good story for journalists and thus the case may receive more media attention than it might otherwise do' (Innes, 2003: 58). The parents of Holly Wells and Jessica Chapman, Sarah Payne and Milly Dowler – all indirect victims in child abduction and murder cases – made emotional television appeals for the safe return of their children, and in some cases for information regarding the identity and whereabouts of their child's killer. Madeleine McCann's parents went further still and appointed media advisors to help manage the news agenda. The risk, as they learned to their cost, is that once inside the media spotlight it can be impossible to step back out. Their punishing trial by media is clear evidence that, even with professional help, it is impossible to control the news process with any certainty, still less manage wider social media speculation and debate. Because these cases featured ideal victims, media interest was automatic. In stark contrast, Stephen Lawrence's parents were faced with a clear lack of media interest in their son's murder. They had to campaign to raise the case's profile and keep it in the public imagination when media attention was sparse (Cottle, 2004). Their efforts paid off. With the continuing support of the *Daily Mail*, two men were convicted of Stephen Lawrence's murder and sentenced to life imprisonment in 2012. The newspaper's editor, Paul Dacre (2012), had the following to say:

> I don't think it's an exaggeration to say that if it hadn't been for the *Mail*'s headline in 1997 – 'Murderers: The Mail accuses these men of killing' – and our years of campaigning, none of this would have happened. Britain's police might not have undergone the huge internal reform that was so necessary. Race relations might not have taken the significant step forward that they have. And an 18-year-old A-Level student who dreamed of being an architect would have been denied justice. The *Daily Mail* took a monumental risk with that headline. In many ways, it was an outrageous, unprecedented step.

Ultimately, in each of these cases articulate and 'respectable' parents were not only able, but willing, and in some cases driven to engage with the media and withstand the constant and potentially blinding glare of its spotlight. Their suitability and capability in this regard made the stories more newsworthy and, crucially, kept the cases in the public eye. Those less willing or able to engage with the media, those the police consider less suitable for media exposure, or those the media themselves are less interested in reporting, may find that attention quickly dries up.

Potentially even more powerful than press conferences, victim photographs familiarise media audiences, instantly and enduringly, with victims of crime in a way that words cannot. 'Photographs', Susan Sontag (2004: 2) argues, 'have an insuperable power to determine what people recall of events'. Gerrard (2004: 14), writing about the murders of Holly Wells and Jessica Chapman, suggests that 'We understand with words and stories, through the linked chain of events. But we recollect in pictures. Memory freeze-frames. Our lives are held in a series of vivid stills inside our head, and so it is with more public events.' And in the words of one journalist, 'If the public can see ... a victim, it adds something. There is nothing to a name. When you see a picture, you see the life, the potential' (cited in Chermak, 1995: 104). In missing persons and murder cases, victim photographs are rendered more poignant still by the understanding that those featured may be, or already are, dead. They present an idealised personification of innocence and loss. At the same time, they serve indirectly to highlight the monstrosity of the offender and the extent to which that monstrosity should inform a retributive justice response (Pickett et al., 2013). In Western culture so attuned to the visual (Carrabine, 2012; Young, 2014), photographs simultaneously humanise and memorialise crime victims, creating affective connections between image and spectator, victim and viewer, with potential to evoke a more visceral and emotionally charged reaction than might be produced by words alone.

Thus it is not only what is known or imagined about victims, in terms of background, life history, future potential, but also how vividly – how *visually* – that history and potential can be communicated to media audiences. In high-profile crimes featuring 'ideal victims', whose innocence is uncontested and whose potential is palpably felt, photographs may take on an iconic status, becoming an instant, powerful and lasting reference point. The photograph of Holly Wells and Jessica Chapman posing in their matching Manchester United shirts, the school portrait of Sarah Payne, or the picture of Madeleine McCann (Figure 3.2) are examples of victim photographs which were used relentlessly throughout each case and its aftermath, and became deeply embedded in the popular imagination. The power of these images, the newsworthiness of the crime type, the social characteristics of the primary victims, and the suitability and willingness of the indirect victims to engage with the news media coalesced with other factors to produce a compelling narrative that connected deeply and on a profoundly personal level with media consumers. A further reason why many of these cases maintained a high-profile news media presence was evidence of serious failure by key institutions and agencies tasked with the role of 'public protection'.

CRIME VICTIMS AND INSTITUTIONAL FAILURE

A key element in the construction of a compelling crime narrative is the attribution of blame (Chibnall, 1977). Blame for serious and violent crimes may be individual and directed at offenders, or less often social and directed at society. Importantly, however, it can also be institutional. When there is evidence that official agencies and state bodies assigned to protect the innocent have somehow failed in this task, the potential to develop and sustain a compelling narrative is increased considerably. Media interest in the deaths of Stephen Lawrence, Sarah Payne, Holly Wells and Jessica Chapman was maintained in part by evidence of serious institutional failings – variously implicating the police, the courts, the education system – which were portrayed either as serving to maintain the conditions that allowed the offence to occur in the first place, or impeding the police investigation and prosecution of the alleged offenders afterwards. Now sensationally located at the heart of a scandal, the victims' symbolic power extended beyond their individual cases and they became representative of wider issues and debates on public safety, social and criminal justice, or the nature of society itself.

When crime victims come to symbolise a problem that resonates with and potentially affects many in society – school safety, racist violence, knife crime, institutional child sexual abuse – mediatised campaigns, particularly when launched in the victim's name, are likely to garner high levels of public support (Chancer, 2005). Faced with collective moral outrage and a barrage of critical media coverage, agencies publicly implicated as part of the problem, or the authorities to which those agencies are answerable, are required to respond. In each of the cases discussed above, the response was some form of official inquiry which, in turn, led to recommendations for change across structures of training and accountability, professional practice, and criminal justice and public policy. The Macpherson Report (1999) investigating the mismanagement of the Stephen Lawrence murder case branded the London Metropolitan Police 'professionally incompetent and institutionally racist' and called for fundamental change to police training and accountability, and engagement with black communities across the UK (Hall et al., 2013). Sarah Payne's abduction and murder by a convicted paedophile generated mediatised debate and public outrage, which informed the legislative changes embodied in the Sex Offences Act 2003 and resulted in the nationwide launch of the Child Sex Offenders Disclosure scheme – also known as Sarah's Law – across the UK in 2012 (Lipscombe, 2012; Jones and Newburn, 2013). The murders of Holly Wells and Jessica Chapman resulted in the Bichard Inquiry (2004), which scrutinised the police's 'intelligence-based record keeping, vetting practices and information sharing with other agencies' and made recommendations relevant for police, social services, education establishments, vetting services and government aimed at improving national child protection. The Savile scandal resulted in most far-reaching public inquiry in British history. With victims potentially numbering in the thousands, the Independent Inquiry into Child Sexual Abuse (IICSA) has been launched not in the name of an individual 'ideal victim', but in the name of *all* victims of institutional child sexual abuse in England and Wales in the post-War period (Greer and McLaughlin, 2016). The IICSA is committed to 'identify institutional failings where they are found to exist' and to 'demand accountability for past institutional failings' (www.iicsa.org.uk/). It is arguably leading to a re-writing of British post-War history as a growing body of evidence forces British society to acknowledge that: a) the sexual victimisation of children has been widespread across UK public and private sector institutions throughout the post-War period; and b) in many cases senior figures knew abuse was taking place and either failed to act or, still worse, actively covered it up.

The extent to which the changes or recommendations for change following these cases have been appropriate, effective or adequately implemented remains a matter for debate (Hall et al., 2013; Foster et al., 2005; Roycroft et al., 2007; Price et al., 2013). For current purposes, what is important is the role news media played in generating, sustaining and shaping the preceding debate. In each case news media were instrumental in publicly defining the cases, rooting the victims' images in the popular imagination, generating and focusing collective moral outrage and support for change, and, crucially, keeping the stories alive in both political and popular consciousness, in some cases long after the initial investigation had closed.

Revisit your list of crime victims.

What is it that you recall about each case? Is it the details of the offence; the news coverage – social media, television, press, radio, internet; the images that were released during the investigation; evidence of institutional failure?

Do some research and make a list of any investigations, inquiries or policy outcomes that resulted from these cases.

Why do some murder victims bring about transformations in policy, practice and public understanding, while most receive little media or public attention?

What other forms of criminal victimisation, not discussed in this chapter, are reported in the news? What characterises those news constructions?

SUMMARY

This chapter has identified and explored some of the key influences that shape the construction of crime victims and criminal victimisation in the news media. It has explored the relationship between social divisions, inequality and 'ideal' or 'legitimate' victim status, and examined how changes in the media environment and the news production process have impacted on the construction of primary and indirect crime victims. More specifically, it has sought to demonstrate the complexity of the interconnections between these factors and the impact they can have on the attribution of legitimate or ideal victim status, media interest, the public construction of particular murder cases and the policy outcomes that may result from victim-driven news media campaigns. These closing paragraphs offer a few points by way of summary, raise some questions which seem pertinent at the present time, and suggest a number of potentially fruitful areas for further research and investigation.

Over the past forty years or so, shifts in 'official' and 'academic' thinking, accompanied by wider political and cultural change, have contributed to generating a climate in which 'system discourses' are often pitched in vain against 'victim discourses' (Garland, 2000). At a time of widespread intolerance, anxiety and fear of the unknown 'other', those who are seen to represent the interests of offenders occupy an uncomfortable and, at times, deeply unpopular place within public hearts and minds (Greer, 2012). In stark contrast, those who speak for victims are seen to speak for us all. Yet the victim voices that find resonance in the media represent only a fraction of those suffering criminal victimisation. What this chapter demonstrates, along with the other contributions in this collection, is that those who feel the pains of victimisation most acutely are often those whose voices are stifled rather than amplified in news media discourses.

It is not simply the case that race, gender or any other social division retains an immutable defining influence over media interest in crime victims and their subsequent construction in the news. Reporting criminal victimisation is fluid and dynamic, and can change from case to case and over time. Implicitly promoting the view that news media, like any other institution, are capable of reflexive learning, many journalists would contend that since Stephen Lawrence the news media have learned how to 'do race', if perhaps not yet 'class'. That there is evidence both for and against this claim – some of which has been discussed in this chapter – serves further to highlight the variability of news reporting and the dangers of settling for blanket generalisations about the prejudices of the 'the press' or 'the media'. Nevertheless, it remains the case that much news coverage of criminal victimisation both reflects and reinforces social divisions and inequalities, and in so doing feeds into the wider structures of power, dominance and marginalisation from which they derive.

Despite the growing scholarly interest in the construction of crime victims and criminal victimisation in the media, a number of key questions remain under-researched:

- How do different individuals and groups go about soliciting and sustaining media interest in particular crime victims, or types of criminal victimisation?
- What are the necessary conditions for victimised members of marginalised and powerless groups to be deemed worthy of media attention and public sympathy?
- How might you evaluate the everyday impact on crime consciousness of the selective representation of crime victims?
- How might you go about researching the influence of social media on the representation of crime victims in the news?

The answers to these questions are complex and difficult to research, but this does nothing to diminish their importance. In the digital age, news and social media debates are a key influence in shaping popular notions of who can rightly claim legitimate victim status, informing victim policy formation and, ultimately, helping to shape the structures of training, accountability and professional practice directed at protecting the public and responding to victims of crime. Deconstructing the power dynamics, information flows, social relations and political struggles between all those involved in the news production process is an important criminological project. Just like so many crime victims who remain marginalised or ignored in official discourses, understanding the role of media in constructing and representing crime victims and criminal victimisation cannot remain on the periphery of academic enquiry. Rather, it should be a central concern for all those wishing seriously to engage with the contemporary construction and meaning of crime, control and social order.

FURTHER READING

Chermak, S. (1995) *Victims in the News: Crime and the American News Media*. Boulder, CO: Westview Press.

One of the few book-length studies on the topic, Chermak presents an in-depth qualitative analysis of the often contested processes through which crime victims are socially constructed in American news media.

Cottle, S. (2004) *The Racist Murder of Stephen Lawrence: Media Performance and Public Transformation*. Westport, CT: Praeger.

A sophisticated book-length analysis of the Stephen Lawrence case and its construction and 'performance' in the media, exploring the rhetoric of journalism, the dynamics and contingencies within both politics and storytelling, and the strategic interventions of various groups, interests and identities.

Crime, Media Culture: An International Journal. London: Sage.

This journal offers a forum for exchange between scholars who are working at the intersections of criminological and cultural inquiry. It promotes a broad cross-disciplinary understanding of the relationship between crime, criminal justice, media and culture, and regularly features article on media methodology, news production, and crime victims and criminal victimisation.

Greer, C. (2003/2012) *Sex Crime and the Media: Sex Offending and the Press in a Divided Society*. London: Routledge.

This book presents an in depth quantitative and qualitative analysis of the press reporting of sex crime, including detailed discussion of victims and offenders, and interviews with all the key players in the news production process.

REFERENCES

Bichard, Sir M. (2004) *The Bichard Inquiry: Report*, HC653. London: The Stationery Office.

Blair, I. (2009) *Policing Controversy*. London: Profile.

Brown, M. and Carrabine, E. (eds) (2017) *The Routledge International Handbook of Visual Criminology*. London: Routledge.

Carrabine, E. (2012) 'Just images: aesthetics, ethics and visual criminology', *British Journal of Criminology*, 52(3): 463–89.

Carter-Ruck (2008) 'Kate and Gerry McCann: Statement in Open Court'. Available at www.carter-ruck.com/news/read/kate-and-gerry-mccann (accessed 7.11.16).

Chancer, L. (2005) *High-Profile Crimes: When Legal Cases become Social Causes*. Chicago, IL: University of Chicago Press.

Chermak, S. (1995) *Victims in the News: Crime and the American News Media*. Boulder, CO: Westview Press.

Chibnall, S. (1977) *Law and Order News: An Analysis of Crime Reporting in the British Press*. London: Tavistock.

Christie, N. (1986) 'The ideal victim', in E. Fattah (ed.), *From Crime Policy to Victim Policy*. Basingstoke: Macmillan.

Cottle, S. (2004) *The Racist Murder of Stephen Lawrence: Media Performance and Public Transformation*. Westport, CT: Praeger.

Cottle, S. (2005) 'Mediatized public crisis and civil society renewal: the racist murder of Stephen Lawrence', *Crime, Media, Culture: An International Journal*, 1(1): 49–71.

Dacre, P. (2012) 'A glorious day for justice: How the Mail's monumental risk could have put editor Paul Dacre in court ... but instead did 'a huge amount of good and made a little bit of history', *Daily Mail*, 4 January.

Davies, N. (2011) 'Missing Milly Dowler's voicemail was hacked by News of the World', *Guardian*, 4 July.

Davies, N. (2014) 'Phone-hacking trial failed to clear up mystery of Milly Dowler's voicemail', *Guardian*, 26 June.

Driessens, O. (2013) 'The celebritization of society and culture: understanding the structural dynamics of celebrity culture', *International Journal of Cultural Studies*, 16(6): 641–57.

Duschinsky, R. (2013) 'The emergence of sexualization as a social problem: 1981–2010', *Social Politics*, 20(1): 137–56.

Foster J., Newburn, T. and Souhami, A. (2005) *Assessing the Impact of the Stephen Lawrence Inquiry*, Home Office Research Study 294. London: Home Office.

Fracassini, C. (2002) 'Missing', *Scotland on Sunday*, 18 August.

Galtung, J. and Ruge, M. (1965) 'Structuring and selecting news', in S. Cohen and J. Young (eds), *The Manufacture of News: Deviance, Social Problems and the Mass Media*. London: Constable.

Garland, D. (2000) 'The culture of high crime societies: some preconditions of recent "Law and order" politics', *British Journal of Criminology*, 40: 347–75.

Gekoski, A., Gray, J. and Adler, J. (2012) 'What makes a homicide newsworthy?', *British Journal of Criminology*, 52(6): 1212–32.

Gerrard, N. (2004) *Soham: A Story of Our Times*. London: Short Books.
Gibson, O. and Dodd, V. (2006) 'Met Chief labels media institutionally racist', *Guardian*, 27 January.
Greer, C. (2004) 'Crime, media and community: grief and virtual engagement in late modernity', in J. Ferrell, K. Hayward, W. Morrison and M. Presdee (eds), *Cultural Criminology Unleashed*. London: Cavendish.
Greer, C. (2012) *Sex Crime and the Media: Sex Offending and the Press in a Divided Society*. London: Routledge.
Greer, C. and Jewkes, Y. (2005) 'Extremes of otherness: media images of social exclusion', *Social Justice*, 32(1): 20–31.
Greer, C. and McLaughlin, E. (2011) 'Trial by media: policing, the 24–7 news mediasphere, and the politics of outrage', *Theoretical Criminology*, 15(1): 23–46.
Greer, C. and McLaughlin, E. (2012a) 'Trial by media: riots, looting, gangs and mediatised police chiefs', in J. Peay and T. Newburn (eds), *Policing, Politics, Culture and Control: Essays in Honour of Robert Reiner*. London: Hart. pp. 19.
Greer, C. and McLaughlin, E. (2012b) 'Media justice: Madeleine McCann, intermediatisation and "trial by media" in the British press', *Theoretical Criminology*, 16(4): 395–416.
Greer, C. and McLaughlin, E. (2013) 'The Sir Jimmy Savile scandal: child sexual abuse and institutional denial at the BBC', *Crime Media Culture: An International Journal*, 9(3): 243–63.
Greer, C. and McLaughlin, E. (2016) 'Theorizing institutional scandal and the regulatory state', *Theoretical Criminology*, DOI: 10.1177/1362480616645648.
Greer, C. and Reiner, R. (2012) 'Media made criminality: the representation of crime in the mass media', in M. Maguire, R. Morgan and R. Reiner (eds), *The Oxford Handbook of Criminology* (3rd edn). Oxford: Oxford University Press.
Hall, N., Grieve, J. and Savage, S. (eds) (2013) *Policing and the Legacy of Lawrence*. Cullompton: Willan.
Hall, S. (1973) 'The determination of news photographs', in S. Cohen and J. Young (eds), *The Manufacture of News: Deviance, Social Problems and the Mass Media*. London: Constable.
Hall, S., Critcher, C., Jefferson, T., Clarke, J. and Roberts, B. (1978) *Policing the Crisis: Mugging, the State and Law and Order*. London: Macmillan.
Hillyard, P., Pantazis, C., Tombs, S. Gordon, D. (eds) (2004) *Beyond Criminology: Taking Harm Seriously*. London: Pluto Press.
Howarth, G. and Rock, P. (2000) 'Aftermath and the construction of victimisation: "the other victims of crime"', *Howard Journal*, 39(1): 58–77.
Innes, M. (2003) 'Signal crimes: detective work, mass media and constructing collective memory', in P. Mason (ed.), *Criminal Visions: Representations of Crime and Justice*. Cullompton: Willan.
Jewkes, Y. (2015) *Media and Crime* (3rd edn). London: Sage.
Jones, T. and Newburn, T. (2013) 'Policy convergence, politics and comparative penal reform: sex offender notification schemes in the USA and UK', *Punishment & Society*, 15(5): 439–67.
Katz, J. (1987) 'What makes crime "news"?', *Media, Culture and Society*, 9: 47–75.
Leveson, Lord Justice (2012) *The Leveson Inquiry: Culture, Practice and Ethics of the* Press. Available at http://webarchive.nationalarchives.gov.uk/20140122145147/http:/www.leveson inquiry.org.uk/ (accessed 6.10.16).
Levi, M. (2009) 'Suite revenge? The shaping of folk devils and moral panics about white-collar crimes', *British Journal of Criminology*, 49(1): 48–67.

Lipscombe, S. (2012) *Sarah's Law: The Child Sex Offender Disclosure Scheme*. House of Commons Library, Standard Note SN/HA/1692.

Machin, D. and Mayr, A. (2013) 'Corporate crime and the discursive deletion of responsibility: a case study of the Paddington rail crash', *Crime Media Culture*, 9(1): 63–82.

Macpherson, Sir W. (1999) *The Stephen Lawrence Inquiry: Report of an Inquiry by Sir William Macpherson of Cluny*. London: HMSO.

Maguire, M. and Pointing, J. (eds) (1988) *Victims of Crime: A New Deal?* Milton Keynes: Open University Press.

Marsh, H.L. (1991) 'A comparative analysis of crime coverage in newspapers in the United States and other countries from 1960–1989: a review of the literature', *Journal of Criminal Justice*, 19(1): 67–80.

McLaughlin, E. and Murji, K. (2001) 'Ways of seeing: the news media and racist violence', in M. May, E. Brunsden and R. Page (eds), *Understanding Social Problems: Issues in Social Policy*. Oxford: Blackwell.

Peelo, M. (2006) 'Framing homicide narratives in newspapers: mediated witness and the construction of virtual victimhood', *Crime, Media, Culture: An International Journal*, 2(2): 159–75.

Pickett, J., Mancini, C. and Mears, D. (2013) 'Vulnerable victims, monstrous offenders, and unmanageable risk: explaining public opinion on the social control of sex crime', *Criminology*, 51: 729–59.

Price, S., Hansen, R. and Tagliani, L. (2013) 'Screening procedures in the United Kingdom for positions of trust with children', *Journal of Sexual Aggression*, 19(1): 17–31.

Reiner, R., Livingstone, S. and Allen, J. (2000) 'Casino culture: media and crime in a winner-loser society', in K. Stenson and D. Cowell (eds), *Crime, Risk and Justice*. Cullompton: Willan Press.

Rock, P. (2004) *Constructing Victims' Rights: The Home Office, New Labour and Victims*. Oxford: Oxford University Press.

Roycroft, M., Brown, J. and Innes, M. (2007) 'Reform by crisis: the murder of Stephen Lawrence and a socio-historical analysis of developments in the conduct of major crime investigations', in M. Rowe (ed.), *Policing Beyond MacPherson: Issues in Policing, Race and Society*. Cullompton: Willan.

Silverman, J. and Wilson, D. (2002) *Innocence Betrayed: Paedophilia, the Media and Society*. Cambridge: Polity Press.

Smolej, M. (2010) 'Constructing ideal victims? Violence narratives in Finnish crime-appeal programming', *Crime Media Culture*, 6(1): 69–85.

Sontag, S. (2004) 'What have we done?', *Guardian G2*, 24 May, pp. 2–5.

Steele, J. (2006) 'Met Chief: Why the fuss over Soham murders?', *Daily Telegraph*, 27 January.

Whyte, D. (ed.) (2015) *How Corrupt is Britain?* London: Pluto.

Young, A. (2014) 'From object to encounter: aesthetic politics and visual criminology', *Theoretical Criminology*, 18(2): 159–75.

4 HISTORICAL PERSPECTIVES IN VICTIMOLOGY

Barry Godfrey

Research into victims of crime has been closely related to the development of criminology (Miers, 1978; Holstein and Miller, 1990), and particularly critical victimology (Walklate, 1996, 1992; Mawby and Walklate, 1994). Only in 1948 was the first detailed study of victims published. In describing 13 psychological and sociological classes of victim, von Hentig's *The Criminal and His Victim* (1948) was an important but rather solitary foray into an area of criminology which would only fully emerge some years later (Mawby and Walklate 1994: 69). Ironically, research into the experiences of victims emerged at a historical moment when the part played by victims in the criminal justice system was around its lowest. In 1985 the historian George Rude famously answered his own question: 'What do we know about the characters or attitudes of victims? The answer is very little' (1985:76). Thirty years on, however, we can be a little more confident that we know a little more about victims, partly because of the development of victimology and the emergence of criminological research into victims, and partly because of the willingness of researchers to interrogate historical sources which are able to throw much more light on to the changing role of victims in the criminal justice system.

This chapter follows a broadly chronological framework while exploring some of the key issues about the practical circumstances that restricted the options of victims of crime to take their cases to court: the orientation of the criminal justice system towards victims, first as active prosecutors and later as 'ideal victims' for whom the system worked. It will introduce some contradictions, including the times when victims took action themselves outside of official routes to justice, and when the boundaries between victims and offenders became blurred. Last, given the huge gaps in our knowledge of victims, it will look at the ways in which the new digital media can, at last, offer some opportunities for research into the lives and experiences of victims of crime in the last 200 years. In doing all of this, the chapter will illustrate the confused and contradictory position that victims have occupied as both symbolic and real actors in the detection and prosecution of crime from the 18th to 20th centuries, and in particular it will focus on three important questions:

- What role did the victim have in the 18th and 19th century criminal justice system?
- How and why did victims change from being active prosecutors into symbolic but absent actors in the system?
- How has historical research complicated and undermined our conceptions of 'the ideal victim'?

ACTIVE VICTIMS?

Until fairly recently criminologists have portrayed the victim as a backstage helper in the theatre of criminal justice, emphasising the passivity and marginality of those who had suffered some kind of criminal victimisation in the process of justice (Miers, 1978; Hoyle and Young, 2002). However, recent historical research has now substantially challenged this view of the 'marginality' of victims by pointing to court and trial records created from the 18th century onwards. The work of King (1984, 2000) and Hay and Snyder (1989: 25–6) has shown that it was largely through the actions and impetus of individual victims that cases were brought to court at all. The victim wasn't marginal but pivotal, indeed indispensable, to the criminal justice system until the late 19th century. Victorian commentators (notably Sir James Fitzjames Stephen, the most noted Jurist of his age in 1883: 493–504) simply accepted that victims of crime initiated a prosecution and then testified in the court case. Only sentencing was to be reserved for the judiciary to determine. So, if one was unfortunate enough to suffer some form of harm outlawed by legislation, what pathways to justice were available in the 18th and 19th centuries?

PAUSE FOR REVIEW

What options were available to victims of crime in the 18th and 19th centuries?

This question is asking not only what kinds of responses were available to victims of crime – the Thief Takers and the Prosecution Associations and so on – but also questioning the expectations of victims. What did victims want from the process? How did private agencies fulfil their needs, and how useful were they generally to society?

PROSECUTION ASSOCIATIONS AND THIEF TAKERS

Victims that had a considerable pot of money to dip into could undertake a prosecution. That is if they could run the expense of applying to a **magistrate** for a summons to apprehend the suspect (for a fee), and also, perhaps surprisingly to modern thinking, pay for the detention of the suspect, the travel and expenses of witnesses, and sometimes even the court costs. This was clearly a costly business, and even more so if private agencies were involved in any part of the detection and apprehension of the suspect – **The Bow Street Runners**, or Additional Constables, for example, were available to anyone who could afford the appropriate fee (Steedman, 1984; Cox, 2012). Thief Takers were another option. Their title was something of a misnomer, as they were more concerned with the return of stolen property than capturing the perpetrator – indeed, both Thief Takers and the thieves themselves often agreed to take a share of the fee in return for the property going back to its rightful owner. Obviously this suited all parties to some extent – the property was safe, as were the thieves and their disreputable captors – but it was hardly a satisfactory system (Hay and Snyder, 1989: 301–340).

By banding together, individuals could purchase a kind of insurance against the considerable costs of prosecution. 'Associations for the Prosecution of Felons' sprung up across the country from the 1760s and were very firmly established by the mid-19th century (Gatrell et al., 1980: 179). For an annual subscription, Prosecution Associations would advertise the loss of people's property, offer a reward for its return, sometimes provide a detecting inspector to track down the suspect, pay for counsel to prosecute the case in court and, on occasion, pay compensation when these duties were not met (Hay and Snyder, 1989; Philips, 1989). The Prosecution Associations therefore provided a service to victims and made prosecutions possible in many cases where previously it would have been impossible. However, clearly the costs of belonging to Associations were unaffordable for the masses. They were the equivalent of an army of private armed butlers that served but a section of the community (Beattie, 1986; Philips, 1989; Gatrell et al., 1980; Palmer, 1988). What other options were open to those who could not pay for Thief Takers or Bow Street Runners, or to join exclusive Prosecution Associations?

PAUSE FOR REVIEW

Why did some victims have greater access to justice in this time?

Relating to the question above, private agencies required a subscription that only wealthy victims could afford, but was lack of funds the only barrier to victims' obtaining justice? What part did gender play; did women face barriers to justice which men did not? If so, what were they?

OPTIONS FOR LESS WEALTHY VICTIMS?

As we have seen, private action by aggrieved victims was for centuries the mechanism that initiated and sustained legal proceedings, but a victim's response was conditioned by the type of crime they had suffered, their place in society, and their gender. The statistics of victimhood are indicative of a network of hidden decisions made by victims themselves, but also by various actors throughout the criminal justice system, and it seems that gender biases within the system are ahistorical, and global. A recent British Academy-funded research project ('Prosecution and sentencing processes in international perspective, 1880–1940, 2007–2009) collected together details of 120,000 prosecutions in the court records of towns and cities in the UK, Channel Islands, the US, Canada, New Zealand and Australia. The gendered nature of victimisation shown in this research may not be surprising, but it is nonetheless stark. In the 19th century, the victims of property crime were overwhelmingly male (because men were overwhelmingly property owners). The gender patterns of victims of violence was more mixed, since many women were victims of various types of violence in this period, but their chances of bringing the cases to court were still less likely than were men's, although the situation in the UK was much better than it was in other Anglophone countries (see Table 4.1).

Victims (usually women) of domestic violence faced structural, familial, economic and religious barriers to prosecuting their abusive partners (D'Cruze, 1998; Ross, 1982; Tomes, 1978). Research on women's experience of violence in the family home has demonstrated that a huge number of victims never reached the courts, and that when sexual and domestic violence were brought to the courts, the impact on the victim was often ignored or downplayed (Godfrey, 2003; D'Cruze, 1998; Stanko, 1985). So, even when victims of domestic violence did manage to persuade the police to intervene (and that was often a large barrier to prosecution), they then often fell victim to patriarchal attitudes in the courtroom. Judges and magistrates were loathe to undermine the traditional authority of husbands (including their right to physically discipline their wives and children).

Table 4.1 Victims of crime by gender and type of offence, in the UK, US, Canada and Australasia, c.1880–1940

	UK	US	Canada	Australia	NZ
Percentage of men as victims of property crime	86	86	91	94	97
Percentage of women as victims of property crime	14	14	9	6	3
Percentage of men as victims of violent crime	52	81	64	74	82
Percentage of women as victims of violent crime	48	19	36	26	18
Number of cases	7,642	311	1,354	905	4,064

Victims of violent husbands had their cases adjourned (never to return to court) or simply dismissed if the magistrates felt that reconciliation was possible. Indeed, many victims had their cases informally settled in court by the magistrates:

> In January 1900, for example, the *Staffordshire Advertiser* reported that relations between a son and his father had become so strained that, in a drunken fit, the son took out his pocket knife and threatened to stab his father to death. In court, 'His Worship reminded the prosecutor that his son would have a conviction that would stand against him all of his life. Could they not, he enquired, 'make friends?'. (Godfrey, 2008)

A large number of victims settled their differences with their adversaries even before the court was convened. Since prosecutions were expensive, the decision not to prosecute was an attractive proposition for many victims, at least until the 1850s when the growth of the local magistrates' courts system made prosecution cheaper. Before the mid-19th century, victims could go so far as to get a violent husband or neighbour arrested, but withdraw their prosecution at the last moment. This practice shamed the abuser but didn't break the bank; disputing parties could come to terms (sometimes with an exchange of money in damages – a process known as **compounding**, which was actually illegal but quite common); or victims could be persuaded or threatened not to take any formal action.

So, although dominated by men, it was increasingly the case, especially after the mid-19th century, that the majority of victims of crime had access to local courts, and that many working people could afford to have their cases and disputes heard before the courts. King (1984, 2000), for example, found that complainants in assault cases in the 18th century were drawn from a fairly wide cross-section of society, including the working population. For the 19th century it was the same. 'Working-class' prosecutors accounted for between one-fifth and one-quarter of all prosecutions for theft during the 1860s and 1870s (Davis, 1984; Hay and Snyder, 1989: 413). It seems that legitimate means or pursuing a case were denied only to the lowest strata of society, and even they still found other routes to try and achieve some kind of justice.

VIGILANTISM

Victims could take direct action if they felt the courts were unavailable to them for reasons of cost, or because it was simply easier and more effective to them to distribute extra-legal justice. The general public in the 18th and 19th centuries accepted that justice could be handed out by the victim themselves in regard to certain types of crime – particularly shop-lifting and petty thefts when juvenile offenders were often just punched or kicked by the victim, or their friends and neighbours, as a punishment (Wood, 2003: 111, 114; Beattie, 1986: 135; Emsley, 2005: 182). 'Rough Music' (a form of public shaming ritual such as villagers banging pots and pans outside the houses of abusive husbands, adulterous wives or local 'gossips') was equally common and generally accepted within local communities (Hammerton, 1991, 1992: 15–33). Again, by the mid-19th century these kinds of direct action became less acceptable to the authorities (who labelled it as vigilantism) or the general population. Around this time, it might be said that more 'civilised' attitudes began to take hold (Wood, 2003); the costs of bringing offenders to trial had been reduced because of the availability of an expanded system of magistrates' courts (which did massively increase the number of cases formally prosecuted), and by the mid-1850s every town and borough in England and Wales now had a police force to keep the peace and have crimes reported to them.

PAUSE FOR REVIEW

How did victim's options become enlarged to some extent after the mid-19th century, and to some extent reduced?

Again, relating to the question above, the position of some types of victims may have changed as the 19th century progressed (e.g. female victims of domestic violence), but what changes in the administration of justice around the mid-19th century encouraged more victims to report offences, and to take their cases to court? As the century progressed, why did fewer and fewer 'real' victims appear in court?

WHAT'S HAPPENED TO REAL VICTIMS OF CRIME?

When the **New Police** were introduced progressively from 1835 onwards, to the extent that a local 'Bobby' patrolled all parts of the country by 1856, they offered a new option for victims of crime to report offences. Some victims were slow to take up this option, since the traditional methods of exacting justice described above were still working, or were easier to control and manipulate. Storch (1975, 1976) stated that acceptance of the police as a legitimate force in working-class communities for the reporting of offences and dealing with offenders only came when people realised that they offered a better (or at least alternative) option for solving neighbourhood disputes. The police then gradually became the first point of contact for everyone who believed they had been criminally victimised (Johnson and Monkonnnen, 1996; Jones, 1982; Taylor, 1998a, 1998b), and over time the range of offences they were prepared to prosecute in court (rather than just acting as the mechanism for arresting and detailing suspects) became greater and greater.

In the mid-19th century, the police had mainly acted as the prosecutors in cases of indictable felonies (murders, serious sexual violence, woundings, burglaries, larcenies and other serious property offences). However, in the 1870s and 1880s, the police routinely prosecuted a much wider range of less-serious offences. In England and Wales, public order offences rose particularly between 1890 and 1920 as the police attempted to control public space and curb drunken disorder and, since there was no clear victim other than the community or the notion of public order, the police would take the lead in prosecuting these offences (drunkenness, disorderliness, fighting etc.). They were also taking the lead on 'victimless' crimes, prosecuting cases for the 'public good' including the **Contagious Diseases Acts** (1864, 1866 and 1869), which gave the police the power to detain women suspected of engaging in prostitution; a range of regulatory offences, weights and measures, market bylaws and so on. There were no individual victims in these cases, instead the perceived harm was caused to the community or the nation – a notion which was new and which would cause a huge shift to the way that victims would be able to access justice.

By 1914 the police led 90 per cent of prosecutions over this period. Even in cases of assault, where, until around the 1880s, one complainant usually prosecuted one defendant, the police prosecuted one-fifth of offenders between 1880 and 1940 (with that proportion growing as the period went on so that by 1940 they comprised only 4 per cent of the total number of cases). In all categories of offending, private prosecutions by individuals were becoming ever rarer occurrences (Devlin, 1960; Sigler, 1974; Lidstone et al., 1980). Therefore, by the First World War, the police or a range of local authority prosecutors (i.e. education and truancy officers) had become the dominant and active prosecutor in the courtroom, a system which was only altered when the **Crown Prosecution Service** (CPS) was created in 1985 (Emsley, 2005: 195, 2007: 272). However, until that time the police represented victims in the criminal justice system – but where did this system leave the victims of crime, and how did the absence of victims in the courtroom alter public perceptions of victimhood?

What impact has the emergence of 'symbolic victims' had on the criminal justice system?

If real victims were disappearing from the courtroom, were they replaced by ideas of ideal victims, and if so how? What part did the media play in the process of developing symbolic groups of potential victims? What part did the police play in facilitating the victim's path to justice? What were the long-term impacts of these changes in the options available to victims of crime across the whole of the 19th century? In what ways were victims sometimes less than ideal?

SYMBOLIC VICTIMS

Paralleling the disappearance of victims from the courtroom, a few victims were receiving ever greater prominence in the media. A small selection of victims in the 1860s and 1870s were used in local and national newspapers as vehicles to mobilise public outrage, sympathy, condemnation or more punitive attitudes. The growth of **sensationalist reporting** gave colour to victims of crime, and sought to paint a picture of the private lives and past experiences of victims in order to elicit sympathy for poor and unfortunate victims:

Annie Astill, the daughter of respectable parents, made exceedingly miserable by the violence of his [her husband William's] temper and his habits. They had one child, and lived in Northumberland Street, where they had frequent quarrels, and where the poor woman was subject to continual ill-treatment and brutality ... The poor victim of his brutality was found lying on the floor of the house in a state of unconsciousness, and messengers were at once despatched for medical assistance. Dr Souter arrived and dressed her wounds, which were of a fearful character. (*Leicester Chronicle and Mercury*, 15 October 1870)

Newspaper reports, public literature, paintings and lithographs, as well as contemporary social investigations depicted the 'victims' of an uncaring social environment. Taken together with public campaigns in the late-19th century (e.g. against 'white slavery', or protesting the sexual exploitation of young girls in London), the notion was created of actual or potential groups vulnerable to victimisation (Walkowitz, 1992). Moral entrepreneurs were encouraged to create campaign groups which were, in a sense, reincarnations of 18th-century style Prosecution Associations, this time funded by public rather than individual subscriptions. Rather than tasked with recovering men's property, these victim's groups would protect the 'ideal' of Victorian femininity or the purity of children by prosecuting those who violated against them. Both the Society for the Prosecution of Offences Against Women and Children, and the National Society for the Prevention of Cruelty to Children, became active in advancing prosecutions on victims' behalf from the 1880s onwards (Jackson, 2000).

Substantially this kind of moral enterprise created symbolic categories of victim which mirrored and also fed into dominant tropes of Victorian society, dividing groups into the deserving and undeserving poor, those to be pitied, and those to be condemned. Thus, in the context of victims of crime, this moved the focus onto ideal types of victim – particularly the vulnerable widow, the 'plucky' orphan, the innocent maiden seduced into a life of vice – rather than real men and women who suffered some kind of criminal harm (Hendler, 2001). It seems that real victims were no longer the best vehicle to arouse sympathy for social reform, or necessary to active prosecutors in order to secure convictions in court.

By the end of the First World War this symbolic/mythic centrality of the victim in criminal justice narratives (underscored by the de facto marginalisation of **real** victims of crime from criminal justice processes) was firmly embedded, and remained so for most of the 20th Century. Indeed it could be argued that the Victimology that emerges in the last quarter of the 20th Century sets out to critique and problematise precisely the construction of the victim that is symbolically constructed during this period. (Kearon and Godfrey, 2007: 25)

A central plank of the modern criminological critique of the production of ideal or symbolic victims was that victims were not always as 'ideal' as they appeared, although the contradictory social status of many victims only slowly emerged as a subject of research.

VICTIMS AS OFFENDERS

As noted previously, the courts were used as places to demonstrate one's respectability; forums in which to continue feuds, to shame violent husbands or drunken wives, to solve, prosecute, or develop grudges, and so on. The prosecutors in such cases with those kinds

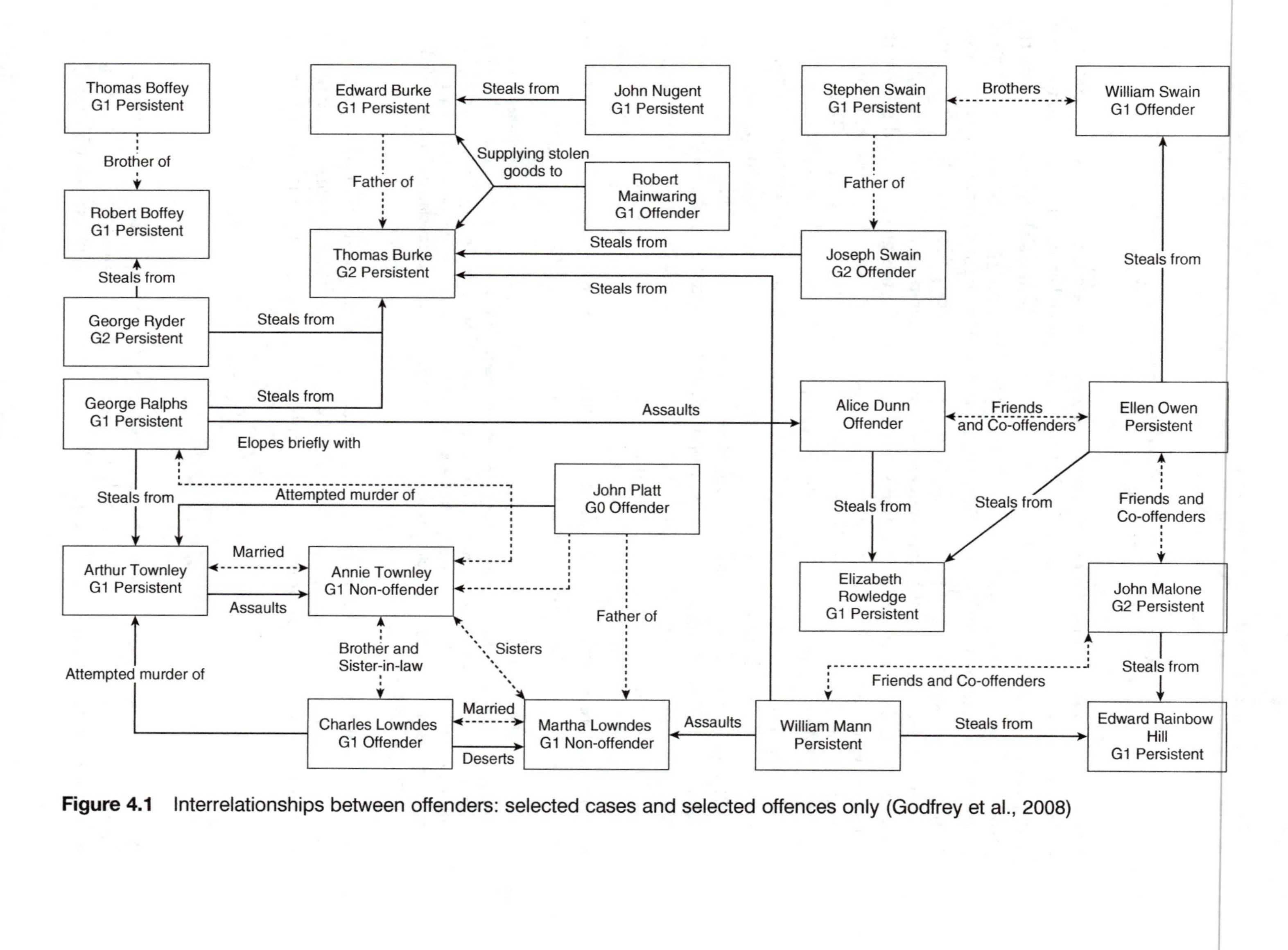

Figure 4.1 Interrelationships between offenders: selected cases and selected offences only (Godfrey et al., 2008)

of motivations seem far from our simple conception of them as poor victims seeking redress. Historians have been prompted by the work of criminologists such as Newburn and Stanko (1994: 161) who noted that a fully realist victimology needs to acknowledge and explore the fact that there are not simply 'victims' *and* 'offenders', but rather people who are *both* victims and offenders. The online site London Lives (https://www.londonlives.org) illustrates these points with reference to the case of Mary Harvey, a vexatious litigant from 18th century London who prosecuted two of the constables that were making her life difficult as a brothel-owner (a keeper of disorderly houses where sex may be appropriated) (https://www.londonlives.org). Although her prosecutions failed, they cast a slur upon the character of the constables, and therefore undermined the quality of evidence against her in subsequent trials. Some victims were clearly less than ideal, and failed to live up to their image as innocent and vulnerable.

In the 19th century, socio-economic conditions such as the growth of large towns and cities with hundreds of thousands of residents living in high-density cramped housing brought people into close daily contact with workmates, neighbours and strangers. Daily interactions sometimes turned into arguments, arguments into fights, fights into assaults, and a long feud between former friends and neighbours conducted over a number of years. For the combatants in these feuds, they were sometimes the victim of assaults, and sometimes they gave out a measure of violence themselves. Moreover, close-knit working-class communities provided a market and a conduit for burglars and thieves to fence stolen goods. Godfrey et al. (2007) produced a schema of the complex interrelationships of victims and assailants in a small northern town (see Figure 4.1).

DIGITAL VICTIMS

Historical research has helped to develop new perspectives on victimology, but now digital online resources have the capacity to greatly improve our knowledge of victims. For example, The Old Bailey online website (www.oldbaileyonline.org/), which records details of every trial held at London's **Central Criminal Court** until 1913, has a search engine which allows us to quickly find out information about hundreds of victims. Written and deposited trial records have always recorded the bare bones about victims or complainants. Magistrates courts registers, for example, will give the name, and sometimes the age or address of the victim in a case, but researchers have found it time-consuming to aggregate enough details to carry out analysis of, say, gender and age in cases of violence and so forth. Digital resources allow researchers to do this very quickly, and therefore it is now relatively easy to carry out analysis of the social status or gender of victims, and to an unprecedented degree. Moreover, a large amount of contextual detail on victims can be discovered by consulting the online census records and the digitised newspaper databases. For example, see the case in Box 4.1 which came into the Old Bailey in November 1911.

BOX 4.1 EXAMPLE OF INFORMATION RETREIVED FROM A DIGTAL RESOURCE

Detective-Inspector ARTHUR NEILL. At 12.30 p.m. on October 12 I was in conversation with prisoner's wife in Brewery Road, when prisoner came up. I said to him, 'Is your name Thomas Collins?', he said 'Yes.' I said, 'I am a police officer and I shall have to arrest you for attempting to murder your wife last evening.' He said, 'Quite right; I intended to do it. She summoned me at the police court yesterday for persistent cruelty. The case was adjourned and we went home together. We had a drink on the way and, going upstairs when we got home, I lost my temper and pulled her hat off. She went into a room where her mother was. I went into the other room and got the knife and tried to cut her throat. Her mother interfered and I left.' The mother was living in a room in the same house. On the way to the station he said, 'It is all her own fault. She has been going into public-houses with other women drinking, and I heard she was going to leave me and go with the lodger. I did it more to frighten her than anything else. After I had done it I went and got some money owing me at my work and I have been on the drink ever since.' He certainly had been drinking when I arrested him. He said, 'I have spent 3s. on the drink since.'

Cross-examined. There is no doubt that prisoner's wife was on a day or two previously in a public-house with Mrs. Gray, but she behaved herself properly; she is regarded there as a very peaceable woman.

SUSANNAH HILL, 96, Brewery Road. I live on the first floor. Prisoner and his wife, my daughter, lived on the second floor; they have been married three years, and she has had three children, of whom one is alive. About 5 p.m. on October 11 they came back home having been to the police court. Outside my kitchen door he hit her, took her hat off and tore it up. I had heard them rushing up the stairs, and I opened the door. I took my daughter into my kitchen and prisoner went upstairs. About fifteen minutes later he came, knocked at my door and asked for a match. I gave him one and said, 'Why don't you be quiet and leave off. She has been and summoned you and of course you have got to go through it'. My daughter said, 'If you hit me again, I will go and fetch a policeman. I am going out and I won't come back any more.' He said, 'You don't go out of this place alive,' and he rushed over to her with a knife in his hand; I do not know where he got it from; I have seen it in his room. My daughter fell back in the chair and screamed. She put her hands up to save her throat, and I rushed up to him and held him while she ran downstairs. The knife fell on the ground; it had only cut her hand.

Cross-examined. He had complained of her going out to drink with Mrs. Gray; he said that Mrs. Gray was the cause of all the trouble between them. He told her that he had been told she was going to go away with Mr. Gray. She is living with him now as his wife. He accused her of drinking with other men …

ELLEN COLLINS. Prisoner is my husband. On October 11 I took out a summons against him for cruelty. It was adjourned till the 17th. We left the police court to go home. On the way I had drink with him as he said he would break my neck if I did not. On reaching home I was going upstairs when he pulled my skirt. I ran up the stairs and outside my kitchen door he tore my hat off and knocked my head against the door. I screamed, and my mother came to my assistance. He went up to his room, and returned after 10 minutes. I was sitting in a chair in my mother's kitchen. He asked for a match and mother gave him one. He looked as if he was coming towards me, and I said, 'If you don't leave me alone, I shall call a policeman.' He said, 'You don't go out of this house alive,' and he pulled this knife from his breast pocket and rushed at me, saying, 'I will cut your throat.' I put my hands up and the knife caught my thumb. Mother pulled him away. He left the house.

Verdict: Guilty of unlawful wounding under great provocation.

Prisoner received a good character.

Sentence: Three months' 'hard labour.'

Source: Old Bailey Online (https://www.oldbaileyonline.org/browse.jsp?id=def1-17-19111107&div=t19111107-17#highlight)

Online digital resources not only provide details of the cases and the victims of the offences that were dealt with in court, a mass of incidental information of all kinds can also be gained through online searching. For example, in the same month and in the same court that Ellen Collins's case was prosecuted, Private Albert Hambleton and Private Charles Mundy were accused of raping Annie Vincent. Annie's case was dismissed because she failed to prove her respectability – she had been drunk when the men were upon her – and a search of the military records of Private Hambleton of the Coldstream Guards on the Commonwealth War Graves website (www.cwgc.org) shows that he was killed in the line of action, dying a hero in 1917 in the service of his country. A researcher looking to see how symbolic victimhood was created, negotiated and operationalised in courtroom and media settings could not do better than further exploring cases of heroism and disrepute such as these.

SUMMARY

Historical research has complicated our traditional view of the part of the victim always being passive and marginal. Although only very few victims had the financial means to find redress in the 18th and early 19th centuries, they were central to the process of prosecution. Enabled by private agencies, wealthy victims could secure the return of property, even if they could not always manage to propel the offender into court. The options available to working- and middle-class victims of crime were increased when a public police force took on many of the costly services provided by Prosecution Associations in the mid-century. Victims were therefore still a central plank of a prosecution system which relied on individual victims prosecuting individual offenders. However, victims then started to play a lesser and lesser part in the prosecution process until, by the First World War, they were essentially witnesses to their own complaint, and not much more. From the 1880s onwards, at almost every stage of the criminal justice system, professional bodies were starting to act for or represent individual victims.

King (2000) has used the analogy of separate rooms leading to conviction, with people leaving rooms at various points in their journey to court, to characterise the prosecution system in the 18th century. For the 19th century we may think of the criminal justice system as a set of canal locks with the complainant skippering their boat through each lock-gate. Each gate they passed through moved them closer to an end conviction. In the 18th and for most of the 19th century the complainant was key to moving the whole process forward. However, throughout the late 19th century, the pressure that victims felt able to exert on the process was gradually reduced as police and other professional bodies began to organise first the means of detecting crime and apprehending offenders, and later the prosecution process. It is clear that the police did not 'capture' or 'take over' the system so much as inherit the duties of the prosecutor.' (Godfrey, 2008:188)

The withdrawal of real victims was accompanied by the symbolic construction of ideal victims or groups of victims, one might more accurately term them 'categories' of victims – women and children, or respectable men, who were firmly in the victim category and never in the offender category. In reality, however, life was not that simple. In the 19th century, many of those who appeared as complainants had also been on the other side of the dock. Possibly because research on victims was only very limited until recently, this victim/offender overlap has not been well-researched. Certainly it has not permeated the public consciousness, where victims and offenders are still seen as discrete categories. It is possible that criminology (particularly victimology) can now use historical data to try to interrogate these complex issues a little more thoroughly in the future.

FURTHER READING

Emsley, C. (2010) *Crime and Society in England, 1750–1900* (4th edn). Harlow: Longman.
Godfrey, B. and Lawrence, P. (2005) *Crime and Justice, 1750–1950*. Cullompton: Willan Press.

Both of these crime history textbooks contain good chapters on victims or prosecutors.

King, P. ([1984] 2000) *Crime, Justice and Discretion in England, 1740–1820*. Oxford: Oxford University Press.

This provides more detailed analysis of the victims' use of the law in the 18th and 19th centuries.

Kearon, T. and Godfrey, B. (2007) 'Setting the scene: the history of victims', in S. Walklate (ed.), *The Handbook of Victims and Victimology*. Cullompton: Willan Press. pp. 17–37.

Discusses the transformation of the victim into a symbolic cipher, and the effect this had on both criminal statistics and court practices.

Godfrey, B. (2008) 'Changing prosecution practices and their impact on crime figures, 1857–1940', *British Journal of Criminology*, 48(2): 171–90.

This article contends that when the police took over the prosecution of violent offenders in the late 19th century, the number of violent offences reduced rapidly and victims of crime were denied their day in court.

REFERENCES

Beattie, J. (1986) *Crime and the Courts in England 1660–1800*. Oxford: Clarendon Press.

Cox, D. (2012) *A Certain Share of Low Cunning: A History of the Bow Street Runners, 1792–1839*. London: Routledge.

D'Cruze, S. (1998) *Crimes of Outrage: Sex, Violence and Victorian Working Women*. London: University College London Press.

Davis, J. (1984) 'A poor man's system of justice? The London Police Courts in the second half of the 19th century', *The Historical Journal*, 27(2): 309–335.

Devlin, P. (1960) *The Criminal Prosecution in England*. London: Baron Patrick.

Emsley, C. (2005) *Crime and Society in England, 1750–1900* (3rd edn). Harlow: Longman.

Emsley, C. (2007) *Crime, Police and Penal Policy: European Experiences 1750–1940*. Oxford: Oxford University Press.

Gatrell, V.A.C., Lenman, B. and Parker, G. (eds) (1980) *Crime and the Law: A Social History of Crime in Early Modern Europe*. London: Europa.

Godfrey, B. (2003) 'Counting and accounting for the decline in non-lethal violence in England, Australia and New Zealand, 1880–1920', *British Journal of Criminology*, 43(2): 340–53.

Godfrey, B. (2008) 'Changing prosecution practices and their impact on crime figures, 1857–1940', *British Journal of Criminology*, 48(2): 171–90.

Godfrey, B. Cox, D. and Farrall, S. (2007) *Criminal Lives: Family, Employment and Offending*, Clarendon Series in Criminology, Oxford University Press, pp. 214.

Godfrey, B.S., Lawrence, P. and Williams. C.A. (2008) *History and Crime*. London: Sage.

Hammerton, J. (1991) 'The targets of "rough music": respectability and domestic violence in Victorian England', *Gender and History*, 3(1): 23–44.

Hammerton, J. (1992) *Cruelty and Companionship: Conflict in 19th-Century Married Life*. London: Routledge.

Hay, D. and Snyder, F. (eds) (1989) *Policing and Prosecution in Britain, 1750–1850*. Oxford: Oxford University Press.

Hendler, G. (2001) *Public Sentiments: Structures of Feeling in 19th Century American Literature*. Chapel Hill, NC: University of North Carolina Press

Holstein, J. and Miller, G. (1990) 'Rethinking victimization: an international approach to victimization', *Symbolic Interaction*, 13: 103–122.

Hoyle, C. and Young, R. (2002) 'Restorative justice: assessing the prospects and pitfalls', in M. McConville and G. Wilson (eds), *The Handbook of The Criminal Justice Process*. Oxford: Oxford University Press.

Jackson, L. (2000) *Child Sexual Abuse in Victorian England*. London: Routledge.

Johnson, P. and Monkonnnen, E. (1996) *The Civilization of Crime*. Champaign, IL: Illinois University Press.

Jones, D.V. (1982) *Crime, Protest, Community and Police in 19th-century Britain*. London: Routledge.

Kearon, T. and Godfrey, B. (2007) 'Setting the scene: the history of victims', in S. Walklate (ed.), *The Handbook of Victims and Victimology*. Cullompton: Willan Press.

King, P. (1984) 'Decision makers and decision-making in the English criminal law 1750–1800', *Historical Journal*, 27: 25–58.

King, P. (2000) *Crime, Justice and Discretion in England, 1740–1820*. Oxford: Oxford University Press.

Lidstone, K., Hogg, R. and Sutcliffe, F. (1980) *Prosecutions by Private Individuals and Non-Police Agencies*. London: HMSO.

London Lives (2010a) 'Prosecutors and litigants'. Available at www.londonlives.org/static/ProsecutorsLitigants.jsp (accessed 7.10.16).

London Lives (2010a) 'Mary Harvey, fl. 1727–1733'. Available at www.londonlives.org/static/HarveyMaryC1727-c1733.jsp (accessed 7.10.16).

Mawby, R.I. and Walklate, S. (1994). *Critical Victimology*. London: Sage.

Miers, D. (1978) *Responses to Victimisation*. Abingdon: Professional.

Newburn, T. and Stanko, B. (1994) 'When man are victims: the failure of victimology', in T. Newburn and B. Stanko (eds), *Just Boys Doing* Business. London: Routledge.

Palmer, S. (1988) *Police and Protest in England and Ireland 1780–1850*. Cambridge: Cambridge University Press.

Philips, D. (1989) 'Good men to associate and bad men to conspire: associations for the prosecution of felons in England 1750–1860', in D. Hay and F. Snyder (eds), *Policing and Prosecution in Britain 1750–1850*. Oxford: Oxford University Press. pp. 113–70.

Ross, E. (1982) '"Fierce questions and taunts": married life in working-class London', *Feminist Studies*, 8(3): 575–602.

Rude, G. (1985) *Criminal and Victim: Crime and Society in Early 19th-century England*. Oxford: Clarendon Press.

Sigler, J. (1974) 'Public prosecution in England and Wales', *Criminal Law Review*, 642.

Stanko, E. (1985) *Intimate Intrusions*. London: Virago.

Steedman, C. (1984) *Policing the Victorian Community: The Formation of English Provincial Police Forces, 1856–80*. London: Routledge and Kegan Paul.

Stephen, Sir J. (1883) *A History of the Criminal Law of England*, Vol. I. London: Macmillan.
Storch, R. (1975) 'The plague of blue locusts: police reform and popular resistance in northern England 1840–57', *International Review of Social History*, 20: 61–90.
Storch, R. (1976) 'The policeman as domestic missionary: urban discipline and popular culture in northern England, 1850–1880', *Journal of Social History*, 9: 481–511.
Taylor, H. (1998a) 'Rationing crime: the political economy of criminal statistics since the 1850s', *Economic History Review*, 49(3): 569–90.
Taylor, H. (1998b) 'The politics of the rising crime statistics of England and Wales', *Crime Histoire and Societies: Crime, History and Societies*, 1(2): 5–28.
Tomes, N. (1978) 'A torrent of abuse: crimes of violence between working-class men and women in London, 1840–1875', *Journal of Social History*, 11: 328–45.
von Hentig, H. (1948) *The Criminal and His Victim*. New Haven, CT: Yale University Press.
Walklate, S. (1992) 'Appreciating the victim: conventional, realist or critical victimology?', in R. Matthews and J. Young (eds), *Issues in Realist Criminology*. London: Sage.
Walklate, S. (1996) 'Can there be a feminist victimology?', in P. Davies, P. Francis and V. Jupp (eds), *Understanding Victimisation*. Newcastle: Northumbria Social Science Press.
Walkowitz, J. (1992) *City of Dreadful Delight: Narratives of Sexual Danger in Late-Victorian London*. London: Virago.
Wood, J.C. (2003) 'Self-policing and the policing of the self: violence, protection and the civilising bargain in Britain', *Crime, History and Societies*, 7(1): 109–128.

5 THEORETICAL PERSPECTIVES IN VICTIMOLOGY

Peter Francis

Victimology is approximately 80 years old. Since its emergence in 1940s Europe it is today an established if contested academic enterprise (Goodey, 2005; Walklate, 2007a). Described as a broad church (Rock, 2010) of 'academics, activists and policy makers' (Walklate, 2007a: 30) victimology comprises a range of models and perspectives each offering their own conceptualisation of the victim, understanding of victimization, its causes and consequences, and policy responses. In this chapter, the purpose of which is to introduce and evaluate the major theoretical perspectives in victimology, two models of victimology are presented and reviewed along with their respective theoretical perspectives.

The first model derives many of its ideas and assumptions from mid-20th century positivism, and can be viewed as the 'orthodox' or conventional way of thinking about victims and victimization. It is a model that conceptualizes victims through legal means and one that is home to theoretical perspectives that variously utilise concepts of lifestyle, risk, and vulnerability to explain mostly criminal victimisation. The second model, which emerged in the 1970s onwards, is revisionist in outlook and substance, in that it significantly revises the orthodox model, and is informed by radical, feminist and critical social science ideas and assumptions. It is a model concerned with the social interpretations of victimhood and comprises theoretical perspectives that utilise concepts of power, politics and representation to uncover and explain victimisation.

The structure of the chapter is as follows. First, it introduces the origins of victimological theory in mid-20th century Europe. Second, it describes how a number of key intellectual and social factors converged during the late 20th century in the US and England and Wales to shape contemporary thinking about victims and victimisation.

Third, the chapter critically assesses the orthodox model and its theoretical perspectives, detailing how many of the ideas and assumptions of early victimologists have been repackaged and rebranded today as lifestyle exposure. Fourth, it critically examines the ideas and assumptions that have combined to inform a revisionist model of victimology, along with the key radical, critical, feminist and cultural perspectives on victims and victimisation. Finally, the chapter presents key differences between orthodox and revisionist thinking in order to highlight why, despite the dominance and impact of the former, revisionist victimology provides perhaps a more constructive narrative in light of its willingness to challenge taken-for-granted concepts and assumptions, and engage in meaningful critique about who constitutes the victim and how best to understand and respond to their experiences.

THE ORIGINS OF VICTIMOLOGICAL THOUGHT

The early pioneers of thinking about victims of crime and victimisation were academic lawyers and human scientists, many of whom worked on the fringes of law, criminology and psychiatry (Rock, 2010). Many were critical of the partiality offered by criminological theory (focusing on the offender at the expense of other factors, including that of the victim) (MacDonald, 1939; von Hentig, 1948; Ellenberger 1955; Garafalo, 1914). Von Hentig (1948) noted the potential that an understanding of 'victim' attributes, their motives and experiences could bring to understanding crime and its control. Through the creation of a victim typology, made up of various classes of victim types, underpinned by the notion of 'victim proneness', von Hentig postulated the role victims play in their own victimisation through the identification of motivational/psychological (inherited or acquired) and functional/societal factors (Fattah, 1986: 29). It was von Hentig's view that:

> Looking into the genesis of the situation, in a considerable number of cases, we meet a victim who consents tacitly, co-operates, conspires or provokes. The victim is one of the causative elements. (von Hentig, 1948, cited in Fattah, 1986: 30).

By involving victims in his analysis, von Hentig was attempting to transform thinking about crime by opening up for examination all aspects of the crime process. However, his primitive methodology based upon incomplete data and speculation offered little robust empirical insight nor analysis. Working from a more legalistic perspective, yet a similarly flawed methodological approach, Mendelsohn (1958) suggested a typology underpinned by the idea of 'victim culpability', ranging from the completely innocent victim to an offender who subsequently becomes a victim through the committal of an act of aggression. Box 5.1 provides a summary of the various typologies constructed by von Hentig and Mendelsohn.

BOX 5.1 TYPOLOGIES OF VICTIMS OF CRIME

von Hentig, 1948	Mendelsohn, 1958
• Young people, females, the elderly.	• The completely innocent.
• The mentally defective, 'dull' normals, the depressed.	• Those with 'minor' guilt.
• Immigrants, members of minority groups.	• Those as guilty as the offender.
• The acquisitive, the wanton, the lonely and heartbroken.	• Those as more guilty than the offender.
• The tormentor, the fighting victim.	• Those who are the most guilty.

Source: Walklate, 2007c

It was the systematic empirical research of Wolfgang (1958) on homicide and by his PhD student Amir (1967, 1971) on forcible rape that really brought to the fore thinking about victims of crime. It is the subject matter, the research approach, the conceptualisation and the conclusions that they derived from their findings that secure Wolfgang and Amir's footnote in the history of thinking about victims and victimisation. Both studied police data in Philadelphia, USA. Both were interested in victim–offender relationships. For Wolfgang, over one-quarter of all cases of homicide involved some form of 'victim precipitation' in the event, while Amir estimated that the figure was 16 per cent for rape cases. Amir went on to offer a victim typology that detailed that 20 per cent of victims had some form of record for sexual misconduct, and a further 20 per cent had bad reputations. It is this body of work that went on to influence the development of theorising about victims and victimisation in the latter part of the 20th century onwards (Walklate, 2007a, 2007c; Spalek, 2006; Miers, 1989; Meier and Miethe, 1993). It introduced the idea that victims could in some way initiate their victimisation. It identified that time and location were important factors in understanding risk and vulnerability, two key variables of later victimological thinking. It also brought forward the notion of victim responsibility.

PAUSE FOR REVIEW

In what ways can victims be a causative element of crime? What are the major problems with such an approach to understanding victimisation?

What is meant by victim proneness, victim culpability and victim precipitation, and what do they say about the causes of victimisation and about victim–offender relationships?

TAKING VICTIMS AND VICTIMISATION SERIOUSLY

From the mid to late 1970s onwards, theorising about victims and victimisation in Europe, England and Wales, and the US, experienced an unprecedented intensive period of development (Rock, 2010; Zedner, 1994). Four factors can be identified as to the reasons for this. First, criminology's response to the growing problem of crime and crisis of etiology. Second, the influence of second-wave feminism's exploration of women's experience of victimisation. Third, the introduction of the crime survey and its contribution to uncovering the nature, extent and impact of victimisation. Fourth, the growing mediatisation of crime, and its impact on crime and victim representation. Each of these is discussed below.

Up until the post-war period, criminology had directed little attention towards the victim of crime, preferring to study the activities of men and boys (for it was mostly they who were the subject of study) through the lens of sociology and psychology to identify the 'clues' as to why they engaged in offending (Zedner, 1994). It was an era in which there were relatively low levels of offending and crime, and criminologists variously presented both to be resultant from poor material living standards and individual psychosocial conditions (e.g. resultant from poor socialisation, broken homes and paternal/maternal deprivation). Criminologists at this time also viewed the solution as involving social intervention accompanied by effective police, criminal justice and prison systems.

However, the inexorable rise in crime in both the US and England and Wales from the 1960s to the 1990s called into question many of these ideas and assumptions. Crime grew during the post-war Keynesian economics of the 1950s and 1960s aimed at creating a stable and sustainable welfare society. It also grew during the 1970s, 1980s and 1990s, this time accompanied by an emerging global neo-liberal economic model underpinned by conservative politics and policies, discourses of efficiency, and competition and marketisation. Significantly, it grew despite huge financial and human investment in policing, criminal justice, and prisons and punishment. The challenge for criminologists was that crime had increased during years of boom and slump, and recession and recovery. Jock Young (1997) describes the period as one of etiological crisis; a failure of criminology to explain why crime occurs. It is on the back of criminology's search for answers to this crisis that thinking seriously about victims and victimisation entered centre stage.

The response amongst many conservative criminologists to the etiological crisis was to probe the failure of the police and prisons to maintain order and protect the victim through effective deterrence, enforcement and incapacitation (Wilson, 1975), and to locate the causes of crime as lying in bio-social and psycho-social factors (Wilson and Herrnstein, 1985; Wilson and Kelling, 1982; Gottfredson and Hirschi, 1990). For those conservative criminologists of a more administrative persuasion the response was more about what could be done to prevent crime occurring, and this meant a focus on deterrence mechanisms, particularly through situational and victimisation prevention (Felson, 1994; Cornish and Clark, 1986).

The response amongst radical criminologists to the problem of rising crime was similarly twofold. Rising crime was viewed as a result of the greater targeting of individuals by the police, creating more victims, and secondary victimisation (Quinney, 1972). A second response was that whilst crime was inevitably an outcome of policing and recording practices, victimisation was not merely a crude social construction born out of state interventions. Crime was deeply intra-class rather than inter-class, victimisation was destructive, and criminology had to take rising crime and thus rising victimisation seriously (Young, 1979; Taylor, 1981).

Whereas conservative and radical criminology all but ignored the gender dimension during this period, second-wave feminists (Rock, 2010; Walklate, 2007a) began to highlight the gendered nature of victimisation and the needs of the female victim. Academics such as Carol Smart (1976) articulated the neglect of women in criminological research either as offenders or as victims. The impact was considerable. This is not the place to assess the impact of feminism on thinking about crime (see Walklate, 2007a), nor the development of victimology because of feminist thinking (see Davies, 2011, for a good discussion here); suffice to say:

> the first stirrings of the new victimology supplied an appropriate butt not only for contesting the meanings of victimization, gender and power but also for establishing a countervailing feminist criminology. Like The New Criminology (Taylor et al., 1973) before it, early feminist criminology was elaborated through what was called 'immanent critique', a series of running criticisms which amounted through accretion to the provision of an alternative theory, and one of its prime objects was the failing of criminology and victimology to comprehend female victimisation. (Rock, 2010: 472)

Accompanying the emerging realisation amongst criminologists of the importance of taking victims and victimisation seriously was a clamour for the problems of official police data to be addressed (Sparks, 1982; Rock, 2010). It was not long before calls to survey victims of crime emerged, and crime surveys were introduced in 1973 in the US, in 1981 in Canada and in 1982 in England and Wales. Victim surveys began to 'provide detailed information about the ecology of crime' (Meier and Miethe, 1993: 465), such as victim characteristics, the nature and extent of victimisation, as well as the distribution of crime and its impact on individuals and communities. The dark figure of unreported and unrecorded crime was exposed, fear of crime uncovered, as was the high levels of victimisation amongst particular social groups, often those also experiencing hardship in welfare, education, employment and the economy. And local crime surveys provided evidence of people's experiences of problems as they lived them (Lea and Young, 1984), drawing out the key intersectionalities of class, race, age, gender and so on.

A final factor that helped capture the victimological imagination amongst criminologists was the media's growing interest in and construction of crime and victimisation as bad news, often as more bad news and sometimes as really bad news. For Greer (2007: 21), 'the foregrounding of crime victims in media representations is one of the most significant qualitative changes in media representations of crime and control since the second world war.' While those victims that do find themselves represented within the media are but a minor element of those who experience victimisation, the importance of the mediatisation of victims and victimisation in this period concerns the influence it had on public perceptions of crime, on the reportage of fear of crime, on the development of particular crime control activities, and importantly, on research and policy agendas of criminology, as well as local and national governments.

What are the key factors that helped shape victimological thinking in the second half of the 20th century?

What is meant by the etiological crisis and why is it important to the development of thinking about victims and victimisation?

How and in what ways did the development of the crime survey address the problems of official data on crime and contribute to theorising about victims and victimisation?

How did the mediatisation of crime in the last quarter of the 20th century impact on academic thinking about victims and victimisation?

THINKING SERIOUSLY ABOUT VICTIMS AND VICTIMISATION: TWO MODELS OF VICTIMOLOGY

Clearly the interplay between the social and the intellectual (Young, 1997) during the second half of the 20th century helped bring debates about the victim and victimisation to the fore. Criminologists and victimologists of all persuasions began to acknowledge the importance of understanding victimisation, the interrelationship between perpetrator and victim, and of structure and agency, to the study of crime (for a discussion here see Rock, 2010; Spalek, 2006; Karmen, 1992). Many of the ideas and assumptions promoted by the early theorists such as von Hentig and colleagues were picked up by the conservative and administrative criminologies of the 1970s and 1980s onwards to form what can be described as an orthodox model of thinking about victims and victimisation. At the same time, Marxist, radical, feminist and critical social scientists began to form alternative revisionist viewpoints (and standpoints), particularly about the nature of victimhood, and the role of the state and its agencies in the process of victimisation. It is to an assessment of these two models and the perspectives that make up each that the chapter now turns. Box 5.2 provides a diagrammatic representation of the key elements of each model.

BOX 5.2 TWO MODELS OF VICTIMOLOGICAL THOUGHT

	Orthodox	**Revisionist**
Key Features	Concerned with: • the identification of non-random patterns of victimisation • interpersonal crimes (public rather than private) • interest in victim responsibility and vulnerability Origins in 1930s and 1940s Europe and positivist social science of the 1950s and 1960s	Concerned with: • the victimisation of individuals by the state and their agencies, corporations, often (but not exclusively) in alternative sites for victimisation (home, workplace etc.) • impact of marginalisation, globalisation and structural relations on crime and victimisation • power, politics and representation in the construction of victims and victimisation Origins in 1960s and 1970s Marxist, radical, feminist and critical social science
Definition of victim	Victim as legally defined, and crime victimisation	Victim defines their experiences, but also interested in the social construction of victimhood and victimisation from social harms
Extent of victimisation	Patterned geographically, spatially and temporally, and underpinned by vulnerability and risk	Ubiquitous; much of which remains hidden and invisible from view, especially that within private, institutional and corporate settings
Approach	• Police data and criminal victimisation surveys nationally and internationally • Focus on the individualistic nature of victimisation	• Documentary and visual analysis, together with ethnographies of victims • Local crime surveys • Focus on the shared lived experiences of victims and victimisation socially and structurally
Causes of victimisation	An individual's: • lifestyle and routine activities reflective of societal changes • risk and vulnerability • irrationality and irresponsibility at given moments • initiation and participation in the event (e.g. retaliation) • lack of capable security, inappropriate guardianship, ineffective crime control and regulation	• Absolute and relative deprivation, and marginalisation deriving from neo-liberal and predatory capitalist society creating an unjust and unequal society • Criminalisation of individuals through the victimising actions of the state and its agencies • Patriarchy, masculinity, and power inequities of late modern society • Global, social and economic change
Policy implications	**Deterrence through:** • targeted policing, sentencing and incarceration • situational and victimisation prevention • individual changes of behaviour and attitude • victim avoidance and changes in lifestyle/routine activities	**Transformation of society through:** • social policy • economic and social change • fundamental revision of crime control industry • reconciliatory, peacemaking and restorative measures and mechanisms

ORTHODOX PERSPECTIVES

The central tenets of orthodox thinking on victims and victimisation are: an emphasis on the victim of crime; on the ordinary, conventional, normal, ordered, regular and public forms and patterns of victimisation (Walklate, 2007a); concern with the fear of crime and disorder; and identification of the causes of victimisation within the routine everyday lifestyles and activities of individuals (Spalek, 2006). Its empirical basis derives from the manipulation, aggregation and disaggregation of 'official' data collected by police or local criminal justice organisations, through crime surveys carried out in specific geographic and sometimes 'hot spot' locations – usually nationally and internationally, and more recently from geographic information systems (GIS). Its policy solutions are essentially concerned with managing the probability of criminal victimisation occurring or re-occurring through forms of victimisation and situational prevention, regulation and control. Social policy is articulated as being about managing risks, vulnerability and fear at individual and neighbourhood levels.

Lifestyle exposure perspective

The most developed form of thinking is that articulated by Hindelang et al. (1978) (Walklate, 2007b). Becoming a victim (or not) is, for Hindelang et al., a consequence of an individual's lifestyle and their level of exposure to high-risk 'victimisation' situations. An individual's lifestyle, such as vocational activities (work, school, housework) and leisure pursuits, and the routine activities that underpin and inform them, is core to this way of thinking. An individual's structural position, role expectations and demographic characteristics all help inform their lifestyle and routine activities and thus inform their levels and patterning of risk and potential levels of vulnerability. Hindelang et al. predict victimisation occurring at the point a suitable victim and likely offender converge, in specific situations and under certain conditions, where the offender views force as advantageous and is willing to use it. Such interactions underpin, for Hindelang et al., personal crime victimisation, and they further support their thesis by eight propositions as detailed in Box 5.3 (see Walklate, 2011).

BOX 5.3 EXPERIENCE OF VICTIMISATION

Experience of victimisation is dependent to an extent on:

1 Time spent in public places, particularly at night.
2 Time spent in public is a product of lifestyle.
3 Social contact and interactions – these occur disproportionately among individuals who share similar lifestyles.
4 Chances of personal victimisation – these are dependent partly on shared demographic features.

(Continued)

(Continued)

5 The proportion of time spent with non-family members – this varies according to lifestyle.
6 Personal victimisation – increases as a proportion of time spent away from family.
7 Variations in lifestyles – associated with variations in the ability of individuals to isolate themselves from offenders.
8 Variations in lifestyle – associated with variations in the convenience, the desirability, and that variability of a person as a target for personal victimisation.

Routine activity, rational choice and crime science perspectives

In a similar vein, albeit under the heading 'routine activity theory', Cohen and Felson (1979), Felson and Cohen (1980) and Felson and Santos (2010) argue that criminal victimisation occurs when there is a convergence between a likely offender and a suitable target (victim) in specific material and historical times and spaces where there is insufficient capable guardianship either to intercede on behalf of the victim or to demotivate the likely offender. Routine activities are described as recurrent and prevalent activities that help an individual address their needs (work, leisure, consumption and human interaction). The basic premise is that societal changes influence a victim's exposure to and risk of victimisation: for example, victimisation opportunities increase with the development of accessible, light and easily concealed electronic items such as mobile phones; car theft decreases with better and more sophisticated security equipment; burglary opportunities increase with more households working – but also decrease with the introduction of better security (Meier and Miethe, 1993).

Lifestyle exposure and routine activity perspectives are very similar; the difference is that the former was developed to understand victimisation rates amongst social groups, and the latter to explain crime rates over time (Meier and Miethe, 1993). Meier and Miethe (1993) have attempted to integrate both perspectives into a structural choice model of victimisation in an attempt to understand not only why victimisation may occur, but also the reasoning behind specific targets and choices of victim, assessing both predisposing and precipitating factors informing risk and vulnerability.

Rational choice theory (Cornish and Clark, 1986) emphasises the decision making of offenders and victims. It is a model that down-plays assessment of the motivations of the offender in favour of a more specific event focus, exploring the potential victim, in situ, and their decisions such as taking avoidance and preventative actions. Similarly, crime science (Clarke, 2010) suggests that crime, and thus victimisation, is a rational outcome of the interaction between motivation and opportunity in an environment where forms of intervention can influence the nature of the opportunities and can modify or enhance the precipitators.

Critical assessment

The appeal of the orthodox model is substantial. It offers a 'commonsense' approach to understanding victim decision making and promoting problem solving. It focuses on the everyday realities of public life and it supports the maintenance of the status quo and social order. It is empirically grounded, utilising victim information generated by crime surveys alongside official crime recording, and is supported by analysis of crime and victimisation data. Its interest in the patterning of victims and victimisation, and its symbiosis with evidence-based intervention has secured for itself a scientific reputation. It is applied, offers policy implications and shifts thinking towards aligning individual victims' experiences to their personal, material and structural characteristics.

However, it adopts a narrow and often legal definition of the victim of crime, and promotes a passive idea of the victim being determined by their demographic, role and structural positioning, and therefore lifestyle and routine activities. It has overly functionalist overtones, particularly regarding an individual's decision making, suggesting that individuals merely adapt to circumstance. While never overtly 'blaming' the victim for their own victimisation, each perspective within this model inadvertently draws attention towards the role victims play in their own misfortune, alongside their own responsibility for victimisation prevention. In particular, its bloated scientific underbelly suggests a world of regularity, patterning and precipitative characteristics of victimisation that may well hide as much as elucidate understanding of victimhood. Its predominant focus on public lifestyles, and activity defined as criminal, neglects the private and corporate as locations for much victimisation, such as within the home, in organisations and institutions including at boardroom levels.

PAUSE FOR REVIEW

What are the key elements of orthodox thinking on victims and victimisation, and what are the key differences between the various orthodox perspectives in victimology?

In what ways can an individual's victimisation result from their lifestyle and routine activities, and what issues does this form of thinking give rise to?

How does orthodox victimology provide a passive view of the victim of crime?

REVISIONIST PERSPECTIVES

At the core of revisionist thinking is: a deconstruction of the term 'victim'; a focus on the materiality of victimhood; examination of victimisation as a consequence of late modern, global, neo-liberal predatory capitalism; and the uncovering of victimisation generated by the actions of the state and its agencies, corporate organisations and private institutions, often in hidden locations such as the home, the boardroom and the workplace (Davies et al., 2014; McLaughlin, 2010; McShane and Williams, 1992). Methodologically, qualitative, ethnographic and visual criminological approaches are used to give voice and meaning to victims' experiences, exploring the lived realities of victimisation, including those that are invisible and going on behind a person's back in order to capture, record and challenge the dynamic processes and relations that give rise to victimisation (Mawby and Walklate, 1994). Its policy solutions are often transformatory rather than pragmatic. It is interested less in making changes to systems and processes already in existence and more in economic, cultural, social and political change.

There is a wide array of competing perspectives within the revisionist strand. What solidifies them is an espoused focus on the concepts of power, politics and representation, be they articulated through analyses of social divisions, social structural relations, globalisation, patriarchy, postmodern conditions or cultural signifiers. The authors variously embrace the ideas, concepts and assumptions of social interactionism, critical sociology, Marxism, gender studies and postmodernism. Three of the most important perspectives are the radical criminology arising from the work of Quinney (1972), feminist perspectives on victimology (see Davies, 2011) and critical victimology (Mawby and Walklate, 1994). Mythen (2016), Walklate et al. (2011) and Arfman et al. (2016) have also articulated a case for cultural victimology.

Radical and feminist victimology and the reconceptualisation of the victim

Quinney's (1972, 1977) early reflections on the victim as a social construction has proved pivotal in allowing radical victimology to be entrusted to re-imagine the victim beyond that claimed by orthodox victimology. Thinking seriously about the victim involved for Quinney 'Breaking out of the theory of reality that has dominated criminological thought' by conceiving 'of the victims of police force, the victims of war, the victims of the "correctional" system, the victims of state violence, the victims of oppression of any sort' (1972: 321). It is an approach that has influenced the work of Elias (1986) into human rights, Pearce's (1976) examination of victimisation in commercial settings, and Cohen's (2001) exploration of atrocities and states of denial. In each it is the state, or its agencies, corporations and big business that are viewed as perpetrating crime and injustice, and therefore victimisation.

Kauzlarich et al. (2001: 76) offers a radical victimology of state crime, defining victims as 'individuals or groups of individuals who have experienced economic, cultural or physical harm, pain, exclusion or exploitation, because of tacit or explicit state actions or policies which violate law or generally defined human rights.' Within this work, Kauzlarich et al. posit a number of propositions as detailed in Box 5.4.

BOX 5.4 PROPOSITIONS REGARDING STATE CRIME

- Victims of state crime tend to be the less powerful socially.
- Victimisers usually fail to understand institutional policies or they are neutralised.
- Victims of state crime are often blamed for their suffering.
- Victims of state crime usually have to rely on the victimiser for redress.
- Victims are easy targets for repeat victimisation.
- Illegal state policies and practices are the manifestation of achieving institutional goals.

(Kauzlarich et al., 2001) (see Westervelt and Cook, 2010)

At the about same time as Quinney was asking pertinent questions about the role of the state in the construction and creation of the victim, second-wave feminism also influenced victimological thinking by highlighting the needs and rights of the female victim (Rock, 2010; Walklate, 2007a; Heidensohn, 1985). It was not long before feminist victimologies (there are more than one) began to challenge orthodox agendas around victims and victimisation, helping focus research for rather than on women, exploring the intersectionalities of class, race, age, gender, and theorising about inequality, patriarchal power, and hegemonic masculinities (see Davies, 2011). Box 5.5 provides a simplified diagrammative representation of the various strands of feminist victimological thought.

BOX 5.5 FEMINIST PERSPECTIVES ON VICTIMS AND VICTIMIZATION

	Liberal	Radical	Socialist	Postmodern
Key features	Against inequality and discrimination For equal opportunities	Against men's oppression and power over women For women's knowledge and contribution	Against one dimensional analyses and standpoints For structural analysis, understanding intersectionalities of class, race, age, gender, sexuality etc.	Against the uncritical and the universal dimensions of all-encompassing grand narratives For women as the other and celebrating difference
Definition of victim	Victim	Survivor	Victim/survivor	Victim/survivor

(Continued)

(Continued)

	Liberal	Radical	Socialist	Postmodern
Extent of victimisation	As reported in official police recorded data and crime surveys	Ubiquitous; much of which remains hidden and invisible from view, especially that with private and corporate settings	Ubiquitous; much of which remains hidden and invisible from view, especially that with private and corporate settings	Ubiquitous; defined through individual narratives
Approach	Challenge positivism but can come across as positivistic	Radical and critical social sciences; symbolic interactionism and labelling theory	Left realism	Postmodern perspectives drawn from a mix of humanities and social science disciplines
Causes of victimisation	Patriarchy, inequality and power	Power relations and marginalisation a result of neo-liberal and predatory capitalism Criminalisation of particular acts and behaviours	Social and relative deprivation; marginalisation Criminalisation of particular acts and behaviours	Individual victim narratives have their own causal factors
Policy implications	Challenges sexism in theory, and promotes equality	Focuses on violence and intimate and domestic relations	Campaigns for social justice and social policy interventions	Challenges conventional links between science and policy making; promotes peacemaking approaches

Source: Davies, 2011

Critical victimology, left realism and cultural criminology

Both radical and feminist perspectives offer considerable advances on orthodox thinking about victims and victimisation. They deconstruct the notion of the 'victim'; elucidate understanding through assessment of the processes of social construction; offer structural analyses; utilise gender, power and politics as key conceptual tools to capture the depth of victim's narratives; and theorise in context (social, economic, political, cultural, historical etc.). Yet, for Walklate (2007a: 48) they do not capture adequately the processes that 'go on behind our backs', but are nevertheless still home grown in the form of the activities of the state and/or those that go on within the 'safe haven' of our own homes. Along with Rob Mawby, Walklate has attempted to address this through the development of a critical victimological perspective that gets beyond the mere appearance of things. It is a perspective that attempts to understand

> people's conscious activity, their 'unconscious' activity (that is routine activities people engage in which serve to sustain and sometimes change, the conditions in which they act), the generative mechanisms (unobservable and unobserved) which underpin daily life, and finally, both the intended and unintended consequences of action which feed back into people's knowledge (Mawby and Walklate, 1994: 19)

Critical victimology involves understanding the complex interplay and interrelationship between agency and structure, and of how individual actions and experiences take place in particular material conditions. It calls for appreciation of human interaction in time and space, analysis of representation (and misinterpretation), and articulates an empirical research agenda involving mixed methodologies and methods, comparative and longitudinal studies.

In a not dissimilar vein, left realism (Matthews, 2014, 2009; Currie, 2007, 2010) provides further opportunity to critically understand crime and victimisation. For left realists, crime and victimisation are outcomes of processes of action and reaction involving offenders, victims, communities and the state and its agencies (see Figure 5.1). Crime is not merely a consequence of social reaction but a complex outcome of the interplay of relative deprivation, marginalisation and criminalisation informed by a series of fundamental organising concepts including class, the state and social structure. Neoliberal Capitalist free market societies create the conditions for relative deprivation, and crime and victimisation are an outcome of processes of marginalisation and criminalisation. To theorise victimisation involves understanding the actions of the offender and victim at particular times, and in specific locations, alongside the responses of the public (community) and the state and its agencies. Who the victim is, how the victim is labelled

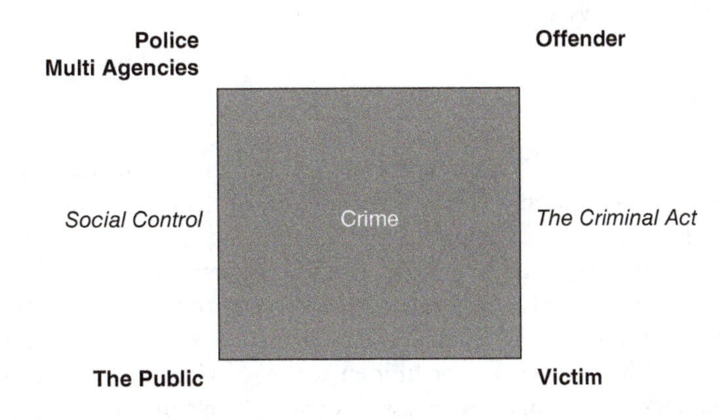

Figure 5.1 The square of crime (Young, 1997)

(or not), how the victim manages the victimisation, and how they are responded to (or not) is an outcome of this dynamic process. Victimisation is a consequence of social, economic and political inequalities (Lea and Young, 1984; Lea, 2010; and Matthews, 2014).

In line with the cultural turn in criminology (see e.g. Ferrell et al., 2008; Hayward and Young, 2007; Hayward and Presdee 2010; Presdee 2000), attempts have also been made to capture a cultural analysis of victims and victimisation (Mythen, 2016; Walklate et al., 2011; Arfman et al., 2016). For Ferrell et al. this means

> a victimology attuned to human agency, a symbolic display, and shared emotion. Such a victimology would consider performances of victimization and enactments of grief through which the meaning of victimization is constructed. It would explore the symbolic environments created by victims, their families and their friends as they come to terms with their experiences. And it would trace the path of personal pain as it moves through the mass media and the criminal justice system, and so re-emerges as a collective accomplishment. (Ferrell et al., 2008: 190)

Mythen (2007) examines the use of the term 'new terrorism', a concept used by many in positions of power and influence such as journalists, policymakers and politicians to differentiate the activities of contemporary radical Islamic groups and older European organisations that have used terrorist tactics (e.g. the IRA). The former is presented as attempting to perpetrate mass killings throughout the world, working in cells, with untold access to an extensive array of dangerous weapons. In contrast, the latter are portrayed as single-issue groups, targeting specific people and locations. For Mythen (2007) the potential victims of the new terrorism are defined as anyone and everyone who is white, urban, Christian, Anglo Saxon and so on. The construction of this universal victim, for Mythen (2007), using the 'new terrorist' threat has allowed those with vested interests to promote significant and fundamental changes in the regulatory and security systems, approaches and mechanisms aimed at containing and preventing terrorism. It exaggerates fear, magnifies risk and diminishes other potential threats (crime, disorder etc.) (Mythen, 2007). See also Mythen and Walklate (2006) and Walklate et al. (2011) for further explorations of aspects of cultural victimology.

Critical assessment

The revisionist model helps unpack the way in which victims and victimisation are represented and misrepresented, and constructed and reconstructed. It allows for the social construction of victimhood to be exposed and understood. It uncovers and presents new perpetrators (or victimisers), and provides greater understanding of the lived experiences of those victimised. Importantly it notes the role power, politics and representation plays alongside structural and temporal variables. The impact of this strand has been considerable in unearthing hitherto invisible or hidden forms of victimisation (such as domestic violence). It challenges the impact of excess at various levels of the state and its agencies, corporations and organisations and highlights the role of gender and politics in constructing and defining victimhood. The responses from this perspective range from peacemaking approaches, through reconciliatory mechanisms through to social structural changes. Social policy is viewed as a transformatory activity.

However, in its deconstruction of the victim, and identification of the victimiser, revisionist thinking can sometimes appear to be more interested in the aggressor, be it men, organisations, corporations, state governed institutions, and governments, than the lived experiences of those victimised. Often less depth and detail concerning the nature and extent of the victim and victimisation is presented. Often the power relations underlying a particular act or acts are under exposed, with the voice of the victim remaining understated. Sometimes, the transformatory ambitions read as though it is the state, and its agencies, alongside late modern predatory capitalism that are to 'blame' for victimisation.

PAUSE FOR REVIEW

What are the central tenets of revisionist thinking about victims and victimisation? Does it do more than merely invert orthodox thinking about victims and victimisation? How?

What are the key feminist perspectives in victimology and what are the key differences between each in terms of theorising about women as victims and survivors?

What are the key elements of critical social science and what do they offer to an understanding of victims and victimisation?

ORTHODOXY AND REVISIONISM: THEMES AND REFLECTIONS

Orthodox and revisionist victimologies have shadow-boxed over the last 50 or so years in relation to answering the questions: Who is the victim? Why does victimisation occur? What is the nature, extent and impact of victimisation? What should be done in response to the victim's lived experiences? Orthodox thinking remains the dominant strand of victimology exerting considerable intellectual, political and policy weight in the US, Europe and the UK. Yet, in many respects revisionist victimology offers an advance on such thinking. It locates victimhood and victimisation in a broader analysis of social conflict in order to explore the dynamic interplay between power, politics, representation and social divisions. This section examines three key problems associated with orthodox thinking in order to outline the major benefits that a revisionist approach offers those wishing to take victims and victimisation seriously.

The necessity of deconstructing the victim and victimisation

Orthodox victimologies utilise a narrow definition of the victim, often using legal means. It is usually criminal victimisation that is in focus. While this may provide clarity as to what is and what is not in scope, it is problematic. It shuts out assessment of those who experience harm but who do not achieve formal victim status. It narrows the potential number of people whose lived experiences indicate that they have been a victim of injustice, harm, force or fraud. It limits the nature, form and shape that victimisation can take. It contributes to a particular narrative about public crimes and individual victims, and of criminal victimisation, underscored more by data than lived experience, and it can drive a particular view of victim responsibility, and sometimes victim blaming. It also informs policy and practical interventions that are pragmatic, situationalist and short-termist. Certainly as a way of thinking it undervalues the impact that power, politics, representation and inequality can and does play in determining who the victim is, and of how they are received.

Not all activities that are harmful are criminalised, and those victimised may not acquire the term 'victim' because of who they are, even though they may well wish to define themselves as such. Alternatively, some individuals' who do acquire the term 'victim' may not define themselves as such, wishing to reject the label and the implications that may arise from its application (Christie, 1986; Carrabine et al., 2004). Deconstruction of the term 'victim' is therefore both welcome and necessary. For feminists when the word 'victim' is gendered, it connects notions of powerlessness and passivity with being female, and it is for these reasons that many feminists prefer to use the term 'survivor' (Walklate, 2007c). The notion of victimless crime has received criticism from feminists who note the wider social and political aspects of power and domination that give rise to the 'crime' in the first place, whether it is drug use or prostitution (Walklate, 2007c). For many critical victimologists the term 'social harm' is preferred, as the term 'victim of crime' is believed to exclude many serious or mass harms as well as many petty events (Hillyard et al., 2005). It is also the view that the criminal law has an individualising focus. Certainly 'social harm' better reflects the broader aspects of social and political victimisation (Davies et al., 2014). For Hillyard et al. (2004, 2005) the term social harm:

- acknowledges the multitude of harms that affect people from birth to death including physical, financial/economic, emotional and psychological, sexual, cultural;
- recognises individual, group, corporate and collective harms and actions/non-actions;
- allows for a greater understanding of who or what might be responsible, and who might also be a victim;
- prioritises social rather than criminal justice policy, on restorative, reconciliatory, informal and re-integrative approaches located in the community;
- confronts power structures and powerful interests.

Yet, at the same time, it is important that some parameters are employed in defining who the victim is and what is meant by victimisation, otherwise there is a danger that everyone can be defined as victims and the clarity of illustration and circumstance would diminish considerably. As Walklate (2012: 173), has articulated, 'the questions raised by Quinney not only centred the importance of appreciating the ways in which victims were socially constructed, but also raised significant questions about the relationship between these social constructions and morality.' Thinking about victims and victimisation should not fall into the trap of relativism and essentialism.

It is here that revisionist victimology has the potential to really contribute to a better understanding of victims and victimisation. Matthews (2009), for example, noted earlier for developing a left-realist perspective, articulates what he refers to as a 'soft constructionism', whereby concepts such as crime and victim are viewed neither as top-down constructs, nor just bottom-up processes of feeling, emotion and tolerance. Rather, for Matthews, they are a result of a complex relationship between four determinants: those who do (the offender); those that experience (the victim); the state; and the local community. The role of theory, for Matthews is to help uncover and explore the underlying processes and determinants, acknowledging the importance of social divisions, including race, gender, age and so on, alongside the relative centrality of class in understanding social divisions and inequality. Only revisionist victimology can do this.

Moreover, Arfman et al. (2016) argue that the terms 'victim' and 'victimhood' are cultural rather than legal or psychological concepts, and that victimhood should be seen as a cultural object of study. They present three reasons for this argument. First, because victimhood is an increasingly complex and global issue a strictly legal approach can hide how the law itself can victimise; second, because victim definitions differ by legal systems and such systems emerge in particular cultural contexts; and third because victimhood today has a public aspect beyond that of the individual victim. This latter point is also highlighted by Furedi (1998).

The limitations of positivist victimology

Positivism remains the golden thread connecting the pioneering work of von Hentig and much contemporary orthodox victimology today (Goodey, 2005: 99). It provides some of the conceptual and theoretical frameworks within which orthodox victimological thinking is undertaken, and it continues to influence many of the decisions concerning what is studied, why, how, as well as the questions asked. The impact of positivism can be seen in the ongoing search for the 'causes' of criminal victimisation that focus on the individual, and on their differentiation and lifestyles. The repackaging of early victimological concepts, such as victim proneness, culpability and precipitation as victim 'lifestyle', 'vulnerability' and 'risk' is further evidence of the continuing influence of positivism (Goodey, 2005). Moreover, the victim survey, and more recently the use of GIS in victim studies has ensured that the traditions of positivistic science, and the conceptual and methodological techniques associated with it, are synchronistic with much victimological research and thinking today. The lasting impact of positivist thinking is considerable in contributing to victimology's enduring appeal as a 'science' (Francis, 2016).

Yet, the limitations of positivism have led to significant problems arising, many overt. It has led to accusations of 'victim blaming' through orthodox victimology's focus on the participation of victims in their own victimisation, alongside their active contribution to specific incidents. It has been pilloried for its limited assessment of 'invisible' victims, of actions that go on behind victims' backs (Walklate, 2003), and for its lack of analysis of state, government and corporate victimisation. Withering criticisms have also been levelled at its gendered assumptions, lack of wider structural and social analysis, and reliance on conventional strategies of crime control (Francis, 2016). And, whilst helping shape knowledge about the nature, extent and impact of crime and victimisation, and concerning the distribution of crime by class, race, age, gender, sexuality and so on, surveying victims of crime is acknowledged as a flawed methodology, especially as a tool to uncover, to expose, to listen and to contextualise victim experiences, especially those which cannot be clearly legally defined.

What revisionist thinking has achieved is not merely a critique of orthodox victimology, and its positivist undertones, but rather a fundament reorientation of victimological thinking, from crime victims, to victims of harm and injustice, to survivors in a socially stratified society as well as towards the sites and places where victimisation may occur, including hidden and private places. It has fostered criticality, challenge and reflection as tools to get behind the mere appearance of things and to expose, to uncover and to critique taken-for-granted ideas and assumptions. Through a focus on victims' narratives, revisionist perspectives have promoted a view from below, of the injustices arising from an unequal and unjust capitalist society. Revisionist thinking has allowed the voices of the marginalised to be heard and has helped ensure that victims lived experiences are crucial in understanding and developing interventions. Finally, it has confirmed the importance of qualitative mixed-method approaches to studying victims and victimisation. Researching victims of crime and victimisation is a necessary and important aspect of theorising, and debates about method should not be constrained by particular approaches but rather reflect what is being studied and the research questions posed (Matthews, 2010).

The importance of the interplay between theory, research and practice

Orthodox victimology is, today, often presented as a scientific discipline, one that is objective, valid and reliable in approach. For many victimologists this is to be applauded. Fattah (1992: 48), for example, writing in the late 20th century, bemoaned what he saw as victimology's shift from an academic research orientated discipline into a humanistic movement, from one involved in 'scholarly research to political activism'. It was Fattah's belief that victimology was becoming overrun by the victim's movement, with its emphasis on victims' needs, helping propagate the ideas and philosophy of right-wing criminology, and their calls for greater deterrence and harsher punishments. There was only one solution for Fattah (2012: 93), the separation of the academic from the humanist, in order to defend the scientific nature of victimology:

> The future of victimology will thus depend on its ability to return back to its original scientific mission, to shed its ideological mantle and to resume its role as a scholarly discipline as an integral part of criminology. It is the need to separate research from action and science from activism that dictates that victimology be separated from victim policy. To restore the neutrality of victimology and to regain and maintain its scientific integrity it has to detach itself from politics and ideology.

Yet, the outcome of such demarcation is, it could be argued, often an atheoretical, highly-quantitative victimology that is technical in nature. This is certainly the case in much lifestyle, routine activity and crime science research on victims and victimisation. It is also a view that fails to understand the importance of the interconnectivity between, theory, research and practice. As Matthews (2009: 342) has noted, 'The division of labour that identifies some people as theorists and others as researchers or activists involves the breakdown of the relation between theory and practice which in turn serves to undermine the policy relevance and coherence of the subject'.

It is within this context that revisionist victimology, and its robust promotion of the necessary interrelationship between theory, research and practice, should be applauded. Over 30 years ago, Phipps (1986: 114) made the case for a radical victimology that integrated theory, evidence and practice: 'My concern here, however, is not just with a theoretical development but with the development of a radical socialist criminology which has practical relevance to the struggle for justice and against socially generated harms of which criminal harms are a part.' More recently, Goodey (2005: 120), has highlighted how the interconnections between victimological theory, research and practice offer real opportunities for a developing praxis, whereby 'academic research needs to inform victim advocacy and policy initiatives that, in due course, can feed back into new research avenues'.

Radical, feminist and critical perspectives have all helped bring debates about the victim into sharp focus intellectually, politically and in terms of policy (Goodey, 2005). As a consequence victims of hate crime, domestic violence as well as youth victimisation have all received considerable attention (Goodey, 1997, 2005; Walklate, 2007b; Francis, 2007). A key example is the pioneering work of feminist victimologists, which arose from feminist concerns about the lack of academic research on the experience of women, alongside a political ambition to challenge women's experience of patriarchal forms of control be it in the home, at work or the criminal justice system. One study that confirms the importance of engaging at the nexus of theory, research and policy is that by Phil Scraton into the Hillsborough football disaster (see Box 5.6).

BOX 5.6 HILLSBOROUGH: THE TRUTH

On 15 April 1989, 96 Liverpool football fans lost their lives at Leppings Lane, Hillsborough, home to Sheffield Wednesday Football club in the north of England. At some time around 3 p.m. on that Saturday afternoon, Britain's worst football disaster had started to happen. Some 27 years later the truth about Hillsborough started to be told, as a consequence of the activism and lobbying of the parents and family members of those who died on that fatal day (Hillsborough Independent Panel 2012), the research of Scraton and colleagues (see for example Scraton et al., 1995; Scraton, 1999, 2009), and because of a changing political agenda. Scraton's study examines how 'truths' were constructed through a powerful combination of organisational, institutional, political, and media factors. It details how 'institutionalised injustices' and 'systemic biases' left victims mourning long after the event. It highlights the way in which politics and media influenced the reporting and subsequent state, political, institutional responses. It notes the way in which 'myths' become the popular perception of what happened. Hillsborough, and what we know today highlights the ways in which myths were constructed; how the establishment closed ranks; and the consequences for getting to the truth of power, politics and representation lying in the wrong hands.

(see www.hillsborough.independent.gov.uk)

PAUSE FOR REVIEW

What are the key elements of positivism and what factors demonstrate its continuing influence on orthodox thinking on victims and victimisation?

What is meant by 'deconstructionism' and why is it important to the study of victims and victimisation?

What are the key reasons for combining theory, research and practice in thinking critically about victims and victimisation?

SUMMARY

This chapter has outlined the development since the mid-20th century of theorising about victims and victimisation, and its contemporary presence in two competing models, orthodox and revisionist victimology. It has demonstrated how the development of theorising about victims and victimisation received a much needed boost in the late 20th century from a criminology keen on reinventing itself in the light of its failure to explain rising crime in the postwar period of social change and political instability. Two victimological models have been presented, along with the key perspectives that make up them, and the chapter has made clear how each model and perspective has contributed to a better understanding of victims, crime and society. However, in noting this, the chapter has also raised various challenges to each model, and highlighted the very real opportunities that a revisionist victimology can provide. The chapter concludes by suggesting that it is only through a revisionist approach that a fully social theory of victims and victimisation can be developed, one that is theoretically rich, politically informed, and practice aware, able to develop evidence-based interventions that are responsive to the needs of those that are victims.

FURTHER READING

Walklate, S. (2007) *Understanding Criminology: Current Theoretical Debates*. Buckinghamshire: Open University Press, Ch.7.

Chapter 7 of this book provides a concise, critical oversight of theories and perspectives in victimology.

Meier, R.F. and Miethe, T.D. (1993) 'Understanding theories of criminal victimisation', *Crime and Justice*, (17): 459–99.

Offers an excellent summary of early orthodox thinking.

McShane, M.D. and Williams, F.P. (1992) 'Radical victimology: a critique of the concept of victim in traditional victimology', *Crime and Delinquency*, 38(2): 258–71.

Details clearly the development of early radical thinking.

Davies, P. (2011) *Gender, Crime and Victimisation*. London: Sage.

Provides an excellent overview of the development of feminist thinking on victims and victimisation.

Walklate, S., Mythen, G. and McGarry, R. (2011) 'Witnessing Wootton Bassett: an exploration in cultural victimology', *Crime, Media, Culture*, 7(2): 149–65.

The best starting point to begin to understand cultural victimology.

Walklate, S. (2006) *Imagining the Victim of Crime*. Buckinghamshire: Open University Press.

This book provides an excellent overview of the key theoretical debates in victimology, in an accessible and well written way.

REFERENCES

Amir, M. (1967) 'Victim-precipitated forcible rape', *Journal and Criminal Law, Criminology and Police Science*, 58: 493–502.

Amir, M. (1971) *Patterns of Forcible Rape*. Chicago,IL: University of Chicago Press.

Arfman, W., Mutsaers, P., Van der Aa, J. and Hoondert, M. (2016) The Cultural Complexity of Victimhood Tilburg Papers in Culture Studies Paper 163. Tilberg University.

Carrabine, E., Iganski, P., Lee, M., Plummer, K. and South, N. (2004) *Criminology: A Sociological Introduction*. London: Routledge.

Christie, N. (1986) 'The ideal victim', in E.A. Fattah (ed.), *From Crime Policy to Victim Policy*. London: Macmillan.

Clarke, R.V. (2010) 'Crime science', in E. Mclaughlin and T. Newburn (eds), *The Sage Handbook of Criminological Theory*. London: Sage.

Cohen, L.E. and Felson, M. (1979) 'Social change and crime rate trends: a routine activity approach', *American Sociological Review*, 44: 588–608.

Cohen, S. (2001) *States of Denial*. London: Routledge.

Cornish, D. and Clark, R. (1986) *The Reasoning Criminal: Rational Choice Perspectives on Offending*. New York: Springer-Verlag.

Currie, E. (2007) 'Against marginality: arguments for a public criminology', *Theoretical Criminology*, 11(2): 175–90.

Currie, E. (2010) 'Plain left realism: an appreciation of some thoughts for the future', Crime, *Law and Social Change*, 54: 11–124.

Davies, P. (2011) *Gender, Crime and Victimisation*. London: Sage.

Davies, P., Francis, P. and Wyatt, T. (eds) (2014) *Invisible Crimes and Social Harms*. Basingstoke: Palgrave Macmillan.

Elias, R. (1986) *The Politics of Victimization*. Oxford: Oxford University Press.

Ellenberger, T. (1955) 'Psychological relationships between the criminal and his victim', *Archives of Criminal Psychology*, 2: 257–90.

Fattah, E.A. (ed.) (1986) *From Crime Policy to Victim Policy*. London: Macmillan.

Fattah, E.A. (ed.) (1992) *Towards a Critical Victimology*. Basingstoke: Palgrave Macmillan.

Fattah, E.A. (2012) 'From victimology of the the act to victimology of action and the resulting impoverishment of the scholarly discipline of victimology' in Groenhuijsen, M., Letschert, R. and Hazenbroek, S. (eds) Liber Amicorum in honour of Professor dr. Jan van Dijk. Nijmegan: Wolf Publishing. (accessed 27 March 2017)

Felson, M. (1994) *Crime and Everyday Life*. London: Sage.

Felson, M. and Cohen, L. (1980) 'Human ecology and crime: a routine activity approach' *Human Ecology*, 8: 389–406.

Felson, M. and Santos, R. (2010) *Crime and Everyday Life*. London: Sage.

Ferrell, J., Hayward, K. and Young, J. (eds) (2008) *Cultural Criminology*. London: Sage.

Francis, P. (2007) 'Young people, victims and crime', in P. Davies, P. Francis and C. Greer (eds), *Victims, Crime and Society*. London: Sage.

Francis, P. (2016) 'Positivist victimology', in K. Corteen, S. Morley, P. Taylor and J. Turner (eds), *A Companion to Crime, Harm and Victimization*. London: Policy Press.

Furedi, F. (1997) *Culture of Fear: Risk Taking and the Morality of Low Expectation*, London: Continuum International Publishing Group.

Garafalo, R. (1914) *Criminology*. Boston: Little Brown.

Goodey, J. (2005) *Victims and Victimology: Research, Policy and Practice*. London: Longman.

Goodey, J. (1997) 'Boys don't cry: masculinities, fear of crime and fearlessness', *British Journal of Criminology*, 37(3): 401–148.

Gottfredson, M. and Hirschi, T. (1990) *A General Theory of Crime*. Stanford, CA: Stanford University Press.

Greer, C. (2007) 'News media victims and crime', in P. Davies, P. Francis and C. Greer (eds), *Victims, Crime and Society*. London: Sage.

Hayward, K. and Presdee, M. (eds) (2010) *Framing Crime: Cultural Criminology and the Image*. London: Routledge.

Hayward, K. and Young, J. (2007) 'Cultural criminology', in M. Maguire, R. Morgan and R. Reiner (eds), *The Oxford Handbook of Criminology*. Oxford: Oxford University Press. pp. 102–120.

Heidensohn, F. (1985) *Women and Crime*. London: Macmillan.

Hillsborough Independent Panel (2012) *The Report of the Hillsborough Independent Panel*. London: The Stationery Office. Available at http://hillsborough.independent.gov.uk/repository/report/HIP_report.pdf (accessed 7.10.16).

Hillyard, P., Pantazis, C., Tombs, S. and Gordon, D. (eds) (2004) *Beyond Criminology: Taking Harm Seriously*. London: Pluto.

Hillyard, P., Pantazis, C., Tombs, S., Gordon, D. and Dorling, D. (2005) 'Criminal obsessions: why harm matters more than crime' monograph. London: Crime and Society Foundation.

Hindelang, M. Gottfredson, M. and Garofalo, J. (1978) *Victims of Personal Crime: An Emprical Foundation for a Theory of Personal Victimisation*. Cambridge, M.A: Ballinger.

Kauzlarich, D., Matthews, R.A. and Miller, W.J. (2001) 'Toward a victimology of state crime', *Critical Criminology*, 10: 173.

Lea, J. (2010) 'Left realism, community and state-building', *Crime, Law and Social Change*, 54(2): 141–58.

Lea, J. and Young, J. (1984) *What is to be done about Law and Order*. Harmondsworth: Penguin.

MacDonald, R. (1939) *Crime is a Business*. Palo Alto, CA: Stanford University Press.

Matthews, R. (2009) 'Beyond "So what?" criminology: rediscovering realism', *Theoretical Criminology*, 13: 341.

Matthews, R. (2010) 'Realist criminology revisited', in E. McLaughlin and T. Newburn (eds), *The Sage Handbook of Criminological Theory*. London: Sage.

Matthews, R. (2014) *Realist Criminology*. London: Sage.

Mawby, R. and Walklate, S. (1994) *Critical Victimology*. London: Sage.

McLaughlin, E. (2010) 'Critical criminology', in E. McLaughlin and T. Newburn (eds), *The Sage Handbook of Criminological Theory*. London: Sage.

McShane, M.D. and Williams, F.P. (1992) 'Radical victimology: a critique of the concept of victim in traditional victimology', *Crime and Delinquency*, 38(2): 258–71.
Meier, R.F. and Miethe, T.D. (1993) 'Understanding theories of criminal victimisation', *Crime and Justice*, 17: 459–99.
Mendelsohn, B. (1958) Victimology (163) The Origins of the Doctrine of Victimology Excerpta Criminologoca Vol 3 (May June) 239-44.
Miers, D. (1989) 'Positivist victimology: a critique', *International Review of Victimology*, 1: 3–22.
Mythen, G. (2007) 'Cultural victimology: are we all victims now?', in Walklate, S (ed). *Handbook of Victims and Victimology*. Cullompton: Willan.
Mythen, G. (2016) Terrorism and War: Interrogating Discourses of Risk and Security. In S. Walklate and R. McGarry (eds), *The Handbook of Criminology and War: Critical Themes and Approaches*. Basingstoke: Palgrave Macmillan.
Mythen, G. and Walklate, S. (2006) 'Communicating the terrorist risk: harnessing a culture of fear?', *Crime Media Culture*, 2(2): 123–142.
Pearce, F. (1976) *Crimes of the Powerful*. Harmondsworth: Penguin.
Phipps, A. (1986) 'Radical criminology and criminal victimization', in R. Matthews and J. Young (eds), *Confronting Crime*. London: Sage.
Presdee, M. (2000) *Cultural Criminology and the Carnival of Life*. London: Routledge
Quinney, R. (1972) 'Who is the victim?', *Criminology*, 10(3): 309–329.
Quinney, R. (1977) *Class, State and Crime: On the Theory and Practice of Criminal Justice*. New York: McKay.
Rock, P. (2010) 'Approaches to victims and victimization', in E. Mclaughlin and T. Newburn (eds), *The Sage Handbook of Criminological Theory*. London: Sage.
Scraton, P. (1999/2009) *Hillsborough: The Truth*. London: Mainstream.
Scraton, P. Jemphrey, A. and Coleman, S. (1995) *No Last Rights: The Denial of Justice and the Promotion of Myth in the Aftermath of the Hillsborough Disaster*. Liverpool: Liverpool City Council
Smart, C. (1976) *Women, Crime and Criminal Justice*. London: Routledge and Kegan Paul.
Spalek, B. (2006) *Crime Victims*. Basingstoke: Palgrave Macmillan.
Sparks, R. (1982) *Research on Victims of Crime: Accomplishments, Issues, and New Directions*. Rockville, MD: US Dept of Health and Human Services.
Taylor, I. (1981) *Law and Order: Arguments for Socialism*. London: Polity.
Taylor, I. Walton, P. and Young, J. (1973) *The New Criminology*. London: Routledge.
von Hentig, H. (1948) *The Criminal and His Victim*. New Haven, CT: Yale University Press.
Walklate, S. (1989) *Victimology*. London: Unwyn Hyman.
Walklate, S. (2003) 'Can there be a feminist victimology?'. in P. Davies, P. Francis and V. Jupp (eds), *Victimisation: Theory, Research and Policy*. Basingstoke: Palgrave Macmillan.
Walklate, S. (2007a) *Imagining the Victim*. Buckingham: Open University Press.
Walklate, S. (2007b) *Understanding Criminology*. Buckingham: Open University Press.
Walklate, S. (2007c) 'Men, victims and crime', in P. Davies, P. Francis and C. Greer (eds), *Victims, Crime and Society*. London: Sage.
Walklate, S. (2011) *Criminology: the basics*. London: Routledge.
Walklate, S. (2012) 'Who is the victim of crime? Paying homage to the work of Richard Quinney', *Crime, Media, Culture*, 8(2): 173–84.

Walklate, S. Mythen, G. and McGarry, R. (2011) 'Witnessing Wootton Bassett: an exploration in cultural victimology', *Crime, Media, Culture*, 7(2): 149–66.

Westervelt, S.D. and Cook, K.J. (2010) 'Framing Innocents: the wrongly convicted as victims of state harm', *Crime, Law, and Social Change*, 53: 259–275.

Wilson, J.Q. (1975) *Thinking About Crime*. New York: Vintage.

Wilson, J. and Herrnstein, R. (1985) *Crime and Human Nature*. New York: Simon and Schuster.

Wilson, J. and Kelling, R. (1982) 'Broken windows', *Atlantic Monthly*, March: 29–38.

Wolfgang, M.E. (1958) *Patterns of Criminal Homicide*. Philadelphia, PA: University of Pennsylvania Press.

Young, J. (1979) 'Left Idealism, Reformism and the Law' in B. Fine et al. (eds) *Capitalism and the Rule of Law*. London: Hutchinson.

Young, J. (1997) 'Left realist criminology: radical in its analysis, realist in its policy', in M. Maguire, R. Morgan and R. Reiner (eds), *The Oxford Handbook of Criminology* (2nd edn). Oxford: Oxford University Press.

Zedner, L. (1994) 'Victims', in M. Maguire, R. Morgan and R. Reiner (eds), *The Oxford Handbook of Criminology*. Oxford: Oxford University Press.

6 GLOBAL PERSPECTIVES IN VICTIMOLOGY

Matthew Hall

This chapter examines three key areas in the development of policy and practice – across jurisdictions and at the international level – concerning victims of crime, their role in criminal justice and the support mechanisms made available to them. These areas are: recognition of different categories of 'victims' in national and international policy instruments; affording 'rights' to victims of crime; and facilitating compensating and redress. Through a critical discussion of these areas the chapter provides a global snapshot of the substantive and theoretical issues faced by commentators and policy makers. The chapter draws examples from a number of jurisdictions including: England and Wales; the US; the Netherlands; Scotland; Australia; Canada; New Zealand and South Africa. One criticism which might be levied at this sample is that, aside from the Netherlands, all these jurisdictions are what Cavadino and Dignan (2007) refer to as 'neo-liberal' states characterised by right-wing political orientations, a commitment to free-market principles, and where imprisonment rates are relatively high and there exists extreme income differentials. As such, the Netherlands was chosen not only because it has been a major centre for victimological research and policy but also because it serves as a comparator 'conservative corporatist' jurisdiction. Cavadino and Dignan describe such countries as characterised by a focus on rehabilitation in the penal system with a moderately generous welfare state.

DEFINING VICTIMS IN A GLOBAL CONTEXT

In examining the development of victim-based polices across jurisdictions, it is clear that the scope of official notions of victimhood is expanding (Hall, 2010). In terms of **victimological** theory, this development in the understanding of victimisation may reflect so-called **critical victimology** and its expanded notions of victimhood beyond simple, criminal classifications (Dignan, 2005). Yet uncertainties remain, and in 2009 Victim Support Europe made the point that 'not even a common definition of a "victim" has been fully affirmed' at a national or international level (Victim Support Europe, 2009: 8).

A review of the varying national and international definitions of 'victimisation' confirms the above observations. Key differences between definitions include whether or not victimisation is expressly linked to *criminal* activities, whether such victims are defined as suffering 'harm' or whether the more specific notion of 'injury' is employed. Some definitions draw on notions of human rights and/or 'damage'. Box 6.1 draws on examples of national and international definitions of 'victimisation' to illustrate a continuum ranging from relatively narrow definitions to much wider understandings employed in different parts of the globe.

BOX 6.1 GLOBAL UNDERSTANDINGS OF 'VICTIMISATION'

State/organisation	Source of definition	Understanding of 'victimisation'	Features
New Zealand	Victims' Rights Act, 2002 (s.4); Victims' Rights Amendments Act 2011	'those suffering physical injury, or loss of, or damage to, property ... as a result of criminal actions'	• Based on 'injury', narrowly defined
Québec (Canada)	Act Respecting Assistance for Victims of Crime 1988 (s.1)	'a natural person who suffers physical or psychological injury or material loss by reason of a criminal offence committed in Québec, whether or not the perpetrator is identified, apprehended, prosecuted or convicted'	• Based on 'injury', defined broadly to include non-material loss
Victoria (Australia)	Victim Charter Act 2006 (s.3)	'a natural person who has suffered injury as a direct result of a criminal offence, whether or not that injury was reasonably foreseeable by the offender.' Here, injury means actual physical bodily injury; mental illness; pregnancy; grief, distress, trauma or 'other significant adverse effects'; loss or damage to property; or any combination of these'	• Based on 'injury', defined broadly and also including 'other adverse effects'
China	See Guo-An (2001)	'a citizen, a legal person or an organisation that has directly suffered harm as a result of the criminal act'	• Based on the notion of 'harm' • Includes 'legal persons' (companies)

(Continued)

(Continued)

State/organisation	Source of definition	Understanding of 'victimisation'	Features
USA	Crime Victims' Rights Act 2004 (18 USC 3771)	'a person directly and proximately harmed as a result of the commission of a federal offense or an offense in the District of Columbia'	• Based on the notion of 'harm' (the meaning of which is left ambiguous)
European Union	Directive establishing minimum standards on the rights, support and protection of victims of crime 2011 (Art.2(a))	'a natural person who has suffered harm, including physical or mental injury, emotional suffering or economic loss directly caused by a criminal offence'	• Includes both 'harm' and 'injury' • Restricted to 'directly' affected victims
Canada (Federal)	Corrections and Conditional Release Act 1992 (s.2(1))	'a victim is someone who was harmed or who suffered physical or emotional damage as the result of an offence' (s.2(1))	• Based on the notion of 'harm', which here includes emotional 'damage'
South Africa	Department of Justice (2008a)	'a person who has suffered harm, including physical or mental injury; emotional suffering; economic loss; or substantial impairment of his or her fundamental rights, through acts or omissions that are in violation of our criminal law' (p.23)	• Based on the notion of 'harm', widely defined • Also includes human rights violations
United Nations	1985 UN Declaration on Victims of Crime and Abuse of Power (para.18)	'persons who, individually or collectively, have suffered harm, including physical or mental injury, emotional suffering, economic loss or substantial impairment of their fundamental rights, through acts or omissions that do not yet constitute violations of national criminal laws but of internationally recognised norms relating to human rights, (para.18)	• Includes harms perpetrated by the *state* which are not officially categorised as 'crimes' • Based on human rights violations

Such differences in wording between definitions may have significant implications. Williams (1996), for example, argues that 'injury' is a far more concrete concept than 'harm', and as such more useful to lawyers and those wishing to achieve the actual incorporation of victims within criminal justice and sentencing processes. Nevertheless, it is notable from the overview in Box 6.1 that victims are increasingly being defined by the *harm* they suffer. Much victimological literature has commented on the fact that the definition of 'victims' employed is also at least partly dependent on the political and economic context of any given jurisdiction (Harland, 1978). It has also been argued that political expediency has had an important role to play in prompting many jurisdictions to recognise various categories of victims in their official definitions (Walklate, 2012). Inevitably this means other forms of victimisation receive less attention. Examples include: state crime (Matthews and Kauzlarich, 2007), environmental crime (Hall, 2013) and, as I have discussed elsewhere in this volume, elderly victims of crime. Others receiving press coverage at the time of writing are victims of disablist hate crime (HMCPSI et al., 2015).

The politicisation of the victims issue in many jurisdictions is well illustrated by the example of families of homicide victims (Walklate, 2007). For policy makers in a number of countries, the recognition of this group by state criminal justice agencies has been spurred on not only by academic observations concerning the impact of crime on such **survivors**, but also as a response to media campaigning in their support (Rock, 1998; Kenney, 2003). Another recent example from England and Wales concerns the political capital being afforded to victims of press intrusions: prominent figures in the debate have been the parents of the murdered schoolgirl Milly Dowler and the missing youngster Madeleine McCann (BBC, 2013). Furedi (1998) has questioned the apparent authority afforded to victims, as 'moral custodians', to influence policy debates.

In most jurisdictions, much of the victim reform agenda has also been focused on addressing **secondary victimisation** at the hands of the criminal justice process (South African Department of Justice, 2008b). There is a clear criticism to be made in that in Britain we know the majority of victims of crime never report their victimisation (Home Office, 2011). This adds to the impression that much of this agenda is focused on so-called 'ideal victims' who are entirely blameless and cooperative with the criminal justice system (Christie, 1986; Hall, 2010). Ellison (2001) argues that secondary victimisation is impossible to substantially address in countries adhering to **adversarial** justice models (notably England and Wales and the US). That said, when Brienen and Hoegen (2000) reported on a wide-scale comparison of European criminal justice systems and their treatment of victims, they could find little evidence that **inquisitorial** systems were inherently 'better' for victims of crime.

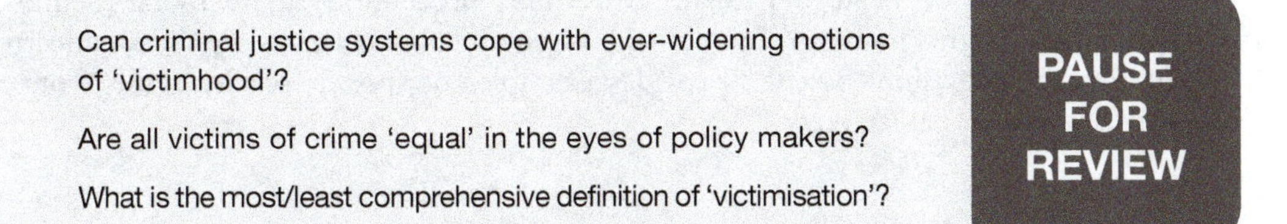
Can criminal justice systems cope with ever-widening notions of 'victimhood'?

Are all victims of crime 'equal' in the eyes of policy makers?

What is the most/least comprehensive definition of 'victimisation'?

PAUSE FOR REVIEW

DO VICTIMS OF CRIME HAVE 'RIGHTS'?

The provision of 'rights' to victims is a controversial issue. Most resulting discussions have concerned themselves with the degree to which victims can be permitted to influence decision making within criminal justice while still safeguarding defendants' right to due process. A common distinction is that drawn by Ashworth (1998) between so-called 'service rights' for victims and 'procedural rights'. The service rights Ashworth has in mind include: respectful and sympathetic treatment; support; information; the provision of facilities at court; and compensation from the offender or state. Procedural rights, on the other hand, afford victims the ability to make a practical contribution to the criminal justice process, most often in relation to prosecution decisions or sentencing.

Much of the modern victim policy agenda in most jurisdictions traces its roots back to the 1985 UN Declaration of Basic Principles of Justice for Victims of Crime and Abuse of Power. The Declaration speaks of victims being afforded:

- Access to justice.
- Fair treatment and compassion.
- Respect for their dignity.
- Information about their role and about the scope, timing, and progress of proceedings, as well as the disposal of their case.
- Assistance from the criminal justice system (including information that such assistance is available), as well as formal and/or informal procedures providing them with redress, restitution and compensation.
- Protection from unnecessary delay or inconvenience.

Generally speaking, other rights found in the various forms of victims' charter adopted across most jurisdictions since the 1985 Declaration fall within four broad categories:

1. Information provision.
2. Protection.
3. Compensation/restitution.
4. Consultation.

Of these, only the fourth category usually constitutes 'procedural' rights. By far the most numerate of such rights found in national and international documents are those concerning information provision. Box 6.2 provides examples of specific service rights from a number of international sources.

BOX 6.2 EXAMPLES OF 'SERVICE RIGHTS' AFFORDED TO VICTIMS OF CRIME

Type of right	State/ organisation	Description	Source
Information	Scotland	Victims are entitled to understand the information being presented to them by criminal justice actors.	Scottish National Standards for Victims of Crime (Scottish Executive, 2005: 3)
	England and Wales	Prosecutors must meet with victims personally, prior to court proceedings, to offer explanations and answer questions.	Code of Practice for Victims of Crime (para.7.7)
	South Africa	Victims have a right to receive information, including information concerning victims' rights *as victims*.	South African Victims Charter (p. 7)
Protection	European Union	Member states shall ensure that measures are available to protect victims and their family members from secondary and repeat victimisation, from intimidation and from retaliation, including against the risk of emotional or psychological harm, and to protect the dignity of victims during questioning.	Directive establishing minimum standards on the rights, support and protection of victims of crime 2011 (Art.18(a))
	USA (Federal)	A right to be 'reasonably protected from the accused'.	USA Crime Victims' Rights Act 8 U.S.C. § 3771(a)(1)
	New Zealand	Judicial officers may withhold part of statement from offenders to protect victim's physical safety or security.	Victims' Rights Act 2002 (s.4); Victims' Rights Amendments Act 2011
Compensation	European Union	Victims are entitled to obtain a decision on compensation by the offender, within a reasonable time.	Directive establishing minimum standards on the rights, support and protection of victims of crime 2011 (Art.16)
	Netherlands	It is possible for the court to impose a fine for any criminal offence. If damages are awarded, the person convicted has to pay a sum of money to compensate for the harm incurred by the victim.	Victims' Status (Legal Proceedings) Act 2011 (s.4)
	Canada (Federal)	Includes compensation to direct and indirect victims of crime as well as, in some circumstances, witnesses of crime.	Canadian Statement of Basic Principles of Justice for Victims of Crime 2003

The majority of individual countries, both in Europe and beyond, have relied on combinations of minimum standards and 'legitimate expectations' (JUSTICE, 1998) as a means of affording rights to victims within their criminal justice systems, although the degree to which the term 'rights' is employed to describe such provisions varies between jurisdictions. The exception is the US, where individual states have been more inclined to incorporate victims of crime within state constitutions, or to produce separate victims' bills of rights. The extent to which such bills are in practice different or more enforceable than the charters used elsewhere is, however, open to dispute.

As reflected in Box 6.2, most 'rights' afforded to victims are service rights. Nevertheless, many charters do provide for a limited degree of participation for victims of crime within the criminal justice system, mainly through an obligation placed on criminal justice actors to *consult* victims when making specific decisions. Box 6.3 provides a summary of key examples in relation to prosecution decisions. It should be noted, however, that in all cases expectations are tempered by clear statements to the effect that victims will not be permitted to *dictate* prosecution decisions.

BOX 6.3 CONSULTATIVE PARTICIPATION BY VICTIMS ON PROSECUTION DECISIONS

Country	Source	Description
South Africa	South African Charter	Victims have a general right to 'offer information'
Scotland	Scottish Executive (2005: 4)	Victims to be consulted on decisions affecting them at all times
England and Wales	Prosecutors Pledge, Crown Prosecution Service (2013)	Victims have the right to request a review of a decision by the prosecutors not to pursue a trial
New Zealand	Prosecution Guidelines of New Zealand and New Zealand Crown Law Office (2010): para.3.3.2(m)	Lists the 'attitude of the victim of the alleged offence to a prosecution' as a matter which 'may arise for consideration'
Netherlands	See Government of the Netherlands (2013)	Anyone with an interest in a prosecution has the right to complain to the Court of Appeal

The other widespread development in terms of victims' participation in the criminal justice process is the rollout of victim impact statements (VIS): allowing victims to communicate the impacts of crime to a court at the sentencing stage. These have caused great controversy in the literature ranging from argument that the VIS can negatively impact on the rights of defendants (Ashworth, 1993) to debates over whether they increase the proportionality of sentences (Erez, 2004; Sanders et al., 2001). Despite continued confusion over the purposes of such statements, provision for their use is now found in most jurisdictions listed above and are also now the subject of court judgements.

One particularly significant decision in the US Supreme Court (*Payne* v *Tennessee*[1]) holding that the use of victim impact statements in capital cases was constitutional, the implication being that in extreme cases the VIS could contribute to the imposition of the death penalty.

The above discussion notwithstanding, the question of whether these developments afford victims of crime genuine 'rights' is a complex one. Jackson (2003), for example, has argued that whatever form they might take, robust and workable enforcement mechanisms are a prerequisite to make any talk of 'victims' rights' meaningful. A number of enforcement mechanisms have been tried in various jurisdictions, as presented in Box 6.4.

BOX 6.4 ENFORCEMENT MECHANISM FOR VICTIMS' RIGHTS

State	Source	Description
England and Wales	The Code of Practice for Victims of Crime	Complains to individual CJS agencies followed by complaint to Parliamentary Commissioner for administration
Netherlands	Terwee Guidelines	Judicial review procedure
US	Crime Victims' Rights Act 2004	Direct enforcement in trial courts

Notably the examples in Box 6.4 reflect increasing involvement of the *judiciary* as opposed to extra-judicial enforcement mechanisms as we progress down the table, albeit that the majority of jurisdictions have elected for a model similar to that of England and Wales.

One particularly significant example of the enforcement of victims' rights is that under the Crime Victims' Rights Act 2003, which has been heralded as a major breakthrough by proponents of a more judiciable form of victims' rights, containing as it does the Crime Victims' Rights Act, introducing such rights into the US penal code (Doyle, 2008). The Act restates standard service rights of information protection and compensation, as well as a procedural rights for victims 'to be reasonably heard at any public proceeding in the district court involving release, plea, sentencing, or any parole proceeding' (18 U.S.C. §3771(a)(4)). The most significant feature of the legislation, however, is its enforcement mechanisms. Here, individuals or the federal government may assert victims' rights at the District Court level. If the victim or the government are still not satisfied with the enforcement of these rights they may file a petition with the Court of Appeals for a writ of mandamus. A court's decision to deny any of these rights may be asserted as an error by the prosecution in the case. Even more significantly, in limited circumstances a victim may move for a new trial on the basis of the denial of their rights (Doyle, 2008).

Aside from the creation of new 'victim rights', another relevant development is the consideration of victims' issues in relation to human rights concerns, especially by the European Court of Human Rights (ECtHR). Key cases from the ECtHR dealing with the question of victims' rights are presented in Box 6.5 (see also Doak, 2003).

BOX 6.5 KEY VICTIMS' RIGHTS CASES FROM THE EUROPEAN COURT OF HUMAN RIGHTS

Case name(s)	Principle
Baegen v *Netherlands*[2] and *Doorson* v *Netherlands*[3]	• Keeping witnesses (including victim witnesses) anonymous in order to reduce intimidation and enhance protection does not breach a defendant's Article 6 rights under the Convention[4]
Sn v *Sweden*[5]	• Article 6 does not grant the defence an unlimited right to secure the appearance of witnesses in court • Witnesses can give evidence through recorded interviews without breaching Article 6
T and V v *UK*[6]	• The parents of a young murder victim were permitted to make representations to the Court about how the crime had impacted upon them

On a wider scale, Oda J. of the International Court of Justice has referred to victims having rights in his dissenting opinion in the case of LaGrand (*Germany* v *United States of America*). Victims' participation rights have also been recognised in the first criminal trial of the International Criminal Court, where 93 victims were permitted to present impact statements. Nevertheless, McDermott (2009) has criticised the fact that these statements contained information about war crimes not listed in the official indictment.

PAUSE FOR REVIEW

Why do criminal justice systems seem to have such difficulty with the notion of 'victims' rights yet accept that defendants have rights?

What does it mean to 'participate' in a criminal justice system?

Should criminal justice systems react more to the wishes of victims; for example, should they proceed with prosecutions against the wishes of victims of crime in domestic violence cases?

COMPENSATION AND REDRESS FOR VICTIMS OF CRIME

Young (1997) highlights state (i.e. publicly-funded) compensation for victims of crime as an important factor in the development of the international victims' movement. Paul Rock (1986, 1990) similarly notes compensation as a key influence on the development of victim policy making in England and Wales and Canada specifically. Discussed here is the trend whereby governments have moved from state compensation, to the introduction of offender-based compensation or 'restitution' schemes and the establishment of victims' funds financed by surcharges imposed on offenders. Most recently, many jurisdictions have experimented with restorative justice as a means of affording redress to victims of crime.

STATE COMPENSATION SCHEMES

In England and Wales and elsewhere, the introduction of state compensation was largely based on a presumption that victims wanted it (Rock, 1990). The implications of this are that compensation originally surfaced on the policy scene in a most ad hoc manner, far removed from the modern focus on evidence-based policies. Certainly the justifications for using public money to fund compensation for victims of crime in most jurisdictions are somewhat eclectic. In Texas, for example, the primary purpose of the state's Crime Victims Compensation Program are presented as 'encouraging greater victim participation in the apprehension and prosecution of criminals' (Office of the Attorney General of Texas, 2009). In the Netherlands, justifications are based on social welfare arguments as well as the collective responsibility of the state and the community to care for victims, which is in keeping with that country's 'conservative corporatist' background. There is also a recognition that state compensation to some extent acknowledges the victim in a way the criminal justice system previously did not. In almost all cases, governments emphasise that these schemes in no way amount to an acknowledgement of *state* liability for criminal injuries.

Miers (1997: 3) claims that the justifications in different jurisdictions for state-based compensation are 'to varying degrees unconvincing'. Both Miers (1997) and Elias (1986) emphasise the heavily political character of state compensation. This echoes the earlier concerns of Harland (1978), discussed above, whereby state compensation schemes are said to emanate from interest group protests and press coverage. Clear examples and comparisons of the mediatised effect Miers and Harland have in mind can be drawn from the US and the UK and the compensation schemes set up in the aftermath of the terrorist attacks in New York and London in 2001 and 2005 respectively, as well as the compensation system set up in the wake of the Gulf of Mexico Oil Spill in 2010.

One common characteristic of most state compensation schemes is that they tend to be relatively restrictive in terms of the scope of victimisation and the impacts of crime they cover; indeed, usually they are aimed at victims of *violent* crime who suffer *physical* injury. Both the Anglo-Welsh and the New Zealand systems employ the term 'injury', which encompasses physical and mental injury, although eligibility to claim for the latter category is typically restricted in all jurisdictions. It is usually envisaged that mental injury will have occurred in addition to physical injury, thus preserving the essential violent crime/physical injury core to these schemes, although there are limited circumstances where mental injury alone can be compensated. In Ireland the scheme refers to 'personal injury where the injury is directly attributable to a crime of violence' (Irish Criminal Injuries Compensation Tribunal, 2009: para.1). It is clear that a link between the compensated harm and a violent crime must be present in most of the aforementioned schemes. North American and Canadian state-based compensation schemes (Californian Victim Compensation and Government Claims Board, 2009) tend to be especially prescriptive in this regard, providing schedules of specific 'qualifying offences', most of which are crimes of violence or sexual crimes. The New Zealand system has a similar list. This approach can be compared to those in several Australian jurisdictions, and in particular New South Wales, where the relevant legislation (Victims Support and Rehabilitation Act 1996) provides lists of *injuries suffered* as opposed to *crimes committed*. This is also the approach of the English and Welsh system. Rock (1990) acknowledges that the general restrictiveness of most state compensation schemes reflects budgetary limits, as exemplified in Box 6.6.

BOX 6.6 THE UK CRIMINAL INJURIES COMPENSATION SCHEME 2012

In January 2012, the UK Ministry of Justice published a consultation paper *Getting It Right for Victims and Witnesses* proposing changes to the State Compensation system, last updated in 2008. Key changes now in force include:

- Increased focus on the distinction between eligible 'deserving victims' and ineligible 'less deserving' ones.
- Reduced the number of injuries qualifying under the lowest tariff amounts (£1,000–£2,000). As the vast majority of payments are made at this level, this will effectively reduce the number of payments substantially.
- Placed further restrictions on the compensation victims can obtain for loss of earnings.
- Re-emphasised that victims need to cooperate with the criminal justice system in order to qualify for compensation under the scheme.

The reforms clearly reduce the scope of the scheme and are perhaps representative of the greater importance (or economic necessity) of alternative means of providing redress and compensation to victims of crime in 21st century.

It is also significant that these schemes tend to judge the victim as well as the victimisation. Many schemes exclude victims who have previously had criminal convictions or were not entirely 'innocent' in their victimisation. According to a critical perspective, this type of victim might be considered atypical given the frequent overlap between 'offenders' on the one hand and 'victims' on the other.

RESTITUTION FROM OFFENDERS

Over the last 30 years, many jurisdictions have developed restitution schemes whereby offenders provide monetary compensation to victims, either though the imposition of court-based compensation orders or through offender surcharges or fine payments. Such developments tend to be applauded by victimological scholars who hold that payments from offenders themselves carry greater symbolic value to victims of crime than monies allocated from taxation (Wright, 1998).

Restitution has become an integral component of many criminal justice systems globally. For example, in Canada the courts have established in *The Queen* v *Zelensky*[7] that compensating victims of crime is a key objective of sentencing. The Canadian criminal code allows courts to make restitution orders at the time of sentencing an offender.[8] In South Africa a victim's right to both compensation and restitution have more recently been set out in the South African Victims' Charter. Here the term 'compensation' is taken to mean financial payments from offenders for 'loss or damage to property' (South African Department of Justice and Constitutional Development, 2008a: 13). 'Restitution' in this instance means the return or repair of property by the offender 'in order to restore you [the victim] to the position you were in prior to the commission of the offence' (p. 15). This was also the rationale given for the introduction of compensation orders in the Netherlands in the Terwee Act 1995. In South Africa, it is notable that neither the governing legislation nor the Victims' Charter include crimes of violence and the associated medical costs under the headings of restitution or compensation, as is the case with the US and Canadian schemes. As in all jurisdictions, the limited means of most offenders will inhibit the effectiveness of restitutive measures. Box 6.7 looks at offender-based restitution from a global perspective.

BOX 6.7 OFFENDER-BASED RESTITUTION – GLOBAL COMPARISONS

One of the most wide-ranging systems of offender-based restitution is found in New Zealand where, as in the US and Canada, the Sentencing Act 2002 includes a strong statutory presumption in favour of restitution, and a judge must give reasons when restitution is *not* ordered in specific cases. Under the legislation, such reasons must demonstrate

(Continued)

(Continued)

that the imposition of an order would 'result in undue hardship for the offender or the dependents' or that 'any other special circumstances would make it inappropriate' (s.12(1)). The New Zealand Law Commission (2008) has suggested that, unlike the US system, this latter provision means that an offender's lack of earnings can be used to justify a refusal to make an order. The same is true in England and Wales, where the Powers of Criminal Courts Sentencing Act 2000 requires courts to give reason when an order is not made (s.130(3)), but there is no presumption in favour of granting restitution as in the US and Canada.

In addition to compensation orders, a number of jurisdictions have also introduced levies on all offenders to be paid into general victims' funds used to pay for services and support mechanisms for victims. Hence the Californian Victims Compensation Program is funded by 'restitution fines and orders, penalty assessments levied on persons convicted of crimes and traffic offenses, and federal matching funds' (Californian Department of Corrections and Rehabilitation, 2009). In England and Wales, under the Domestic Violence Crime and Victims Act 2004 (s.14) a court must impose a £15 surcharge on offenders in cases where it also imposes a fine and/or a compensation order. A similar fund has been set up in Scotland funded by charitable donations (Victim Support Scotland, 2009). In New South Wales, Australia, Part 5 of the Victim Support and Rehabilitation Act 1996 requires a levy of either AUS$30 or AUS$70 (depending on the mode of trial) to be imposed on adult offenders convicted of imprisonable offences. As is the case in England and Wales, this levy takes precedence over any other financial payment imposed on the offender by the court. This can be contrasted to the system in Ontario, Canada where, under the Provincial Offences Act 1990, a victim's surcharge is based on the amount of fine payable. However, such fines take precedence over the surcharge itself.

Despite the advantages of the restitutive approaches discussed above, such funding of victims recompense brings difficulties. In the US, for example, authorities have faced considerable problems in *enforcing* restitution fines and orders since the enactment of the Mandatory Victims Restitution Act of 1996. One set of figures put the amount of uncollected federal criminal restitution debt at $50 billion by the end of 2007 (Criminal Justice Transition Coalition, 2009). In addition, much depends on the cultural attitude of the courts to direct compensation to victims. Prosecutors may also lack information about what constitutes suitable amounts of compensation.

RESTORATIVE JUSTICE

Restorative justice typically encompasses victim–offender mediation schemes; family group conferencing; community conferencing; restitution panels; sentencing circles; and problem-solving initiatives designed to address conflicts between citizens. Most jurisdictions have some form of restorative justice within or outwith their criminal justice process and restorative justice is proliferating across the globe. A wide variety of interrelated factors have influenced this development, from the increased focus on the harms caused by crime discussed earlier in this chapter, to the growing costs of incarceration seen in all countries.

In practice restorative justice is often conceived principally as an offender-based development. This interpretation is supported by the difficulties faced in some jurisdictions in getting victims involved in the process (Crawford and Newburn, 2003). Even in New Zealand, where restorative justice has a long history, the Law Commission has advocated caution in relation to 'forcing' restorative justice on unwilling victims or on offenders who lack the skills that would make the process meaningful (New Zealand Law Commission, 2008).

Restorative justice has so far had only limited success, with little influence beyond what are generally viewed as the most minor offences. For example, South Australia and New Zealand are the only jurisdictions in the world that routinely use conferencing to process youth accused of sexual assault. In all other jurisdictions sexual assault has deliberately been placed off the restorative justice agenda because it is widely considered too sensitive or too risky to be handled via conferencing or to be diverted from court prosecution (Coates and Umbreit, 2000). This focus of restorative justice on what are generally considered less serious crimes represents a departure from the general observation that victims who have suffered most are generally receiving greater recognition in reform agendas.

Robust empirical evidence is now beginning to emerge as to the strengths and weaknesses of restorative justice mechanisms, and increasingly policy makers at local and national levels are adopting these principles in a number of jurisdictions. Following a major pilot of restorative justice schemes in England and Wales, Shapland et al. (2011) concluded that the schemes brought significant advantages to victims of crime in terms of satisfaction and perceptions of **procedural justice**. Restorative justice is also increasingly thought to have a positive impact on recidivism rates: in particular when restorative justice schemes are non-coercive and are aimed at lower-risk offenders (Bonta et al., 2005). Restorative justice is also thought to bring significant cost savings compared with traditional criminal justice processes (Sherman and Strang, 2007).

As a conscience of such findings, the application of restorative justice in various jurisdictions is continually extending. Many states have initially elected to experiment with restorative justice in relation to youth justice (see Cunneen and White, 2011), but increasingly adult schemes are being rolled out. As well as the UK pilots there are many examples in Australia of adults schemes (Strang, 2001). Roche (2006) reports that restorative justice has also been influential in Latin America as a means of increasing confidence justice. In the pacific region (Maxwell and Hayes, 2006) and the middle-east (Van Ness, 2005) restorative justice mechanisms have been associated with and developed from traditional cultural practices of community justice. Furthermore, restorative justice has been proposed as a means of coping with novel situations and problems faced by modern criminal justice systems, including environmental crime (Rivers, 2012).

PAUSE FOR REVIEW

If offenders are statistically unlikely to be in a position to offer meaningful compensation to victims in economic terms, what benefits are there to forcing them to pay restitution?

How should public money be used to compensate victims of crime?

Is restorative justice suitable for all crimes and all offences?

SUMMARY

This chapter has mapped the key conceptual and practical debates and associated policy developments related to the official recognition of victims of crime across the globe. Perspectives on East Asian jurisdictions are largely absent from the literature, though Liu (2007) has discussed how alternative East-Asian philosophies are far quicker to incorporate issues like community, apology and honour, which may be highly instructive in light of the discussions here. Nevertheless, it is clear that victims remain a key policy concern across many jurisdictions. However, that policy makers are talking about victims and enacting legislation and service standards does not imply that in practice victims are experiencing such benefits. Walklate (2012: 12) sums up this gap between policy and practice: 'There is a tendency to assume that the various initiatives introduced are in place and working, but, in practice, this is far from the case'.

While the official recognition of 'victimhood' is expanding, the prevailing focus of the international victims movement is around traditional notions of suffering and the 'ideal' victim. Furthermore, while much appears to have changed for victims falling within this category, it is notable that the advent of truly robust, justiciable rights even for these victims is elusive, and are substantively absent for victims falling outside this category.

FURTHER READING

Walklate, S. (2007) *Imagining the Victim of Crime*. Maidenhead: Open University Press.

Delivers an excellent overview of victimology and victimisation.

Hall, M. (2009) *Victims of Crime: Policy and Practice in Criminal Justice*. Cullompton: Willan.
Details the role of the victim in criminal trials.

Hillyard, P. (2006) 'Crime obsessions: crime isn't the only harm', *Criminal Justice Matters*, 62: 26–46.

Recommended for insights into critical victimology.

The major dedicated journal in the field is the *International Review of Victimology* (http://irv.sagepub.com/).

REFERENCES

Ashworth, A. (1993) 'Victim impact statements and sentencing', *Criminal Law Review*, 40: 498–509.

Ashworth, A. (1998) *The Criminal Process: An Evaluative Study* (2nd edn). Oxford: Oxford University Press.

BBC (2013) 'Leveson: Hacking victim welcomes press regulation deal'. Available at www.bbc.co.uk/news/uk-wales-21838337 (accessed 28.3.13).

Bonta, J.P., Jesseman, R., Ruffe, T. and Cormier, R. (2005) 'Restorative justice and recidivism: promises made, promises kept?', in D. Sullivan and L. Tift (eds), *Handbook of Restorative Justice: A Global Perspective*. London: Routledge. pp. 8–118.

Brienen, M. and Hoegen, H. (2000) *Victims of Crime in 22 European Criminal Justice Systems: The Implementation of Recommendation (85) 11 of the Council of Europe on the Position of the Victim in the Framework of Criminal Law and Procedure*. Niemegen: Wolf Legal Productions.

Californian Department of Corrections and Rehabilitation (2009) 'Restitution responsibilities, information for adult offenders'. Available at www.cdcr.ca.gov/Victim_Services/restitution_responsiblities.html (accessed 14.3.13).

Californian Victim Compensation and Government Claims Board (2009) *Victim Compensation Program (VCP) Regulations*. Sacramento, CA: Californian Victim Compensation and Government Claims Board.

Cavadino, M. and Dignan, J. (2007) *The Penal System: An Introduction* (4th edn). London: Sage.

Christie, N. (1986) 'The ideal victim', in E. Fattah (ed.), *From Crime Policy to Victim Policy*. Basingstoke: Macmillan. pp. 17–30.

Coates, R. and Umbreit, M. (2000) *Restorative Justice Circles in South Saint Paul, Minnesota*. St. Paul, MN: Centre for Restorative Justice and Peacemaking.

Crawford, A. and Newburn, T. (2003) *Youth Offending and Restorative Justice: Implementing Reform in Youth Justice*. Cullompton: Willan.

Criminal Justice Transition Coalition (2009) *Improving Likelihood of Victim Restitution*. Available at http://2009transition.org/criminaljustice/ index.php?option=com_content&view=article&id=63&Itemid=62 (accessed 15.3.13).

Crown Prosecution Service (CPS) (2005) *The Prosecutors' Pledge*. Available at www.cps.gov.uk/publications/prosecution/prosecutor_pledge.html (accessed 3.10.13).

Crown Prosecution Service (CPS) (2013) 'DPP enshrines victims' right to review of prosecution decisions'. Available at http://cps.gov.uk/news/latest_news/victims_right_to_review/ (accessed 11.10.13).

Cunneen, C. and White, R. (2011) *Juvenile Justice: Youth and Crime in Australia*. Oxford: Oxford University Press.

Dignan, J. (2005) *Understanding Victims and Restorative Justice*. Maidenhead: Open University Press.

Doak, J. (2003) 'The victim and the criminal process: an analysis of recent trends in regional and international tribunals', *Legal Studies*, 23: 1–32.

Doyle, C. (2008) *Crime Victims' Rights Act*. New York: Nova.

Elias, R. (1986) *The Politics of Victimization: Victims, Victimology and Human Rights*. New York: Oxford University Press.

Ellison, L. (2001) *The Adversarial Process and the Vulnerable Witness*. Oxford: Oxford University Press.

Erez, E. (2004) 'Integrating restorative justice principles in adversarial proceedings through victim impact statements', in E. Cape (ed.), *Reconcilable Rights? Analysing the Tension between Victims and Defendants.* London: Legal Action Group. pp. 81–96.

Furedi, F. (1998) 'A new Britain – a nation of victims', *Society*, 35: 80–84.

Guo-An, M. (2001) 'Victims in the criminal justice system in China', *The Victimologist*, 5(June): 1–2, 5, 8–9.

Hall, M. (2010) *Victims and Policy Making: A Comparative Approach*. Cullompton: Willan.

Hall, M. (2013) *Victims of Environmental Harm: Rights, Recognition and Redress Under National and International Law*. London: Routledge.

Harland, A. (1978) 'Compensating the victim of crime', *Criminal Law Bulletin*, 14: 203–224.

HMCPSI et al. (Her Majesty's Crown Prosecution Service Inspectorate, Her Majesty's Inspectorate of Constabulary, Her Majesty's Inspectorate of Probation) (2015), *Joint Review of Disability Hate Crime Follow Up*. London: Criminal Justice Joint Inspectorate.

Home Office (2011) *Crime in England and Wales 2010/11*. London: HMSO.

Irish Criminal Injuries Compensation Tribunal (2009) *Scheme of Compensation for Personal Injuries Criminally Inflicted – As Amended from 1st April 1986*. Dublin: Irish Criminal Injuries Compensation Tribunal.

Jackson, J. (2003) 'Justice for all: putting victims at the heart of criminal justice?', *Journal of Law and Society*, 30: 309–326.

JUSTICE (1998) 'Victims in criminal justice', Report of the JUSTICE Committee on the Role of Victims in Criminal Justice. London: JUSTICE.

Kenney, J. (2003) 'Gender roles and grief cycles: observations of models of grief and coping in homicide survivors', *International Review of Victimology*, 10: 19–49.

Liu, J. (2007) 'Principles of restorative justice and Confucius philosophy in China', *European Forum for Restorative Justice*, 8(1): 2–3.

Matthews, R. and Kauzlarich, D. (2007) 'State crimes and state harms: a tale of two definitional frameworks', *Crime, Law and Social Change*, 48: 42–55.

Maxwell, G. and Hayes, H. (2006) ‘Restorative justice developments in the Pacific region: a comprehensive survey’, *Contemporary Justice Review*, 9(2): 127–54.
McDermott, Y. (2009) *The Lubanga Trial at the International Criminal Court*. Available at www.lubangatrial.org/contributors/ (accessed 9.4.10).
Miers, D. (1997) *State Compensation for Criminal Injuries*. London: Blackstone.
Ministry of Justice (2012) *Getting It Right for Victims and Witnesses.* London: The Stationery Office.
New Zealand Law Commission (2008) *Compensating Crime Victims*, Issues Paper 11. Wellington: New Zealand Law Commission.
Office of the Attorney General of Texas (2009) *Crime Victims' Compensation*. Available at www.oag.state.tx.us/victims/about_comp.shtml (accessed 13.3.13).
Rivers, L. (2012) ‘Shareholder return – a ‘Nuremberg defence’? Ecocide and restorative justice’, *Environmental Law & Management*, 24(1): 17–19.
Roche, D. (2006) ‘Dimensions of restorative justice’, *Journal of Social Issues*, 62(2): 217–38.
Rock, P. (1986) *A View from the Shadows: The Ministry of the Solicitor General of Canada and the Making of the Justice for Victims of Crime Initiative*. Oxford: Clarendon Press.
Rock, P. (1990) *Helping Victims of Crime: The Home Office and the Rise of Victim Support in England and Wales*. Oxford: Oxford University Press.
Rock, P. (1998) *After Homicide: Practical and Political Responses to Bereavement*. Oxford: Clarendon Press.
Sanders, A., Hoyle, C., Morgan, R. and Cape, E. (2001) ‘Victim impact statements: don't work, can't work’, *Criminal Law Review*, June, 437–58.
Scottish Executive (2005) *National Standards for Victims of Crime*. Edinburgh: Scottish Executive.
Shapland, J., Robinson, G. and Sorsby, A. (2011) *Restorative Justice in Practice*. London: Routledge.
Sherman, L. and Strang, H. (2007) *Restorative Justice: The Evidence*. London: Smith Institute.
South African Department of Justice and Constitutional Development (2008a) *Service Charter for Victims of Crime in South Africa*. Pretoria: DoJCD.
South African Department of Justice and Constitutional Development (2008b) *Understanding the South African Victims' Charter: A Conceptual Framework*. Pretoria: DoJCD.
Strang, H. (2001) *Restorative Justice Programs in Australia: A Report to the Criminology Research Council*. Canberra: Australian National University.
United Nations (1985) ‘Declaration of basic principles of justice for victims of crime and abuse of power’. Available at www.unodc.org/pdf/compendium/compendium_2006_part_03_02.pdf (accessed 10.10.16).
Van Ness, D. (2005) ‘An overview of restorative justice around the world’, *Criminal Justice*, 18: 25.
Victim Support Europe (2009) *A Manifesto for Europe*. Utrecht: Victim Support Europe.
Victim Support Scotland (2009) ‘Victims' fund launched’. Available at www.victimsupportsco.org.uk/page/latestnews.cfm/Scotland-victims'-fund.htm (accessed 15.3.13).
Walklate, S. (2007) *Imagining the Victim of Crime*. Maidenhead: Open University Press.
Walklate, S. (2012) ‘Courting compassion: victims, policy and the question of justice’, *Howard Journal of Criminal Justice*, 51(2): 109–121.

Williams, C. (1996) 'An environmental victimology', *Social Science*, 23(1): 16–40. Reprinted in White, R. (2009) *Environmental Crime: A Reader*. Cullompton: Willan. pp. 200–222.
Wright, P. (1998) '"Victims' Rights" as a stalkinghorse for state repression', *Journal of Prisoners on Prisons*, 9: 1–4.
Young, M. (1997) 'Ideological trends within the victims' movement: an international perspective', in R. Davis, A. Lurigio and W. Skogan (eds), *Victims of Crime* (2nd edn). Thousand Oaks, CA: Sage. pp. 115–26.

NOTES

1. 501 US (1991).
2. Series A no 327-B (1995) 77.
3. Reports of Judgments and Decisions 1996-II, [1996] 23 EHRR 330.
4. Convention for the Protection of Human Rights and Fundamental Freedoms, Rome, 4.XI.1950.
5. (2004) 39 EHRR 13.
6. [2000] Crim. L.R. 287.
7. [1978] 2 S.C.R. 940.
8. R.S., 1985, C-46.

FEAR, VULNERABILITY AND VICTIMISATION

Murray Lee

Since it was 'discovered' in the late 1960s, fear of crime has largely been understood as a destructive force, both for individuals who experience this fear, and for social well-being and cohesion more generally. However, research has consistently suggested that some socio-demographic groups experience fear of crime to greater degrees than others; that is, fear of crime is not evenly distributed. In particular some groups are likely to report being more fearful of crime if they feel more vulnerable. Women and the elderly, for example, report higher levels of fear of crime than do men and the young. Moreover, those who have previously been victims of crime are more likely to express fear than those who have not. This chapter critically engages with the concept of fear of crime. After exploring the emergence of fear of crime and victims research, the chapter explores a range of models through which the relationship between victims and fear of crime has been conceptualised. It also discusses the conceptual and methodological confusion that has surrounded the relationship between victimisation and fear of crime. Following this the political and policy responses to fear of crime are discussed. After a discussion of more recent critical scholarship into fear of crime the chapter concludes by suggesting that fear of crime has provided a convenient discourse on which to base victim experiences, and that is has limited other possibilities that might include victims being positioned as resilient subjects with productive capacities as opposed to fearing subjects whose plight might be best described as a 'politics of pity'.

MEASURING AND COUNTING VICTIMS AND FEAR

During the 1960s amid calls to develop more sophisticated tools for understanding the hidden dimensions of crime in the US, the President's Commission on Law Enforcement and the Administration of Justice commissioned crime and victim surveys. These were trialled as part of three major pilot projects and their finding published in three reports (Biderman et al., 1967; Ennis, 1967; Reiss, 1967)[1]. As data sets, these new victim surveys aimed to augment recorded crime data. Such surveys can be conceptualised as part of a broad movement to collect and enumerate an increasing range of social indicators in the US as the cold war began to thaw and social data was democratised during the 1960s (Lee, 2007). They also aimed to tell social researchers much more about the 'dark figure of crime', the extent of victimisation, and the characteristics of victims and victim cohorts. Such surveys coincided with, and indeed helped facilitate, the 'rediscovery of the victim' (Karmen, 2013) and the development of victims' rights movements (Morgan, 1987). Victims became more empirically visible as the victim survey model became more universally deployed.

However, these early victim surveys, on the advice of the President's Crime Commission (1967), also asked respondents about their anxieties, concerns or fears in regard to crime and victimisation. At the time this seemed mundane and unremarkable – an extension of the opinion poll model that had gathered momentum since the 1940s. As can be seen from Box 7.1 and Table 7.1, the surveys uncovered a significant amount of 'fear of crime'. However, even in discussions about the surveys by the researchers it was clear that they were unsure what these questions were actually measuring. Biderman et al. (1967), for example, in the report of the first survey, noted that questions meant to elicit a respondent's fear of crime actually measured much more (see Box 7.1).

BOX 7.1 THE FEAR OF CRIME

This article from 1967 by Biderman et al. clearly outlines the emerging social scientific interest in fear of crime.

> Whether more concerned about adult or juvenile crime, most people think that the crime situation in their own community is getting worse, and while substantial numbers think the situation is staying about the same, hardly any-one sees improvement. A Gallup survey, in April 1965, showed that this pessimistic perception of the problem prevailed among men and women, well educated and less well educated, and among all age, regional, income, and city-size groupings. When citizens in Washington, D.C., were interviewed by the Bureau of Social Science Research (BSSR) the next year, 75 per cent thought that crime had been getting worse in that city during the past year; 16 per cent thought that it was about the same. (McIntyre, 1967: 36)

As Farrall et al. (2009: 24) noted more recently that survey questions about fear of crime clearly 'elicited an unstructured range of attitudes'. Consequently, early critics suggested the measures of Biderman et al. (1967) and Ennis (1967) were too broad and captured not only concerns about crime, but a range of other worries and concerns (Garofalo and Laub, 1978). Later, critics suggested that the more standardised measures produced evaluations

Table 7.1 Fear and safety: findings of Ennis (1967: 73) in relation to the question: 'How safe do you feel walking alone in your neighbourhood after dark?'

	White (%)		Non-white (%)	
Response	**Male**	**Female**	**Male**	**Female**
Very safe	65	35	33	16
Somewhat safe	22	24	25	19
Somewhat unsafe	9	23	22	28
Very unsafe	4	18	20	37
Total (%)	100	100	100	100
Total (no.)	(4,628)	(7,495)	(646)	(1,033)

of risk, rather than fear, and were misleading (Ferraro, 1995; Ferraro and La Grange, 1987). Even those researchers working on such surveys were often circumspect about what their findings meant or how much could be drawn from them (see e.g. Maxfield, 1984). The President's Commission had suggested that there was a need for a 'scientific and technological revolution' in criminal justice. The Commission heralded a turning point in the reorientation of mainstream criminology towards the collection of knowledge about victims of crime (Phipps, 1986).

The idea of measuring fear of crime was transported from the US to Britain in the mid-1970s (Lee, 2007) and a scenario-based question became a standard of surveys like the British Crime Survey (BCS). A version of these questions and the Likert scales on which it can be answered is reproduced in Box 7.2.

BOX 7.2 STANDARD FEAR OF CRIME SCENARIO QUESTION

The British Crime Survey has used a number of different items to measure concerns or fears about crime victimisation. One standard question concerns feelings of safety while walking alone at night. Another concerns the worry of becoming a victim of a specific crime. Indicative questions are reproduced below:

How safe would you feel walking alone in this area after dark?

1. very safe
2. fairly safe
3. a bit unsafe
4. very unsafe

(Continued)

(Continued)

How worried are you about ... having your home broken into and something stolen?

1. very worried
2. fairly worried
3. not very worried
4. not at all worried

By the early 1980s, such questions were being cemented into large-scale crime surveys such as the British Crime Survey that collected data in time series – so despite acknowledged and inherent problems with the question there was little appetite to erase or amend it. The time-series data being produced became an end in itself, quite apart from what the data were actually reflections of (Farrall, 2004; cf. Hough, 2004), and the concept of fear of crime held firm despite intense debate amongst criminological schools of thought as to its worth (Walklate, 1998). Fear of crime amongst a population could now be enumerated (Lee, 2009). Such research completely refigured our criminological understandings of the socio-cultural impact of crime, and fear of crime was in a sense 'discovered' (Ditton and Farrall, 2000; Lee, 2001, 2007). An encyclopaedic review of the research and literature on fear of crime by Chris Hale (1996) clearly demonstrates how entranced criminology became in this newly discovered concept. Indeed, for many researchers and policy makers, explaining and reducing fear of crime became equally important a project as explaining and reducing crime itself.

This background is quite telling about both understandings of fear of crime and of contemporary conceptualisations of the nature of **victimage**. There is great cross-over and interdependence in these genealogies as objects of criminological knowledge. Without the victims survey, fear of crime clearly would not have taken on the same discursive characteristics that it has developed. Moreover, the 'haunting' fear of crime that crime victims might experience provided victims and victims movements with a seemingly tangible way to explain an important element of the trauma of victimisation.

VICTIMS, VULNERABILITIES AND FEAR OF CRIME

It would come as no great surprise that victims of crime might be concerned about crime, and in particular about becoming re-victimised. Such concerns seem very reasonable. Indeed, the measured risk of victimisation is clearly higher amongst those previously victimised. As crime and victim profiles tell us, an individual's past victimisation is a good predictor of his or her subsequent victimisation, and the greater the number of prior victimisations, the higher the likelihood the victim will endure future crime (Pease and Laycock, 1999). We might say that victims are therefore vulnerable to future victimisation. However, it should not automatically follow that there is a causal relationship between victimisation, vulnerability and fear of crime. A risk of revictimisation – or indeed concern arising from a person's victimisation – could reasonably be expected to take any range of forms. Moreover, ones' risk and/or vulnerability might be contingent on a range of personal, social and cultural factors. In the next section we discuss a range of models that have been used conceptually to understand the relationship between fear of crime, victimisation and vulnerability.

PAUSE FOR REVIEW

How is fear of crime linked to studies of victimisation?

When did fear of crime first become a policy issue and why?

THE VICTIMISATION THESIS

The notion of a somewhat causal relationship between fear of crime and victimisation has been called the 'victimisation thesis' (Farrall et al., 2009). This 'victimisation thesis' has been a strong and enduring one in the research and literature concerned with fear of crime. It can be conceptualised as operating on two levels. First, and perhaps most simply, an individual's concern of being victimised originates in their previous experiences as a victim. Second, that a community's general fear of crime originates in the level of criminal activity in that community, or indeed in what residents hear about criminal activity in a community from either other citizens or the mass media. In essence, high levels of victimisation and/or high levels of the perceived threat of victimisation are said to lead to higher levels of fear of crime (Bennett, 1990).

Such theses are said to explain why some people report being anxious or worried about crime while others do not, or at least do so to a greatly reduced extent (Lewis and Salem, 1980). There is a simple and clear logic to this approach to understanding crime fear, and this logic can be traced back to the relationship between fear of crime and victimisation found in the structure of victim surveys. As Farrall et al. (2009: 82) put it, 'this model is by far the simplest model of fear: levels of fear within a community are caused by the level of criminal activity within that community'. Or put another way, the higher the risk of victimisation, the higher the chance of individuals or communities reporting fearfulness about crime.

However, this simple victimisation thesis papers over significant complexity. As Maxfield (1984: 47) noted, 'the differences in fear by sex and age are so substantial that something other than direct victimisation experience must be involved'. Indeed, it takes only a review of the fear of crime literature to discover that not all victims or likely victims of crime express or experience fear of crime. Accordingly, many of those least at risk of being victimised express high levels of fear of crime. That is, it appears that victimisation (or the threat of victimisation) is by no means the only variable related to expressions of fear of crime.

In the fear of crime literature this phenomenon has been called the 'risk–fear paradox', whereby many socio-demographic groups who are least likely to be victimised report higher levels of fear of crime in victim surveys. Take young men as an example. They are the most likely victims of violent crime, yet this socio-demographic group is least likely to express high levels of fear of crime (Goodey, 1997) – at least if we are to believe the surveys. One the other hand, women and the elderly, the less likely victim demographics taken as a whole, are more likely to both express higher levels of fear of crime and exhibit avoidance behaviours (Gordon and Riger, 1989; Madriz, 1997; Stanko, 1990). Stanko (1996: 81) has noted that the 'gender differential is the most consistent finding in the literature on fear of crime'. Specifically, there is seemingly no identifiable statistical relationship between those who are the most at risk of becoming victims of crime, and those that report being the most fearful (Hough and Mayhew, 1983). I have argued elsewhere that this paradox has been extremely alluring for criminologists and others in studying fear of crime (Lee, 2007). That is, the apparent paradox has been partly responsible for the amount of attention fear of crime has received as an object of inquiry. Yet, this paradox begins to look less convincing and much more complex when a range of mixed research findings are explored in more depth as we do below.

PAUSE FOR REVIEW

What is the victimisation thesis and why is it problematic?

Explain the problem of measuring fear of crime.

EVERYDAY VIOLENCE AND FEAR OF CRIME

The risk–fear paradox has been explained quite differently by left realist criminology, radical feminism and feminist criminology[2]. Such approaches posit that official recorded crime statistics, victimisation surveys and questionnaires, and the fear of crime literature more broadly, has failed to capture or to take into account the full extent and broadly submerged nature of victimisation – particularly women's victimisation. Victimisation for women, it is argued, is an ongoing **sub-legal** (Goodey, 1994) process that includes being stared at, harassed at home and in the workplace, and shouted at in the street (Gordon and Riger, 1989; Stanko, 1990; Young, 1988). Advocates of this position also stress the fact that women are much more likely to be the victims of hidden crime such as sexual assault and domestic violence, both of which are highly under-reported in official statistics and victim surveys.

Stanko (1990), for example, argues that women's fears about crime cannot be understood quantitatively, and only qualitative methods can reveal the extent 'everyday violence', or constant (often low-level) harassment that serves to increase women's concerns. If low-level harassment is cumulative, then methodological issues are exacerbated by the survey model which normally asks only about victimisation in the prior 12 months. Left-realist researchers forwarded a similar thesis. For example, Jones et al. (1986, cited in Sparks, 1992a: 122) argue that:

> To take only the most important and controversial issue in the area, namely women's fear of crime, 'realist' social surveys indicate that a proper account of women's subjection to domestic, work related, and other peripherally visible forms of victimisation, their experience of other harassments and marginally criminal incivilities, their unsatisfactory experience of police protection and the multiplication of each of these problems by factors of race, class and age, entirely dispels the apparent disparity between risk and fear.

Further, it is suggested that women have lower rates of victimisation primarily because they are less likely to place themselves in risky situations than men (Goodey, 1997; Sacco, 1990). This suggests that women's victimisation rates should be 'adjusted up' to account for the gendered differences in exposure to risks that are not reflected in the statistical data. These accounts (re)rationalise women's fears (Jones et al., 1986; Stanko, 1990; Young, 1988).

Sutton and Farrall (2005, 2009) argue that the risk–fear paradox can be explained in part by the way in which men suppress expressions of fear in line with expected masculine stereotypes (see Box 7.3). They suggest that the gender disparity between men and women in measured levels of fear might be both an artefact of the survey method and of social values and gendered expectations. Taken together, these arguments around gender might strengthen the argument in favour of a broader kind of victimisation thesis of fear of crime, which problematises exactly what we count as crime.

BOX 7.3 EXPRESSIONS OF FEAR

Passage adapted from Sutton and Farrall (2009):

> 93 respondents were asked 10 questions about their own fear of crime ... They responded on much the same five point scale used in previous investigations. Respondents were then asked to answer the questions as if they were 'the average male', and as if they were 'the average female'. When we average across men and women, we see that respondents attributed much more fear to the average female than the average male, $p < .001$. This provides strong direct evidence of the existence of a stereotype that women experience more fear than men. Respondents, regardless of their own gender, also attributed more fear to the average female than themselves, $p < .001$. In contrast, respondents attribute roughly as much fear to themselves as to the average male.

Of course, the problematic nature of the notion of 'crime' itself also clouds the risk–fear paradox in other ways. What types of crime are we actually talking about? Perhaps if we are more specific about offence types the paradox disappears? Again, research findings are confused with Miethe and Lee (1984) finding a relationship between victimisation and violent offences, and Smith and Hill (1991) suggesting the link is stronger with property offences.

There is also a question about whether broad sub-legal victimisation, rather than simply causing expressions of fear amongst victims, might actually become **normalised.** My own work in high crime areas in Western Sydney suggested that when qualitative methods were used, fear or worry about crime was not commonly expressed as a key concern for residents in high crime areas (Lee, 2011). Rather, these respondents knew what and whom to avoid and managed high crime situationally while still expressing a strong desire to see crime reduced. For them, victimisation was largely 'demystified' or 'neutralised' (Agnew, 1985; Innes and Jones, 2006). This suggests once again that there are complexities at play beyond the victimisation thesis which also confound the idea of a risk–fear paradox. It also raises questions about whether the survey methods themselves provide respondents with a language of fear of crime quite different to what they might express under normal circumstances. We return to these critical questions below where we explore the risk–fear paradox with reference to the questions of vulnerability.

PAUSE FOR REVIEW

Why might men under-report levels of fear of crime?

Why might women seem to over-report levels of fear of crime?

What does it mean to suggest that fear of crime might be managed situationally?

THE RISK–FEAR PARADOX AND VULNERABILITY

Maxfield (1984) begins to capture what vulnerability might be in regard to fear of crime, suggesting it refers to an individual's capacity to resist attack and the likelihood of suffering injury from a given level of violence: 'In the rather complex calculus of perceived threats to one's safety, the likely *consequences* of victimisation are as important as subjective assessment of risk' (1984: 47).

The concept of vulnerability and its relationship to fear of crime can be broken down into three discrete factors, according to Killias (1990). First, high levels of fear of crime are related to exposure to non-negligible risk. That is, a sense of vulnerability reflects the higher levels of risk faced by those such as the previously victimised – essentially the victimisation thesis. Second, that higher levels of fear of crime reflect the sense of a loss of control, a lack of an effective defensive or protective measure against victimisation, and/or the absence of an escape mechanism. That is, a general sense of vulnerability is likely to become fear when one has an inability to exercise agency in freeing oneself from danger. Third, high levels of fear reflect the anticipation that serious consequences could follow victimisation. This could relate to the frailty of an individual or a sense of a clearly uneven power distribution between victim and imagined offender.

Vulnerability also has physical, social and situational components (Killias 1990). These can include such things as the long-term consequences of sexual assault for women or injury for the elderly (both physical and social), the lack of adequate support services for victims (social), or that some kinds of work may place individuals such as bank tellers and late-night petrol station attendants (situational) at risk. Moreover, some individuals will experience more than one of these variables of vulnerability. Thus, vulnerability can be conceptualised as being multi-faceted. 'The relatively powerless situation of women: economically, socially and physically makes them more unequal victims than men' (Young, 1988: 175). Furthermore, Carach and Mukherjee (1999) found women's exclusion from the labour force was a significant factor in women's fear of crime. Grabosky (1995: 8) suggests that socialisation processes might be such that 'traditional sex roles have been learned in a manner which fosters in females a lesser degree of self-confidence and autonomy than those roles learned by men.' According to these accounts, crime fears can outstrip the reality of risk when vulnerability is a factor.

THE POLITICS OF FEAR AND VULNERABILITY

The problem of exaggerated levels of fear of crime, or personal assessments of risk, has led to a range of policy interventions. By the mid-1990s in many jurisdictions, police became responsible for not just reducing crime but reducing fear of crime. Reassurance policing became an important policing strategy and reducing fear of crime became a key performance indicator for many police organisations. For example, a key performance indicator for the New South Wales Police Force was to 'increase the per cent of the community who feel safe walking/jogging alone after dark' (NSW Police Force, 2009: 5). Indeed, NSW Police articulate in their *Annual Report* that to 'reduce perception and fear of crime' was a 'core strategy' (2009: 23).

This model, and assumptions embedded within it, has also been embraced by a variety of policy makers and so-called administrative criminologists. Weatherburn et al. (1996: 1) argue that

> public opinion about the risk of criminal victimisation is probably more influential in shaping state government spending priorities in law and order than the actual risk. If public concern about crime is driven by an exaggerated assessment of the risks of victimisation then strategies need to be in place to address the problem.

This governmental concern about fear of crime also saw policies specifically aimed at those feeling the most vulnerable. Stanko (1996: 80–81) demonstrates with clarity how these policies were essentially exercises in political economy:

> The high levels of fear disclosed by so-called vulnerable groups have provided the impetus for government concern. ... programs designed to reduce fear may well be a reflection of the state's worry that their image as public protectors is being undermined. After all, if the public had confidence in the police's ability to protect them, then anxiety about encountering criminal violence should be low.

These policy responses were intimately linked to a political economy of fear. Sandra Walklate (1995: 55) also highlights this politicisation of the victim and the way in which, by the 1980s, processes of 'invoking the imagery of the crime victim' became a basis on which to formulate policy. Sparks (1992a: 119) had likewise noted that fear of crime was no longer just a topic of empirical disagreement; rather, it 'assumed a heavy polemical charge in theoretical and political disputes'. Clearly fear of crime has long left its conceptual roots as a social scientific category through which to simply understand concerns about crime. It is rather part of a political discourse which is often deployed in the name of tougher responses in criminal justice interventions.

THE QUALITATIVE TURN AND THE DECONSTRUCTION OF FEAR OF CRIME

While, as we have seen above, feminist criminology and left realism had already been critical of the survey model that was driving fear of crime research, by the early 1990s and into the 2000s a body of critical literature developed around the 'deconstruction' of the risk–fear paradox. These authors began undermining the very idea that fear of crime can be a useful conceptual framework through which to explore gendered crime concern. Some work used a survey method but experimented with a variety of new questions to establish just what was being captured by the established surveys (Ditton et al., 1999a, 1999b; Farrall et al., 1999). Other researchers used altogether different qualitative techniques either through in-depth interviews or focus groups (Hollway and Jefferson, 1997a, 1997b, 2000; Tulloch et al., 1998a, 1998b; Loader et al., 2000). Still other authors attempted to place fear of crime in an historical (Lee, 1999, 2001, 2007) or cultural (Sparks, 1992b; Possamai and Lee, 2004) context (see Box 7.4 for Lee's account).

BOX 7.4 THE 'FEAR OF CRIME FEEDBACK LOOP'

By *fear of crime feedback loop* I mean the following: that research into fear of crime – through crime and victim surveys – produces the criminological object fear of crime statistically, and discursively a concept is constituted. This information then operates to inform the citizenry they are indeed fearful, information that the *fearing subject* can reflect upon. The law and order lobby and politicians use fear to justify a tougher approach on crime (they have to, the citizenry are fearful apparently), a point on which they grandstand and produce more fear. The concept feeds the discourse and the discourse in turn justifies the concept. All the while the fields of criminology can use their new concept to measure and assess (Lee, 2007: 77).

Hollway and Jefferson (2000), for example, suggested that the structure of the questions in the British Crime Survey produced the very gendered differences in crime fear it pertained to report. The results were, the authors argued, driven by the question 'How safe do you feel walking alone in this area after dark?'. This scenario question, and the subsequent coding and quantification of results, was said to strip the context from any responses (2000: 166).

Alternatively, Tony Jefferson with both Wendy Hollway (1997a) and David Gadd (2009) sought to understand fear of crime qualitatively, using frameworks drawn from psychoanalysis. The authors suggest that anxiety is a key human trait, and the emotional responses to anxiety can only be understood in the complex biographies of individual lives. They suggest that individuals defend against the anxieties of late-modern existence by displacing fear and concerns on to convenient and known objects of hate. The 'criminal other' is one such receptacle that is both convenient but also reinforced as a legitimate site by broader social and cultural discourses of risk and fear. In the face of ontological insecurity the construction of an 'other' on which to project fears provides some certainty for the self.

If this is the case, fear of crime as a discourse becomes one in which these defended subjects will have a stake. The expression of fear of crime and vulnerability to victimisation becomes a resource in the face of feelings of powerlessness. In the victim survey we have an instrument to provide access to this resource. As Gadd and Jefferson (2009: 139) put it:

> In essence then, what we are arguing is that subject positions are negotiated in relation to the individual's biography and attendant anxieties, the discursive fields available to the individual (often constrained by their class, ethnicity and gender), and intersubjectively through the responses to others. Whether someone invests in the position of the fearful subject preoccupied with the ever-growing threat of victimisation depends, in part … on how available that position is to him or her.

Tulloch et al. (1998a, 1998b) developed a similar qualitative method using focus groups, which questioned the direct connection between the 'fear' and 'crime'. Both of these research teams suggested that a range of social, economic, aesthetic and existential biographical variables could influence one's likelihood of having a stake in what I might call a fear of crime discourse.

Stephen Farrall's work, first with Ditton et al. (e.g. 1999a, 1999b; Farrall et al. 1999) and later with Jackson and Gray (eg. Farrall et al. 2009), shows that by asking different survey questions the levels of 'fear' as measured can differ very significantly. For example, many surveys now ask questions about specific crimes such as burglary. Such a question might be: 'How worried about being burgled are you?' However, once the researchers asked how *frequently* respondents felt worry about robbery in the past 12 months, those expressing worry dropped from around 40 per cent of those sampled to around 8 per cent of those sampled. Such findings are significant. They indicate that experiential fear (i.e. fear as actually experienced) only contributes minimally to what surveys count as fear or worry about crime. Where, then, does all this other fear come from? The authors account for this by connecting experiential (often local) fears to more *expressive* fears. These are local, social, cultural, national and global concerns (Farrall et al., 2009: 209). This argument is perhaps best summed where the authors argue that concerns about crime have

> become intertwined in the public mind with the less dramatic but more everyday matter of social cohesion, consensus and relations. Concerns about crime would consequently be driven not just by aspects of risk perception and circulating mass-media images of frightening and unsettling events, but also by signs of social stability and moral order. Such concerns may be just as much about moral outrage as they are about explicit threat perceptions. (Farrall et al., 2009: 220)

In summary, Farrall et al.'s revised survey measures suggest that fear of crime as measured is a composite of experiences, beliefs and expressions. As such for many people living in areas of higher levels of disorder and crime, fear of crime as measured is often a reflection of personal experience. On the other hand, for the more comfortable middle classes, fear of crime as measured is often an expression of broader social and moral concerns.

Many of Farrall's suggestions have now found their way into the Crime Survey for England and Wales (CSEW).[3] This is good news as it certainly allows for a more specific and targeted measure of concerns about crime. However, while many of the new measures of fear of crime can be seen as extremely positive developments, they are not without their problems in relation to victimisation. For example, while Farrall et al.'s (2009) measures that filter out 'expressive fear' in using frequency variables and the like, they might also filter out the very 'everyday fears' that make women's concerns about crime somewhat gender specific. In this sense, by focusing in on the specifics of fear reported (experienced, frequency, intensity), it may push other broader, less specific victims' experiences further into the *dark figure* of crime.

PAUSE FOR REVIEW

Why do feelings of vulnerability differ between groups and between individuals?

What do qualitative studies tell us about fear of crime and vulnerability?

What are expressive and experiential fears? Why is the distinction important?

One of the less remarked upon findings that the critical work on fear of crime has established is that some people have a stake in the discourse of fear of crime. In other words, that expressing fear of crime provides a voice – whether for the victimised who feel their plight needs to be taken seriously, the vulnerable who feel a physical or psychological sense of insecurity, and even those who might be ontologically insecure about their place or the pace of change in the modern world. And while a 'composite' model of fear is complex and multifaceted, the problem is that at the level of political economy fear of crime can seem a simple and self-evident concept.

While we are willing to acknowledge a broader political economy of fear and propensity to *govern through crime*, we are much less likely to acknowledge a personal politics of fear. Partly this is because we don't feel comfortable questioning the judgements and perceptions of the vulnerable, particularly crime victims. However, to say there is a personal politics of fear is not to suggest that fear of crime is somehow false or manufactured. Rather, I refer to this personal politics of fear in the way Foucault might speak of a **bio-politics**, which also includes a micro-physics of power. That is, the way in which bodies become imbued with particular capacities. This entails us thinking not of fears as a somehow innate physiological or psychological response to the threat of victimisation, but something that's form is made possible by bio-political discourse. Essentially the possibilities of fear of crime are embedded in the knowledge and practices of victimage and vulnerability we have come to accept as true.

Walklate (2011), drawing from the work of Aradau (2004), conceptualises this in terms of understanding the power of the 'politics of pity'. To this end she highlights the 'constructed' side of suffering, or to be more precise, what suffering is deemed deserving, and so legitimate. As she puts it, 'the politics of pity ... needs to be put alongside the politics of vindictiveness. Taken together they contribute in different ways to the contemporary punitive sentiments' (Walklate, 2011: 190). The point is that discourses of fear, along with notions of vulnerability support, take support from both the politics of pity and the politics of vindictiveness. They are not the same thing and can certainly co-exist with alternative discourses; nonetheless they can easily co-exist and support particular forms of legitimate or 'ideal' victimage over others (Christie, 1986). This brings us back to the entwined nature of fear of crime and the victim: their shared genealogies.

FEAR AND POLITICS

The rediscovery of the victim and the concept of fear of crime have intimately intertwined genealogies. That is, they were born in the 1960s and grew as siblings through the 1970s and 1980s. Their emergence was contingent on a range of factors that include the politicisation of law and order, and the gradual decay of a post-Second World War social, cultural and political consensus. But, importantly, they also rely on the development of new social scientific methods of enumerating crime, specifically the victim survey. Victimage and fear of crime were both enumerated in the crime and victim surveys that emerged out of the President's Commission in the US in the 1960s. It was not surprising that victimage was seen as a key variable in fear of crime research, and that fear of crime became part and parcel of understanding the victim. The relationship has exercised criminological scholarship, particularly when variables related to vulnerability such as gender and age were also seen as key associations with fear of crime.

The politics of victimisation – and the notion that victims are *fearing subjects* – has helped fuel this and has resulted in something of a politics of pity. This has limited the possibilities of victimage and, as Walklate (2011) has argued, also limits the ways in which victimisation might be understood in terms of resilience; the positive capacities for victims to 'bounce back' after victimisation. Moreover, it helps create a hierarchy of victimage where 'ideal victims' are preferenced over those constructed as less worthy of their victim status (Stanko, 2000). This is not to propose that victims do not feel vulnerable, nor that they should not experience fear and concerns about re-victimisation. Rather, that the focus on the negative experiences of victimisation, and the politics of pity that can accompany this focus, creates a situation where the positive resilient capacities of victims to 'bounce back' is compromised. If we follow Foucault in believing that subjects 'take up positions' that are created through discursive conditions of possibility, the politics of pity is likely to influence the nature of such positions considerably for victims. To this end it is perhaps useful to think of fear of crime as a discourse that has been offered through the political economy of fear, and sustained empirically through the victim survey. The critical and qualitative research into fear of crime and victims clearly demonstrates that there is by no means a simply causal link between victimisation, vulnerability and fear of crime.

SUMMARY

This chapter has critically engaged with the concept of fear of crime. Having explored the emergence of fear of crime and victims research, the chapter examined a range of models through which the relationship between victims and fear of crime has been conceptualised. It has discussed the conceptual and methodological confusion that has surrounded the relationship between victimisation and fear of crime, the political and policy responses to fear of crime and, finally, after a discussion of more recent critical scholarship into fear of crime the chapter reflects that fear of crime has provided a convenient discourse on which to base victim experiences, and that is has limited other possibilities that might include victims being positioned as resilient subjects with productive capacities as opposed.

FURTHER READING

Farrall, S., Jackson, J. and Gray, E. (2009) *Social Order and the Fear of Crime in Contemporary Times*. Oxford: Oxford University Press.

Provides both an extensive overview of the research into fear of crime and draws together over a decade of research by the authors themselves. The work is theoretically informed and methodologically sophisticated.

Ditton, J. and Farrall, S. (eds) (2000) *Fear of Crime*. Aldershot: Ashgate.

An extensive resource in bringing together an extensive body of fear of crime research from the 1960s to the late 1990s.

Hope, T. and Sparks, R. (eds) (2000) *Crime, Risk and Insecurity*. London: Routledge.

An excellent edited collection that interrogates questions of fear of crime and victims from a broad range of theoretical and methodological perspectives.

Hale, C. (1996) 'Fear of crime: a review of the literature', *International Journal of Victimology*, 4: 79–150.

This is still a very useful prima and great resource.

Lee, M. (2007) *Inventing Fear of Crime: Criminology and the Politics of Anxiety*. Cullompton: Willan.

This author situates the historical emergence of fear of crime as a criminological concept and with Stephen Farrall has edited a contemporary collection of critical articles:

Lee, M. and Farrall, S. (2009) *Fear of Crime: Critical Voices in an Age of Anxiety*. Milton: Routledge-Cavendish.

REFERENCES

Agnew, R. (1985) 'Neutralising the impact of crime', *Criminal Justice and Behaviour*, 12: 221–39.
Aradau, C. (2004) 'The perverse politics of four-letter words: risk and pits in the securitisation of human trafficking', *Millennium: Journal of International Studies*, 33(2): 251–77.
Bennett, T. (1990) 'Tackling fear of crime', *Home Office Research and Statistics Bulletin*, 31(28).

Biderman, A., Johnson, L., McIntyre, J. and Weir, A. (1967) 'Report on a pilot study in the District of Columbia on victimisation and attitudes toward law enforcement', *President's Commission on Law Enforcement and Administration of Justice, Field Surveys I*. Washington, DC: US Government Printing Office.

Carach, C. and Mukherjee, S. (1999) 'Women's fear of violence in the community', in A. Graycar (ed.), *Trends and Issues in Crime and Criminal Justice*. Canberra: Australian Institute of Criminology.

Christie, N. (1986) 'The ideal victim', in E. Fattah (ed.), *From Crime Policy to Victim Policy*. London: McMillan.

Ditton, J. and Farrall, S. (2000) 'Introduction', in J. Ditton and S. Farrall (eds), *Fear of Crime*. Aldershot: Ashgate.

Ditton, J., Bannister, J., Gilchrist, E. and Farrall, S. (1999a) 'Afraid or angry? Recalibrating the "fear" of crime', *International Review of Victimology*, 6: 83–99.

Ditton, J., Farrall, S., Bannister, J., Gilchrist, E. and Pease, K. (1999b) 'Reactions to victimisation: why has anger been ignored', *Crime Prevention and Community Safety: An International Journal*, 1(3): 37–54.

Ennis, P. (1967) 'Criminal victimisation in the United States: a report of a national survey', *President's Commission on Law Enforcement and the Administration of Justice, Field Surveys II*. Washington, DC: Government Printing Office.

Farrall, S., Bannister, J., Ditton, J. and Gilchrist, E. (1999) 'Social psychology and the fear of crime: re-examining a speculative model', *The British Journal of Criminology*, 40(4): 692–709.

Farrall, S. (2004) 'Can we believe our eyes? A response to Mike Hough', *International Journal of Social Research Methodology*, 7(2): 177–9.

Farrall, S., Jackson, J. and Gray, E. (2009) *Social Order and the Fear of Crime in Contemporary Times*. Oxford: Oxford University Press.

Ferraro, K.F. (1995) *Fear of Crime: Interpreting Victimisation Risk*. Albany, NY: State University of New York Press.

Ferraro, K.F. and La Grange, R. (1987) 'The measurement of fear of crime', *Sociological Inquiry*, 57: 70–101.

Gadd, D. and Jefferson, T. (2009) 'Anxiety, defensiveness and the fear of crime,' in M. Lee and S. Farrall (eds), *Fear of Crime: Critical Voices in and Age of Anxiety*. Milton: Routledge-Canendish.

Garofalo, J. and Laub, J. (1978) 'The fear of crime: broadening our perspective', *Victimology*, 3: 242–53.

Goodey, J. (1994) 'Fear of crime: what can children tell us?', *International Review of Victimology*, 3: 195–210.

Goodey, J. (1997) 'Boys don't cry: masculinities, fear of crime, and fearlessness', *The British Journal of Criminology*, 37(3): 401–418.

Gordon, M.T. and Riger, S. (1989) *The Female Fear*. New York: Free Press.

Grabosky, P.N. (1995) 'Fear of crime, and fear reduction strategies', *Current Issues in Criminal Justice*, 7(1): 7–19.

Hale, C. (1996) 'Fear of crime: a review of the literature', *International Journal of Victimology*, 4: 79–150.

Hollway, W. and Jefferson, T. (1997a) 'Eliciting narrative through the in-depth interview', *Qualitative Inquiry*, 3(1): 53–70.

Hollway, W. and Jefferson, T. (1997b) 'The risk society in an age of anxiety: situating fear of crime', *The British Journal of Sociology*, 48(2): 255–66.

Hollway, W. and Jefferson, T. (2000) *Doing Qualitative Research Differently: Free Association, Narrative and the Interview Method*. London: Sage.

Hough, M. (2004) 'Worry about crime: mental events or mental states?', *International Journal of Social Research Methodology*, 7(2): 171–6.

Hough, M. and Mayhew, P. (1983) *The British Crime Survey: First Report*, Home Office Research Study 76. London: HMSO.

Innes, M. and Jones, V. (2006) *Neighbourhood Security and Urban Change: Risk, Resilience and Recovery*. York: Joseph Roundtree Foundation.

Jones, T., MacLean, B. and Young, J. (1986) *The Islington Crime Survey: Crime, Victimisation and Policing in Inner-City London*. Aldershot: Gower.

Karmen, A. (2013) *Crime Victims: An Introduction to Victimology* (8th edn). Belmont, CA: Wadsworth.

Killias, M. (1990) 'Vulnerability: towards a better understanding of a key variable in the genesis of fear of crime', *Violence and Victims*, 5: 97–108.

Lee, M. (1999) 'The fear of crime and self-governance: towards a genealogy', *The Australian and New Zealand Journal of Criminology*, 32(3): 227–46.

Lee, M. (2001) 'The genesis of fear of crime', *Theoretical Criminology*, 5(4).

Lee, M. (2007) *Inventing Fear of Crime: Criminology and the Politics of Anxiety*. Cullompton: Willan.

Lee, M. (2009) 'The enumeration of anxiety: power, knowledge and fear of crime', in M. Lee and S. Farrall (eds), *Fear of Crime: Critical Voices in an Age of Anxiety*. Milton: Routledge-Canendish.

Lee, M. (2011) 'Be careful what you ask for: exploring fear of crime in the field', in L. Bartels and K. Richards (eds), *Qualitative Criminology: Stories From the Field*. Annandale: Hawkins Press.

Lewis, D. and Salem, G. (1980) 'Community crime prevention: an analysis of a developing strategy', *Crime and Delinquency*, 27: 405–421.

Loader, I., Girling, E. and Sparks, R. (2000) 'After success? Anxieties of affluence in an English village', in T. Hope and R. Sparks (eds), *Crime, Risk and Insecurity*. London: Routledge.

Madriz, E. (1997) *Nothing Bad Happens to Good Girls: Fear of Crime in Women's Lives*. Berkeley, CA: University of California Press.

Maxfield, M.G. (1984) *Fear of Crime in England and Wales*. London: Her Majesty's Stationery Office.

McIntyre, J. (1967) 'Public attitudes toward crime and law enforcement', *Annals of the American Academy of Political and Social Science*, 374: 34–46.

Miethe, T. and Lee, G. (1984) 'Fear of crime among older people: a reassessment of the predictive power of crime related factors', *Sociological Quarterly*, 25: 397–415.

Morgan, A. (1987) 'Victim rights: criminal law: remembering the "forgotten person" in the criminal justice system', *Marquette Law Review*, 70: 572–97.

NSW Police Force (2009) *Annual Report 2008–2009.* Parramatta: NSW Police.

Pease, K. and Laycock, G. (1999) 'Revictimisation: reducing the heat on hot victims', *Trends and Issues in Crime and Criminal Justice: Australian Institute of Criminology*, 128.

Phipps, A. (1986) 'Radical criminology and criminal victimisation', in R. Matthews and J. Young (eds), *Confronting Crime*. London: Sage.

Possamai, A. and Lee, M. (2004) 'New religious movements and the fear of crime', *Journal of Contemporary Religion*, 19(3): 337–52.

Reiss, A. (1967) 'Studies in crime and law enforcement in major metropolitan areas, vol. 1', *President's Commission on Law Enforcement and the Administration of Justice, Field Surveys III*. Washington, DC: US Government Printing Office.

Sacco, V.F. (1990) 'Gender, fear and victimisation', *Sociological Spectrum*, 1: 485–506.

Smith, L. and Hill, G. (1991) 'Perceptions of crime seriousness and fear of crime', *Sociological Focus*, 24(4): 108–131.

Sparks, R. (1992a) 'Reason and unreason in 'left realism': some problems in the constitution of the fear of crime', in R. Matthews and J. Young (eds), *Issues in Realist Criminology*, London: Sage.

Sparks, R. (1992b) *Television and the Drama of Crime: Moral Tales and the Place of Crime in Public Life*. Buckingham: Open University Press.

Stanko, E. (1990) *Every Day Violence: How Women and Men Experience Sexual and Physical Danger*. London: Pandora.

Stanko, E.A. (1996) 'The commercialisation of women's fear of crime', in C. Sumner, Israel, M. O'Connell and R. Sarre (eds), *International Victimology: Selected Papers from the 8th International Symposium: Proceedings of a Symposium held 21–26 August 1994*. Canberra: Australian Institute of Criminology.

Stanko, E. (2000) 'Victims R' Us', in T. Hope and R. Sparks (eds), *Crime, Risk and Insecurity*. London: Routledge.

Sutton, R. and Farrall, S. (2005) 'Gender, socially desirable responding, and the fear of crime: are women really more anxious about crime?', *British Journal of Criminology*, 45(2): 212–24.

Sutton, R. and Farrall, S. (2009) 'Untangling the web; deceptive responding in fear of crime research', in M. Lee and S. Farrall (eds), *Fear of Crime: Critical Voices in and Age of Anxiety*. Milton: Routledge-Canendish.

The President's Commission on Law Enforcement and Administration of Justice (1967) *The Challenge of Crime in a Free Society: A Report by the President's Commission on Law Enforcement and Administration of Justice*. Washington, DC: United States Government Printing Office.

Tulloch, J., Lupton, D., Blood, W., Tulloch, M., Jennett, C. and Enders, M. (1998a) *Fear of Crime*, Vol. 1. Canberra: Attorney-General's Department, Commonwealth of Australia.

Tulloch, J., Lupton, D., Blood, W., Tulloch, M., Jennett, C. and Enders, M. (1998b) *Fear of Crime*, Vol. 2. Canberra: Attorney-General's Department, Commonwealth of Australia.

Walklate, S. (1995) *Gender and Crime*. London: Harvester Wheatsheaf.

Walklate, S. (1998) 'Crime and community: fear or trust?', *British Journal of Sociology*, 49(4): 550–69.

Walklate, S. (2011) 'Reframing criminal victimisation: finding a place for vulnerability and resilience', *Theoretical Criminology*, 15(2): 179–94.

Weatherburn, D., Matka, E. and Lind, B. (1996) 'Crime perception and reality: public perceptions of the risk of criminal victimisation in Australia', *Crime and Justice Bulletin*, Vol. 28. Sydney: NSW Bureau of Crime Statistics and Research.

Young, J. (1988) 'Risk of crime and fear of crime: a realist critique of survey-based assumptions', in M. Maguire and J. Pointing (eds), *Victims of Crime: A New Deal?*. Milton Keynes: Open University Press.

Young, J. (n.d.) 'Risk of crime and fear of crime: the politics of victimisation studies'. Available at www.malcolmread.co.uk/JockYoung/RISK.htm (accessed 1.7.13).

NOTES

1. The Bureau of Social Science Research in Washington (Biderman et al., 1967), The National Opinion Research Center (Ennis, 1967) and The University of Michigan (Reiss, 1967) began their work from 1965 and reported in 1967. The reports were titled respectively *Report on a Pilot Study in the District of Columbia on Victimization and Attitudes Toward Law Enforcement – Field Surveys I*, *Criminal Victimisation in the United States: A Report of a National Survey – Field Surveys II*, and *Studies in Crime and Law Enforcement in Major Metropolitan Areas – Field Surveys III.*
2. I acknowledge there are divergences between these schools of thought that have also been the topic of some debate. However, for the purpose of this chapter and their shared critique of the risk–fear paradox I address them collectively.
3. Previously the British Crime Survey.

8 GENDER, VICTIMS AND CRIME

Pamela Davies

The most stable fact about crime in societies across the globe is that it is largely a male activity. Young men in particular are more likely to be convicted of crime than women, have longer criminal careers and commit more serious offences including murder or manslaughter, sexual and violent offences, terrorism, organised, state and corporate crimes. The distinctive male nature of crime warrants explanation and while the gender gap in the commission of crime masks some interesting nuances to the doing of crime by men and women, this feature is stubbornly persistent. Moreover, some crimes are highly gendered in nature. The latter refers to the unequal distribution of victimisation in society and how much interpersonal violence is typically male-on-female.

The purpose of this chapter is to encourage critical thinking around gender, victims and crime. First we define gender and explain what a gendered understanding comprises. Key features of the gender patterning to criminal victimisation are outlined and discussed as we explore the nature, extent and impact of victimisation. Vulnerability and victimisation are then considered through a gendered lens. In this discussion the chapter draws especially upon the concepts of **secondary victimisation** and **victim blaming** to illustrate how social processes shape victims' experiences. By examining these processes and illustrating these concepts in the context of criminal justice, the gendered nature of the **justice gap** is revealed. The emphasis in this chapter is largely on victims of rape, sexual abuse and exploitation. Importantly, the latter allows us to not only move beyond the confines of the criminal justice system, but also to contemplate the intersections of gender and age. Primarily, however, the chapter encourages critical thinking around how a gendered perspective can inform understanding of the social process that give rise to victimisations and what constitutes victimisation. It therefore addresses how cultural constructions of masculinity and femininity are often omnirelevant for making sense of men's and women's experiences of harm, criminal victimisation and justice. The chapter suggests criminal justice might become more gender friendly and sensitive and that a better understanding of gender similarities and differences has yet to be achieved.

BACKGROUND: DEFINITIONS, CONCEPTUALISATIONS AND ASSUMPTIONS

In defining and explaining gender it is helpful to distinguish 'gender' from 'sex'. Walklate's description of sex/gender differences remains useful in this regard: 'sex differences, i.e. differences that can be observed between the biological categories, male and female: they are not necessarily a product of gender. Gender differences are those that result from the socially ascribed roles of being male or being female, i.e. masculinity and femininity' (Walklate, 2004: 94; see also Renzetti, 2013). These categories and differences are represented in Table 8.1.

Table 8.1 Sex/gender

Sex	**Gender**
Male/Female	Masculine/Feminine

The representations above introduce oppositional associations: male/female; masculine/feminine. These are often referred to as 'gender dichotomies' or 'binary categories'. In patriarchal societies, cultural and social cues tend to be overlaid upon sex-based distinctions. The imaginary, yet at the same time very real, dichotomies that extend beyond sex differences to gender traits are important to untangle, not least because they produce rather different political and policy agendas for those adopting different feminist approaches to the study of victims of crime (see Box 5.5). Early liberal feminist approaches were wedded to eradicating inequalities between the sexes, and they sought to achieve equality by preventing differentiation and discrimination between men and women. Equality-based approaches are now complemented by other feminist voices, so that we now have the power of a *gendered* appreciation of the crime and victimisation problem.

Victimologically, a sex-based analysis might start by exploring women and girls' share of the experience of victimisation as compared with men and boys' share. A *gender based* analysis adds another dimension to our understanding. Socialist and radical feminists would be variously concerned with the inequalities and power differentials that complement the sex-based analysis, turning the analysis into one which is gender-wise. Therefore sex-based analyses are important but it is the products of gender that provide a deeper understanding of the significance of power, powerlessness and, in the context of crime and victimisation, vulnerability (Davies, 2017).

Having established what we mean by 'gender' and how we might begin to conduct a gendered analysis of victimisation, it is worth noting from the outset the complex historical juxtapositions that emerge when a gendered lens is adopted. At the same time as we can make claims for **gender blindness** in matters concerning crime and justice (gender blindness or myopia is a failure to consider gender at all, and so the masculine and feminine as well as males and females are indistinguishable), we can also detect implicit assumptions that have a gendered basis. Two chapters in this volume have already drawn attention to both of these threads. In Chapter 5, Peter Francis discusses what he refers to as the 'orthodox strand of thought' about victims of crime, which has its roots in positivist victimology. This strand dominates much academic and political thinking about victims and victimisation, and is broadly characterised by defining victims through legal means and whose perspectives variously use concepts of 'risk', 'vulnerability' and 'lifestyle' to explain mostly criminal victimisation. In Chapter 2, Sandra Walklate elaborates on the origins of these concepts, and both authors illustrate how von Hentig's (1948) typology worked with a notion of **victim proneness** whereby women, children, the elderly, the mentally subnormal and so on were much more likely to be victims of crime than others. Alongside this, Mendelsohn's typology (1956), adopting an underlying concept of **victim culpability**, incorporated a legal understanding of what counts as reasonable with that which the white, heterosexual male would consider to be reasonable. In Chapter 2, Walklate also reminds us that criminal victimisations that are routine, mundane, ordinary and local include family violence and crimes behind closed doors – child abuse, elder abuse and all forms of 'domestic' violence. People's experiences of criminal victimisation are intra-personal and involve others who are not only known to them but also close family members. While violent familial victimisation is described as routine, mundane and ordinary, much of this violence, especially domestic violence and rape, are classic examples of gendered crimes. This is borne out throughout the critical discussion at the heart of this chapter where we explore this perspective and go on to illustrate the legacy and contemporary relevance of being insensitive to gender.

At this juncture the proposition is that for men and women the lasting influence of these orthodox 'domain assumptions' (Walklate, 2007) is inherently problematic. In early victim studies, on the face of it, a homogenous portrayal of the crime victim predominates. Where distinctions between victims are discernible, women are collapsed into a single homogenous group. Men are too, though the implicit representation of men is that even as victims they are fighting victims with affinities closer to those associated with offenders rather than true victims. Women have been broadly characterised as ideal victims (see von Hentig, 1948), whereas men have been characterised as non-victims. These conceptualisations have steered presumptions towards the belief that all victims of sexual violence are female and that perpetrators are male. Thus men tend to be conceived as the victimological other, never vulnerable, fearful or at great risk to victimisation, and ultimately non-victims. White, heterosexual, rational, men have been the norm or yardstick against whom not only females but also all other victims could be compared. We return to the question of problematic masculinities later in the chapter.

The concept of 'victim' is highly contested as has been made evident in the early pages of this volume, and from a gendered perspective this contestation becomes especially troublesome. Dominant understandings of victimhood determine who is recognised in social policy terms as a victim and impact upon how victim services are resourced and who is supported. Though von Hentig characterised women as ideal victims, this has not necessarily ensured that all suffering women have been visible or that support provisions correspond and match criminally victimised women's needs. Over the last 50–60 years, victim-oriented policies and services have emerged as part of a victims' movement. In Britain, developments in the 1960s saw the introduction of the Criminal Injuries Compensation Scheme for, largely, 'deserving victims' (Davies, 2007b). The 1970s–1980s is a period associated with the introduction of victim support schemes. The feminist movement was especially effective in this era too, mobilising support to cater for women victims of domestic violence and abuse via the provision of refuge accommodation and rape crisis centres. Thus generalists as well as more specialist services for women and children escaping domestic violence emerged. However, despite the institutionalisation and mainstreaming of victim support services and the expansion of core initiatives within the official victims' movement, responses to victimisation failed to cater for all victims' needs, or for all types of victim (Spalek, 2006). This chapter, in focusing on the most seriously violent of interpersonal crimes and on sexual abuses and exploitations, makes the case for gender-appropriate and **gender-sensitive** responses and service provisions in order to appreciate the gender difference in victims' experiences, needs and wants.

PAUSE FOR REVIEW

Why might it be useful to move beyond a sex-based inquiry to a gender-based analysis of victimisation?

What is a 'gendered crime'?

Are women, weak or old or as wives, ideal victims?

THE EXTENT, NATURE AND IMPACT OF VICTIMISATION

As noted above, there is an unequal distribution of victimisation in society. Here we illustrate the extent, nature and impact of violent victimisation. In foregrounding sex and gender we acknowledge that these social variables and processes are among several other intersecting and overlocking social characteristics (Daly, 1997). Nevertheless, as several observers have noted, it is impossible to understand the risk of victimisation without considering gender (Brookman and Robinson, 2012; Heidensohn and Silvestri, 2012). Here we extrapolate the headline features with regards to violent crime, drawing on findings from the *Crime Survey for England and Wales (CSEW) 2013/14* (Office for National Statistics, 2015).

Inter-personal Violence and the Effects of Violence on Women

The CSEW commentary continues to claim steady declines in violent crime. Between the 1995 and the 2013/14 surveys, the number of violent crime incidents fell from 3.8 million in 1995 to 1.3 million in 2013/14. However, violent crime covers a wide spectrum of offences including rape, sexual assault and unlawful sexual activity against adults and children, sexual grooming and indecent exposure. The number of sexual offences (64,205) in 2013/14 was the highest recorded by the police since 2002/03. As well as improvements in recording, this is thought to reflect a greater willingness of victims to come forward to report such crimes. Box 8.1 details further findings on intimate partner violence (IPV).

BOX 8.1 VIOLENT CRIME AND INTIMATE PARTNER VIOLENCE, 2013/14

- Males are more likely to be a victim of violent crime than females, as are adults aged 16 to 24 compared with all other age groups.
- Just under two-thirds of homicide victims were male (64 per cent, 331 victims) and one-third were female (36 per cent, 186 victims).
- 8.5 per cent of women and 4.5 per cent of men reported having experienced any type of domestic abuse in the last year – an estimated 1.4 million female victims and 700,000 male victims.
- 6.8 per cent of women and 3.0 per cent of men reported having experienced any type of partner abuse in the last year – an estimated 1.1 million female victims and 500,000 male victims.
- Overall, 28.3 per cent of women and 14.7 per cent of men experienced any domestic abuse since the age of 16 – 4.6 million female victims and 2.4 million male victims.
- Women are more likely than men to have experienced intimate violence across all headline types of abuse asked about; for example, 2.2 per cent of women and 0.7 per cent of men having experienced some form of sexual assault (including attempts) in the last year.

(Office for National Statistics, 2015)

The prevailing message about the rate of violent crime from 1994–2014 is that the rate is falling. Walby and colleagues (2016) challenge this. They report the fall in the rate of violent crime has stopped and argue strongly that this is due to the increase in violent crime against women. At the end of 2015 police data showed a continuing rise in recorded sexual offences (especially marked since 2013), figures up 29 per cent on the previous year (an additional 23,349 offences), bringing the total to 103,614 in a single year for the first time. 2015 showed the numbers of rapes (34,741) and other sexual offences (68,873) were at the highest level recorded since the introduction of the National Crime Recording Standard in 2003. The tightening of police recording practices following HMIC's inspection of crime recording in 2014, which found that sexual offences had been substantially under-recorded (by 26 per cent nationally) and which subsequently provoked police to review their recording processes, is thought to partly explain the higher level of recording. The CSEW also reports that increases seen throughout 2014 and 2015 are due to a rise in current offences and that a rise in the recording of historical offences (those that took place more than 12 months before being recorded by the police) is the reason for the consistent rise in police recorded sexual offences since 2013. Prior to this, and since 2008, the trend in sexual offences was broadly flat. The high-profile coverage of sexual offences and the police response to reports of historic sexual offending during and following Operation Yewtree in 2012 (following the exposure of Jimmy Savile as a prolific and serial paedophile) is also thought to explain this rise, having prompted a greater willingness of victims to come forward to report such crimes (Flatley, 2016).

International data amassed by Hoyle (2012) on the nature and scope of men's and women's victimisations evidences that other continents, particularly Africa, have high endemic rates of sexual violence. In Turkey between one-third and a half of women are victims of physical violence. Hoyle also points towards the growing awareness of particularly heinous forms of domestic abuse including acid attacks and murder resulting from honour killings (p. 403). The World Health Organisation (WHO) has highlighted

> that acts of violence against women are not isolated events but rather form a pattern of behaviour that violates the rights of women and girls, limits their participation in society, and damages their health and well-being. (WHO 2013: 1)

Furthermore, WHO has estimated that more than 35 per cent of women worldwide have experienced either intimate partner violence or non-partner sexual violence in their lifetime. This organisation recognises that there are gendered patterns in both the prevalence and experience of such violence, in that it is overwhelmingly perpetrated by men against women and girls and that violence against women and girls is both a cause and a consequence of gender inequality in society. Drawing on worldwide data, WHO (2013) reports on the extent and impacts of violence against women and girls (see Box 8.2).

BOX 8.2 THE EFFECTS OF VIOLENCE AGAINST WOMEN

- Almost one-third (30 per cent) of all women who have been in a relationship have experienced physical and/or sexual violence by their intimate partner.
- In some regions, 38 per cent of women have experienced IPV.
- Globally, as many as 38 per cent of all murders of women are committed by intimate partners.
- Women who have been physically or sexually abused by their partners report higher rates of a number of important health problems.

(Continued)

(Continued)

- Women who have been physically or sexually abused by their partners are:
    - 16 per cent more likely to have a low-birth-weight baby;
    - more than twice as likely to have an abortion;
    - almost twice as likely to experience depression;
    - in some regions,1.5 times more likely to acquire HIV, as compared to women who have not experienced partner violence.

Men, women and victimisation

In addition to the above, qualitative knowledge is gleaned from a limited number of case studies, several of which are now dated (see Kelly and Radford, 1996; Lees, 1997; Szyockyi and Fox, 1996) and there remain many gaps in our knowledge. Cultural, green and environmental victimologies are in their infancy, yet a scoping exercise by Brody et al. (2008) and research by Wachholz (2007) suggest increased risks to women becoming victims of violence in the wake of disasters. Box 8.3 provides a broad summary of men, women and victimisation where the correlates are gleaned from national and local survey data.

BOX 8.3 MEN, WOMEN AND VICTIMISATION

- Victimisation is generally higher for males than females. The exception to this pattern is rape.
- Men have a much higher risk of homicide than women.
- Women are at a much higher risk of domestic homicide than men – the largest cause of morbidity worldwide in women aged 19–44.
- Risks of violence by strangers and acquaintances are substantially greater for men than for women.
- Black males have the highest rate of violent victimisation and white females the lowest.
- Single, divorced or separated women show higher rates of victimisation than those who are married or widowed.
- For some victimisations age combined with sex renders women more at risk.
- Large numbers of crime committed by non-strangers against women are unreported.
- Levels of violence against women are far higher than official surveys show.
- Women are more vulnerable to domestic violence from current or former partners.
- Women suffer both more serious and more frequent domestic assaults than men.
- Women-on-women incidents are more common in acquaintance violence than in any other type.
- Young homeless women have elevated risks to sexual assault.

- Violence and sexual abuse are major reasons for young women running away from home.
- There are gendered risks to:
    - consumer related victimisations;
    - victimisations at work.
- Gender and age structure fear of crime and victimisation.
- Women are more worried and fearful about crime despite having lower chances of victimisation than men and young people.
- Fear of sexual violence and harassment from men underpins women's higher fear.
- Fear and experience of crime and victimisation impacts upon women's lifestyles and day-to-day activities.

In summary, there are gendered risks to victimisation, and domestic violence is the classic example of a gendered crime. With regard to sexual offences in particular, our knowledges point towards complex victim–offender dynamics and relationships with complex social processes contributing to differential gender patterns in various spatial locations. These dynamics are examined and explored through case examples below and with reference to the concept of vulnerability.

PAUSE FOR REVIEW

What is most striking about the patterns of violence?

What are the most salient features of the patterns to sexual offences?

How does violence differentially impact upon men and women, and how might this be explained?

VULNERABILITY AND VICTIMISATION

In light of the above it would seem that there are links between being recognised as a victim and being vulnerable to victimisation. How victimisation impacts on people in turn affects their status as victims. These links have been explored in the contexts of primary, secondary and indirect victimisation in Chapter 2. In that chapter, we also noted how the story of Doris epitomises the classic image of who is seen to be vulnerable both emotionally and socio-economically: Doris is seen to have inherent vulnerabilities because of her sex and age. The elderly female would find herself in the low-risk, high-harm quadrant according to the axis of vulnerability (Green, 2007) produced by the data derived from victim surveys. Here we look briefly at how vulnerabilities are managed in the context of criminal justice. We then illustrate how vulnerability is manifested and can be exacerbated via gender- and age-insensitive responses.

Vulnerability is an 'intrinsic attribute of children' (Furedi, 2013: 42), yet vulnerability is a multi-dimensional concept and being vulnerable due to being youthful can co-exist with emotional, socio-economic and undiagnosed psychological vulnerabilities. Some victims qualify as 'vulnerable' on entry into the criminal justice system, and since the late 1990s in England and Wales there has been a move to identify and enhance service provision for a particular group of vulnerable and intimidated witnesses (Cook and Davies, 2016). Following the Youth Justice and Criminal Evidence Act 1999, these two groups are eligible for 'special measures'. These allowances can include screens in the courtroom to prevent the defendant and the witness seeing each other, and allowing the defendant to give evidence via a live video link from somewhere outside the court room. In guidance from the Ministry of Justice (2011: 5), intimidated witnesses are defined as 'those whose quality of evidence is likely to be diminished by reason of fear or distress'. The guidance states that in determining whether a witness should be included in this category or not, the court should consider a number of issues:

- The nature and alleged circumstances of the offence.
- The age of the witness.
- Where relevant:
    - the social and cultural background of the witness;
    - the domestic and employment circumstances of the witness;
    - any religious beliefs or political opinions of the witness.
- Any behaviour towards the witness by:
    - the accused;
    - members of the accused person's family or associates;
    - any other person who is likely to be either an accused person or a witness in the proceedings.

The guidelines, furthermore, list the following as vulnerable witnesses:

- Those under 18.
- Those who suffer from a mental disorder (as defined by the Mental Health Act 1983).
- Those who have a significant impairment of intelligence and social function.
- Those who have a physical disability or disorder.

Victims of sexual offences and human trafficking as well as witnesses of knife and gun offences are also entitled to special measures unless they wish to opt out. As we can see with the special measures for vulnerable and intimidated witnesses, qualification and classification as a particular type of witness and/or victim plays an important role in shaping service provision in the criminal justice system and, potentially, in making experiences at court more bearable.

Sexual abuse, vulnerability and victimisation

The tragedy of a sexual abuse victim who committed suicide after giving evidence against her attacker brought the police and the Crown Prosecution Service under scrutiny in England early in 2013. This case exemplifies how women victims of violence remain susceptible to secondary victimisation when in contact with the agencies of the criminal justice system (see Box 8.4).

BOX 8.4 POLICE ARGUE OVER WHO TOLD VICTIM: 'DON'T GET HELP'

Frances Andrade, a talented violinist and victim of sexual abuse, committed suicide six days after testifying against choirmaster Michael Brewer. Despite being a vulnerable witness, police had warned she should not seek psychological counselling to cope with the two-year run up and trauma of going to court. Reluctant to bear witness yet doing so under pressure from the police, in court she was called a liar and a fantasist by the defending barrister. During her cross-examination she said: 'This feels like rape all over again.'

(Barrett, 2013)

Though there are guidelines on vulnerable victim categories, vulnerability remains an intractable problem. Women, children and young people who have experienced sexual violence, exploitation and/or physical abuse, have mental health problems or learning difficulties (often as a result of institutionalisation) comprise a large vulnerable victim population. These categories of victim may be denied access to justice, others will fail to progress through the system without being re-victimised and such victims may be outwith the protection of the criminal justice system (Starmer, 2013). There is little evidence of vulnerable victims proceeding through to satisfactory outcomes (Stern, 2010).

The justice gap and intersections of sex–gender–age

There is little academic research on the 'justice gap' for vulnerable victims but we can make informed judgements based on the evidence of under-reporting of sexual offences, known patterns to victimisation and scholarly research. Hester's research (2013) on adults emphasises how in most rape cases victims were either recently acquainted with their attacker or know their perpetrator as a current or ex-partner, family member or their abuse was historical and in the domestic setting. Not only are there severe levels of under-reporting in these cases but also there is severe attrition (Brennan et al., 2010). These knowledges point towards vulnerabilities that coalesce around the intersections sex–gender–age and to swathes of hidden victims of sexual offences, trafficking and exploitation more broadly (see Chapters 10 and 13 for references to victims of sex trafficking and forced labour). Official records under-count assaults on children and young people for a host of reasons. The close proximity of victims to their offenders and the extent of the coercion exercised by adults over young people contribute to under-reporting. An inquiry into Child Sexual Exploitation, supported by the NSPCC, suggested that in excess of 2,409 children in England are abused every year and a further 16,500 are at high risk of sexual exploitation (Beckett et al., 2012). Few of these will gain access or progress through the criminal justice system.

In 2013, the *Guardian* newspaper reported upon prosecution lawyer Robert Colover QC of the Crown Prosecution Service and Judge Nigel Peters in the case of a 13-year-old girl who they described as 'predatory' (Toynbee, 2013). Toynbee's headline for this article, 'Misogyny runs so deep in this society, it is even used against abused children', captures how culturally embedded and institutionalised such practices are that suggest women and young girls are personally responsible for their own injures and abuse. Children's charities work hard to alter the perception of such extremely vulnerable children as offenders. In the area of child sexual exploitation there are attitudinal and perceptional problems producing tensions and scepticism about whether or not the young person is a passive 'innocent' victim (Pearce, 2009). See Figure 8.1 for how Barnardos represent the child sexual exploitation perception and reality gap.

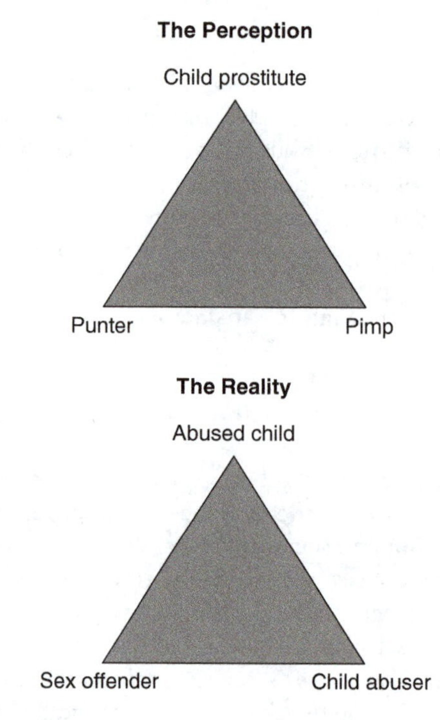

Figure 8.1 Child sexual exploitation: the perception–reality gap

According to these assessments, where children are supported to report acts committed against them there is evidence of them being responded to as offenders and they run the risk of being criminalised. Furthermore, where children and young people do engage with the criminal justice system as victims, despite the entitlements for vulnerable and intimidated witnesses, there is evidence of secondary victimisation and practices which discredit them turning vulnerable child victims into out-of-control, troublesome, often promiscuous or lately even 'predatory' offenders. Victims of child sexual exploitation and street grooming are still being failed, despite a series of high-profile trials (Jay, 2014). New guidelines for prosecutors of cases of child sexual abuse and exploitation set out an approach designed to focus decision making on the credibility of the overall allegation of abuse (Crown Prosecution Service, 2016). These guidelines promote:

- a focus on the credibility of the overall allegation, rather than solely the victim's account, through looking at the wider context;
- a much greater testing of the suspect's account and circumstances;
- a very high level of support for victims;
- the challenging of myths and stereotypes raised in court about the behaviour of the victim;
- assisting the courts to ensure that effective timetabling and case progression takes place that helps victims in court;
- accessing third-party material to build the prosecution case.

PAUSE FOR REVIEW

Who qualifies as a vulnerable victim?

To what extent are female victims of sexual assault protected in court under the vulnerable and intimidated witness measures?

How do the intersectionalities of sex–gender–age help us to understand the dynamics of child sexual exploitation?

WOMEN, VICTIMISATION AND CRIMINAL JUSTICE

Adversarial systems of justice might appear to encourage re-victimisation in the form of hostile police interrogations and similar approaches from defence solicitors, barristers and members of the judiciary. In cases of rape and sexual assault in particular, questioning and cross-examinations have seen criminal justice practice render victim's experience hard to bear. In looking for things that the victim might have done to provoke the crime her legitimacy as a victim may be 'aggressively contested'

(Rock, 2008), to the extent that there is an implication that women invite abuse. As suggested by the example in Box 8.4, the reality of the rape victims experience in court is that she may well be forced to relive her ordeal in the witness box. The onus has been placed on the victim to prove her non-precipitation, thereby disproving that she caused her own rape. Rock (2008: 326) discusses such victim precipitation, in the context of the trial defence, as a 'duet' or an exchange in which the victim contributed to her own fate. Blame is shifted onto the vulnerable victim and removed from the offender. Victim blaming is a particularly insidious form of direct revictimisation which incurs indirect victimisations. It can lead to under-reporting of serious offending by putting other victims off reporting their own experiences and reduces confidence in the criminal justice system.

Rendering rape invisible: silencing agents, attrition and myths

In relation to allegations of rape, women victims have effectively been silenced by, according to Jordan (2012: 254), six key silencing agents: the self, police responses, court and trail processes, formal and informal supports, researchers and academics and the media. These agents contribute to the process of **attrition** or 'drop out' in rape cases, which is stubbornly problematic (see Daly and Bouhours 2010; see also Chapter 12). Rape cases reported to the police can drop out and result in attrition at any one of three stages: at police involvement and investigation, during CPS involvement or at court (Hester, 2013). In Hester's (2013) research into rape cases and the criminal justice system in the North East of England, three-quarters of the cases dropped out at the police stage, with many of these involving very vulnerable victims such as those with extensive mental health problems. The first stage of attrition occurred despite the police having largely adopted the victim-focused approach recommended in the Rape Experience Review (Payne 2009). The Payne review placed an emphasis on believing victims from when they had reported and supporting them to remain in the criminal justice system. In England and Wales, Kelly and colleagues (2005) reported that only three-quarters of rape cases were reported to the police, one-quarter of those were 'no crimed'; the vast majority did not proceed beyond the investigative stage; only 14 per cent reached the trial stage and the conviction rate was 8 per cent. In 2008 only 5.7 per cent of rape cases reported to police lead to a conviction, and research shows that attrition – or cases dropping out – happens at every stage from initial complaint to trial.

As noted above, the persistence of such attrition rates is stubborn and explanations for this can be partially attributed to prevalent myths surrounding rape. Rape myths are commonly-held beliefs about rape that are ill-informed and misconceived. Feminist-inspired commentators and organisations working to support women (Rape Crisis England & Wales, 2004–2016) are concerned to de-bunk such myths. Myths suggest women: lie about it and make false allegations; really want, enjoy rape and provoke it; can prevent rape; should put up a fight and show signs of struggle and will sustain genital injuries; and that women are less traumatised by rape by a non-stranger. Myths abound about male rapists too. These myths suggest that rapists have uncontrollable urges and cannot help themselves, are sex fiends and predatory strangers (Davies, 2017).

Across the globe common rape myths prevail. The commonest five rape myths are summarised in Box 8.5.

BOX 8.5 RAPE MYTHS

Myth I: Sexual assault does not occur often.

Reality: Under-reporting of rape continues and estimates suggest that 1 in 8 women will be raped in her lifetime.

Myth 2: Women lie about being sexually assaulted to get revenge, for their own benefit, or because they feel guilty afterwards about having sex.

Reality: Women rarely make false reports about sexual assault.

Myth 3: Sexual assault is committed by strangers.

Reality: Sexual assault is not most often committed by strangers. Over 80 per cent of sexual assaults are committed by someone known to the victim.

Myth 4: The best way for a woman to protect herself from sexual assault is to avoid being alone at night in dark, deserted places such as alleyways or parking lots.

Reality: Most assaults occur in a private home.

Myth 5: Women who are sexually assaulted ask for it by the way they dress or act.

Reality: No one asks for it. Reports show that there is a lot of diversity in the way women who are assaulted act and dress. Any woman of any age and physical type, in almost any situation can be sexually assaulted.

Rape myths suggest that public opinion is out of touch and ignorant of the high number of women raped every year. Rape myths feed and fuel the practice of 'victim blaming'. Often, and as already illustrated in relation to rape and child sexual exploitation, this practice tends to emerge in cases where the most vulnerable of victims/witnesses are seeking justice. In summary, there is a mis-match between perceptions and the reality of those who are vulnerable and who experience sexual abuse. This mis-match represents a justice gap for victims who are particularly vulnerable due to the nature of the abuse and exploitation and due to their gender and age profile.

MEN, MASCULINITY AND VICTIMISATION

An earlier section of this chapter outlined the patterns to violent crime and IPV. The headlines year on year show young males are more likely than any other group to be a victim of violent attack. So far this chapter has passed this over, having focused on men as offenders for the main part. Here we further explore the levels and types of violence experienced by men. Box 8.6 and Box 8.7 summarise some of the key themes.

Men as victims

BOX 8.6 MEN AS VICTIMS OF SEXUAL ASSAULT AND DOMESTIC VIOLENCE

- In 2013/14, 116,000 men suffered a sexual assault.
- 1 per cent of men and 1.9 per cent of women were victims of force at the hands of their partner during 2014/15.
- Men (5.2 per cent) with a long-term illness or disability were victims of partner abuse in 2013/14 compared to women (11.1 per cent) in the same situation.
- Of those that suffered partner abuse in 2014/15, a higher proportion of men suffered from force (37 per cent) than women (29 per cent) – for emotional and psychological abuse this was 61 per cent and 63 per cent respectively.
- 12 per cent of men and 15 per cent of women who were victims of partner abuse suffered three or more incidents in 2012/13. 1 per cent of men had suffered 50 or more incidents as had 2 per cent of female victims.
- Of those that suffered from partner abuse in 2012/13, 29 per cent of men and 23 per cent of women suffered a physical injury, a higher proportion of men suffering severe bruising or bleeding (6 per cent) and internal injuries or broken bones/teeth (2 per cent) than women (4 per cent and 1 per cent respectively).
- 30 per cent of men who suffer partner abuse have emotional and mental problems (47 per cent women).
- Only 27 per cent of men sought medical advice whilst 73 per cent of women did.
- Male victims (29 per cent) are over twice as likely than women (12 per cent) to not tell anyone about the partner abuse they are suffering from. Only 10 per cent of male victims will tell the police (26 per cent women), only 23 per cent will tell a person in an official position (43 per cent women) and only 11 per cent (23 per cent women) will tell a health professional.
- The percentage of gay or bi-sexual men (6.2 per cent) who suffered partner abuse in 2008/09 is nearly double the number for heterosexual men (3.3 per cent).

Source: Office for National Statistics (2014) Crime Statistics, Focus on Violent Crime and Sexual Offences

Since the advent of the crime survey and its widespread use to determine more accurately experiences of victimisation we have known more about where violence happens. Furthermore, when asked about fear of crime, men in self-report surveys always report lower levels of fear. So, according to this data, risky places are those where men go and where women live (see Boxes 5.3 and 8.3), and men's and women's fear of crime has produced some interesting conundrums whereby fear does not appear to match with risk levels as determined by crime survey data.

Men and victimhood

Threaded throughout this chapter there is a clear theme about men and victimhood. The summary in Box 8.7 together with the information about men's experiences of violence as shown in Box 8.6 suggests we know little about men's experiences of victimisation *as men*; that is, we know little about masculinity and victimisation.

BOX 8.7 MEN AND VICTIMHOOD

- A legal understanding of what counts as reasonable is equated with that which the white, heterosexual male would consider to be reasonable.
- White, heterosexual, rational men have been the norm or yardstick against whom not only females but also all other victims are compared.
- Domain assumptions are as problematic for men as they are for women.
- Men are conceived as the victimological other, never vulnerable, fearful or at great risk to victimisation and ultimately non-victims.

Masculinity and victimisation

Research on gender, masculinities and crime can be traced back only some thirty years or so when new studies focused on criminal masculinities. Inspired by feminist scholarship, the notion of masculinity was employed to help explain men's oppressive power and violence against women. Part of this new thinking suggested men may be acting out, demonstrating and asserting their machismo. This application of the notion of masculinity sought to explain and understand men as victimisers.

Connell's (1987) work on a tripartite structure of gender relations and the gender order was particularly influential, although Messerschmidt is credited with applying the concept of masculinities to the doing of crime by men and thereby importing the concept into criminology. Following this, masculinities emerged as a key theoretical concept in its own right. This influential body of work, following Messerschmidt (1993, 1997), Connell (1987) and West and colleagues (1987, 1995) suggests that violent crime can be understood as a product of masculinities and of men 'doing gender' (see Davies, 2014, 2017).

Masculinities theorising has infiltrated victimology such that a select few scholars now embrace the concepts of hegemonic, hyper and subordinate masculinities. Such masculinities seemingly produce problematic hierarchies of victimhood for men as victims. Walklate usefully reviews a small number of studies that challenge orthodox presumptions about men as non-victims (Walklate, 2007) while research by Lees (1997) remains significant. Two surveys were conducted in 1995, a survey of male victims of rape and the first-ever survey of police recording practices of rape of men by men. The analysis focuses on men's experiences of sexual violence in the context of masculinity (see Lees, 1997: 89–107; Gregory and Lees, 1999: 112–33). Lees presents a persuasive illustration of how hegemonic masculinity is the most feasible explanation for why sexual assaults on men are predominantly perpetrated by men who regard themselves as heterosexual in sexual orientation: 'By sexually humiliating men who do not appear to live up to the dominant form of masculinity, the perpetrator's own masculinity is enhanced' (1997: 13).

As noted above, not only do we know little about men's experiences of victimisation but also we know little about men's experiences of victimisation *as men*. Some of the barriers to knowing more are listed in Box 8.8.

BOX 8.8 BARRIERS TO KNOWING ABOUT MEN, MASCULINITIES AND VICTIMISATION

- Obsessions with positivist research methodologies.
- Prejudices and constraints of time and resources.
- Macho concealment of fear.
- Socially desirable responses in surveys.
- Hegemonic masculinities.
- The stigma of male rape – prevents heterosexual and gay men from reporting their experiences.
- Worries about disclosing vulnerability.
- Being labelled 'victim'.

(Davies, 2007a)

PAUSE FOR REVIEW

How can a gendered perspective in criminology inform our understanding of the social processes that give rise to criminal victimisation?

SUMMARY

This chapter has considered gender, victims and crime. It has explained the distinctions between sex and gender and has examined some commonly held assumptions and perceptions about victimhood and vulnerability. Experiences of criminal justice have been highlighted and in doing so the chapter has explored some complex victimological dynamics, relationships and processes. In the examples used to illustrate the complex ways in which gender is relevant to understanding inter-personal violence, vulnerability is identified as a key concept. For vulnerable women and girls in particular, rape myths are a huge barrier to achieving justice and, combined with stubborn attrition rates and silencing agents, these social and cultural stereotypes and legacies explain the continuing gendered nature of the justice gap. There is a circularity to the way in which rape silencers and gender myths contribute to the practice of 'victim blaming' – arguably the biggest barrier to meaningful reforms in the criminal justice system. This chapter has made the case for **gender-appropriate** and **gender-sensitive** responses and service provisions to reduce the justice gap for vulnerable victims. In this endeavour the chapter encourages readers to 'think critically about' what it is to be a victim-survivor, from a gendered perspective.

FURTHER READING

Davies, P. (2014) 'Gender first: the secret to revealing sexual crimes and victimisations', in P. Davies, P. Francis and T. Wyatt (eds), *Invisible Crimes and Social Harms*. Basingstoke: Palgrave Macmillan.

This provides the reader with a good overview of gender as it relates to sexual crime and victimisation.

Davies, P. (2011) *Gender, Crime and Victimisation.* London: Sage.

This explores gender patterns to offending and victimisation and how these patterns are variously established and represented, researched, explained and responded to by policy makers and criminal justice agencies.

Walklate, S. (ed.) (2017) *Handbook on Victims and Victimology* (2nd edn). London: Routledge.

Various chapters in this Handbook are relevant to an understanding of gender and victimisation including Ch. 6 by Pam Davies entitled 'Feminist voices, gender and victimisation' and Ch. 9 'Sexuality and victimisation' by Les Moran.

REFERENCES

Barrett, D. (2013) 'Police argue over who told victim: "don't get help"', *Sunday Telegraph* 10 February, p. 8.

Beckett, H. with Brodie, I., Factor, F., Melrose, M., Pearce, J., Pitts, J., Shuker, L. and Warrington, C. (2012) *Research into Gang-associated Sexual Exploitation and Sexual Violence*, Interim Report. Luton: University of Bedfordshire.

Brennan, I.R., Moore, S.C. and Shepherd, J. P. (2010) 'Risk factors for violent victimisation and injury from six years of the British Crime Survey', *International Review of Victimology*, 17(2): 209–229.

Brody, A., Demetriades, J. and Esplen, E. (2008) *Gender and Climate Change: Mapping the Linkages – A Scoping Study on Knowledge and Gaps*. Brighton: BRIDGE Institute of Development Studies.

Brookman, F. and Robinson (2012) 'Violent crime', in M. Maguire, R. Morgan and R. Reiner (eds), *The Oxford Handbook of Criminology* (5th edn). London: Oxford University Press.

Connell, R.W. (1987) *Gender and Power.* Oxford: Polity.

Cook, I. and Davies, P. (2016) 'Supporting victims and witnesses', in J. Harding, P. Davies and G. Mair (eds), *An Introduction to Criminal Justice*. London: Sage.

Crown Prosecution Service (CPS) (2016) 'Guidelines on prosecuting cases of child sexual abuse'. Available at www.cps.gov.uk/legal/a_to_c/child_sexual_abuse/ (accessed 7.11.16).

Daly, K. (1997) 'Different ways of conceptualising sex/gender in feminist theory and their implications for criminology', *Theoretical Criminology*, 1(1): 25–51.

Daly, K. and Bouhours, B. (2010) 'Rape and attrition in the legal process: a comparative analysis of five countries', *Crime and Justice: An Annual Review of Research*, 39: 565–650. Chicago: University of Chicago Press.

Davies, P. (2007a) 'Lessons from the gender agenda', in S. Walklate (ed.), *Handbook on Victims and Victimology.* Cullompton: Willan.

Davies, P. (2007b) 'Criminal (in)justice for victims?', in P. Davies, P. Francis and C. Greer (eds), *Victims, Crime and Society*. London: Sage.

Davies, P. (2014) 'Gender first: the secret to revealing sexual crimes and victimisations', in P. Davies, P. Francis and T. Wyatt (eds), *Invisible Crimes and Social Harms*. Basingstoke: Palgrave Macmillan.

Davies, P. (2017) 'Feminist voices, gender and victimisation', in S.L. Walklate (ed.), *Handbook on Victims and Victimology* (2nd edn). London: Routledge.

Flatley, J. (2016) *Crime in England and Wales: Year ending December* 2015. London: Office for National Statistics.

Furedi, F. (2013) *Moral Crusades in an Age of Mistrust: The Jimmy Savile Scandal.* London: Palgrave MacMillan.

Green, S. (2007) 'Crime, victimisation and vulnerability', in S. Walklate (ed.), *Handbook of Victims and Victimology*. Cullompton: Willan. pp. 91–120.

Gregory, J. and Lees, S. (1999) *Policing Sexual Assault.* London: Routledge.

Heidensohn, F. and Silvestri, M. (2012) 'Gender and crime', in M. Maguire, R. Morgan and R. Reiner (eds), *The Oxford Handbook of Criminology* (5th edn). Oxford: Oxford University Press.

Hester, M. (2013) *From Report to Court: Rape Cases and the Criminal Justice System in the North East, Executive Summary*. Bristol: University of Bristol in association with the Northern Rock Foundation.

Hoyle, C. (2012) 'Victims, the criminal process, and restorative justice', in M. Maguire, R. Morgan and R. Reiner (eds), *The Oxford Handbook of Criminology* (5th edn). Oxford: Oxford University Press.

Jay, A. (2014) *Independent Inquiry into Child Sexual Exploitation in Rotherham 1997–2013*. London: Office of the Children's Commissioner.

Jordan, J. (2012) 'Silencing rape, silencing women', in J.M. Brown and S.L. Walklate (eds), *Handbook on Sexual Violence*. Abingdon: Routledge.

Kelly, L. and Radford, J. (1996) '"Nothing really happened": the invalidation of women's experiences of sexual violence', in M. Hester, L. Kelly and J. Radford (eds), *Women, Violence and Male Power*. Buckingham: Open University Press. pp. 19–33.

Kelly, L., Lovett, J. and Regan, L. (2005) *A Gap or a Chasm? Attrition in Reported Rape Cases*, Home Office Research Study 293. London: Home Office.

Lees, S. (1997) *Carnal Knowledge: Rape on Trial*. Harmondsworth: Penguin.

Mendelsohn, B. (1956) 'A new branch of bio-psychological science: la victimology', *Revue Internationale de Criminologie et de Police Technique*, 2.

Messerschmidt, J.W. (1993) *Masculinities and Crime*. Lanham, MD: Rowman & Littlefield.

Messerschmidt, J.W. (1997) *Crime as Structured Action*. Thousand Oaks, CA: Sage.

Ministry of Justice (2011) *Vulnerable and Intimidated Witnesses: A Police Service Guide*. London: Ministry of Justice.

Office for National Statistics (2015) *Crime Survey for England and Wales*, Focus on: Violent Crime and Sexual Offences, 2013/14. London: ONS.

Payne, S. (2009) *Redefining Justice: Addressing the Individual Needs of Victims and Witnesses*. London: Home Office.

Pearce, J.J. (2009) *Young People and Sexual Exploitation: 'It's not hidden, you just aren't looking'*. London: Routledge.

Rape Crisis England & Wales (2004–2016) 'Myths vs realities'. Available at http://rapecrisis.org.uk/mythsvsrealities.php (accessed 11.10.16).

Renzetti, C.M. (2013) *Feminist Criminology*. London: Routledge.

Rock, P.E. (2008) 'The Treatment of Victims in England and Wales', *Policing*, 2: 1–10, in P.E. Rock (2010) *Victims, Policy-making and Criminological Theory: Selected Essays*. Farnham: Ashgate.

Spalek, B. (2006) *Crime Victims: Theory, Policy and Practice*. Basingstoke: Palgrave Macmillan.

Starmer, K. (2013) *The Criminal Justice Response to Child Sexual Abuse: Time for a National Consensus*. London: Crown Prosecution Service.

Stern, V. (2010) *The Stern Review: A Report by Baroness Stern CBE of an Independent Review into How Rape Complaints are Handled by Public Authorities in England and Wales*. London: Home Office.

Szyockyi, E. and Fox, J.G. (1996) *Corporate Victimisation of Women*. Boston, MA: Northeastern University Press.

Toynbee, P. (2013) 'Misogyny runs so deep in this society, it is even used against abused children', *Guardian*, 7 August.

von Hentig, H. (1948) *The Criminal and His Victim: Studies in the Socio-biology of Crime*. New Haven, CT: Yale University Press.

Wachholz, S. (2007) 'At risk': climate change and its bearing on women's vulnerability to male violence', in P. Bierne and N. South (eds), *Issues in Green Criminology Confronting Harms Against Environments, Humanity and Other Animals.* Cullompton: Willan.

Walby, S., Towers, J. and Francis, B. (2016) 'Is violent crime increasing or decreasing? A new methodology to measure repeat attacks making visible the significance of gender and domestic relations', *British Journal of Criminology*, Advance Access February 3.

Walklate, S. (2004) *Gender, Crime and Criminal Justice*. Cullompton: Willan.

Walklate, S. (2007) 'Men, victims and crime', in P. Davies, P. Francis and C. Greer (eds), *Victims, Crime and Society*. London: Sage.

West, C. and Fenstermaker, S. (1995) 'Doing difference', *Gender and Society*, 9(1): 8–37.

West, C. and Zimmerman, D.H. (1987) 'Doing gender', *Gender and Society*, 1(2): 125–51.

World Health Organisation (2013) *Global and Regional Estimates of Violence Against Women: Prevalence and Health Effects of Intimate Partner Violence and Non-partner Sexual Violence*. Geneva: WHO.

9 OLDER PEOPLE, VICTIMS AND CRIME

Matthew Hall

In the relatively short history of victimology older people have, with a few exceptions, largely remained at the periphery of key developments and discussion. While a sizeable body of research has in fact built up over the years exploring various aspects of criminal victimisation and the fear of crime amongst those in later life, this is still not a mainstream subject for many victimologists. Not only is the literature relatively scarce, in more recent years there have developed palpable disagreements as to the nature and extent of victimisation amongst older people, and how the elderly react to crime and the fear of crime. Increasingly the traditional understanding that older people fall victim to crime very rarely yet 'irrationally' have the greatest fear of crime is coming under closer scrutiny (Penhale, 2013).

Recent studies have not only cast further light on the hidden nature of much of the criminal victimisation experienced by older people, they have also exposed the reality that 'fear of crime' amongst the elderly is in fact a complex, multifaceted issue. This chapter introduces some of the key questions facing researchers examining how crime impacts on older people while, at the same time, advocating increased attention to a problem which, given the ageing nature of the world's population, will become increasingly pressing in the 21st century.

DEFINING AND THEORISING THE PROBLEM

Like many of the issues discussed (or in this case, not discussed) by criminologists, it is important to appreciate that 'old age' and 'the elderly' are fluid concepts, much like like 'criminal victimisation' itself. As such, analysis by Powell et al. (2007) exposes the complexities of the interactions between Beck's (1992) notion of the **risk society** and of 'old age' as a social construction. On the latter point, Penhale (2013: 179) notes:

> Of importance also within the field of elder abuse are the societal views and attitudes, which are commonly held concerning older people. The discrimination and lowered social status experienced by older people; the routinized devaluation which elders experience from living in an ageist society can exacerbate vulnerability which may already exist due to deterioration in physical and mental health. The risk of abuse may thus be increased.

For the sake of brevity, this chapter generally follows what has become the convention in many developed countries by understanding 'old age' as beginning at the chronological age of 65 (see World Health Organisation, 2014). It is important, however, to recognise the arbitrary nature of this 'cut-off' point in the light of observations like those above.

Furthermore, while discussion of criminal victimisations perpetrated against older people raises important questions concerning crime and criminal justice, it must be recognised that this represents only one component of the wider problem of elder abuse (see Payne, 2011). Although elder abuse may obviously include victimisation as the result of criminal activities, the term tends to be construed as wider than this. This in turn raises questions of the place of *social harms*, as opposed to *criminal harms* in any discussions of elderly victimisation, and with it the importance of more critical branches of criminological debate, which tend to question why some activities and victims are labelled as 'criminal' while others are not.

The above complexities notwithstanding, several authors have applied mainstream criminological theories to the question of elder victimisation. For example, Payne and Gainey (2006) have argued that violent victimisation perpetrated against elderly residents by staff is consistent with **routine activities theory** because such people have been systematically placed in vulnerable positions, exposed to motivated offenders with an absence of capable guardians or the ability to report their victimisation. On this point Pain (1995) similarly concludes that routine activities have an important role in explaining some elderly victimisation. Pain also argues that **general strain theory** can also be applied in relation to the role of **caregiver burden** in elderly victimisation. Specifically, Pain argues that caregivers may victimise their elderly charges as a result of their situation, leading to failure to achieve positively valued stimuli, the loss of positively valued stimuli and the presentation of negative stimuli. The negative experiences of any of these, including mere emotional distress, can for Agnew (1992) result in criminality.

ELDER VICTIMISATION: THE TRADITIONAL APPROACH

As noted above, the examination of older people as both victims of crime and as fearful of crime has developed steadily, since the late 1970s. Earlier studies, usually based on victim survey data from both the US and England and Wales, emphasised that older people were not in fact the victims of much crime compared to younger age groups

Table 9.1 Victimisation rates (percentage of the population experiencing crime in the last year, by age bands and crime-type) from the 2011/12 CSEW (ONS, 2013)

	Violent crime (%)	Burglary rates (%)	Personal theft (%)
16–24 year olds	8.4	6.4	2.5
25–34 year olds	4.4	3.4	1.5
35–44 year olds	2.6	2.9	0.9
45–54 year olds	2.0	2.6	0.7
55–64 year olds	1.0	2.1	0.7
65–74 year olds	0.4	1.2	0.8
75+ year olds	0.1	1.4	0.7

(Hough, 1986). On the face of it, these findings still hold true according to more recent surveys. Table 9.1 sets out victimisation data from the 2011/12 Crime Survey for England and Wales (CSEW) (Office for National Statistics, 2013) for violent crime, burglary and personal theft.

In an era characterised by evidence-based policy making (Lawrence, 2006) it is therefore little surprise that older people and their experiences of crime, while frequently cited in a rhetorical sense by politicians, has in fact received very little firm policy attention over the years, despite the elderly frequently constituting the archetypal 'ideal victim': blameless, weak and vulnerable (Christie, 1986). The other prevailing theme in much of the early literature is that people in later life are more fearful of crime than younger people (Mayhew et al., 1993). Taken with the apparently reduced vulnerability to crime evidenced from surveys, this had led to a supposition described by Pain (1995: 584) in the following terms:

> [O]ne of the paradoxes arising in criminological discussions of 'risk' and 'fear' remains that while elderly people seem to suffer as much or more from the fear of crime as young people, they appear to be the least likely of all groups to be victimised.

By the turn of the century this paradox had been more thoroughly explored. Pain's (1995) analysis, for example, suggests that gender is far more determinative of a person's perceptions of crime and their perceived risk of falling victim to it than age. In fact Pain's 1995 study suggested that, even then, such fear is largely limited to perceptions *of being in danger* in public places, rather than a fear of *crime*. At the same time, Lindesay (1996), Klaus (2005) and Bulman (2010) have stressed that, while older people may indeed be less prone to the kinds of crime caught by victimisation surveys, this represents only the tip of the iceberg when one considers less visible victimisations occurring in private: including elder abuse perpetrated by relatives in their home, corporate (Powell and Wahidin, 2004) and **white-collar crime** (Croall, 2009) and elder abuse within nursing homes.

Can crime perpetrated against older people be adequately counted or estimated? What are the limits of presently utilised research instruments in this regard?

What do we mean when we speak about 'fear of crime'?

Are the elderly more fearful and more at risk of criminalisation than other social groups?

PAUSE FOR REVIEW

OLDER PEOPLE AS VICTIMS: SOURCES OF INFORMATION

Data from the Crime Survey for England and Wales

It is clear from the recent statistics cited in Box 9.1 that the Crime Survey for England and Wales (CSEW) still implies that criminal victimisation amongst the elderly is, numerically speaking, not a major concern. Nevertheless, it is also clear that such surveys may underestimate such victimisation for a number of reasons. Initially it is worth pointing out more generic criticisms of victim surveys: specifically that they rely on the recollection of victims (which may in the case of elderly people be less reliable than that of most younger victims of crime), their willingness to report crime to the surveyors and their ability to self-define themselves as victims (Lynn and Elliott, 2000). Perhaps more importantly in relation to older people is the fact that the CSEW is a *household* survey – excluding those resident in nursing homes or similar institutions. Estimates by LaingBuisson (2013) put the total number of older and physically disabled people living in such nursing homes in the UK at 432,000. For present purposes it is somewhat ironic that the CSEW has recently extended its remit to younger people (10–15 year olds) at a time when it is the *elderly* population that is expanding the most in the wake of baby boomers reaching older age.

Data from the Crown Prosecution Service (CPS)

The Crown Prosecution Service (2012) now gathers its own data on 'Crimes Against Older People' (CAOP), based on cases forwarded to prosecutors by police. As such, these data are grounded in reported crime figures, which we know themselves are limited (often picking up much less crime than victimisation surveys) largely because most crime is not reported. Nevertheless, these figure are useful as an indicator of how much elderly victimisation is coming to the attention of the criminal justice system and therefore can help to drive institutional acceptance of this issue. The CPS's understanding of crime against older people is presented in Box 9.1.

BOX 9.1 NON-STATUTORY DEFINITION OF 'CRIMES AGAINST OLDER PEOPLE' USED BY THE CPS

Where there is a relationship and an expectation of trust e.g. assault/theft by a carer or family member;

- Which are specifically targeted at the old person because they are perceived as being vulnerable or an 'easy target' e.g. a distraction burglary or a mugging;
- Which are not initially related to the older person's age but later do so e.g. a burglary where the burglar does not know the age of the householder but later exploits the situation on discovering that the householder is an older person and;
- Which appear to be in part, or wholly motivated by hostility based on age, or perceived age e.g. an assault, harassment or antisocial behaviour involving derogatory statements associated with the victim's age.

Where an offender deliberately targets an older person because of his/her hostility towards older people this will amount to an aggravating factor as will targeting anyone who is vulnerable.

(CPS, 2009)

In 2010/11 the CPS (2012) data indicates the following broad trends in CAOP compared with the previous year's (2009/10) figures:

- A rise in the number of cases *referred* to the CPS by police.
- A 4 per cent increase in the proportion of cases *charged* from 2009/10, representing 44 per cent of referred cases (n = 2,213).
- A considerable (38 per cent) increase in the number of *convictions*.
- Guilty pleas were increased to 73.2 per cent of all outcomes.
- Unsuccessful prosecutions represented a reducing proportion of concluded cases in 2010/11 (20.0 per cent as opposed to 21.3 per cent in 2008/09).
- The proportion of cases failing due to victim issues (usually victim reluctance to give evidence) remained reasonably consistent.
- The proportion of cases failing for 'other key reasons' had fallen slightly from 68.2 per cent to 65.7 per cent over the period with acquittal after trial and essential legal element missing representing the largest proportion and the greatest volume of such cases.
- 76.3 per cent of defendants were men in these cases, a figure that had remained consistent over the past three years.

(CPS, 2009)

Research findings on elder victimisation and elder abuse

The absence of CSEW data on victimisation of elderly people resident in care homes is significant not just because of the raw numbers of people excluded from the survey but, more importantly, because it effectively also excludes a whole classification of crime and victimisation occurring within institutional settings. In relation to residential care homes there have been very few definitive studies of such victimisation in the UK. Wolhunter et al. (2009) provide a concise summary of relevant research that has been carried out in residential homes in Germany (Goergen, 2004) and the US (Lachs et al., 2007; Payne and Gainey, 2006). The Wolhunter study concluded that verbal victimisation and neglect at the hands of nursing staff were more regularly reported than physical violence. Lach et al.'s research, however, indicates that when residents do suffer violence, it is often at the hands of other residents competing for scarce resources.

One of the most in-depth evaluations of elder abuse carried out in England and Wales is that conducted by the National Centre for Social Research (NatCen) on behalf of the Department of Health and the charity Comic Relief. In a number of reports from an initial survey of over 2,100 older people aged over 66 and resident in households (including sheltered accommodation but excluding care homes)[1] the research team discusses many aspects of the elder abuse issue (see Mowlam et al., 2007; Speight and Purdon, 2007; Dixon et al., 2009). In total 2.6 per cent of those surveyed reported having experienced mistreatment involving a family member, close friend or care worker in the last year. This expands to 4.0 per cent if incidents involving neighbours and acquaintances are included, equating to about 342,400 older people subject to some form of mistreatment nationally.

One recurring issue arising throughout the NatCen project has been the problem of definitions. Mowlam et al. (2007) conducted 36 follow-up qualitative interviews with survey respondents and comment at some length as to the difficulties of defining elder abuse in a logical and useful way. The definition used in official government policy on elder abuse, entitled *No Secrets* in England and Northern Ireland and *In Safe Hands* in Wales, defines the concept as 'a violation of an individual's human and civil rights by any other person or persons' (Home Office and Department of Health, 2000). The document then lists possible ways this abuse can occur, replicated in Box 9.2.

BOX 9.2 FORMS OF 'ELDER ABUSE' ACCORDING TO *NO SECRETS*

- **physical abuse**, including hitting, slapping, pushing, kicking, misuse of medication, restraint, or inappropriate sanctions;
- **sexual abuse**, including rape and sexual assault or sexual acts to which the vulnerable adult has not consented, or could not consent or was pressured into consenting;

- **psychological abuse**, including emotional abuse, threats of harm or abandonment, deprivation of contact, humiliation, blaming, controlling, intimidation, coercion, harassment, verbal abuse, isolation or withdrawal from services or supportive networks;
- **financial or material abuse**, including theft, fraud, exploitation, pressure in connection with wills, property or inheritance or financial transactions, or the misuse or misappropriation of property, possessions or benefits;
- **neglect and acts of omission**, including ignoring medical or physical care needs, failure to provide access to appropriate health;
- **social care or educational services**, the withholding of the necessities of life, such as medication, adequate nutrition and heating; and
- **discriminatory abuse**, including racist, sexist, that based on a person's disability, and other forms of harassment, slurs or similar treatment.

(Home Office and Department of Health, 2000)

Elder abuse and **elder justice** has a slightly longer history in the US, with legislation coming in the form of the 1965 Older Americans Act. Title VII of the Act (updated in 2006) provides for programmes intended to prevent elder abuse, neglect and exploitation of the elderly. More recently the US stance on elder abuse has been revitalised in a succession of Elder Justice Acts (2002, 2003 and 2009), which have enhanced relevant provisions to achieve these aims in a host of different contexts including: criminal justice, medical services, social services, economic reforms, legal issues, housing and law enforcement (see Blancato, 2004). Interestingly, the preliminaries of the 2009 Act cite a figure of 'between 500,000 and 5,000,000' elders (in this case people over 60) in the US as being abused, neglected, or exploited each year. The breadth of this range is itself indicative of the lack of clear figures and measurement problems surrounding this issue. More recent US research from Acierno et al. (2010) cites a figure of 10 per cent of elder individuals reporting some type of mistreatment in the previous year. Elder Justice has itself grown into something of a political movement: certainly since the World Health Organisation's spearheading of the Toronto Declaration on the Global Prevention of Elder Abuse in 2002. The Declaration highlights that in many parts of the world 'legal frameworks are missing. Cases of elder abuse, when identified are often not addressed for lack of proper legal instruments to respond and deal with them' (WHO, 2002: 2).

Whilst elder abuse is increasingly recognised in its own right, abuse of the elderly in their own homes is also increasingly being acknowledged in the context of domestic violence. According to some estimates, two-thirds of acts of elder abuse are committed at home by someone in a position of trust (Help the Aged, 2008). In the UK, the official definition of domestic violence is not age restricted. It is defined as 'any incident or pattern of incidents of controlling, coercive or threatening behaviour, violence or abuse between those aged 16 or over who are or have been intimate partners or family members regardless of gender or sexuality' (Home Office, 2012). Yet combining investigations of elder abuse with domestic violence research is a matter of some debate in the literature. Penhale (2013), for example, concludes that the term 'elder abuse' hides the gendered nature of much of the activities under discussion; that is, the fact that it is older women who are far more often the victims of such abuse compared to older men. As such, the author argues

> the term elder abuse, by virtue of its gender-neutral status, may disempower older women who are the majority of elders who experience abuse in later life. Links with the feminist movement to end violence against women may serve to empower older women and to promote their rights to full citizenship. (2013: 170)

At the same time, however, Penhale is wary of simply amalgamating the two areas of discussion because 'elder abuse is similar to and yet different from other types of family violence' (p. 179). The author continues:

> The spectrum of elder abuse, if viewed as a continuum, encompasses both abuse between partners in later life and child abuse and many variations in between. It also encompasses abuse that occurs within institutions, either due to the regime within the institution, or abuse that occurs directed at an individual in that setting (from a relative, paid carer, or indeed another resident). This form of abuse is indeed different from violence occurring within the domestic setting.' (p. 179)

Notwithstanding such reservations, one further link between the issues of elder abuse and domestic violence is the realisation that the latter may constitute a long-term continuation of the former. This was a key conclusion presented by Hightower et al. (2001) following a major empirical study of abuse and violence in the lives of older women in British Columbia and Yukon.

Returning to the 2011/12 CSEW (Office for National Statistics, 2013), we see again that this particular kind of violence is more prevalent amongst younger age groups, is shown in Table 9.2

As in previous sweeps of the survey, splitting the results by gender reveals that women are more likely than men to have fallen victim to domestic violence in the younger age groups (0.7 per cent of men compared with 1.3 per cent of women in the 16–24 age bracket). That said, it is notable that the prevalence of domestic violence amongst those aged 55 and over was practically identical for both men and women. On the face if it, such figures may indicate that domestic violence amongst the elderly is less gender dependent than that of younger victims. Again, however, such a finding would be quite misleading given the very low numbers in that age bracket.

Table 9.2 Prevalence of domestic violence, by age group – CSEW 2011/12 (ONS, 2013)

Age range	Percentage of age range reporting DV victimisation in the last year
16–24 year olds	1.0
45–54 year olds	0.5
55–64 year olds	0.1
65–74 year olds	0
75+ year olds	0.1

Comparing prevalence rates between older and younger victims of domestic violence, or indeed any other form of crime, is not straightforward, not least because simplistic analyses may ignore the possibility that when older people do fall victim to crime, they are differently affected than younger people. Pain (1995: 584), for example, argues 'that there are dimensions to the vulnerability of elderly people other than the physical'. Certainly there is evidence that, owing to increased frailty and lack of social support mechanisms, the impacts of both property crime and personal crime hit elderly victims the hardest (Mawby, 1988). For example, Donaldson (2003: 1) concludes that, although people over the age of 60 are less likely to become victims of burglary,

> elderly victims of burglary decline in health faster than non-victims of similar age and the impact of burglary is typically great. Two years after the burglary, they were 2.4 times more likely to have died or to be in residential care than their non-burgled neighbours.

Pantazis (2000) also concludes that when older people feel vulnerable and fearful, their ability to withstand victimisation may be substantially reduced. Regarding burglary it should also be noted that whilst older people are apparently at lower risk from 'standard' burglaries, they appear to be at higher risk of falling victim to so-called distraction burglary whereby the method of entry is via some form of trick or deception (Thornton et al., 2003). In sum, these points indicate that the impact of crime on the elderly has become largely subsumed by discussions of their fear of crime with insufficient attention on other impacts – physical, psychological, social or otherwise.

ELDER ABUSE AS HATE CRIME

Another aspect of elderly victimisation and/or elder abuse that has received some attention in recent years is the conceptualisation of such victimisation as hate crime. Garland (2011) has reflected on both the advantages and disadvantages of such a classification. On the positive side the author notes that hate crime and elder abuse do share some key characteristics:

> [J]ust as forms of recognized hate crime, such as homophobic or transphobic (for instance), occur within a social context characterized by open or latent hostility towards those groups, arguably elder abuse also occurs in a social context in which older people are not valued. Instead, they are stigmatized by, and marginalized from, mainstream society in a fashion similar to that of the acknowledged hate crime victim groups. (2011: 30)

Sherry (2010) also laments the failure to explore the clear overlap between elder abuse and disability hate crime. That said, Garland also acknowledges that notions of 'hate crime' inevitably tend to compartmentalise victims into set social groupings with assumed, homogenous characteristics. Given the great variation in wealth and social status amongst the elderly, he argues, this would be a mistake. Indeed, this is particularly significant in light of evidence presented by Pantazis (2000) that amongst older people it is still the poorest members of this group that suffer the most crime. In concluding his discussion of elder abuse Garland notes that 'debating victimisation via the framework of "groups", which can homogenize diverse communities and lead to broad assumptions about them' (2011: 32) may be unhelpful. In a more recent contribution Policastro et al. (2013) has emphasised how the characteristics of elder victims vary significantly along with the different types of crime they experience. As such, the authors distinguish four types of victimisation suffered by older people: elder abuse; elder domestic violence; elder white-collar crime; and general crime. They therefore critique the existing literature in the following terms:

> A tendency exists, however, to treat all of the offense types within a single broader category of elder mistreatment or some variation thereof. Such an approach potentially masks the differences between these offense categories. (2013: 5)

The authors' main findings in terms of correlations between different offence types and different personal and wider characteristics of older victims (and the relevant offenders) are reproduced in Box 9.3.

BOX 9.3 POLICASTRO ET AL.'S (2013) KEY FINDINGS ON ELDER VICTIMISATION

- A higher percentage of male victims were found in elder domestic violence cases than in elder abuse cases.
- A higher percentage of non-white victims were found in abuse by other relatives/ caregivers.
- Psychiatric problems were identified more often in white-collar crime victims than in elder abuse, elder domestic violence, and abuse by other relatives/caregivers.
- Elder domestic violence and white-collar crime cases more frequently involved physical abuse cases and daughters tended to be accused of exploitation more often.
- Caregiver burden was more frequent in elder domestic violence cases and elder abuse cases by daughters.
- While white-collar crimes were more likely than the other offenses to occur in long-term care settings, a sizable proportion (about a fourth) of the white-collar crimes occurred in the victim's home.

It is clear from these findings that treating *all* elder victimisation as one vulnerable category of victims is clearly insufficient. It is submitted that more work is now needed to investigate the differing needs of older victims of crime as individuals, and in a way that does not infanticise them. This is particularly important, as this demographic group is both increasing in size and becoming ever more diverse in character (see Wray, 1991).

Is it useful to 'borrow' ideas from other 'areas of crime' (hate crime, domestic violence, sexual violence etc.) in our studies of older people's victimisation? What advantages/disadvantages can this bring?

To what extent are labels like 'elder abuse' useful/restrictive?

Criminologists tend to think about crime and victimisation in terms of specifically defined 'groups' of victims/offenders. What are the advantages/disadvantages of this approach?

PAUSE FOR REVIEW

OLDER PEOPLE'S FEAR OF CRIME AND VICTIMISATION

As noted earlier, the suggestion that people in later life are more concerned about crime dominates much of the earlier literature on this topic. The most recent CSEW data on those respondents expressing 'high levels' of worry about crime in fact show little indication of a definite spike in levels of concern amongst the elderly in relation to worries about burglary, car crime or violent crime (Office for National Statistics, 2013). The figures for those reporting that they felt it was 'highly likely' they would fall victim to burglary, car crime or violent crime in the next year tell a similar story. Such concern is broadly similar across age ranges for all burglary and car crime for everyone under 75. The same is broadly true for crimes of violence, although here the 16–24 age group report slightly greater concern that they will experience such crime in the next year. When one looks at the over-75 category such concern drops markedly in all three cases. In sum, therefore, there is little indication from these data that older people are more concerned about crime.

Following a review of US data from the 1990 Fear of Crime in America Survey, Ferraro and LaGrange (1992: 242) concluded that 'there is no evidence in this recent national sample of adults that older people are now the age group most afraid of crime.'

As with the types of victimisation experienced by the elderly, however, these basic figures mask a great deal of underlying complexity, including the fundamental difficulty acknowledged in much of the work concerning fear of crime: what exactly is it we are measuring, or indeed trying to measure (see Farrall et al., 1997)? Just as 'older people' are not a homogenous group, 'fear of crime' is a complex and multifaceted issue. Therefore it could be argued that just because a respondent feels it is highly likely that he or she will fall victim to a particular type of crime over the next year, that is not to say they *fear* the consequences of that crime any more or less than someone who feels their risk to be much lower. Furthermore, just as the impacts of crime are known to spread out to an ever widening group of **indirect victims**, so too can others be made fearful for the safety of elderly friends and family. Heber (2009) discusses the concept of *altruistic fear*, whereby surveyed respondents expressed concerns about their elderly parents being vulnerable to bag-snatching, theft, mugging and assault, as well as the parent's concerns about their children falling victim to crime.

There are other difficulties arising from the way questions in surveys – most commonly 'Are you afraid to be out of your house alone after dark' (Farrall et al., 1997) – tend to be equated (unproblematically) with fear of crime. In critiquing such assumptions we would be wise to bear in mind the observation by Fattah (1993: 8) that

> [e]motions, such as fear, are not based on rational objective assessments of the chances of becoming victim. There is no sense, therefore, in trying to determine whether they are proportionate or disproportionate to the real dangers and the objective risks of victimisation.

The above notwithstanding, underlying much of the existing literature there remains an assumption that there is a 'proportional' level of fear of crime amongst any given demographic group. On this point, however, the other complicating dimension to the measurement of fear (as with criminal victimisation itself) lies in how we define the group of people we wish to investigate. Pain's (1995) analysis, already noted above, attempts to deconstruct crime survey figures with a greater focus on the distinctions between 'risk of crime' and 'fear of crime' amongst the elderly while also highlighting the importance of gender over age in the equation. One highlight of her findings is that there was no evidence to suggest that elder women were more fearful of violent crime (as a whole) compared to younger women, and in fact such women were less afraid of street violence than their younger counterparts. Elder women were, however, more afraid of falling victim to harassment than younger women and were roughly equal to them in their fear of violence taking place in the home.

Pain's explanation of these findings constitutes a useful indication of the true complexities of the issue. For her, gender is far more indicative than age in determining fear of crime. Her conclusion concerning fear is that older women essentially fear crime for the same reason as younger women: because of the actual risks of violence in the home and the sexual harassment that they face. In other words, for Pain it is 'structural vulnerability shaped by gender rather than the ageing process which creates the perception of public places as dangerous' (1995: 594) amongst both older *and* younger women. For Pain, older women are more at risk of actual victimisation than is traditionally believed because, first, there is a great deal more elder abuse occurring behind closed doors than the crime survey reveals and, second, because, having lived longer, older women build up a wealth of knowledge and understanding about the nature of the risks they face from crime, which is reflected in the answers they give about fear. For this reason, Pain concludes, elder women's fear of crime is in fact more *realistic* than that of younger women. Elderly women's concerns tend to be more 'realistic' than younger women's in that they are less fearful of being attacked outside, equally worried about violence in the home, and more worried by the prospect of harassment. On the basis of the experiences of violent and abusive behaviour among women in the survey, the relationship of elderly women's concerns with risk is closer than that of younger women's, rather than more distant. This assertion is dependent upon the survey's acknowledgement of experiences over a lifetime (1995: 590).

Pantazis (2000), along similar lines, argues that feelings of being unsafe among older people are conditional upon their level of *multiple deprivations* including the effect of gender, but also poverty, along with age.

Certainly not all scholars accept such interpretations. Fattah (1993), for example, argues that the estimates of elder abuse going on behind closed doors (both at home and in care institutions) are 'widely exaggerated' and generally accepts the low(er) risk/higher fear dichotomy. For Fattah, however, it is the heightened fear amongst the elderly that partly (if not entirely) explains their lower levels of victimisation, because this results in associated crime avoidance techniques. Thus, it is argued, fear of crime may have positive as well as negative connotations.

The notion that crime can be both avoided and prevented by focusing more on promoting risk-avoidance activities amongst potential or actual victims is now a mainstream of the crime prevention literature (see Walklate, 2007), although such an approach risks becoming a form of victim-blaming. The contention that not all fear is 'bad' certainly exemplifies once again that this is a complex, multifaceted issue, Fattah himself acknowledging that 'it would be foolhardy to claim that the low victimisation rates of the elderly are entirely due to their high level of fear of crime' (1993: 20).

PAUSE FOR REVIEW

Consider what is meant by 'fear of crime'. Does it always mean the same thing? How can we measures it, and is it useful to do so?

Do older people react to crime differently than younger people?

Who/what are the indirect victims of elder abuse?

SUMMARY

The above discussion demonstrates that the interaction between the older population and crime goes far beyond the simple low risk/high fear dichotomy to encompass a wide variety of complicating factors, of which gender is an especially important issue. Definitions of key concepts like 'elder abuse' require refinement and agreement and further research is clearly needed at a time when more people than ever are entering old age and are resident in nursing homes and other care institutions. The extent of the 'hidden' victimisation of the elderly both in care and in their own homes is still largely unknown, but it is unlikely that reliance on methodologies like the CSEW are adequate measures. Furthermore, simply amalgamating current elder abuse knowledge with those of domestic violence or sexual violence is unlikely to produce the detailed, tailored results that are needed to form the basis of policy on this issue. As such, the challenges of elder victimisation are as methodological as they are practical and social. Critical brands of victimology clearly point to the need to bring these less-visible victims 'in from the cold' (Shapland, 2003), just as the wider victimological project has from its inception cast light on victims as a 'forgotten group' as a whole. In the interests of evidence-based policy making, such a change of approach is vital if we are to present the case for policy revision in this area.

FURTHER READING

Payne, B. (2011) *Crime and Elder Abuse: An Integrated Perspective* (3rd edn). Springfield, IL: Charles C. Thomas.

Now in its 3rd edition, this is still one of the only book-length integrated works on the issue of older people and criminal victimisation, covering a broad range of matters, including a useful discussion of theory and crime prevention.

Penhale, B. (2008), 'Older women, domestic violence, and elder abuse: a review of commonalities, differences, and shared approaches', *Journal of Elder Abuse & Neglect*, 15(3–4): 163–84.

This journal article is also extremely insightful in relation to the overlaps between 'elder victimisation' and other classifications of crime.

Powell, J. and Wahidin, A. (2008) 'Understanding old age and victimisation: a critical exploration', *International Journal of Sociology and Social Policy*, 28(3): 90–99.

This offers a more sociologically inspired perspective on understanding old age.

Department of Health (2007) *UK Study of Abuse and Neglect of Older People*, The NatCen/KCL Report. London: Department of Health. Available at www.dh.gov.uk/en/Publicationsandstatistics/Publications/PublicationsPolicyAndGuidance/DH_076197 (accessed 12.10.16).

This is also a must for those wishing to have an overview of relevant issues.

REFERENCES

Acierno, R., Hernandez, M., Amstadter, A., Resnick, H., Steve, K., Muzzy, W. and Kilpatrick, D. (2010) 'Prevalence and correlates of emotional, physical, sexual, and financial abuse and potential neglect in the United States: the national elder mistreatment study', *American Journal of Public Health*, 100(2): 292–97.

Agnew, R. (1992) 'Foundation for a general strain theory of crime and delinquency, *Criminology*, 30(1): 47–88.

Beck, U. (1992) *Risk Society: Towards a New Modernity*. New Delhi: Sage.
Blancato, R. (2004) 'The Elder Justice Act: a landmark policy initiative', *Journal of Elder Abuse & Neglect*, 14(2–3): 181–3.
Bulman, P. (2010) 'Elder abuse emerges from the shadows of public consciousness', *National Institute of Justice Journal*, 265: 4–9.
Christie, N. (1986) 'The ideal victim', in E. Fattah (ed.), *From Crime Policy to Victim Policy*. Basingstoke: Macmillan. pp.17–30.
Croall, H. (2009) 'White collar crime, consumers and victimization', *Crime, Law and Social Change*, 51(1): 127–46.
Crown Prosecution Service (CPS) (2009) *Policy for Prosecuting Crimes against Older People*. London: CPS.
Crown Prosecution Service (CPS) (2012) *Hate Crime and Crimes Against Older People Report 2010–2011*. London: CPS.
Dixon, J., Biggs, S., Tinker, A. and Stevens, M. (2009) *Abuse, Neglect and Lack of Dignity in the Institutional Care of Older People: Definitional Issues*. London: National Centre for Social Research.
Donaldson, R. (2003) *Experiences of Older Burglary Victims*, Home Office Research Findings No.198. London: Home Office.
Farrall, S., Bannister, J., Ditton, J. and Gilchrist, E. (1997) 'Questioning the measurement of the "fear of crime": findings from a major methodological study', *British Journal of Criminology*, 37(4): 658–79.
Fattah, E. (1993) 'Victimisation and fear of crime among the elderly: a possible link?'. Paper presented at the *Crime and Older People Conference*, 23–25 February, Australian Institute of Criminology, Griffith, ACT. Available at www.aic.gov.au/media_library/conferences/olderpeople/fattah.pdf (accessed 2.3.13).
Ferraro, K. and LaGrange, R. (1992) 'Are older people most afraid of crime? Reconsidering age differences in fear of victimization', *Journal of Gerontology*, 47(5): S233–S244.
Garland, J. (2011) 'Difficulties in defining hate crime victimization', *International Review of Victimology*, 18(1): 25–37.
Goergen, T. (2004) 'A multi-method study on elder abuse and neglect in nursing homes', *The Journal of Adult Protection*, 6(3): 15–25.
Heber, A. (2009) '"The worst thing that could happen"': on altruistic fear of crime', *International Review of Victimology*, 16: 257–75.
Help the Aged (2008) *The Financial Abuse of Older People: A Review of the Literature*. London: Help the Aged.
Hightower, J., Smith, M. and Hightower, H. (2001) *Silent and Invisible: A Report on Abuse and Violence in the Lives of Older Women in British Columbia and Yukon*. Vancouver: BC/Yukon Society of Transition Houses.
Home Office (2012) 'A new definition of domestic violence', Press Release of 18 September. Available at www.homeoffice.gov.uk/media-centre/news/domestic-violence-definition (accessed 3.3.12).
Home Office and Department of Health (2000) *No Secrets: Guidance on Developing and Implementing Multi-agency Policies and Procedures to Protect Vulnerable Adults from Abuse*. London: Department of Health.

Hough, M. (1986) 'Victims of violent crime: findings from the British Crime Survey', in E. Fattah (ed.), *From Crime Policy to Victim Policy*. London: Macmillan. pp. 117–34.
Klaus, P. (2005) *Crimes Against Persons Age 65 or Older, 1993–2002*. Washington, DC: US Department of Justice, Bureau of Justice Statistics.
Lachs, M., Bachman, R., Williams, C. and O'Leary J. (2007) 'Resident-to-resident elder mistreatment and police contact in nursing homes: findings from a population-based cohort', *Journal of American Geriatrics Society*, 55: 840–45.
LaingBuisson (2013) *Care of Elderly People UK Market Survey 2012/13*. London: LaingBuisson.
Lawrence, R. (2006) 'Research dissemination: activity bringing the research and policy worlds together', *Evidence & Policy*, 2: 373–84.
Lindesay, J. (1996) 'Elderly people and crime', *Reviews in Clinical Gerontology*, 6(2): 199–204.
Lynn, P. and Elliott, D. (2000) *The British Crime Survey: A Review of Methodology*. London: National Centre for Social Research.
Mawby, R. (1988) 'Age vulnerability and the impact of crime', in M. Maguire and J. Pointing (eds), *Victims of Crime: A New Deal?* Milton Keynes: Open University Press. pp. 101–111.
Mayhew, P., Maunc, N. and Mirrlees-Black, C. (1993) *The 1992 British Crime Survey*. London: HMSO.
Mowlam, A., Tennant, R., Dixon, J. and McCreadie, C. (2007) *UK Study of Abuse and Neglect of Older People: Qualitative Findings*. London: National Centre for Social Research.
Office for National Statistics (2013) *Focus On: Violent Crime and Sexual Offences, 2011/12*. London: ONS.
Pain, R. (1995) 'Elderly women and fear of violent crime: the least likely victims? A reconsideration of the extent and nature of risk', *British Journal of Criminology*, 35(4): 584–98.
Pantazis, C. (2000) '"Fear of crime", vulnerability and poverty: evidence from the British crime survey', *British Journal of Criminology*, 40(3): 414–36.
Payne, B. (2011) *Crime and Elder Abuse: An Integrated Perspective* (3rd edn). Springfield, IL: Charles C. Thomas.
Payne, B. and Gainey, R. (2006) 'The criminal justice response to elder abuse in nursing homes: a routine activities perspective', *Western Criminology Review*, 7(3): 67–81.
Penhale, B. (2013) 'Older women, domestic violence, and elder abuse: a review of commonalities, differences, and shared approaches', *Journal of Elder Abuse & Neglect*, 15(3–4): 163–83.
Policastro, C., Gainey, R. and Payne, B. (2013) 'Conceptualizing crimes against older persons: elder abuse, domestic violence, white collar offending, or just regular "old" crime', *Journal of Crime and Justice*. Online pre-access only at time of writing, available at www.tandfonline.com/doi/full/10.1080/0735648X.2013.76753 (accessed 2.3.13).
Powell, J. and Wahidin, A. (2004) 'Aging and corporate crime', *Journal of Societal and Social Policy*, 3(1): 47–59.
Powell, J., Wahidin, A. and Zinn, J. (2007) 'Understanding risk and old age in western society', *International Journal of Sociology and Social Policy*, 27(1): 65–76.
Shapland, J. (2003) 'Bringing victims in from the cold: victims' role in criminal justice', in J. Jackson and K. Quinn (eds), *Criminal Justice Reform: Looking to the Future*. Belfast: Queens University Belfast. pp. 48–69.

Sherry, M. (2010) *Disability Hate Crimes: Does Anyone Really Hate Disabled People?* Farnham: Ashgate.
Speight, S. and Purdon, S. (2007) *UK Study of Abuse and Neglect of Older People: A Feasibility Study in Care Homes*. London: National Centre for Social Research.
Thornton, A., Hatton, C., Malone, C., Fryer, T., Walker, D., Cunningham, J. and Durrani, N. (2003) *Distraction Burglary Amongst Older Adults and Minority Ethnic Communities*, Home Office Research Study 269. London: Home Office.
Walklate, S. (2007) *Imagining the Victim of Crime*. Maidenhead: Open University Press.
Wolhunter, L., Olley, N. and Denham, D. (2009) *Victimology: Victimisation and Victims' Rights*. London: Routledge.
World Health Organization (2002) *The Toronto Declaration on the Global Prevention of Elder Abuse*, Toronto: WHO. Available at: http://www.who.int/ageing/projects/elder_abuse/alc_toronto_declaration_en.pdf.
World Health Organisation (2014) *Definition of an Older or Elderly Person*. Geneva: WHO. Available at www.who.int/about/contacthq/en/ (accessed 1.5.14).
Wray, L. (1991) 'Public policy implications of an ethnically diverse elderly population', *Journal of Cross-Cultural Gerontology*, 6(2): 243–2.

NOTE

1. The sample was representative of older people in the UK with these characteristics.

10 SOCIO-ECONOMIC INEQUALITIES, VICTIMS AND CRIME

Hazel Croall

Crime has long been associated with lower socio-economic status, with poverty and worklessness and with deprived and 'dangerous' areas. 'Crime' tends to be associated with 'offenders', although 'high crime areas' are also 'high victimisation areas', and one noted criminologist has described crime as a 'regressive tax on the poor' (Downes, 1983). Indeed, the focus on offending serves to downplay the victimisation of the most disadvantaged citizens.

The relationships between socio-economic inequality and victimisation are complex. All citizens are potential crime victims, and the affluent have more to steal, yet poorer victims suffer more severely from crimes which they are less able to protect themselves from. The most deprived and marginalised are also less likely or able to seek help from the police or victim support agencies. Criminal justice processes and policies also exacerbate processes of social exclusion and polarisation affecting offenders, victims and communities.

This chapter will explore these issues, starting with an outline of victimological perspectives. It will go on to explore what we know about victimisation and socio-economic inequalities before looking at the situation of some of the most deprived. It will then briefly consider the impact of criminal justice policies before locating these, and crime and victimisation, in the context of social structural change.

The emphasis in this chapter will be largely on victims of 'conventional' crimes of interpersonal violence and property, whereas victimisation from crimes of the powerful, which also impacts severely on the most disadvantaged, is the subject of Chapter 13 in this volume. It will be noted that in the title and elsewhere the terms 'socio-economic inequalities' and 'socio-economic status' are used in preference to terms such as 'lower class', 'social class' or 'social exclusion', all widely used to express the unequal impact of crime. This is largely because the term 'socio-economic' can encompass the different and interrelated dimensions of social inequality often used in surveys such as income, area of residence or economic activity (Croall, 2011). They also avoid the more pejorative and subjective ways in which terms such as 'social exclusion' or the 'underclass' have been used. Nonetheless, to avoid tedious repetition, the chapter will refer to contrasts, for example between the 'affluent' and the 'poor'.

BACKGROUND: CONCEPTUALISING SOCIO-ECONOMIC INEQUALITY, CRIME AND VICTIMISATION

Positivist victimology and quantitative victim surveys tend to focus on the individual characteristics of victims rather than socio-economic or structural factors. This has been widely criticised. The left-realist approach, for example, challenged the impression given by earlier versions of the British Crime Survey (BCS) that there was a low *average* risk for burglary as this concealed higher risks in poorer areas. Although in turn criticised for their reliance on quantitative victim surveys, they did call for more studies of the 'lived reality' of crime, particularly amongst the poor, and did raise important questions about the wider socio-economic framework of victimisation (Davies et al., 2003; Walklate, 2003).

Critical victimology also asks many relevant questions in relation to economic inequality (Walklate, 2003; Mawby and Walklate, 1994). It asks us to look 'behind our backs' and to reflect on victimisation which we 'do not see' and argues that the processes of victimisation are socially, economically and culturally situated, thus relating victimisation to broader questions of social structure and power and exploring the interconnected links between social class, gender, race and crime (Davies et al., 2007). Walklate also criticises the dualism between victims and offenders by recognising that they are more often drawn from the same social groups. Offending and victimisation are seen as part of a process rather than as single events involving individual offenders and victims. These points are all highly relevant to the exploration of socio-economic status and victimisation.

One factor underlying the relative invisibility of victims from lower socio-economic status is how victimisation is 'counted' by the large-scale victim surveys which form a major source of information. These exclude groups who lack a stable address, such as the homeless, and other marginal and deprived groups. Moreover, they underestimate the extent and impact of repeat victimisation. While, therefore, these surveys do produce a plethora of statistical correlations between victimisation and indicators of socio-economic status such as income, economic activity and living in areas variously described as 'deprived', 'perceived to have high levels of disorder' or 'constrained by circumstances', they fail to capture the essence of the 'lived reality' of crime, victimisation and the role which they play in the life and culture of these areas (Young, 2011).

Furthermore, detailing the 'risks' of victimisation stripped of their social context can lead to 'victim blaming'. Many surveys associate the likelihood of being a victim with living in or walking through 'risky areas' or leading 'risky lifestyles', yet many cannot choose to avoid these risks. Indeed, the inhabitants of these areas, and many of the most deprived are seen as a major part of 'the problem'. They, along with victims who are also known as or perceived to be likely offenders, can be 'blamed' for their victimisation and seen as less credible witnesses. These perceptions can be reflected in the mass media. Greer (2007), for example, contrasts the saturation coverage of the Millie Dowler case in 2002, and the many appearances of her parents, who clearly belonged to a well-to-do, stable home with the sparse attention paid to the working-class, low-income family of a girl whose body was found during the investigation. According to a police spokeswoman, her mother 'wasn't really press-conference material' (see also Chapter 3). Victims of low socio-economic status therefore can become less 'equal', 'deserving' or 'ideal' victims (Walklate, 2007).

DIMENSIONS OF VICTIMISATION AND SOCIO-ECONOMIC INEQUALITY

Unpacking the relationships between socio-economic status and victimisation

The main sources of information about socio-economic factors and victimisation in Britain are crime surveys such as the BCS, which covers England and Wales, the Scottish Crime and Justice Survey (SCJS), and the Northern Ireland Crime survey (NICS). These provide varying amounts of detail on socio-economic factors, with, for reasons of population size, the BCS being able to provide more in-depth breakdowns (Mooney et al., 2010). Generally, they tend to compare inhabitants from the 'most deprived' and 'least deprived' areas, the highest and lowest income groups, and economic activity. The BCS uses the Acorn consumer classification descriptions of areas. See Box 10.1 for some examples.

BOX 10.1 VARIATIONS IN RISKS OF CRIME AND SELECTED INDICATORS OF SOCIO-ECONOMIC STATUS IN BRITAIN

Scotland (2010/11)

Property crime: adults living in the 15 per cent most deprived areas had a higher risk (21 per cent) than elsewhere in Scotland (17 per cent).

Violent crime: no difference in risk by area deprivation (3 per cent).

England and Wales (2009/10)

All crime: households living in the most deprived areas had a higher risk (19 per cent) than those in the least deprived areas (14 per cent).

Specific crimes: vandalism (8 compared to 6 per cent); vehicle related theft (7 compared to 5 per cent); burglary (3 compared to 1 per cent).

Violent crime: 3 per cent reported victimisation with higher rates for the 20 per cent most deprived areas (3.6 per cent); blue collar (3.9 per cent); city living (3.8 per cent) and 'constrained by circumstances' (3.9 per cent) area classifications; lone-parent households (4.4 per cent) and the unemployed (7.7 per cent).

Burglary: 2.2 per cent reported victimisation with higher rates for young people aged under 24 (7 per cent); those with no or less than basic security (5.3 per cent); living in areas with high levels of social disorder (4.3 per cent); lone-parent households (5.9 per cent); students (5.7 per cent); the long-term or temporary sick (4.8 per cent); those with an income of less than £10,000 (3.6 per cent) and those in the 20 per cent most deprived areas (3.3 per cent).

Vandalism: 6.7 per cent reported victimisation, with higher rates including single-parent households (8.4 per cent); the long-term sick (8.7 per cent); blue-collar communities (9.1 per cent); living in areas characterised as having high levels of physical disorder (9.4 per cent) and living in the 20 per cent most deprived areas (7.7 per cent).

Northern Ireland (2011/12)

Households in areas perceived to have a high level of anti-social behaviour were more likely than any other socio-demographic group to have been victims of burglary (6.1 per cent); vehicle-related theft (5.2 per cent for vehicle-owners) or vandalism (10.5 per cent). The average rates were 1.8, 2.1 and 2.9 per cent respectively.

Burglary: those with a household income of less than £10,000 (3.4 per cent) were more likely to be victims with 0.6 per cent of households with an income of over £50,000 being victims.

Vandalism: households within the 20 per cent most deprived areas were more likely to be victims of vandalism (4.3 per cent) compared to the 20 per cent least deprived areas (1.8 per cent).

Violent crime: those who perceived their area to have a high level of anti-social behaviour were much more likely to have been victims of violence (6.5 per cent) compared to low anti-social behaviour areas (1.5 per cent).

(Based on Scottish Government, 2011; Toner and Freel, 2013; Chaplin et al., 2011)

Variations in risks of crime and selected indicators of socio-economic status in Britain provides some selected figures from previous years of these surveys, illustrating some variations and the measures which have been used.

These factors are interrelated and Tilley et al. (2011) point out that:

- those in the *two poorest income groups* (less than £10,000 per annum) are
  - *more* likely to be female; live in households with fewer adults, children and lone parents; be classified as belonging to the occupational classification of those who have never worked; to live in terraced, socially rented accommodation and have a long-standing illness.
  - *less* likely to be in paid work; to be married, cohabiting or divorced.
- Those with an income below £5,000 are *more* likely to be single, separated or widowed; economically inactive; long-term sick, retired or in full-time education and have never worked.

These figures reveal a complex picture, with consistent findings that some forms of crime, particularly property crime, affect *all* social groups and that high rates are found in both relatively affluent *and* poor areas (Bottoms, 2012). The BCS uses complex statistical modelling tools to tease out the independent effect of each variable, although, as outlined above, they are interrelated. In general terms, those in most deprived areas, lower-income groups, those counted as unemployed or who have never worked, single parents and those living in areas characterised by high levels of social disorder do have higher rates of victimisation from many forms of crime. Employment status and occupation are important predictors of violent victimisation, as are living in areas characterised as 'blue collar' and 'constrained by circumstances', and income inequality and social class are related to homicide (Brookman and Robinson, 2012).

A range of factors underlie these figures. The affluent have more possessions to steal, but can also afford to protect themselves better. Areas are not homogenous, and in many towns and cities, areas subject to regeneration, which have higher victimisation rates, are found in close proximity to deprived areas. Research suggests that a large proportion of burglars do not travel far from home, making these areas more at risk (Bottoms, 2012). Avoidance strategies can also affect victimisation rates; for example, vulnerable groups such as the long-term sick, disabled, elderly or poor fear high levels of crime and are less likely to go out, thus reducing victimisation.

The gap between social groups widens when repeat victimisation is considered. While some people experience no criminal victimisation at all, a small group suffer persistent victimisation and can be described as 'chronic' victims (Hope and Trickett, 2008). In Scotland recent quantitative research has estimated that in 2010–11 a small section, around 0.5 per cent of the population, described as 'personal' victims experienced 5 per cent of all crime, 12 per cent of all personal thefts and robberies and 12 per cent of all assaults and thefts (Norris et al., 2014), whereas 82 per cent, described as non-victims, experienced very little crime. Frequent personal victims were more likely to be living in areas characterised by high deprivation (McVie et al., 2015). While there is less widely available information about risks of repeat victimisation and socio-economic factors, studies using BCS and SCJS data sets do suggest that 'hot spots' of crime identified within neighbourhoods are most often those in the poorest local authority estates (Evans and Fraser, 2003) and Hope (2001) found that concentrations of crime risks coincide with concentrations of the 'poor'. Repeat victimisation from both crimes and incivilities is also underestimated in BCS figures, as respondents are restricted to only six forms, whereas some report 'too many' incidents to recall (Tilley et al., 2011).

Repeated victimisation from incivilities is also important. While often regarded as minor, when repeated, incivilities – which include persistent intimidation or harassment, sometimes on the basis of gender, poverty, race, mental illness or disability, stone throwing and noise, along with exposure to the detritus associated with illegal drug markets – can have a serious impact on feelings of insecurity. These experiences have been associated with the poorest communities and 'hard-pressed' areas. Taking all this into account Bottoms (2012: 263) comments:

> [P]eople living in deprived areas are at risk of suffering relatively high rates of victimisation for household crimes and very high rates of repeated incivilities .... it requires little imagination to recognise that living in the most socially deprived areas can be tough.

It is hardly surprising, therefore, that those of lower socio-economic status score more highly on indicators associated with the 'fear of crime'. Pantazis (2000), using BCS data, found that older people living in areas of multiple deprivation were seven times more likely to feel unsafe than those in less deprived areas, and poor households were more than twice as likely as rich to feel unsafe when alone either at home or in the street after dark. Box 10.2 illustrates these differences. In general, those living in most deprived areas or those perceived to have high levels of disorder, and those with lower incomes are more likely to feel unsafe, to view crime as a problem and be worried about different kinds of crime and anti-social behaviour. This is in turn linked to factors such as home security, insurance and the greater impact of crime on the poor.

BOX 10.2 SOCIO-ECONOMIC STATUS AND FEARS AND WORRIES ABOUT CRIME AND SAFETY

Scotland (MacLeod et al. 2009)

Compared to those living elsewhere in Scotland, those living in the 15 per cent most deprived areas were more likely to:

feel unsafe: 46 compared to 30 per cent;

see crime rates as increasing in their local area: 33 compared to 27 per cent;

view crime as 'a bit of a problem': 62 compared to 51 per cent.

(Continued)

(Continued)

England and Wales in 2008–09 (Walker et al., 2009)

Those in the *lowest income group* (earning under £10,000) compared to the highest (earning over £50,000) were more likely to:

be worried about burglary (18 compared to 6 per cent);

car crime (14 compared to 8 per cent);

violent crime (21 compared to 8 per cent).

Those living in the most deprived areas were also more likely to be worried than those in the least deprived areas about:

burglary (18 compared to 7 per cent);

violent crime (22 compared to 8 per cent).

Northern Ireland (Freel and Campbell, 2012)

People living in *the 20 per cent most deprived areas* were more likely to perceive anti-social behaviour as a problem in their area (33 per cent), along with adults living in social rented accommodation (31 per cent).

Respondents from *low-income households* (under £10,000) expressed higher levels of worry about **crime overall** (14 per cent) and **violent crime** (26 per cent) compared to 8 and 1 per cent.

Respondents from the 20 per cent most deprived areas displayed higher levels of worry about all types of crime and personal safety than those living in the least deprived areas including:

burglary (24 compared to 11 per cent);

car crime (22 compared to 10 per cent);

violent crime (29 compared to 15 per cent);

walking alone after dark (16 compared to 6 per cent).

There was a strong positive correlation between a high level of worry about crime and personal safety and being from a high anti-social behaviour area.

Fear of crime

People in lower income groups were more likely to say their lives are greatly affected by 'fear of crime': 9 in the lowest income group compared to 2 per cent in the highest.

Those living in the 20 per cent most deprived areas were more likely to claim that 'fear of crime' had a detrimental effect on their quality of life, with 9 per cent claiming 'fear of crime' had a great impact and 34 per cent reporting a moderate effect. These proportions compare with 3 and 26 per cent (respectively) within the 20 per cent least deprived areas.

Irrespective of socio-economic factors, home security emerges as a key risk factor for burglary, and is related to household income in that low-income households are most likely to be without *basic* security and the availability of *enhanced* security increases with income. Examining BCS data, Tilley et al. (2011) describe a widening 'vulnerability gap' in the risks of burglary faced by the most and least affluent *despite* an overall reduction in risk due to the 'crime drop' (burglary rates fell around 58 per cent from the mid-1990s) *and* an increase in security amongst the poorest. In Scotland, the research cited above also suggests a growing inequality in victimisation as those described as personal victims have not experienced the reduction in victimisation associated with the crime drop (Norris et al., 2014). Enhanced as opposed to basic security acts as a greater prevention for the worse off and, explain Tilley et al. (2011: 310),

> [t]he better-off can afford more and better security devices .... and they are at lower risk because they live beyond the routine activities and awareness spaces of offenders, who tend to reside in poorer neighbourhoods. That enhanced security confers the least protection to the most affluent may be due to the fact that they are at less initial risk .... and/or their houses are targeted by the most experienced and determined burglars who can outwit security devices. By contrast, the least affluent share the same deprived environments with potential offenders and they may be victimized by opportunistic burglars who could have easily been deterred by elaborate security devices.

Insurance is also related to socio-economic status as its cost generally deters the lowest income groups (Victim Support, 2002), and many insurance companies will not insure those who have been previously victimised, charge higher premiums in some areas (particularly those associated with high crime rates) or insist on the installation of expensive security measures (Victim Support, 2002; Goodey, 2004). Dixon et al. (2006), using BCS figures for 2002/03, found that only 11 per cent of the lowest income households (below £10,000) made an insurance claim following a burglary, compared to 37 per cent of high-earning households (over £30,000).

All of these factors are related to the greater impact of crime on poorer households who report that crimes have affected them very much (Maguire and Kynch, 2000). In a report prepared for the Institute of Public Policy Research (IPPR), Dixon et al. (2006) point out that the impact of crime is most severe for the poorest because, for example, they are less able to replace goods, and if essentials are lost or urgent repairs are required, may fall into debt, having few assets to draw on in emergencies.

There is, therefore, a gap in the risks of victimisation between those of lower and higher socio-economic status, which widens when repeat victimisation and security are considered. The poor suffer most because they are least able to protect themselves and recover from crime, and they fear it most. These factors are interrelated, as Dixon et al. (2006:13) point out:

> [T]he more affluent can afford to live in safer areas, invest in home security devices and take private transport late at night. Their ability to avoid victimization may make them less concerned. On the other hand, poorer households have less choice about where they live, cannot afford to pay for expensive alarm systems or take taxis home in the evenings ... [they] cannot control risks which can in turn exacerbate stress levels.

Furthermore, it can be argued that this research is likely to underestimate the victimisation of the most deprived. It has been seen, for example, that aspects of repeat victimisation are missed, and a reliance on statistical correlations and phrases such as affected 'a little' or 'a lot' may underplay the emotional impact of victimisation while living in a highly stressful and deprived environment. Moreover, it excludes the victimisation of some of the most marginal and deprived – which will be explored below.

Look at the findings of the most recent crime surveys in relation to risks and fear of crime.

- What socio-economic factors are included? How are risks distributed?
- What evidence is there to support the argument that the poor suffer more from crime?
- Outline the main limitations of national crime surveys for exploring crime victimisation and socio-economic status.

EXPOSING THE VICTIMISATION OF THE MOST DISADVANTAGED

Attention now turns to the victimisation of some of the most marginal and disadvantaged groups, some of whom may be caught in a vicious circle of victimisation, disadvantage and more victimisation, leading in some cases to crimes of survival. Many are unable or unwilling to report crimes and suffer from criminalisation. This process is illustrated in Box 10.3.

BOX 10.3 THE VICIOUS CIRCLE – CRIME, VICTIMISATION, DISADVANTAGE AND EXCLUSION

- Victimisation can cause or exacerbate social and economic exclusion. Victims of violence in the home may leave home to escape, 'chronic' victims may make themselves 'intentionally homeless' (Victim Support 2002), and political and state violence and poverty may force people to leave their home countries and seek refuge or work in other countries.
- This increases risks of victimisation. Those who have left home may have to live in poorer and high crime areas, and migrants are vulnerable to exploitation and forced labour by gangmasters, employers or landlords. All of these groups face forms of 'hate crime' – adding to their experiences of victimisation.
- Many are less likely to report crime as they fear the police and other 'authorities' who may not believe them, see them as having contributed to their victimisation, and as offenders rather than victims.
- They are less likely to be offered support or to know about support services.
- Many are subject to 'criminalisation' and seen as a threat – for example, 'beggars', 'street people', 'unwanted migrants'.
- In some cases this can lead to committing crime to obtain basic necessities.
- When caught they are likely to be subject to punitive, exclusionary, responses.

Selected examples are outlined below.

The Homeless

The homeless lack the most basic forms of security and shelter, and have higher rates of victimisation (Pain et al., 2002; McDonagh, 2011). Young homeless people are often victims of violence in the home and are subject to high rates of multiple and repeat victimisation on the streets, in hostels or temporary accommodation and often distrust the police who label them as offenders and do not report crimes (Pain et al. 2002). Being perceived as a threat, they face being forcibly excluded from public spaces, and face violence and harassment from public and private police (Coleman and Sim, 2013).

The Mentally Ill

A report by Victim Support (2013) illustrates the experiences of mentally ill victims who are five times more likely to be victims of assault and three times more likely to be victims of household crimes even after socio-demographic factors are taken into account. Mental illness is related to other forms of disadvantage. The mentally ill suffer from high rates of sexual and domestic violence and can be victimised in psychiatric in-patient settings in which some

(Continued)

(Continued)

report feeling unsafe. Some felt that their illness contributed to violence against them and experienced 'hate crime'. While some reported positive experiences with the police, others feared them, the possibility of being sectioned, felt that they were being blamed for their victimisation and that their mental health problems were being used to discredit them.

Migrants

Migrants, whether legal or irregular, are subject to criminalisation, but face higher rates of victimisation, including that from 'hate crime'. Many are victims of crimes in their countries of origin and some, particularly from poorer countries, face high risks when travelling to Europe – with well-publicised cases of migrants dying in dangerous forms of transport. These issues are related to gender, sexuality, race, religion and globalisation, and this chapter only illustrates highly-selected examples such as:

- *European migrants*: Baker et al. (2013) found that a group of mainly Polish and Portuguese migrants defined themselves as victims, reporting racial discrimination and negative experiences in the workplace and community. A combination of language, understanding, distrust, independence and cultural mores acted as barriers to reporting crime. Geddes et al. (2013), in a detailed report for the Joseph Rowntree Foundation, also found that many Eastern European migrants, including the Roma, were subject to forced labour.
- Goodey (2003, 2004, 2010) has highlighted the victimisation of *irregular migrants* who have either entered Western Europe through smuggling (in which case they have paid for their passage) or trafficking, in itself associated with victimisation. Both groups face multiple forms of victimisation which they are reluctant to report, being afraid of being deported. Many have little or no knowledge of the 'host' country's language and norms of behaviour, do not know about support agencies, and fear the police. Their status denies them the rights associated with citizenship, and unwanted immigrants can be criminalised. Therefore, she comments, 'Illegal migrants are ... at the mercy of individuals and groups who take advantage of their vulnerable situation ... from the human smugglers who profit from people's desire for economic betterment, through to employers who escape health and security payments for illegal workers' (2003: 416).
- *'Sex trafficking'* in which women are typically recruited with attractive offers of (legitimate) employment yet can suffer rape, assault and bullying by traffickers and pimps; being held in brothels and forced to 'service' clients; and having passports removed has received considerable attention (Lee, 2007). As well as the aforementioned problems of contacting agencies, women fear repeat victimisation or intimidation.
- *'Forced labour'* (Geddes et al., 2013), sometimes referred to as 'new slavery', exceeds sex trafficking and affects men, women and children, legal and irregular migrants. Women may be forced to work in 'dirty, dangerous and degrading' industries

(Lee, 2007: 4), often characterised by low pay and casual, seasonal work. Geddes et al. (2013) provide many examples across Britain, in sectors such as domestic labour, restaurants, nail bars, hotel and catering, cleaning and care homes, construction, agriculture and food production. The issue has been highlighted by the then Home Secretary, Teresa May, who introduced a Modern Slavery Bill at the end of 2013. Its provisions, however, have been criticised on the grounds that, while victims were said to be 'at the heart' of the Bill, the rights of victims to protection and support are undefined and victim support is patchy and lacks accountability (Robinson and Falconer, 2013).

PAUSE FOR REVIEW

Identify examples of the victimisation of one particularly marginal group. Outline the spiral of victimisation and further disadvantage this group faces.

THE LIMITATIONS OF CRIMINAL JUSTICE AND VICTIM SUPPORT

Recent decades have seen a raft of measures introduced to place the victim 'at the heart' of the criminal justice process in the UK and elsewhere. While these have made considerable improvements (Hall, 2009), victims can still be characterised as the 'poor relation' (Victim Support, 2011) and continue to express dissatisfaction with aspects of their experiences with criminal justice and support agencies. While there is sparse information specifically about socio-economic status, it can reasonably be deduced that the most deprived and marginal will be more severely affected. In general terms, socio-economic status and class are related to cultural and educational differences, which affect people's ability to negotiate with those perceived to be in authority. The more affluent are more likely to know about their rights as victims (Zedner, 2002) and seek advice about giving evidence. As Goodey (2004: 138) points out, 'the most marginalised and, arguably, the most vulnerable victims have no access to private services they can ill afford, and are often unaware of public services to which they may be entitled.' Some examples follow.

Victims and the police

As seen above, many of the most marginal groups distrust and fear the police. Victims complain about requests for protection not being taken seriously, of not being sufficiently informed about the progress of their case, and in general express less satisfaction with the police than non-victims (Victim Support, 2011). The SCJS (Scottish Government, 2011) found that those living in the most deprived areas were significantly more negative towards the police than others, being less likely to agree that people in their area had confidence in the police and feeling that community relations were poor.

Victim support

A key role of the police is to refer victims to support agencies but levels of referral vary across the country (Victim Support, 2011), and an earlier study suggested that the police may 'filter' out young men from 'rough' areas in the belief that they are aggressors (Maguire and Kynch, 2000). Dixon et al. (2006: 43) refer to a 'support gap', finding that

> nineteen per cent of victims in households with incomes of less than £5,000, surveyed in 2002/03, wanted support but did not receive it, compared to 13 per cent of households with incomes of more than £30,000'

and

> low-income households want a different kind of support service to better-off households ... the former are less likely to be concerned about receiving information about protection and much more likely to ask for more intensive (and costly) help, such as moral support or protection from further victimisation.

Victims in court

Victims' experiences in court have been widely recognised as a problem and it can be argued that lower socio-economic groups are likely to be more adversely affected by some of the most commonly reported areas of dissatisfaction:

- The practical aspects of attendance at court including loss of earnings and the cost of childcare and attending court (Hunter et al., 2013).
- Experiences in the waiting room and environs of the court particularly where encounters with offenders are likely, and where there are long delays (Hall, 2009; Hunter et al. 2013).
- The occupational culture of court professionals in which lower-status victims, who may be regarded as offenders, fall short of conceptions of 'ideal' victims. Hall (2009) cites the example of victims not being given pagers should the case be delayed on the grounds that they might steal them.
- Coping with the often confusing legal language of the court and courtroom proceedings where rules of evidence impede the way in which victims can tell their 'story' (Hall, 2009; Victim Support, 2013). Cross-examination can be particularly stressful, particularly where victims feel that their credibility is being questioned or are suspected to have contributed to their victimisation.
- Vulnerable witnesses often lack explanation of this language, the roles of participants and the processes involved, and some victims have reported a lack of information – about, for example, the provision of special measures or the recording and use of victim impact statements (Hunter et al., 2013).

Victim compensation

Victim compensation arrangements have been found to disadvantage poorer victims in a variety of ways:

- The Criminal Injuries Compensation Scheme (CICS) in England and Wales distinguishes between 'deserving' and 'non-deserving' victims and does not make awards to anyone considered to have contributed to the offence or with a criminal record (Zedner, 2002). This reflects a tendency to segregate 'victims' from 'offenders', which does not well reflect the situation in areas with high concentrations of crime and where violence can follow a long history of intimidation (Victim Support, 2002).
- CICS has a minimum level of awards, over £1,000 in 2005, which excludes the majority of victims of minor assaults and robberies, and a much smaller award could be of considerable benefit to those on a low income (Dignan, 2005).
- Court-ordered compensation may also disadvantage the least affluent as poorer victims are most often victimised by offenders who are also on low incomes or dependent on state benefits. Therefore victims may only receive small amounts over a long period of time (Davies et al., 2003).

Restorative Justice

A victim-centred approach is implied in restorative justice schemes which aim to involve offenders, victims and communities in mediation and reconciliation. Yet they have had severe limitations, particularly in relation to the most marginalised. Restorative justice is, for example, inevitably limited to reported crimes with a known offender (Goodey, 2004), whereas the most excluded groups may not report crimes and are intimidated by offenders. Many victims do not take up their options to participate, some feeling that they do not wish to face 'their' offender (Goodey, 2004).

PAUSE FOR REVIEW

Taking one aspect of criminal justice, outline the limitations of 'victim-centred' policies in helping the most deprived victims.

Taking one aspect of victim support, outline the limitations of 'victim-centred' policies in helping the most deprived victims.

EXCLUDING THE POOR: CRIME, VICTIMISATION, POLICY AND EXCLUSION

The greater and often invisible victimisation of the most disadvantaged and their experiences with agencies can be associated with the widening social inequality and polarisation of social classes linked to globalisation and de-industrialisation. Some social commentators talked of a distinct 'underclass' and 'social exclusion' – both related to increasing levels of crime. At the same time penal policy was characterised by a 'punitive turn', discussed below. Policies, such as high rates of imprisonment, seemed to promise reduced levels of victimisation but have arguably exacerbated social divisions. Moreover, it is important to recognise that polarisation and social exclusion are also affected by political choices. Governmental policies which fail to reduce income and housing inequalities or the current preference for austerity have a more adverse impact on the most disadvantaged. These have very often involved low income and poor-quality work, which in turn are associated with personal debt and exclusion from forms of consumption which are considered as the social norm. This may well trigger crime and exacerbate victimisation (Croall and Mooney, 2015). Box 10.4 summarises the late Jock Young's conception of the exclusive society which highlights these processes.

BOX 10.4 THE EXCLUSIVE SOCIETY

Young argues that there has been a shift from an **inclusive** to an **exclusive society.**

An **inclusive society** is associated with:

- material and ontological security, for example *security of employment and feelings of safety*;
- incorporating members;
- attempts to assimilate deviance and disorder;
- 'deviants' are dealt with in communities and families.

An **exclusive society** is associated with:

- material and ontological precariousness, for example *loss of secure employment and feelings of unsafety*;
- response to deviance involves more exclusion, for example *higher rates of imprisonment*.

Young also talks of a **bulimic society** in which cultural inclusion (all are encouraged to aspire to the same material goals disseminated through mass media and culture) is accompanied by structural exclusion which leads to emotions such as humiliation and degradation.

Relative deprivation accompanied by a culture of individualism leads to

increasing crime which in turn leads to:

further exclusion which is associated with:

- fear of crime, which leads to public avoidance of 'risky' situations;
- rising prison rates involving penal exclusion;

- exclusion from public spaces of groups suspected of 'crime' which can lead to
    - 'barriers' between areas in cities;
    - a cordon sanitaire separating 'winners' from 'losers';
    - the 'outgroup' become scapegoated/defined as 'underclass';
    - processes of demonisation.

Criminology and criminal justice policies based on 'risk management' play a part in this exclusion.

(Based on Young 1999, 2003, 2007)

'Conservative' approaches in criminology and victimology stress the role of human agency and individual responsibility, seeing the 'poor' as responsible both for their economic situation and their crimes – and, by implication, for their victimisation. This view has been reflected in popular notions, from that of the 'criminal underclass' (Murray, 1996), which portrayed a 'culture of dependency' on welfare in which 'families without fathers' lacked clear role models, to the theme of 'Broken Britain' associated with the Centre for Social Justice (2008), which stressed the role of families, individuals and the 'disease' of worklessness. In cities around the world entire areas, often described as 'neighbourhoods from hell', are identified as 'dangerous places' with 'dangerous people' (Mooney, 2008) associated with high levels of incivilities and disorder and inhabited by 'urban outcasts' (Wacquant, 2008, cited in Mooney, 2008: 111).

Polarisation was implicit in the concept of social exclusion, which virtually replaced the term 'poverty' (Grover, 2008) and incorporated wider economic and spatial dimensions. The first 'New Labour' Government set up a Social Exclusion Unit, one of whose targets was the perceived concentration of social problems including crime and incivility in social housing areas (Crawford and Evans, 2012). While appearing to recognise structural economic inequalities, 'weak' and 'strong' versions of social exclusion were identified, with the former stressing the role of individual responsibility, family and economic inactivity and the latter stressing justice, rights and structural inequalities. Many policies of New Labour Governments were seen to reflect the former, weaker, version (Young, 2002; Grover, 2008).

The well-documented 'punitive turn' in penal policy was associated with perspectives emphasising individual responsibility, reflected in notions of:

- *Popular punitivism* (Bottoms, 1994): with all political parties seeking to be 'tough on crime'.
- *Responsibilisation* (Garland, 1996): whereby individuals and communities are expected to take more responsibility for protecting themselves from crime by, for example, installing security devices and taking out insurance policies.

- *Actuarial justice* (Feeley and Simon, 1994): involving concerns with costs and efficiency, risk management and crime reduction targets.
- *Crime prevention*, *reduction* and '*community safety*' policies.

These shifts were accompanied by the so-called 'rediscovery of the victim' and the introduction of more 'victim-centred' policies, with the victim survey being a tool to identify crime 'risks'. Some policies stressed technological security and prevention strategies and others, such as 'community crime prevention' and 'community safety', invoked notions of 'community', which, while seemingly inclusive, raised questions about 'whose safety' was being prioritised (Gilling, 2001), as the most victimised groups such as the homeless were generally excluded from participation. The Social Exclusion unit was phased out in 2002, and New Labour's approach became more punitive, focusing on 'problem groups' and incivilities (Crawford and Evans, 2012).

SECURITY AND EXCLUSION

The security gap between the most and least affluent can be linked to wider exclusionary processes. The more affluent, for example, buy homes in safer, 'exclusive' neighbourhoods, insure these homes, use private security and spatially and culturally distance themselves from high crime areas (Hope, 2000, 2001; Goodey, 2004). To Hope, this reflects the use of economic and social capital, also reflected in participation in schemes such as Neighbourhood Watch, found to work better in more affluent areas. This in effect traps the poor in neighbourhoods with less security. Therefore Hope (2001: 216), concludes, 'in a risk society ... the threat of crime victimization is not just a consequence of social exclusion but also a contributory cause', and Jones (2012: 756) comments that

> effective crime prevention in middle class districts .... work[s] to exclude the poor at the same time as further displacing crime and disorder to disadvantaged areas .... [thus] ... it exacerbates economic disadvantage and social disorganisation in disadvantaged neighbourhoods, and increases the likelihood of further expansion of offending and incivilities.

CITY CENTRES

Recent decades have seen the privatisation of public space in city centres with the spread of, for example, shopping malls and regeneration schemes which aim to promote consumption by the better off (Crawford and Evans, 2012). This can involve the exclusion of the 'suspect population' (Jones, 2012) by, for example, the use of CCTV, with some malls having used formalised exclusion policies. To McCahill and Norris (2003) some groups can be seen as 'victims of surveillance', and Norris and Armstrong (1999: 201) argue that CCTV systems

> rather than contributing to social justice through the reduction of victimization ... may become a tool of injustice through amplification of differential and discriminatory policing.

Looking at Liverpool, which contains some of the most deprived areas of England, Coleman and Sim argue that discourses of regeneration reinforce the moral boundaries between 'regenerated' citizens and those who cannot or will not be psychologically or socially regenerated – the mendicant. The policing of shopping malls includes the targeting of the homeless and, they argue, in these regenerated spaces, idealised citizens stand in binary opposition to the 'degenerate other' – 'the poor' and 'regeneration is likely to intensify already existing injustices and social inequalities' (2013: 30).

PENAL POLICY

Many penal policies are also exclusionary. Prisons and policies such as curfews, electronic tagging and anti-social behaviour orders all aim to exclude those perceived to pose a threat to 'order', a depiction which, as seen above, includes many victims. In Scotland, Houchin (2005) found that a disproportionate number of prisoners were drawn from the most deprived wards and calculated that one in nine young men from the most deprived communities will spend time in prison at the age of 23. Indeed, it has been argued that prisons can be used as part of a process of 'managing the poor' as high rates of imprisonment are not related to rates of crime or victimisation and can be, argues Wacquant (2012: 40), linked to the 'penalisation of poverty', therefore

> you cannot understand trends in offending without factoring in the sea changes in welfare provision, public housing .... and related state programmes, including the oversight of irregular migration, that set the universe of life options of the populations most susceptible to street crime (as both perpetrators and victims).

Outline the way in which crime prevention and penal policies can be regarded as increasing the risks of victimisation for the most disadvantaged.

PAUSE FOR REVIEW

SUMMARY

This chapter has sought to expose the often hidden victimisation of the most disadvantaged in society and has outlined many gaps in experiences between those of low and high socio-economic status, with the former consistently suffering more adversely from victimisation, repeat victimisation, feelings of insecurity and in negative experiences with criminal justice and related areas. These gaps are at their most extreme when the situation of the most deprived groups who are often framed as offenders rather than victims, or at least as less deserving victims, is explored. It has also been seen that much of this victimisation is underestimated in conventional crime surveys, which exclude many victims along with experiences of white-collar crime or crimes of the powerful which also have a more severe impact on the poorest (Croall, 2010, 2011; see also Chapter 16).

Moreover, there are many gaps in the available information. Despite the welter of data provided by victim surveys, there are few breakdowns by socio-economic status on aspects of repeat victimisation and victim satisfaction with support services (Croall and Mooney, 2015). There is also a lack of what Foster (2002) describes as the 'people pieces', qualitative studies exploring the day-to-day experiences of crime, victimisation and social deprivation in areas rather blandly described as 'most deprived' or 'constrained by circumstances'. The late Jock Young (2011), for example, has been extremely critical of the prevalence of quantitative surveys and makes an impassioned call for more use of the 'criminological imagination' and qualitative studies exploring the emotional, cultural and structural aspects of crime and victimisation.

FURTHER READING

Very few books or articles look specifically at the relationships between socio-economic status and victimisation. A good starting point is to look at national crime surveys such as these.

Chaplin, R., Flatley, J. and Smith, K. (eds) (2011) *Crime in England and Wales, 2010/11: Findings from the British Crime Survey and Police Recorded Crime* (2nd edn). London: Home Office.

Scottish Government (2011) *2010/11 Scottish Crime and Justice Survey: Main Findings*. Edinburgh: Scottish Government Social Research.

Freel, R. and Campbell, P. (2012) *Perceptions of Crime: Findings from the 2010/11 Northern Ireland Crime Survey*, Research and Statistical Bulletin 1/2012. Belfast: Northern Ireland Department of Justice, Statistics and Research Branch.

Toner, S. and Freel, R. (2013) *Experience of Crime: Findings from the 2011/12 Northern Ireland Crime Survey*, Research and Statistical Bulletin 1/2013. Belfast: Northern Ireland Department of Justice, Statistics and Research Branch.

See also: Croall, H. (2011) *Crime and Society in Britain*. London: Longman.

This includes some relevant information and analysis on crime and victimisation.

Bottoms, A. (2012) 'Developing socio spatial criminology', in R. Morgan, M. Maguire and R. Reiner (eds), *The Oxford Handbook of Criminology* (5th edn). Oxford: Oxford University Press. pp. 450–89.

This provides a good summary of work on crime, victimisation and area.

McAra, L., McVie, S. and Mellon, M. (eds) (2015) 'Poverty, inequality and justice', *Scottish Justice Matters*, 3(3).

This journal article provides interesting reflections on the complexities of the relationships between crime, victimisation and poverty.

REFERENCES

Baker, S., Madoc-Jones, I., Parry, O., Warren, E., Perry, K., Roscoe K. and Mottershead, R. (2013) 'More sinned against than sinning? Perceptions about European migrants and crime', *Criminology and Criminal Justice*, 13(3): 262–78.

Bottoms, A. (1994) 'The philosophy and politics of punishment and sentencing', in C. Clarkson and R. Morgan (eds), *The Politics of Sentencing Reform*. Oxford: Oxford University Press. pp. 17–49.

Bottoms, A. (2012) 'Developing socio spatial criminology', in R. Morgan, M. Maguire and R. Reiner (eds), *The Oxford Handbook of Criminology* (5th edn). Oxford: Oxford University Press. pp. 450–489.

Brookman, F. and Robinson, A. (2012) 'Violent crime', in R. Morgan, M. Maguire and R. Reiner (eds), *The Oxford Handbook of Criminology* (5th edn). Oxford: Oxford University Press. pp. 563–95.

Centre for Social Justice (2008) *Breakthrough Glasgow: Ending the Costs of Social Breakdown*. London: The Centre for Social Justice. Available at www.centreforsocialjustice.org.uk/client/downloads/BreakthroughGlasgow.pdf (accessed 22.9.10).

Chaplin, R., Flatley, J. and Smith, K. (eds) (2011) Crime in England and Wales 2010/11: Findings from the British Crime Survey and Police Recorded Crime (2nd edn). London: Home Office.

Coleman, R. and Sim, J. (2013) 'Managing the mendicant: regeneration and repression in Liverpool', *Criminal Justice Matters*, 92: 30–31.

Crawford, A. and Evans, K. (2012) 'Crime prevention and community safety', in R. Morgan, M. Maguire and R. Reiner (eds), *The Oxford Handbook of Criminology* (5th edn). Oxford: Oxford University Press. pp. 769–805.

Croall, H. (2010) 'Economic crime and victimology: a critical appraisal', *International Journal of Victimology*, 8(2). Available at www.jidv.com/njidv/index.php/archives/150-jidv-23/425-economic-crime-and-victi5mology-a-critical-appraisal (accessed 12.10.16).

Croall, H. (2011) *Crime and Society in Britain* (2nd edn). Harlow: Pearson.

Croall, H. and Mooney, G. (2015) 'Crime and inequalities in Scotland', in H. Croall, G. Mooney and M. Munro (eds), *Crime, Justice and Society in Scotland*. London: Routledge. pp 45–64.

Davies, P., Francis, P. and Greer, C. (2007) *Victims, Crime and Society*. London: Sage.

Davies, P., Francis, P. and Jupp, V. (2003) 'Victimology, victimization and public policy', in P. Davies, P. Francis and V. Jupp (eds), *Victimization: Theory, Research and Policy*. Basingstoke: Palgrave McMillan.

Dignan, J. (2005) *Understanding Victims and Restorative Justice*. Milton Keynes: Open University Press.

Dixon, M., Reed, H., Rogers, B. and Stone, L. (2006) *CrimeShare: The Unequal Impact of Crime*. London: Institute for Public Policy Research.

Downes, D. (1983) *Law and Order: Theft of an Issue*. London: Blackrose.

Evans, K. and Fraser, P. (2003) 'Communities and victimization', in P. Davies, P. Francis and V. Jupp (eds), *Victimization: Theory, Research and Policy*. Basingstoke: Palgrave McMillan.

Feeley, M. and Simon, J. (1994) 'Actuarial justice: the emerging new criminal law', in D. Nelken (ed.), *The Futures of Criminology*. London: Sage. pp. 173–201.

Foster, J. (2002) '"People pieces": the neglected but essential elements of community crime prevention', in G. Hughes and A. Edwards (eds), *Crime Control and Community: The New Politics of Public Safety*. Cullompton: Willan.

Freel, R. and Campbell, P. (2012) *Perceptions of Crime: Findings from the 2010/11 Northern Ireland Crime Survey*, Research and Statistical Bulletin 1/2012. Belfast: Northern Ireland Department of Justice, Statistics and Research Branch.

Garland, D. (1996) 'The limits of the sovereign state: strategies of crime control in contemporary society', *British Journal of Criminology*, 36: 445–71.

Geddes, A., Craig, G. and Scott, S. with Ackers, L., Robinson, O. and Scullion, D. (2013) *Forced Labour in the UK*. London: Joseph Rowntree Foundation.

Gilling, D. (2001) 'Community safety and social policy', *European Journal on Criminal Policy and Research*, 9: 381–400.

Goodey, J. (2003) 'Migration crime and victimhood: responses to sex trafficking in the EU', *Punishment and Society*, 5(4): 415–31.

Goodey, J. (2004) *Victims and Victimology: Research, Policy and Practice*. London: Pearson Longman.

Goodey, J. (2010) 'Human trafficking', in F. Brookman, M. Maguire, H. Pierpoint and T. Bennett (eds), *Handbook on Crime*. Cullompton: Willan. pp. 698–34.

Greer, C. (2007) 'News media, victims and crime', in P. Davies, P. Francis and C. Greer (eds), *Victims, Crime and Society*. London: Sage. pp. 20–49.

Grover, C. (2008) *Crime and Inequality*. Cullompton: Willan.

Hall, M. (2009) *Victims of Crime: Policy and Practice in Criminal Justice*. London: Routledge.

Hope, T. (2000) 'Inequality and the clubbing of private security', in T. Hope and R. Sparks (eds), *Crime Risk and Insecurity.* London: Routledge. pp. 83–106.

Hope, T. (2001) 'Crime victimization and inequality in risk society', in R. Matthews and J. Pitts (eds), *Crime, Disorder and Community Safety: A New Agenda?* London: Routledge. pp. 193–218.

Hope, T. and Trickett, A. (2008) 'Distribution of crime victimization in the population', *International Review of Victimology*, 15: 37.

Houchin, R. (2005) *Social Exclusion and Imprisonment in Scotland: A Report*. Glasgow: Glasgow Caledonian University. Available at www.scotpho.org.uk/downloads/SocialExclusionandImprisonmentinScotland.pdf (accessed 7.11.16).

Hunter, G., Jacobson J. and Kirby, A. (2013) *Out of the Shadows: Victims and Witnesses Experiences of Attending the Crown Court*. London: Victim Support.

Jones, T. (2012) 'Governing security: pluralization, privatization, and polarization in crime control and policing', in R. Morgan, M. Maguire and R. Reiner (eds), *The Oxford Handbook of Criminology* (5th edn). Oxford: Oxford University Press. pp. 743–68.

Lee, M. (2007) 'Introduction: understanding human trafficking', in M. Lee (ed.), *Human Trafficking*. Cullompton: Willan. pp. 1–25.

MacLeod, P., Page, L., Kinver, A., Iliasov, A., Littlewood, M. and Williams, R. (2009) *2008/9 Scottish Crime and Justice Survey: First Findings*. Edinburgh: Scottish Government Social Research. Available at www.scotland.gov.uk/Resource/Doc/296333/0092084.pdf (accessed 12.10.16).

Maguire, M. and Kynch, J. (2000) 'Public perceptions and victims' experiences of victim support: findings from the 1998 British Crime Survey', Home Office Occasional Paper. London: Home Office Research, Development and Statistics Directorate.

Mawby, R. and Walklate, S. (1994) *Critical Victimology: The Victim in International Perspective*. London: Sage.

McCahill, M. and Norris, C. (2003) 'Victims of surveillance', in P. Davies, P. Francis V. and Jupp (eds), *Victimization: Theory, Research and Policy*. Basingstoke: Palgrave McMillan. pp. 121–47.

McDonagh, T. (2011) *Tackling Homelessness and Exclusion: Understanding Complex Lives*. London: Joseph Rowntree Foundation.

McVie, S., Norris, P. and Pillinger, R. (2015) 'Is poverty reflected in changing patterns of victimisation in Scotland?', in *Scottish Justice Matters*, 3(3).

Mooney, G. (2008) '"Problem" populations, "problem" places', in N. Newman and N. Yeates (eds), *Social Justice: Welfare, Crime and Society*. Maidenhead: Open University Press. pp. 97–128.

Mooney, G., Croall, H. and Munro, M. (2010) 'Social inequalities and criminal justice in Scotland', in H. Croall, G. Mooney and M. Munro (eds), *Criminal Justice in Scotland*. Cullompton: Willan.

Murray, C. (1996) 'The underclass', in J. Muncie, E. McLaughlin and M. Langan (eds), *Criminological Perspectives*. London: Sage.

Norris, C. and Armstrong, G. (1999) *The Maximum Surveillance Society: The Rise of CCTV*. Oxford: Berg.

Norris, P., Pillinger, R. and McVie, S. (2014) *Changing patterns of victimization in Scotland 1993–2011*, Research Briefing 2. Edinburgh: Applied Quantitative Methods Network, Edinburgh University.

Pain, R., Francis, P., Fuller, I., O'Brien, K. and Williams, S. (2002) *Hard to Reach Young People and Community Safety: A Model for Participation, Research and Consultation*, Police Research Series Paper 152. London: Home Office Research Development and Statistics Directorate.

Pantazis, C. (2000) '"Fear of crime", vulnerability and poverty: evidence from the British Crime Survey', *British Journal of Criminology*, 40(3): 414–36.

Robinson, C. and Falconer, C. (2013) 'Theresa May's modern slavery bill will fail to provide protection to victims', *Guardian*, 20 December. Available at www.theguardian.com/global-development-professionals-network/2013/dec/20/theresa-may-modern-slavery-bill (accessed 12.12.16).

Scottish Government (2011) *2010/11 Scottish Crime and Justice Survey: Main Findings*. Edinburgh: Scottish Government Social Research.

Tilley, N., Tseloni, A. and Farrell, G. (2011) 'Income disparities of burglary risk: security availability during the crime drop', *British Journal of Criminology*, 51(2): 296–313.

Toner, S. and Freel, R. (2013) *Experience of Crime: Findings from the 2011/12 Northern Ireland Crime Survey*, Research and Statistical Bulletin 1/2013. Belfast: Northern Ireland Department of Justice, Statistics and Research Branch.

Victim Support (2002) *Criminal Neglect: No Justice Beyond Criminal Justice*. London: Victim Support.

Victim Support (2011) *Summing Up: A Strategic Audit of the Criminal Justice System*. London: Victim Support.

Victim Support (2013) *At Risk, Yet Dismissed: the Criminal Victimization of People with Mental Health Problems*. London: Victim Support. Available at www.victimsupport.org.uk/sites/default/files/At%20risk%2C%20yet%20dismissed%20-%20summary.pdf (accessed 7.11.16).

Wacquant, L. (2008) *Urban Outcasts*. Cambridge: Polity Press.

Wacquant, L. (2012) 'The punitive regulation of poverty in the neo-liberal age', *Criminal Justice Matters*, 89: 38–40.

Walker, A., Flatley, J., Kershaw, C. and Moon, D. (eds) (2009) *Crime in England and Wales 2008/09, Volume 1. Findings from the British Crime Survey and Police Recorded Crime*, Home Office Statistical Bulletin. London: Home Office. Available at webarchive.nationalarchives.gov.uk/20110218135832/rds.homeoffice.gov.uk/rds/pdfs09/hosb1109summ.pdf (accessed 7.11.16).

Walklate, S. (2003) 'Can there be a feminist victimology?', in P. Davies, P. Francis and V. Jupp (eds), *Victimization: Theory, Research and Policy*. Basingstoke: Palgrave McMillan.

Walklate, S. (2007) *Imagining the Victim of Crime*. Maidenhead: McGraw Hill/Open University Press.

Young, J. (1999) *The Exclusive Society*. London: Sage.

Young, J. (2002) 'Crime and social exclusion', in M. Maguire, R. Morgan and R. Reiner (eds), *The Oxford Handbook of Criminology* (3rd edn). Oxford: Oxford University Press.

Young, J. (2003) 'Merton with energy, Katz with structure: the sociology of vindictiveness and the criminology of transgression', *Theoretical Criminology*, 7(3): 389–414.

Young, J. (2007) *The Vertigo of Late Modernity*. London: Sage.

Young, J. (2011) *The Criminological Imagination*. London: Sage.

Zedner, L. (2002) 'Victims', in M. Maguire, R. Morgan and R. Reiner (eds), *The Oxford Handbook of Criminology* (3rd edn). Oxford: Oxford University Press.

11 RACE, RELIGION, VICTIMS AND CRIME

Colin Webster

Debates about ethnicity, **race** and crime in the popular and criminological imagination have revolved around the question of whether minority ethnic groups offend at a higher rate than white groups. There has been a particular focus on the prevalence of homicide, gun and knife crime, street robbery and drug-related gang crime among young men and children from minority ethnic backgrounds. This focus on minority *offenders* can be contrasted with a lesser focus given to ethnic groups' experience as crime *victims*, particularly *racist* victimisation (Phillips and Bowling, 2012). The best evidence available about perpetrators and victims among white, black and minority ethnic groups suggests that the greater attention given to ethnically-based offending compared to ethnically-based experiences of being a victim of crime is misplaced (Phillips and Webster, 2014). Apart from the distortion created by an unjustified attention given to the ethnic background of perpetrators, such attention generates racial bias in encouraging us to think of minorities as disproportionately perpetrators of crime rather than – more accurately – disproportionately victims of crime, particularly violence and crimes affecting the person.

This chapter will describe patterns and trends of victimisation and risk by race and ethnic origin; victimisation and risk by religion; hate crime and homicide victims by race and ethnic origin. It will offer some explanations and interpretations of racist victimisation and will introduce some theories and concepts about homicide and violent racism.

PATTERNS AND TRENDS

Ethnic risks of being a victim of crime

A key source of evidence of victimisation remains the Crime Survey for England and Wales (CSEW) for adults and children, and official police recorded statistics for homicide, racist incidents and **racially and religiously aggravated** offences. Data on ethnicity and victim experiences from the CSEW are self-reported based on interviews – whether or not the crime has been reported to the police – whereas for homicides data are based on police recorded ethnic appearance. Police recorded victim experiences depend on victims reporting the incident to the police. The willingness of individuals to report incidents is much less than their actual occurrence, causing a large amount of under-reporting of victims' experiences.

The most recent available data from the Ministry of Justice (2014) about the risks of crime comparing different ethnic groups showed differences in the relationship between victims and offenders, and in the nature and sorts of victimisation between groups. Although the CSEW indicates that the risk of being a victim of personal crime[1] was higher for members of all **Black and Minority Ethnic (BME)** groups than for the White group, the number of ***racist* incidents** and racially or religiously aggravated offences recorded by the police have decreased over the last five years. Over the same period the risk of being a victim of personal crime decreased for whites but remained the same for minority groups. There is, however, little room for complacency, as race and religious hate crimes have significantly increased over the last few years (Office for National Statistics, 2014). This may, according to the Home Office, be partly due to higher levels of hate crime following the murder of Lee Rigby, as well as due to recent Islamist Terrorist attacks in Tunisia in June 2015 and Paris in November 2015.

Highlighting the most significant findings to emerge from previous British Crime Surveys (BCS) and CSEW 2012/13 interviews and police records about ethnicity and victim experiences, there is a somewhat mixed picture (Home Office, 2011; Hoare et al., 2011; Smith et al., 2011; Office for National Statistics, 2013, 2014):

- *Worry about crime*: findings from the 2010 BCS showed that a higher proportion of children in the BME group reported that they avoided travelling on buses because they were worried about their safety or avoided using a mobile phone in public all or most of the time (22 per cent and 30 per cent respectively) than in the White group (14 per cent and 22 per cent respectively).
- *Disproportionate homicide*: of the 2,007 homicides recorded for the period 2007 to 2010, the proportions are very significantly lower for the White group and higher for the Black and Asian groups than reflected in estimates of the general population. In the majority of homicide cases, victims are suspected of being killed by someone from the same ethnic group, which is consistent with previous trends.
- *Racially or religiously motivated crime decline*: there was an 18 per cent decrease in the number of recorded racist incidents and a 26 per cent decrease in racially or religiously aggravated offences across England and Wales over the 5-year period 2006 to 2010/11. There has, however, as already noted, been a recent rise.

The 2011 BCS (see Figure 11.1) and CSEW showed that:

- Only 6 per cent of White adults reporting having been victims of personal crime compared with 8 per cent of those from BME backgrounds.
- The highest proportion of being victimised involving personal crime was reported by the mixed ethnic group, followed by Chinese or Other, Asian and Black (7 per cent).

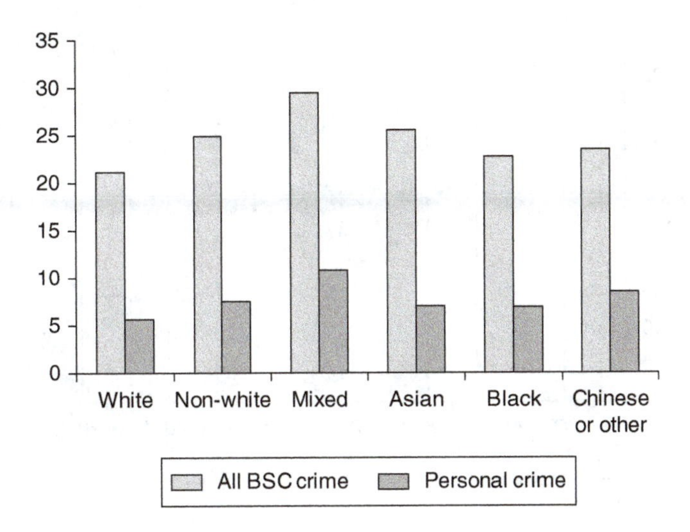

Figure 11.1 Proportion of adults who were victims of all crime and personal crime by ethnicity (Chaplin et al., 2011)

- Between 2006 and 2013, there was a decline in the percentage of respondents in all ethnic groups who had been victims of personal crime but the change was statistically significant only for the White group (see Figure 11.2).

Interpreting CSEW data, it should be noted that differences in the risk of victimisation between ethnic groups may be partly attributable to factors other than ethnicity, although

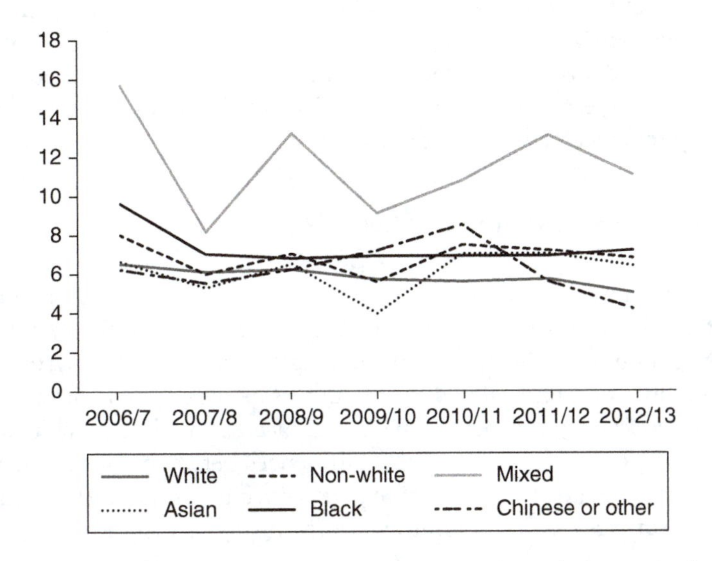

Figure 11.2 Proportion of adults by ethnicity who were victims of personal crime (ONS, 2014)

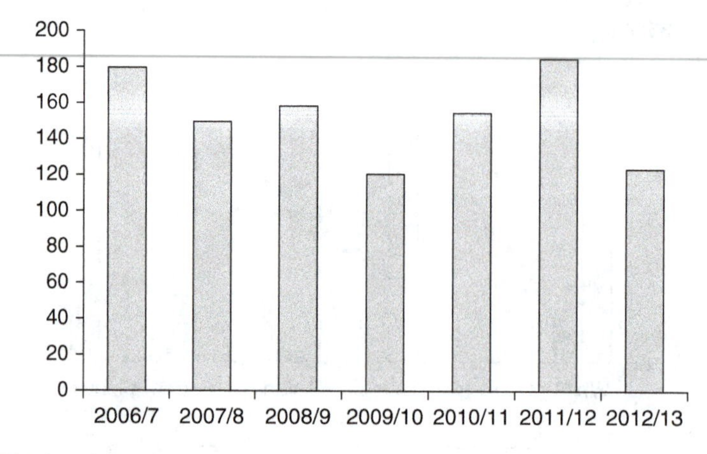

Figure 11.3 Total racially motivated crime (in thousands) (ONS, 2014)

ethnicity seems the overriding factor for people with a mixed ethnic background who are most at risk of crime (Jansson et al., 2007; Salisbury and Upson, 2004). Where the relative contribution of a number of different factors are examined, although ethnicity was associated with the risk of violence, it was less important than other factors such as age, sex and marital status (see Flatley et al., 2010).

Trends in the total number of racially motivated incidents from 2006 to 2013 as reported by adults responding to the BCS are shown in Figure 11.3. Although racially motivated incidents represented a small proportion of all offences reported by adults, their actual and symbolic impact on individuals, places and minority groups over time can be much greater than their relative and absolute numbers compared to other sorts of personal crime and crime overall. Noting the difference between police recorded decreases in incidents mentioned already and racially motivated incidents reported to the BCS and CSEW over the seven-year period 2006 to 2013 it would appear there is a stable pattern of incidents despite fewer being reported to the police.

Children, ethnicity and risk

Until recently our knowledge about the risks of being a victim of crime among children from different ethnic groups has been based on relatively small-scale data. Since 2010 the CSEW has asked about experience of crime and gathered information from children aged 10 to 15 on a number of crime-related topics such as experience and attitudes towards the police, personal safety, being in public spaces and access to leisure facilities (Hoare et al. 2011). In particular, ethnic similarities and differences between children from White and BME backgrounds in regard to fear of crime, exposure to risk, and the precautions taken to avoid becoming a victim. The findings were (Ministry of Justice, 2013):

- A higher proportion of children from the BME group (22 per cent) than White group (14 per cent) reported that they avoided travelling on buses at times of the day because they were worried about their safety or other causing trouble.
- Similarly, 30 per cent of children from a BME background reported avoiding using a mobile phone in public all or most of the time compared with 22 per cent of White children, and 42 per cent of BME children said they avoided using a mobile phone in certain places all or most of the time compared with 36 per cent of White children.
- In contrast, the proportion of children who reported they had experienced bullying in the last year was higher for White children (23 per cent) than for children from a BME background (17 per cent).
- The proportion of children aged 13 to 15 who agreed or disagreed that carrying a knife meant they were more likely to get stabbed themselves was very similar, with 70 per cent of White children and 66 per cent of Non-White agreeing, and 17 per cent from both groups disagreeing with the statement.

RACIST AND RELIGIOUS VICTIMISATION AND HATE CRIME

Racist incidents are recorded by the police and, following the recommendation of the Stephen Lawrence Inquiry (Macpherson, 1999), refer to 'any incident which is perceived to be racist by the victim or any other person'. The Ministry of Justice (2013) shows the majority of racist incidents recorded involve either damage to property or verbal harassment.

Figures for racist incidents reported to the police in England and Wales show that (Ministry of Justice, 2013):

- Overall, 51,187 racist incidents were recorded by the police in 2010/11 – a decrease of almost 18 per cent over the five years 2006 to 2011, the largest reductions in the number of racist incidents recorded in the Metropolitan and West Midlands police forces.
- This overall downward trend for the 5-year period was not shared by all police force areas (PFAs). Eleven PFAs showed an increase, with South Wales recording the largest rise (of 36 per cent). This geographic variation is important and will be returned to below.

Regarding racially and religiously aggravated offences recorded by the police, these comprise the following offences: harassment; actual bodily harm and grievous bodily harm without intent; criminal damage; and assault without injury.

- Harassment was the main type of racially or religiously aggravated offence, accounting for over two-thirds (70 per cent) of all offences recorded for 2010/11, followed by assault without injury (12 per cent), assault occasioning actual bodily harm (9 per cent) and criminal damage (8 per cent). Grievous bodily harm amounted to less than 1 per cent of all recorded offences.
- There was an overall decrease in racially or religiously aggravated offences of 26 per cent over the 5-year period from 2006 to 2011, although this varied geographically.
- For 2010/11, the clear-up rate for racially or religiously aggravated harassment was 10 per cent lower than for non-racially or religiously aggravated harassment (46 per cent compared with 56 per cent) but higher for assault without injury (45 per cent compared with 33 per cent) and actual bodily harm (46 per cent compared with 40 per cent).

Figure 11.4 shows in a fairly spectacular way some of the issues surrounding the discrepancy between reporting and recording crime and the actual incidence of this crime. This discrepancy has been shown to be particularly true of racist victimisation. As the graph shows, dramatic rises in reported racist incidents from 1998/9 can almost certainly be accounted for by a greater willingness on the part of victims to report and changed police recording practices – especially in London – directly as a result of the Macpherson inquiry and changes in the law. The effect of the Macpherson inquiry (Macpherson, 1999) and its endorsement at the time by government and police was to greatly increase confidence among victims that their victimisation would be taken seriously and be dealt with more

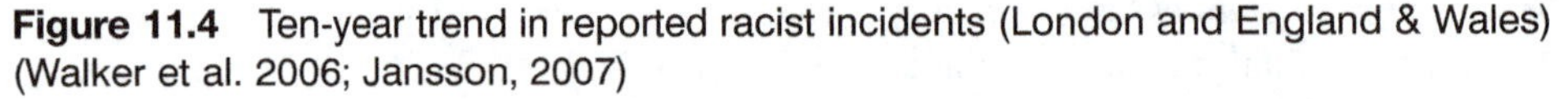
Figure 11.4 Ten-year trend in reported racist incidents (London and England & Wales) (Walker et al. 2006; Jansson, 2007)

sympathetically by the police (or, at the very least that the police were forced to take a victim-centred approach). All reported racist incidents must be interpreted with caution, not only because of a large amount of under-reporting (revealed by Figure 11.4 in the rapid uptake of reporting opportunities that previously hadn't been in place), but because either victims or the police may have considered the offence too trivial, not believed, or deemed not to refer to a criminal offence.

ETHNICITY AND HOMICIDE VICTIMS

There is a marked over-representation of minority ethnic groups among homicide victims. Contrary to what is sometimes thought, the overwhelming majority of homicides are *intra*-ethnic. Figure 11.5 shows the extent to which ethnic minorities are over-represented in the homicide statistics relative to their representation in the general population.

A proper understanding of why this should be the case is, as yet, lacking. So far, the limited amount of research about gun and knife crime within black communities remains undecided whether the growth of homicide in this group – against a general national decline in homicides – is a feature of ethnicity or class. Homicides have generally very significantly increased among young, urban, poor men, particularly since a rapid growth in poverty in certain areas from the 1980s (Bullock and Tilley, 2002; Pitts, 2008). At the same time it should be remembered that gun homicide among black people is relatively rare, so these crimes need to be kept in perspective (Phillips and Bowling, 2012).

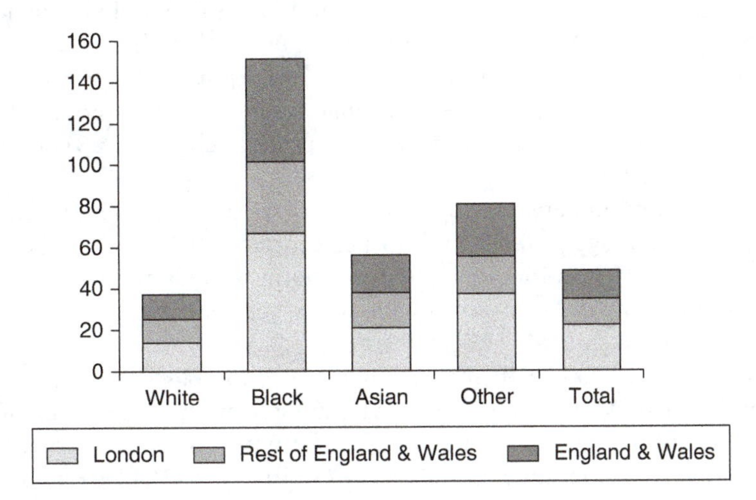

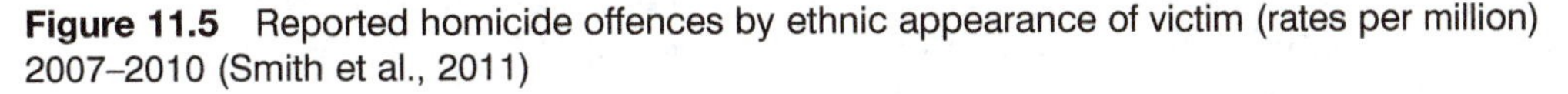

Figure 11.5 Reported homicide offences by ethnic appearance of victim (rates per million) 2007–2010 (Smith et al., 2011)

Information on the ethnic appearance of victims and suspects is available from the Homicide Index, and is a better source of data on these offences than the main recorded crime dataset.[2] Figures for 2007 to 2010 suggest:

- Of the 2,007 homicides recorded over this period, 75 per cent of all homicide victims were White, 12 per cent Black, 8 per cent Asian, 3 per cent were from other ethnic groups, and the ethnicity of 2 per cent of victims was unknown.
- These proportions are broadly similar to those recorded 2001 to 2007, but are lower for the White group and higher for the Black and Asian groups than estimated for the general population (89 per cent of the population were from the White ethnic group, 3 per cent Black and 6 per cent Asian during this 3-year period).
- Homicide by sharp instrument was the most common method of killing across all ethnic groups, but a greater proportion of Black victims were killed this way than other groups, and a greater proportion of Black homicide victims were killed by shooting (25 per cent) compared with other ethnic groups (White 4 per cent, Asian 7 per cent and Other 10 per cent).
- In the majority of homicide cases, victims were suspected of being killed by someone from the same ethnic group, which is consistent with previous trends.
- While data for this period show that homicides for particular ethnic groups are concentrated in particular areas (i.e. with Black homicide victims concentrated in the Metropolitan, West Midlands and Greater Manchester police force areas), these differences reflect, in part, the resident population of these areas and the increased risk of being a victim of homicide in an urban area.

Of key importance from the data is that Black and Asian people have higher homicide rates when compared with White people. For example, Black males, at a homicide rate of 68 offences per million population, are almost six times more likely to be a victim of homicide than White males (12 offences per million population). Although the difference is less, Black females were still nearly three times more likely to be a victim of homicide than White female victims.

In summary, in London between 1999 and 2006, 64 per cent of all homicide victims were young black men aged 10–17 and 58 per cent aged 18–20, yet black men make up only 7 per cent of London's population. Nationally, between 2007 and 2010, 12 per cent of homicide victims were black and 8 per cent Asian. Black victims were much more likely to be children and young people, and homicide by sharp instrument and shooting was much more likely within this group. Black victims were concentrated in London, the West Midlands and Manchester, with 63 per cent of all victims in London, and killings tended to be intra-ethnic with 78 per cent of Black victims killed by someone from the same ethnic group (Smith et al., 2011). Explanations as to why Black young people living in particular places are more likely to rob or be killed than other groups are found in the individual and group dynamics of particular neighbourhoods and geographies (see Box 11.1).

BOX 11.1 YOUNG BLACK PEOPLE AND THE CRIMINAL JUSTICE SYSTEM

Black young people were much more likely to fall victim to violent and weapon-enabled crime, including homicide involving guns, than White people, but no more likely than White people to fall victim to some other sorts of non-violent crime. In London, the largest numbers of homicides in the Black group were of males aged 21–30, but the greatest disproportionality was at younger ages, where Black males accounted for nearly two-thirds of all murders of 10–17 year olds (see Figure 11.5).

Although The British Crime Survey had shown over many years that all ethnic minorities worried more about crime than White people, many of the Committee's witnesses said young Black people live in sustained fear of victimisation:

> 'Many people in my community live in absolute terror, and they have armed themselves in response to that terror.'
>
> 'We heard that the safety of young people travelling to and from schools is an issue which comes up "continually" in some schools.'
>
> 'Throughout the inquiry, it was emphasised to us that young Black people primarily fear being attacked by someone of the same ethnicity.'
>
> 'Young Black people's fear of crime is typically to do with them being attacked by other young Black people.'

(House of Commons, 2007)

How are risk and fear of crime connected to the vulnerability of BME groups?

What factors may affect whether BME group's report their experiences to the police and to victimisation surveys?

What are the advantages and disadvantages of counting racist victimisation?

Summarise and account for recent trends in racist victimisation.

EXPLANATIONS AND INTERPRETATIONS

Patel and Tyrer (2011) provide a particularly useful introduction to different ways of thinking about race, religion, victims and crime. On the one hand, Patel and Tyrer argue that an overwhelming focus on black-on-black crime, especially in the US, diverts our attention away from the criminal justice system and racial oppression, and is in any case uncommon. On the other, that a significant number of studies still show high rates of offending amongst some black and minority ethnic groups, and this must be examined. However, the refocussing on 'black criminality' and 'black-on-black' violence in the contemporary period serves to obscure and detract from the extent of 'white-on-minority' violence and the high numbers of racially motivated attacks against black and minority ethnic people (2011: 7). This argument takes us back to an earlier point at the beginning of this chapter about how public perceptions have emphasised elevated crime rates among visible minorities and immigrants, and downplayed their greater victimisation. Indeed, their wide-ranging discussion of substantive issues and contexts within the race and crime debate shows victimisation of visible minorities are systematically downplayed compared with an all too willing public embrace of an alleged pervasive minority criminality. Similarly, Phillips and Bowling (2012: 378) argue that 'Minority ethnic groups' experience as crime victims has rarely been at the heart of the "race and crime debate"', although suggesting that '*racist* victimisation' (however momentarily) was accorded 'full public recognition' with the publication of the Stephen Lawrence Inquiry. Even this – belated – recognition has recently come under scrutiny with the discovery that the Metropolitan Police were spying on the family and their supporters during their campaign to seek justice. How, then, are we to begin to understand and explain – rather than merely describe – relationships of race, ethnicity and victimisation? The remainder of this chapter focuses on the motivations of perpetrators of race hate in order to explore this question.

CONTEXT: HATE CRIME AND RACIST VIOLENCE

In explaining hate crime and racist harassment and/or violence, a key idea to keep at the forefront of thinking about these sorts of offences is that hate crime and violent racism belong to a social process (Maclean, 1986; Bowling, 1999; Chahal, 1999). Unlike some other sorts of offences whereby individuals are criminally victimised, hate crimes and racist violence are rarely one-off 'incidents' to which the police react and respond. Such 'incidents' usually have a history, context and belong to a process of cumulative incidents against a person, any one of which seen in isolation may appear fairly trivial in the eyes of the police and others but taken together amount to a cumulative and increasingly serious process targeting an individual, household or family. If incidents are perceived by the police as 'one-off', they will be perceived and reacted to by the police inadequately. This is also the situation with other sorts of personal crimes such as domestic violence, which shows the same sorts of ambiguity by the police towards the victim.

Further, even the ground-breaking Stephen Lawrence Inquiry – which brought violent racist victimisation to the centre of public and police attention – failed to really address, locate or explain the racist motivation behind the behaviour:

> The Macpherson definition is 'business as usual' in its misunderstanding of what racist harassment is and why racist incidents occur, and a definition which cannot adequately locate the motivation behind a racist incident is of little practical use to clarifying meaning. The paradox is that the Macpherson Report openly discusses 'racism', and '**institutional racism**', particularly with regard to it disadvantaging minority ethnic people, and yet locating racism as a motivation for suffering a racist incident and its prime target being black and minority ethnic people is generally ignored by the Inquiry Report. In attempting to clarify what institutional racism is, the Inquiry should have also attempted to clarify what a 'racist incident' is, who it is aimed at and why. (Chahal, 1999: Para. 1.6)

Often then the counting of, policy responses to, and common understandings of, hate crimes and racist victimisation have failed to acknowledge that these crimes are against a whole group or community, not just the immediate individual victim(s), as they are perceived by the perpetrator to be representative of the group. As such they are related to wider and deeper causes found in embedded racist ideologies and marginalised white ethnicity and identity (Phillips and Webster, 2014). Hate crimes are implicated in relationships of power and domination between minority and majority communities – relationships, moreover, that are dynamic and change and involve a range of responses from those targeted, not only victimisation but defence and retaliation too. In particular, the implications are that reactive policing responses in themselves are unsatisfactory and more effective responses and prevention may well emerge from the communities affected (Bowling, 1993, Webster, 1996, 1997).

Other writers have pointed to the political contexts and dimensions of hate crime and racist violence. For example, Patel and Tyrer (2011) have suggested that the political context of racist hate crime in the contemporary period has taken a cultural and religious turn from visible racism to anti-Muslim racism. Another aspect of the changed political context in which racist violence may be understood features in the work of Phillips and Webster (2014). They argue that in effect, in the recent period, racism is seen to have left the mainstream and absented itself from institutions and officialdom. Because of this apparent moral censure of racist expression and absence of racial discrimination found in mainstream attitudes – shown by attitude surveys and reinforced by anti-discrimination and formal equality legislation on grounds of ethnicity, race and religion – then residual racism must be exceptional, only found within marginal groups and classes.

Sometimes the thesis that racism has declined in the current period has implied that it belongs to a marginalised, increasingly embattled and shrinking white working-class minority defending white identity from social, cultural and economic change leading to disadvantage. Hate crime is often associated with white working-class disadvantage (Ray and Smith, 2004; Gadd and Dixon, 2011), though the nature of this relationship is unclear. Patel and Tyrer (2011) argue that government's recent though belated recognition and criminalisation of hate crime – particularly since the Stephen Lawrence Inquiry – has been in the face of counter tendencies towards first, rejecting '**multicultural society**' as a model governing ethnic relations, and second, increasing official hostility to immigrants and asylum seekers, as well as the emergence of Muslims as a focus for racism encouraged by successive Terrorism Acts and **Islamophobia**.

RESEARCHING VIOLENT RACISM

It has already been suggested that the failure of many political and policy responses to **violent racism** is often a consequence of relying on surveys of victims rather than understanding the motivations of the perpetrators of violent racism. Nonetheless, some of the best insights about victim experiences have come from qualitative studies rather than surveys such as Chahal and Julienne (1999) (see Box 11.2).

BOX 11.2 RESEARCH BY CHAHAL AND JULIENNE (1999)

Research on the experiences of 74 people in Belfast, Cardiff, Glasgow and London using focus groups and in-depth interviews found that:

- Racism is routine, everyday and varied in its situations, settings and behaviours. The home, shops, the street and school are just some of the places where racist abuse, harassment, insulting behaviour and violence can occur. The home in particular featured as a target for attacks, and experiences of unprovoked threats and assault were by no means unusual.
- Violent racism is a social process. It has a profound effect beyond the actual event or incident influencing a whole range of human relationships from immediate family relations between spouses, parents and children to relatives and friends. Apart from the negative effects on health and well-being, it can lead to extreme household social isolation, children's fear travelling to and from school, and playing outside.
- The experiences of racist victimisation are not captured by the policies and procedures meant to tackle it and support victims. The presence of racist motivation is often questioned or not taken seriously by reporting agencies, and the agencies themselves were limited in encouraging victims to come forward for help and guidance.
- Many victims did not report their experiences to an agency professionally tasked to investigate the complaint, and when they did report were often met with limited feedback about their case and no support as complainants, so support was often sought from within the victim's family.

Leaving aside these assuredly important experiences of victims of racist crime, we now need to turn to the question of who are these racist offenders and what do we know about them given that there are 18 racist incidents to every 1 individual offender either cautioned by the police or convicted of racially aggravated charges by the courts.

Research into racist offenders and perpetrators – particularly their motivations and the varied situations and conditions in which violence occurs – is arguably now generally accepted as the best way forward in devising policies to tackle racist victimisation and violence.

Identifying and understanding the motivations and situations of the source of racism among perpetrators (Webster, 2007; Sibbitt, 1997; Ray and Smith, 2001, 2004; Ray et al., 2003, 2004) is therefore key. Because this sort of research is driven more by a desire to explain the causes and interpret the meanings behind violent racism, approaches tend to take a qualitative in-depth approach rather than a survey approach.

Research carried out by Sibbitt (1997) in two London boroughs emphasised the importance of the 'perpetrator community' or the community context that may encourage or even be unknowingly complicit in violent racism. This suggests 'communities, with their own entrenched problems of socio-economic deprivation and crime, appear to "spawn" violent perpetrators through a mutually supportive relationship between the individual perpetrator and the wider community' (p. 101). Perpetrators then may regard themselves as acting as proxies for the collective racist views of a community. As in other studies of perpetrators a recurring story was the self-perception by perpetrators that they rather than their real victims were the victims by virtue of the presence of visible minorities held responsible for their personal dissatisfaction, frustration and alienation, and relegation to second-class citizens compared to the perceived preferential treatment of black people. Sibbitt argued that racism (if not violence) varies by age and social group experiences and perceptions within the communities studied:

- *The pensioners* having lived in an area for a long time project insecurities from worsening financial and physical local conditions onto black people in general. This scapegoating is reinforced by official hostility to immigration while excluding local black neighbours who they see as 'different'.
- *The people next door* are adults influenced by their parent's racialisation of social problems like unemployment and crime who take a dim view of local authorities' failure to provide the resources to solve these problems while favouring the allocation of resources towards ethnic minorities. The people next door may be racist towards those they deem obtain unfair advantage in, for example, better accommodation.
- *The problem family* experiences poor health, education and abusive relationships intergenerationally, within and without the family such that anti-social behaviour is common, including possibly virulent racism towards ethnic minority neighbours.
- *15–18 year olds* growing up with parents and grandparents having racist views in an area where such attitudes are normal and prevalent, and despite having black friendships, associate with particularly racist older youths who have engaged with a range of violence and anti-social behaviour including racist harassment or violence.
- *11–14 year olds* also grown up among area prevalence of racism who are educationally disengaged – like their parents were – having low self-esteem, engage in bullying other children to gain prestige, including racist abuse of ethnic minority children.
- *4–10 year olds* surrounded by the language of racism in their upbringing and extended familiar and peer networks.

This study began to delineate the complexity of violent racism and point to the need for more refined policy responses beyond a generalised and simplistic binary of 'victims' and 'perpetrators'. A complimentary age- and social-group related study of violent racism by

Colin Webster (1996, 1997, 2007) argued that violent racism is embedded in the drawing of boundaries around real or imagined 'colour-coded' areas from which social relationships form between interdependent minority and majority ethnic groups who come into conflict over power and territory. Such areas define for each ethnic group not only where it is safe to go and who to associate with but help form ethnic and racial identity. Safety and identity were mutually reinforcing touchstones of identity between the groups. In studying adolescent perpetrators and victims of racist harassment and violence, Webster suggested that it was possible to delineate three overlapping levels of racism each roughly corresponding to different typical perpetrator groups:

- *Normal racists* were individuals least involved in violent sorts of racism. Racism was not directed at those ethnic minority individuals – often in the same group – the group knew personally. In this group the use of racist abuse was routine and 'normal', and 'normal' fighting was differentiated from violent racism, the latter condemned and disapproved.
- *Aggressive racists* were teenage men aged between 14 and 15 years at the time who, while having been involved in some violent racism at school when younger (at this age), later after leaving school were less overtly violent in their behaviour. Their attitudes, however, continued to be hostile towards visible minorities.
- *Violent racists* were aged 12 to 13, apart from a couple of older boys, and the majority were from a socially disadvantaged and feared housing estate, with a disproportionate number of the group likely to have experienced acute family pressures, conflicts and loss. Their aggressive racism was palpable, shown whenever the group were in proximity to Asians or Asian areas.

Webster identified a number of analytical themes which, he argued, could help explain different individual and group expressions of racism including violence:

- *The continuum of criminality, violence and violent racism*: Although different levels and intensities of violence were displayed by the three groups, there was a common and strong pattern that linked delinquency and criminality with general violence which predicted an increased likelihood of violent racist behaviours.
- *The continuum of normal, aggressive and violent racists*: The three groups did not express strict categories of racist behaviours. Instead, individuals could move into and out of categories according to changes in age and situation. The normality of racism in the wider youth population in this place at the time of the study did, however, give some legitimacy to a group of hard-core violent racists, which it otherwise may not have had.
- *The influence of locality and territory*: Locality and territory and the policing of their 'boundaries' by aggressive racists in public places defined where it was safe to 'belong', 'be seen' and associate, although boundaries shifted as skirmishes contested, established or 'settled' territories. As a consequence most violent racist assaults occurred at or near these contested boundaries while 'agreed' racialised territories reduced violence. Each ethnic group routinely referred to the others' locality as 'no-go areas'.

- *Process of class as well as race*: These processes relate to the perceived competition over scarce resources – parks, housing, political influence – between poor white and poor British Pakistani/ Bangladeshi communities.
- *Family*: This theme draws attention to the influence of personal loss and family breakdown experienced by a number of the young people, which may exert a negative influence upon their behaviour.
- *School, work and the economy*: There tended to be an element of ethnic segregation between secondary schools and even white flight to a neighbouring authority's schools. At the time of the study (1989 to 1995), youth unemployment was high, and this also impacted on some young people negatively thwarting aspirations and encouraged frustration and resentment.
- *Fear of crime and violent racism*: Asian and white young people were found to have 'more fears in common than they believed but spoke about these fears through the prism and at the boundary of racial and ethnic difference.'

So far we have mostly summarised research into violent racism among young people. Most recently research has extended to analysing violent racism among adults, and to analysing more closely the psychology behind motivations that lead to the expression of racism in violence. For example, Ray and Smith (2001, 2004) and Ray et al. (2003, 2004) argue that violent racism can be understood in terms of unacknowledged shame and its transformation into a certain sort of fury. This occurs according to their interviews with 36 violent racist offenders, because of the shame they felt and their sense of grievance and victimisation coupled with a sense of powerlessness and unfairness compared to the perceived advantages of their neighbouring Asians. Theirs was of a deep sense of exclusion from, and marginalisation to, mainstream social, cultural and economic resources, which it was thought Asians possessed. In truth their prevalent joblessness, poor education, significant criminality, unhappy and disrupted family backgrounds and physical isolation living in peripheral, outlying white estates, meant their violent racism was only an aspect of a wider syndrome of deep disaffection and resentment.

Our most recent study reviewed here is Gadd and Dixon's (2011) *Losing the Race*, which develops the above themes through applying a psychosocial approach to racially motivated crime. As in this chapter, Gadd and Dixon argue that we need to think about the sources of racist victimisation in the motives of racist offenders rather than merely condemning racism and racists as 'bad' or 'wrong', which alone neither explains nor prevents the problem of racist victimisation. Their psychosocial approach looks at the contradictory nature of individual social (including racist) attitudes and the emotional conflicts that may underlie them.

Gadd and Dixon's findings from their interviews with racist violent adult offenders include the following:

- Racism was rarely, if ever, the sole factor motivating their offending behaviour. Rather, it was conjoined with other sorts of violence, general territorial loyalties, alcohol and drug abuse, sometimes mental illness, especially depression and paranoia, and childhood abuse, neglect and violence.

- Feelings of hatred were often inspired by a lack of respect or threatening behaviour on the part of others including disrespect by other adults in authority when they were young people.
- Racist attitudes were widespread among white working-class populations living with the consequences of deindustrialisation so that feelings that they themselves were 'victims' of economic and political discrimination and marginalisation, as well as feelings of personal humiliation, making it difficult to clearly differentiate perpetrators and non-perpetrators despite an abhorrence of racist violence among the wider population.
- Although many among the local white population associated immigration with economic decline, social problems and poor public services and housing, and even a defence against the shame of 'redundancy', others took a darker view.
- In some cases other, more enduring losses, gave racism its more violent features, often connected to coalesced feelings of fearfulness, loneliness, powerlessness, persecution, envy, sadism and humiliation.
- Paradoxically, violent perpetrators tended to locate their grievances in specific conflicts with identifiable individuals on particular occasions rather than all-embracing racist stereotypes. Nonetheless, perpetrators had particularly acute reasons for feeling worthless and fearful, accentuated by troubled childhood histories of school exclusion, parental desertion or neglect and abuse.

We can see from this review of the research about racist violence that the causes of racist victimisation are likely to be found in the complex and myriad motivations of perpetrators. There is an identifiable and discernable pattern to these motivations, which the research has shown and which Gadd and Dixon (2011) in particular seem to summarise. Something that has too long been neglected but which has now come to the fore in tackling victimisation is tackling the underlying reasons why there are willing and motivated offenders in the first place.

RESEARCHING HOMICIDE

Although rare, and seemingly personal in nature, the crime of homicide cannot easily be explained solely in terms of the individual or psychological make-up of perpetrators. Although the trend in homicide is one of decline nationally, the trend among poor, urban, young men has risen (Dorling, 2008). Also, it is by no means obvious that the high homicide rate of Black young men in particular is explained by their **ethnicity** alone. In fact, the 2009/10 British Crime Survey shows that BME groups do not have a higher risk of being a victim of violence after taking other socio-economic factors into account. Flatley et al. (2010), using the survey evidence on all violence from the BCS, showed that ethnic groups other than white do not have a higher risk of being a victim of violence. Analysing the factors involved, Leyland and Dundas (2010), for example, argue for the importance of neighbourhood of residence, alcohol use, the carrying of knives and gang culture. Data from the Office for National Statistics (2013) suggests there are likely to be important socio-economic factors in homicides, and there is evidence from other studies suggesting that ethnicity is just one of many factors in homicides and violent incidents in general. Leyland and Dundas (2010: 437) investigated Scottish homicides between 1980 and 2005, and concluded that 'contextual influences of the neighbourhood of residence might be more important than individual characteristics in determining the victims of assault'.

Webster (2012) argues that it should not be surprising that strong spatial patterns are found within the particularities of ethnicity and crime. These are clearest in relation to homicide. Murder rates have increased in particular places, and for a particular group of people living there. This rise was particularly noticeable among young men living in a poor area from the early 1980s recession (Dorling, 2005). The rise in murders in the rest of the 1980s and 1990s were also geographically concentrated. Most worryingly, in the most recent years the rates for the youngest men have reached unprecedented levels. These men carry these rates with them as they age, and overall murder rates in Britain may continue to rise despite still falling for the majority of the population in most places. There is a strong correlation between homicide rates and levels of poverty and social inequality, and the risk of murder becomes more concentrated spatially, socially and ethnically (Dorling, 2008). In the US, Karen Parker (2008) has shown that changes in the local urban economy influenced homicide rates over time and for specific groups. Local processes of deindustrialisation between 1980 and 1990 directly affected African-American men first, then whites and blacks throughout the 1990s. As the 'new' service economy took hold and joblessness, job stability and inequality reduced, so too did urban violence in the late 1990s. Equally important were the nature of the work available and the segregation of the labour market along racial and gender lines, degrees of housing segregation and competition for jobs, immigration and ethnic diversity. It is to these contexts that we must look to understand the dynamic processes by which crime and homicide rates rise and fall over time.

PAUSE FOR REVIEW

What does research about perpetrators and victims tell us about victimisation processes?

Are policies and practices towards racist victimisation adequate and effective?

What motivates perpetrators of racist crimes?

What do we mean by the 'political context' of racist victimisation?

How do we explain disproportionate homicides among young black men?

RACE, VIOLENCE, VICTIMS AND CRIME

We can begin to look at some of the theoretical implications of the chapter here before summarising the chapter. One way of approaching this is Larry Ray's (2011) analysis in his *Violence and Society*, which offers a useful entry to some broader debates about violence in society. For example, a long observed, long-term decline of violence – or at least a long-term lessening of tolerance towards violence – in western societies needs to be set against situations, groups and places where the risk and frequency of violence continues to be a threat to secure living. These enclaves of residual recorded violence may have seen some recent decline in the level of violence, but levels remain unacceptably high. Divided by poverty, class and race, these economically abandoned urban areas of cities continue to accommodate thriving criminal economies.

More generally, criminal victimisation is geographically concentrated and national rates might not reflect local experiences and risks. This might be especially true of violent crime. Social stress, which includes factors such as racial and ethnic segregation, the proportion of female-headed households, poverty, low education, vacant properties and unemployment – is strongly correlated with locally recorded violence in all its forms. In turn, concentrated poverty is racialised since ethnic minority groups often make up a large proportion of the populations living in such areas. Similar to other findings presented here, Ray's (2011: 79) general conclusion is, 'Relative deprivation and crisis of identity combines with the use of violence as a means of settling problems, which acquires a transgressive edge driven by the energies of humiliation.'

This means that there is a strong association between relative income inequality or deprivation and homicide rates. Here, the readiness to use violence may become an alternative route to status and material resources, especially in more racially segregated areas where social and racial divisions coincide making inequality more severe. In terms of 'hate crime' and hate-based violence, this sort of violence can become a means of social bonding among perpetrators. Here 'retaliation' for 'stepping out of line', crossing boundaries, being in the wrong place, entering the 'wrong' neighbourhood, and a myriad of other 'violations' of local cultural 'rules', can occur (Ray, 2011).

SUMMARY

This chapter began by establishing that there are race and religious differences in fear of crime and that this reflects the rates at which individuals from visible minority groups are at risk of being, and become, victimised by crime. Often it is argued, these greater risks are explained because minorities tend to live in poorer urban areas that experience higher levels of crime and disorder, rather than because of their ethnicity alone. Other aspects of an argument that downplays the significance of race and ethnicity as factors in being a victim is that black and minority ethnic populations tend to be younger, and younger people face more risks.

In respect of hate crime, however, there is little ambiguity that some sorts of violence and harassment are racially motivated and target members of black and minority ethnic groups. Racist victimisation does though seem to have declined, reflecting perhaps a decline in the more overt – and certainly violent – racism since the Stephen Lawrence Inquiry. Explaining and interpreting racist victimisation requires understanding of context that goes beyond the immediate incident itself that can also explain the complex and myriad motivations of perpetrators. Explanations proffered tend to rest upon the thesis that white working-class cultural and economic interests have been disenfranchised in the political system, thwarted and frustrated by an uncaring elite, and finally displaced onto racist and anti-immigration feeling (Ford and Goodwin, 2014). That in a sense, racism and its expression in harassment and violence are extreme forms of grievance in which perpetrators, however mistakenly, feel themselves to be 'victims' of the 'presence' of visible minorities and 'immigrants'.

FURTHER READING

Bowling, B. (1999) *Violent Racism: Victimology Policing and Social Context*. Oxford: Clarendon Press.

An excellent study on racist violence in social and political context.

Phillips, C. and Webster, C. (eds) (2014) *New Directions in Race, Ethnicity and Crime*. Abingdon: Routledge.

An excellent collection of cutting-edge chapters on ethnicity and race, including victimisation.

Webster, C. (2007) *Understanding Race and Crime*. Maidenhead: Open University Press.

This provides a good critical introduction to the key research on the subjects.

REFERENCES

Bowling, B. (1993) 'Racial harassment and the process of victimisation: conceptual and methodological implications for the local crime survey', *British Journal of Criminology*, 33(1): 231–50.

Bowling, B. (1999) *Violent Racism: Victimisation, Policing and Social Context*. Oxford: Clarendon Press.

Bullock, K. and Tillye, N. (2002) *Shootings, Gangs and Violent Incidents in Manchester: Developing a Crime Reduction Strategy*, Crime Reduction Research Series Papers 13. London: Home Office.

Chahal, K. (1999) 'The Stephen Lawrence Inquiry report, racist harassment and racist incidents: changing incidents, clarifying meaning?', *Sociological Review Online*, 4(1). Available at http://socresonline.org.uk/4/lawrence/chahal.html (accessed 17.10.16).

Chahal, K. and Julienne, L. (1999) *We Can't All Be White: Racist Victimization in the UK*. York: Joseph Rowntree Foundation.

Chaplin, R., Flatley, J. and Smith, K. (2011) *Crime in England and Wales 2010/11: Findings from the British Crime Survey and Police Recorded Crime* (2nd edn), Home Office Statistical Bulletin 10/11. London: Home Office. Available at www.gov.uk/government/uploads/system/uploads/attachment_data/file/116417/hosb1011.pdf (accessed 17.1016).

Dorling, D. (2005) 'Murder in Britain', *Prison Service Journal*, No 166.

Dorling, D. (2008) 'Commentary', in *Environment and Planning A*, 40: 255–57.

Flatley, J., Kershaw, C., Smith, K., Chaplin, R. and Moon, D. (2010) *Crime in England and Wales 2009/10: Findings from the British Crime Survey*, Home Office Statistical Bulletin 12/10. London: Home Office. Available at http://webarchive.nationalarchives.gov.uk/20110218135832/rds.homeoffice.gov.uk/rds/pdfs10/hosb1210.pdf, accessed 17/10/16 (accessed 17.10.16).

Ford, R. and Goodwin, M. (2014) *Revolt on The Right: Explaining Support for the Radical Right in Britain*. Abingdon: Routledge.

Gadd, D. and Dixon, W. (2011) *Losing the Race: Thinking Psychosocially about Racially Motivated Crime*. London: Karnac.

Hoare, J., Parfrement-Hopkins, J., Britton, A., Hall, P., Scribbins, M. and Flatley, J. (2011) *Children's Experience and Attitudes Towards the Police, Personal Safety and Public Spaces: Findings from the 2009/10 British Crime Survey Interviews with Children aged 10 to 15*, Home Office Statistical Bulletin 08/11. London: Home Office. Available at www.gov.uk/government/uploads/system/uploads/attachment_data/file/116447/hosb0811.pdf (accessed 13.10.16).

Home Office (2011) *Racist Incidents England and Wales 2010/11*, Home Office Statistical Findings 1/11. London: Home Office. Available at https://view.officeapps.live.com/op/view.aspx?src=https%3A%2F%2Fwww.gov.uk%2Fgovernment%2Fuploads%2Fsystem%2Fuploads%2Fattachment_data%2Ffile%2F116286%2Fhosf0111-xls.xls (accessed 17.10.16).

House of Commons (2007) *Young Black People and the Criminal Justice System*, vol. 1. London: The Stationery Office. Available at www.publications.parliament.uk/pa/cm200607/cmselect/cmhaff/181/181i.pdf (accessed 13.10.16).

Jansson, K. (2007) 'British Crime Survey – measuring crime for 25 years'. Available at http://webarchive.nationalarchives.gov.uk/20110218135832/rds.homeoffice.gov.uk/rds/pdfs07/bcs25.pdf (accessed 7.11.16).

Jansson, K., Budd, S., Lovbakke, J., Moley, S. and Thorpe, K. (2007) *Attitudes, Perceptions and Risks of Crime: Supplementary Volume 1 to Crime in England and Wales 2006/07*, Home Office Statistical Bulletin 19/07. London: Home Office.

Leyland, A.H. and Dundas, R. (2010) 'The social patterning of deaths due to assault in Scotland, 1980–2005: population-based study', *Journal of Epidemiology Community Health*, 64(5): 432–9.

Maclean, B. (1986) 'Critical criminology and some limitations of traditional inquiry', in B. Maclean (ed.), *The Political Economy of Crime: Readings for a Critical Criminology*. Ontario: Prentice Hall.

Macpherson, W. (1999) *The Stephen Lawrence Inquiry*. London: The Sationery Office.

Ministry of Justice (2013) *Statistics on Race and the Criminal Justice System 2012*. London: Ministry of Justice. Available at www.gov.uk/government/statistics/statistics-on-race-and-the-criminal-justice-system-2012 (accessed 13.10.16).

Ministry of Justice (2015) *Statistics on Race and the Criminal Justice System 2014*, London: Ministry of Justice. Available at https://www.gov.uk/government/uploads/system/uploads/attachment_data/file/480250/bulletin.pdf (accessed 8.3.17).

Office for National Statistics (2013) *Focus On: Violent Crime and Sexual Offences, 2011/12*. London: ONS.

Office for National Statistics (2014) *Crime in England and Wales, Year Ending June 2014*, Statistical Bulletin. London: ONS. Available at www.ons.gov.uk/ons/rel/crime-stats/crime-statistics/period-ending-june-2014/stb-crime-stats--year-ending-june-2014.html (accessed 7.11.16).

Parker, K.F. (2008) *Unequal Crime Decline: Theorizing Race, Urban Inequality, and Criminal Violence*. New York: New York University Press.

Patel, T.G. and Tyrer, D. (2011) *Race, Crime and Resistance*. London: Sage.

Phillips, C. and Bowling, B. (2012) 'Ethnicities, racism, crime and criminal justice', in M. Maguire, R. Morgan and R. Reiner (eds), *The Oxford Handbook of Criminology* (5th edn). Oxford: Oxford University Press.

Phillips, C. and Webster, C. (eds) (2014) *New Directions in Ethnicity, Crime and Justice*. London: Routledge.

Pitts, J. (2008) *Reluctant Gangsters: The Changing Face of Youth Crime*. Cullompton: Willan.

Ray, L. (2011) *Violence and Society*. London: Sage.

Ray, L. and Smith, D. (2001) 'Racist offenders and the politics of "hate crime"', *Law and Critique*, 12: 203–221.

Ray, L. and Smith, D. (2004) 'Racist offending, policing and community conflict', *Sociology*, 38(4): 681–99.

Ray, L., Smith, D. and Wastell, L. (2003) 'Understanding violent racism', in B. Stanko (ed.), *The Meanings of Violence*. London: Routledge.

Ray, L., Smith, D. and Wastell, L. (2004) 'Shame, rage and violent racism', *British Journal of Criminology*, 44(3): 350–68.

Salisbury, H. and Upson, A. (2004) *Ethnicity, Victimisation and Worry about Crime: Findings from the 2001/02 and 2002/03 British Crime Surveys*, Home Office Findings 237. London: Home Office.

Sibbitt, R. (1997) *The Perpetrators of Racial Harassment and Violence*, Research Study 176. London: Home Office.

Smith, K., Coleman, K., Eder, S. and Hall, P. (2011) *Homicides, Firearm Offences and Intimate Violence 2009/10: Supplementary Volume 2 to Crime in England and Wales 2009/10*, Home Office Statistical Bulletin 01/11. London: Home Office. Available at www.gov.uk/government/uploads/system/uploads/attachment_data/file/116512/hosb0111.pdf (accessed 13/10/16).

Walker, A., Kershaw, C. and Nicholas, S. (2006) *Crime in England and Wales 2005/06*. Home Office Statistical Bulletin 12/06. London:Home Office.

Webster, C. (1996) 'Local heroes: violent racism, spacism and localism among white and Asian young people', *Youth & Policy*, 53: 15–27.

Webster, C. (1997) 'The construction of British "Asian" Criminality', *International Journal of the Sociology of Law*, 25: 65–86.

Webster, C. (2007) *Understanding Race and Crime*. Maidenhead: Open University Press.

Webster, C. (2012) 'Different forms of discrimination in the CJS', in K. Sveinsson, (ed.), *Criminal Justice v Racial Justice: Over-Representation in the Criminal Justice System*. London: The Runnymede Trust.

NOTES

1. 'Personal crime' covers all crimes against the individual and only relates to the respondent's own personal experience rather than other members of a household. An example of a personal crime would be an assault.
2. The data reported are available in the Home Office Statistical Bulletin 01/11 and can be read in conjunction with Smith et al. (2011). Also see Home Office (2011).

12 SEXUALITY, VICTIMS AND CRIME

Stephen Tomsen and Michael Salter

Aspects of human sexuality have an ongoing link with issues of criminality. From the 18th century, there was a major transition in the regulation of sexuality in western countries from informal social control and Church mandate to the state bureaucracy and the criminal justice system. Male homosexuality and female prostitution were increasingly cast as threats to social order and became the target of intensified surveillance, policing and prosecution. From the mid-20th century, this legal regulation was challenged by more liberal views of what comprises normative sexuality. Nevertheless, the resulting decriminalising impulse has not ended the process of further criminalisation of matters related to sexual behaviour in a new set of relations between sexuality and victimisation. The re-emergence of the feminist movement from the 1960s brought sexual violence against women and children to the forefront of public awareness and generated considerable pressure on state authorities to mount an effective response.

This chapter reflects on such major changes within various liberal legal systems with examples from two key areas. First, we consider the major contemporary drive to further research, highlight and respond to the victimisation of women and children in sexual assaults and the transformations in criminal justice measures that this accompanied. Second, we consider aspects of the criminalisation of violence, harassment and other attacks described as crime motivated on the grounds of sexual identity.

We explain the social movement origins and debates about this, typical legal reforms and protections that have been implemented around the globe, and how the new acknowledgement of this victimisation has shifted understandings of legal citizenship for sexual minorities. We also critically reflect on the mixed achievements and limits of criminal justice attempts to address victimisation from both sexual assaults and sexuality-related hate crimes as principally male forms of offending.

CONCEPTS AND ASSUMPTIONS

The concept of natural sexuality is so common in contemporary society that it has become a taken-for-granted fact about human existence. It is widely assumed that sexuality is a drive that underpins many of our thoughts and actions. However, sexuality does not correspond with a natural fact but rather with modes of authority, social power and control. Historians and other scholars have demonstrated how, during the industrial age, criminal law came to play a key role in the regulation of sexual behavior (Weeks, 2012). Over the last 200 years, sexual desire and practice has become a greater focus of activity by the police and the criminal justice system.

Foucault's (1979) theory of sexuality had a profound impact on the understanding of what had already been called 'victimless sexual crimes', such as consenting adult acts of homosexuality and prostitution. Charges based on moral grounds were seen by reformers and civil libertarians as an unjust form of legal repression. These emphasised the harms of **criminalisation** and the ways in which unnecessary laws authorised police intrusion into sexual life.

Criminalisation was strongly contested in relation to private acts of homosexuality, and there have been ongoing changes and debates over the legal status of prostitution. In the post-war decades and the sexual liberationist ideas that followed, this resonated strongly with liberal norms suggesting that sexual behavior is a private matter and should be placed beyond the purview of state intervention and regulation.

French philosopher **Michel Foucault** (1926–84) rejected the notion that sexuality was a repressed or taboo subject in western societies. From his perspective, the very concepts of sex and sexuality were recent inventions that did not exist until bureaucracies and scientific 'experts' focused so closely on them (Foucault, 1979: 154). Foucault was not denying that people had sex and experienced sexual desire in the past, but rather he argued that the modern concept of 'sexuality' legitimised contemporary configurations of social power.

By contrast, revived feminist thought from the 1960s generally identified sexuality as a medium for **patriarchal** harm to women and children. This insisted that sexual violence against women and children by men was widespread and harmful to women's mental and physical health; a claim further supported by pioneering studies in the 1980s (e.g. Russell, 1984; Koss and Oros, 1982; Stanko, 1985). Findings such as these have prompted renewed state efforts to intervene in intimate relations and to criminalise acts of sexual violence against women and children.

Underpinning feminist advocacy for interventions into sexual violence there was an explicit critique of state inaction as a marker of gender inequality. Most feminist work shared a view of sexual behaviour as a domain of human social practice that reflects power inequities. Gay liberation, queer and sex worker advocates such as Altman, Rubin and Califia have instead usually emphasised the role of sexual agency in breaking through social constraints. This hints at the incongruity of some of the views of sexual practice and experience that are implicit in allied social movement perspectives and debates over sexuality and victimisation. Feminist victimology has maintained a focus on the harms of sexual violence against girls and women, and their revictimisation through invalidating or traumatising criminal justice responses.

However, a key point of convergence has been social mobilisation over both sexually and sexuality-based forms of violence and victimisation. Feminist and gay male and lesbian activists have pursued intersecting strategies to ensure that abusive behaviour on the grounds of gender or sexuality is criminalised. Sexual assaults on women and children and violence linked with sexual identity have commonly been understood as attacks that are usually carried out by disturbed and irrational perpetrators.

Yet research since the 1970s and 1980s (discussed below) indicates that this is a misleading picture of the typical scenarios and risks from such attacks that arise as more everyday phenomena occurring in a range of public and private settings and which involve the enactment of widespread masculine power and privilege. Similarly, evidence indicates that attacks perpetrated on the basis of sexual identity have been an everyday form of victimisation linked to normalised heterosexual male identities (Tomsen, 2009).

PAUSE FOR REVIEW

How do commonsense understandings of sexuality conflict with Foucault's view of sexuality?

What are the similarities and differences between the feminist view of sexuality and those of gay, lesbian and sex worker movements?

RESEARCHING AND RESPONDING TO VICTIMHOOD: SEXUAL VIOLENCE AGAINST WOMEN AND CHILDREN

The notion of a specifically sexual form of violence has a long history in European culture and is closely linked to the status of girls and women. Rape was generally seen as a very serious crime and it was punishable by death well into the 19th century in most jurisdictions. However, the strong denunciation of rape evident in its legal status was undermined by the ways in which sexual assault matters were policed and adjudicated. The social and legal assessment of the credibility and seriousness of a rape allegation was not necessarily determined by the circumstance of the alleged assault, but instead by factors pertaining to the history, behaviour, class and race of both complainant and defendant (see Chapter 9).

It was only with the advent of the second-wave feminist movement in the 1960s and 1970s that the prevalence of sexual violence in female life became a social issue. The women's movement developed strategies to overcome the disbelief and inaction that characterised institutional and community responses to sexual violence, including consciousness raising groups (women's only groups that met to discuss women's issues in feminist terms) and organisations to address rape and domestic violence. Feminists produced a range of explanations of sexual violence that linked rape to women's subordinate social and legal status. These explanations were advanced in a number of pioneering books that generated significant media and political debate over rape, child sexual abuse and women's rights. Millet's (1971) book *Sexual Politics* argued that non-consensual sex was not an aberration but normalised in western culture and literature. Brownmiller (1975) linked the frequency of rape to male structures of social power and control of women. Subsequently, Rush (1980) challenged prevailing theories of child sexual abuse that saw children as 'seducers' and responsible for their own victimisation, by arguing that adults were responsible for abuse and that this abuse also served to socialise girls into subordinate social roles.

By the 1970s available theories of criminal offending, which addressed factors such as age, class, upbringing and individual psychology, were unable to account for the evidence of widespread gender-based violence. The major strands of feminism to emerge during this period included radical, liberal and socialist accounts of sexual violence. Liberal explanations for sexual violence focused on the disadvantages faced by girls and women which placed them in a disempowered position vis-à-vis boys and men. For feminists drawing on liberal political theory, the solution lay in increasing the individual opportunities available to girls and women, reforms to the law and policing, as well as new patterns of socialisation and education for boys and men. Socialist (and Marxist) feminists were more likely to view sexual violence as a symptom of female oppression linked to an inherently unfair social and economic order that needed to be transformed or overthrown.

Attempts to categorise feminist thought have been contested since feminist discourse involves innovation drawing on multiple sources and influences. However, it is useful to identity the particular strands evident in second-wave feminism. **Liberal perspectives** emphasised the failure of society to provide women with the same opportunities for autonomy and fulfillment as men. **Socialist** and **Marxist feminists** drew on Marxist theory to emphasise the exploitation of women's paid and domestic labour, particularly linking the oppression of working class and poor women to the prevailing capitalist order. **Radical feminism** developed the notion of 'patriarchy' to describe societies fundamentally based on masculine domination in which women were systemically disempowered on the basis of gender.

It was ultimately the radical feminist account of sexual violence that emerged as the most enduring although also the most controversial. Brownmiller (1975) argued that sexual violence was a form of group terror that operated to reproduce gendered inequity by maintaining women in a state of fear and shame. While not all men were perpetrators of sexual violence, radical feminists argued that the prevalence of related behaviour such as sexual harassment, as well as in the disinterest and disbelief of male-dominated authorities, suggested a broader complicity. Hence male sex offenders assaulting women and children were not a perverse minority but seen as representatives of normative masculinity, while sexual violence fulfilled a cultural function in that it prepared girls and women to embody the feminine 'ideal' of the docile, passive and obedient wife.

Importantly, the radical feminist view of wide sexual violence found empirical support in expanding international research conducted from the 1970s onwards. Victimisation surveys reported high rates of child sexual abuse and rape, often by 'known men' (e.g. family members, friends or intimate partners) rather than predatory strangers (Koss, 1987; Finkelhor, 1979; Finkelhor and Yllo, 1985). Research with violent offenders and sex offenders suggested that they rationalised their crimes by drawing on common understandings of male sexuality (Scully and Marolla, 1985). Feminist criminologists such as Smart (1976) noted the line between consent and non-consent was blurred in a culture where coercion or pressure was often implicit or assumed in heterosexual relations. The research of Stanko (1985) and Kelly (1988) into women's lived experience of male violence emphasised a continuum of sexual coercion from childhood to adulthood, and from the legal to the illegal. From this perspective, criminal sexual offences were viewed as symptomatic of the broader spectrum of fear, harassment and abuse produced by gendered inequity.

However, the position that men were using rape as a political weapon against women came under criticism for a tendency to stigmatise all men as potential perpetrators, a failure to recognise the full complexities of male offending, and a conspiratorial view of male domination. These concerns about the extended radical agenda also coincided with a **backlash** against such feminist views of violence in the late 1980s and early 1990s.

Despite this, solutions to sexual victimisation began to be integrated into policy making in an effort to reduce victimisation rates, increase reporting and prosecution, and provide victims with more responsive health care systems. In the last three decades, legal definitions of sexual abuse and rape (see Box 12.1) have been expanded to acknowledge more fully the varieties of sexual violence, including rape by acquaintances, boyfriends and husbands (Frank et al., 2009). Judicial suspicion of women's testimony had been exemplified in the warnings and instructions that judges issued to jurors about the need for corroboration in rape cases; however, such warnings are no longer considered necessary. Investigation and evidence-gathering in rape cases has improved and in a growing number of jurisdictions there are more measures available to minimise the potential trauma of testifying and cross-examination for children and adults.

BOX 12.1 DEFINING RAPE

The traditional common-law definition of rape was 'unlawful carnal knowledge of a women by force and against her will' (Futter and Mebane, 2001), and comprised vaginal-penile intercourse. In most jurisdictions with reform since 1945, this definition has expanded to include a number of offences graded via circumstance and physical act (Frank et al., 2009). For example, laws against rape may now cover oral, anal and non-penile penetration as well as attacks on male victims. 'Marital rape' has now become criminalised as such in places where the consent implied in the marital contract previously reduced charges to lesser sexual assault.

Social mobilisation by the women's movement has had far-reaching impacts on national and international responses to sexual violence. It has generated new understandings around sexual violence through which girls and women can frame their experiences as harmful and unjust, and seek redress. However, the limitations of legal reform and state intervention are becoming clear. Reports of rape and sexual abuse to the police and other authorities have increased over the last 30 years, although it remains the case that most incidents go unreported, and rape and sexual abuse complaints have a high rate of **attrition** and low rate of successful prosecution compared to other offences (see also Chapter 9). The proportion of successful prosecutions for rape and sexual abuse has in fact been falling in many jurisdictions since the 1970s (Daly and Bouhours, 2010).

Entrenched cultural mythologies about gender and sexuality can continue to impact on official responses to sexual violence even where legislation and policy has been changed (Stubbs, 2003). For many police officers, jurors and judges, 'real' rape is still defined by the stereotypical stranger rape in which the predatory assailant stalks and attacks a victim (Jordan, 2004). Reports of sexual assault where the perpetrator and victim know one another, and/or where the victim is considered to have engaged in 'unfeminine' behavior (such as drinking, flirting or casual sex) can fall within the legal definition of rape but still be considered as outside the sphere of legitimate victimisation. Sexual abuse within the family continues to be managed primarily as a child protection or mental health issue, while the sexual abuse of children by perpetrators outside the family is more likely to be reported to the police and successfully prosecuted. This effectively reproduces the 'public' and 'private' divide again by characterising sexual violence in intimate life as outside the purview of the law and maintaining focus on forms of sexual violence such as stranger rape or **extra-familial abuse**.

Victims of sexual assault have critiqued the ways in which rape prevention and safety campaigns have held girls and women responsible for preventing their own victimisation. Some feminist prevention initiatives have included calls for increased government regulation and oversight of media imagery, and increased intrusion into private life through child protection and family support interventions. However, efforts to bolster the responsiveness of authorities have had a mixed reception among feminist groups in light of evidence that increased involvement of the police and the law, and welfare authorities, does not necessarily prevent sexual violence and can result in negative outcomes for victims (Walklate, 2008).

A reliance upon policing and criminal justice responses to sexual violence overlaps problematically with law and order politics and the drive to mass incarceration in several nations. Such responses also tend to differentially target men from racial and ethnic minority groups in ways that have destructive secondary effects upon their families and on the disadvantaged communities they are drawn from, while more privileged perpetrators have the resources to obstruct or avoid such punitive responses (Coker, 2004). See Box 12.2 for an example of organised child sexual abuse.

BOX 12.2 RESEARCH EXAMPLE – ORGANISED CHILD SEXUAL ABUSE

In the 1980s, feminist advocacy generated unprecedented public awareness of child sexual abuse that translated into substantial increases in reports of child abuse to the authorities, including reports of multiple offenders who conspired to abuse multiple children. This included cases where community and family networks engaged in the serious sexual abuse of multiple children (Hechler, 1988). It was also becoming clear that a small number of children's institutions were harbouring cultures of abuse in which staff arranged with those within and outside the institution to sexually exploit the children in their care (Finkelhor and Williams, 1988; Crossmaker, 1991; Doran and Brannan, 1996).

These cases included strong forensic evidence of organised sexual abuse (Oates, 1996) but they proved difficult to prosecute. The seriousness of the allegations appeared to provoke disbelief in the community and among investigators. There were few, if any, protections offered in court for the alleged victims, including very young and traumatised children who were subject to prolonged and hostile cross-examination. Meanwhile these cases required a cooperative style of investigation between police and social-work agencies, and the strain of these matters could lead to breakdowns in communication and trust (Campbell, 1988). While some cases of organised abuse were successfully prosecuted in the 1980s and 1990s, many attempts at prosecution failed. Allegations of organised abuse could be substantiated by a child protection investigation but not prosecuted, since child protection interventions are based on a lower standard of evidence than a criminal prosecution.

However, in 1996 global attention became focused on the marches that brought upwards of 275,000 Belgians to the streets in protest against perceived corruption and interference in an investigation into allegations of an organised child sexual abuse ring. Six children were abducted and raped, four of whom subsequently died in captivity. Other rapes, abductions and murders were linked to the case but ultimately only two people were convicted and the case was characterised by allegations of a high-level cover-up (Kelly, 1998). Further evidence that child sexual abuse could take an organised aspect was accumulating in multiple criminal investigations around the world, and the potential complicity of authorities was starkly illustrated in the clergy abuse scandals that have dogged the Catholic Church (Keenan, 2012). The slow acknowledgement of organised abuse has led to international police cooperation in relation to online child pornography as well as police units focused specifically on child solicitation and exploitation via the Internet.

Against this backdrop of new concern about organised abuse, Salter (2013) conducted a novel study in which he interviewed adults reporting sexual abuse in childhood by multiple perpetrators acting in concert. He found that, while authorities typically focused on the threat of 'paedophile rings' outside the home or on the Internet, organised abuse is often orchestrated by family members and other adults with a socially legitimate place in the private lives of children. This points to a hidden population of victims who are unlikely to be detected since their abusers are parents and others who exercise routine control over their victims. This group of victims is characterised by severe mental illness, developmental delays and learning disabilities as well as non-accidental injury, self-harm and suicide (Salter and Richters, 2012).

Allegations of extra-familial sexual abuse and exploitation mobilise public outrage very quickly, and this has led to controversial laws about the extended supervision or indefinite detention of a small number of sexual offenders deemed at high risk of reoffending. (For example, in October 2013, the state of Queensland in Australia passed new laws that gave the Attorney General the discretion to keep sex offenders in gaol indefinitely.) This issue is also now feeding some angry populist forms of victim politics posing a threat to the rule of law and specifically focusing public opprobrium on offenders within disadvantaged or marginalised communities. More recently, this has been tempered by sexual abuse allegations surrounding Jimmy Savile, Rolf Harris and other celebrities throughout 2012–16. This represents an important shift in what had previously been considered possible or credible in the field of child sexual abuse. However, it does also illustrate the enduring emphasis on the threat of victimisation as 'stranger danger' alongside the discomfort that often attends reports of severe sexual violence in the family and local community sphere.

How have changes in the legal definition of rape reflected changes in the status of women?

What are the pros and cons of the liberal, socialist and radical feminist views of sexual assaults on women and children?

Suggest and discuss alternatives to increased police intervention and criminal justice sanctions that might prevent sexual victimisation.

'HATE' VIOLENCE AGAINST SEXUAL MINORITY VICTIMS

Violence against people with sexual minority status has been common in a range of societies and periods of history. The institutional violence directed against homosexuals in Nazi Germany, or even the abuses carried out to 'cure' people of 'sexually abnormal' desire under the ostensibly more humane banners of medicine and psychiatry in many nations, stand as reminders that this form of violence is not novel. Nevertheless, broad awareness of the victimisation from violence grew from the emergence of a new Gay Liberation movement (spreading from the US in the late 1960s) and a subsequent broader gay and lesbian (or **GLBTI**/queer) mobilisation around the globe.

This has placed great emphasis on both the prejudice and the structural disadvantage experienced by members of sexual minorities in their daily lives. Intimidation and cultural stigma had a direct repressive role but were also seen as signalling the boundaries of acceptable sexual and gendered behaviour for men and women built on the central importance of opposite sex desire and relationships. Activists suggested that hostility was reflected at all levels of society. In fact, the criminal justice system was seen as especially problematic for the positioning of sexual minorities and efforts to directly tackle violence. Widespread under-reporting of violence against these groups was reproduced by complacent or hostile police attitudes to victims.

Nevertheless, from the 1980s there was dramatic international growth in research on hate (or bias) crime and violence directed at gay men, lesbians and other sexual minorities producing evidence of a high level of attacks directed against these groups (Herek and Berrill, 1992; Mason and Palmer, 1996; Mason and Tomsen, 1997; Jenness and Grattet, 2001; Herek et al., 2002; Moran et al., 2004). Surveys of the sexual minority experience of violence and perceptions of safety were pioneered by researchers from the US, and soon emulated in Western Europe, Australia, South Africa, Brazil, Canada and Eastern Europe. North American studies in this area include victim surveys conducted by community organisations in the 1980s and the pioneering work of Comstock (1991). See Box 12.3 for an overview of hate or bias crime.

BOX 12.3 HATE/BIAS CRIME

Hate or bias crime generally refers to the vilification, harassment, assault or destruction of property, motivated by hostility towards victims on the basis of their membership of a disadvantaged racial, ethnic, religious or sexual minority group. When viewed as moments of 'social terror', such targeted attacks are seen as symbolic warnings about any open expression of minority identity and as intimidation against the broader membership of the minority.

The significant common findings of studies included a higher rate of victimisation of homosexual men and lesbians as compared with heterosexual populations, and relative low rates of reporting which reflected a marked lack of faith in the criminal justice system. Studies revealed that whereas lesbians have been subjected to harassment and violence in public places, the levels of public attacks against gay men are even higher. Attacks in the form of random street violence and actual physical battery are more typical for gay male victims than for lesbians, and anti-lesbian attacks occur more often in private contexts with known perpetrators, such as incidents that occur at home or work (Mason, 2001).

In most jurisdictions the new official interest in this violence was a result of concerted activist efforts (see Jenness and Grattet, 2001; Moran et al., 2004). Internationally it was community research, protest rallies and other publicity that provided the catalyst for making violence and harassment directed at gay men and lesbians into a public issue. This generally followed a community organising model that evolved in the US (Herek and Berrill, 1992).

In many nations, this came to loom large as an issue for gay and lesbian organisations which dealt with such diverse matters as discrimination and law, education, personal health and counselling. Specific local groups evolved an array of strategies to counter violence and its threat. These included the community monitoring of attacks, closer (though often still mistrustful) cooperation with police, politicians and public officials dealing with housing, education, health and discrimination. This was reinforced by publicity and preventive education in the gay and lesbian press with information on safety, risk and rights, and even 'anti-homophobia' campaigns in the mainstream media intended to target young heterosexual men as potential assailants. The experience of violence became the basis of determined efforts at community building and the promotion of political coalitionism. Conflicts about the inclusion of bisexual, transsexual/transgender and intersex people in these changes ensued, but overall the issue was heralded for its success in uniting the gay and lesbian or queer community and raising the awareness of this form of victimhood.

The social movement classification of this violence as a type of 'hate crime' has meant mixed outcomes for understanding and countering such crimes. In a typical hate crime the perpetrator has been conceived as a stranger to the victim and only concerned with the victim's membership of a despised minority. This definition best fits the scenario of a public attack carried out by an extremist perpetrator. In reality, many victims of such crimes know their assailants as acquaintances, neighbours, work colleagues or even family relatives. They are attacked or harassed in a range of community and private settings. A definition stressing attacks by strangers excludes much violence and abuse directed at lesbians. Many attacks with female victims suggest a misogynist motive. There is no consensus among feminists about the issue, but some commentators (see Jenness and Grattet, 2001) even insist that much or all anti-female violence is actually a form of 'hate crime'.

It is also the case that many of these crimes are carried out with mixed motives. These incidents may not feature naked hatred and may instead reflect a perpetrator awareness of the marginal social status of victims and their reduced likelihood of reporting an offence or being taken as credible by authorities. The 'hate crime' model may also disregard the societal aspects of the motivating bias with an individualistic notion of crime causation and prevention. It often lacks a systemic perspective regarding the marginalisation of groups and minorities subjected to violence and harassment, or the widespread social basis for prejudiced outlooks as simply encouraging the protection of 'normal' sexualities. This means a focus on exceptional causes of prejudice rather than the everyday nature of such intolerance and its links to the dominant views in the wider society.

In the US, activism and measures to counter hate crime were much advanced by the 1990 federal legislation to monitor these offences, and subsequent state-level reforms that sought to lift the police response to victims. The most politically controversial changes have been laws that prohibit the expression or dissemination of vilification or 'hate speech' inciting or likely to incite acts of violence and harassment, and measures to enhance the penalties imposed if a hate motive is deemed proven. Critics of these changes regard them as a serious infringement of the liberal right to free speech and may even decry what they claim on dubious grounds is the pernicious extension of 'special protections' (Jacobs and Potter, 1998) to victims drawn from minority groups which are in fact seeking the sorts of protection and safety that are assumed by others as an expected citizen's right. Alongside this disagreement about the threat to civil liberties entailed by anti-vilification provisions and penalty enhancement, debates concern the actual definition of any typical or actual hate crime and which groups of victims this term could reasonably refer to.

It can be seen that references to these incidents as hate crimes has usefully assisted the mobilisation of a gay and lesbian community response to such forms of victimisation. Claiming a legitimate victimhood in regard to the experience of sexuality-related violence has become an important element of associated political action in many nations. Police consciousness has shifted in many locations (Jenness and Grattet, 2001; Tomsen, 2009), and more courts appear willing to denounce and seriously punish openly prejudice-driven attacks. Of course, this sort of approach to understanding oppression as 'hate' has a more obvious fit with social-movement demands built on liberal models of justice and minority rights. It has also seemed to be ready-made for the most effective community mobilisation against violence, harassment and discrimination.

Yet it is the case that these historical shifts should not be too much exaggerated. Levels of prejudice against gay and lesbian victims still persist in the police agencies, courts and general culture of all nations and this blocks the abatement of violent attacks. There are strict limits to any over-reliance on law and legal protections rather than a multi-pronged strategy pushing greater sexual tolerance. Furthermore, it is the case that publicity and campaigns against this violence are often around the recognition of certain high-profile victims rather than others. This campaigning can even create a new form of normative pressure on gay men and lesbians to absorb safety messages and pursue risk avoidance that could make them feel blameworthy (e.g. as promiscuous, intoxicated, drug using or foolhardy) in relation to their own victimisation. See Box 12.4 for an example of anti-homosexual killing and justice.

BOX 12.4 RESEARCH EXAMPLE – ANTI-HOMOSEXUAL KILLINGS AND THE CRIMINAL JUSTICE RESPONSE

The mixed outcomes of the mobilisation to counter violence against sexual minorities are evident in specific aspects of anti-homosexual killing and the legal response to these crimes. The global response to killings with homosexual, lesbian and transgender victims in the 1990s signalled the internationalisation of concern about these crimes and the extensive activism that emerged around them. In the US, the best known of these has been the killing of Mathew Shepard.

(Continued)

(Continued)

Mathew Shepard (1976–98) was a gay University of Wyoming student who was tortured and killed after accepting the offer of a ride home from two men he met in a local bar. His death became a stimulus for efforts to strengthen hate crime laws and for the cultural aspects of anti-hate activism, with the murder and its aftermath depicted in film, songs and theatre productions around the globe.

In this and most other cases, it has been the stress on hatred as a key motive among perpetrators that has prevailed in activist views.

Although a mobilisation around different killings has proven to be politically galvanising, the new research on violence and sexual prejudice has included a smaller emphasis on anti-homosexual killings. Tomsen's research (2009) set out to fill these gaps by studying homicides in which victims were selected by their killers on the basis of perceived homosexuality. This was achieved by a use of information from overlapping sources, and detailed analyses of perpetrator motive and evidence about the unfolding of different fatal incidents as interactive encounters between victims and perpetrators. Seventy-four anti-homosexual killings that occurred over two decades in the Australian state of New South Wales were uncovered. The research analysed trial records and transcripts, as well as court exhibits, witness statements and sentencing judgements. Whereas some of these trials had resulted in murder convictions, in other cases pleas of provocation and self-defence resulted in manslaughter convictions and even some full acquittals.

The evidence indicated that anti-homosexual killings occur mostly as either an overt group hate attack on a victim selected from the targeted social group, or they result instead from a violent personal dispute between two men with subsequent allegations of a homosexual advance by the deceased. In killings that conform to the scenario of a public group attack, claims about an unwanted homosexual advance are less credible. In cases resulting from the second scenario of a private conflict arising typically during an episode of socialising by male friends or recent acquaintances, such allegations are more difficult to counter. In cases where such claims appear plausible and 'hatred' is difficult to assert, an extreme perpetrator response often exceeds what was needed to reject or repel an unwanted sexual pass.

This may be seen to reflect commonplace masculine violent sensitivity to affronts against personal honour, providing a backdrop to a legal interpretation of this violence that normalises the irrationality of this perceived threat and a violent over-reaction to it. Trial outcomes suggest that this close linking of violence with protection of social respect from a 'homosexual advance' is far more excusable than the overt forms of violent hatred that courts have been increasingly pressured to respond to by hate crime activism (Tomsen, 2009). As with many trials concerning male-on-female rape, it is these homosexual advance cases that are more often marked by a focus on the risk behaviour of the victim and their sexual histories. Various trials in Australia and other nations have been characterised by an additional negative depiction of gay/homosexual victims as threatening, predatory or sexually corrupted (see Tomsen, 2006). To a certain extent these are instances where it is the actual victim of a homicide who is effectively 'on trial'.

As homosexual objectification and unwanted advances are still viewed as matters that can be expected to naturally trigger a violent protection of male honour, a partial excusing of that aggression within law and the wider culture will continue to undermine challenges to violence on the basis of sexual identity. Overall, the mixed outcomes of these legal matters suggest that courts have become more responsive to the demands of a newly mobilised pressure group demanding legal equality. However, the traditional masculinism of the law inscribed in legal doctrines and formal defences (particularly the provocation plea) regarding male violence has still meant dubious outcomes among cases in which perpetrators allege a sexual advance by a homosexual victim. Activism to abolish such defences in relation to anti-homosexual violence on a 'jurisdiction by jurisdiction' basis will be a long further road to victim equality around the globe.

PAUSE FOR REVIEW

Why do you think that victims of hate attacks related to sexual prejudice are often blamed for their own victimisation?

Mathew Shepard's killing attracted a very high level of public and media interest. Why was this the case?

To what extent are these attacks motivated by hatred and/or by gender norms?

SUMMARY

In recent decades, there has been a major push for reform in favour of victims of sexual assaults who commonly experienced lax policing and the failure to criminalise and punish offending. Successive women's movements have challenged the omissions of criminal justice systems in protecting women and children from sexual victimisation by men. In an analogous way, but with unsettled shifts around what sexual practices and identities should or should not be deemed as criminal, formerly deviant gay, lesbian, bisexual, transgender/transsexual and intersexed (GLBTI) categories have also now been linked to the experience of victimisation on the grounds of those very sexual identities that previously led to criminal justice repression.

Research has demonstrated how criminal justice systems have served to reproduce societal sexism and homophobia. Nevertheless, criminal justice is conceived as both the problem and a key solution to these social ills. In both of the examples explored in this chapter it can be seen how researchers and community advocates have struggled with and contested conventional understandings of victimisation. Feminists and GLBTI/queer activists have now taken these issues to the national and international stage and highlighted how both forms of crime have deep links with the protection and enactment of everyday and frequently normalised masculine heterosexual identities. Significant changes to cultural understandings and institutional reactions in relation to sexual violence and violence stemming from sexual prejudice are remarkable contemporary examples of the complex political and social processes that are involved in the recognition of legitimate victimhood in relation to criminal violence and victimisation from crime.

FURTHER READING

Herman, J.L. (2005) 'Justice from the victim's perspective', *Violence Against Women*, 11(5): 571–602.

Journal article based on qualitative research with 22 adults who had experienced or witnessed physical and/or sexual violence. It examines how each understood justice responses, and also how these can fail to acknowledge the complex needs of victims.

Jordan, J. (2008) *Serial Survivors: Women's Narratives of Surviving Rape*. Sydney: Federation Press.

This describes the experiences of 15 women who survived sexual violence by the same serial rapist. Drawing on interviews with the women, the book describes their experiences of rape and its aftermath to study the effects of victimisation and the court process on survivors, families and the wider community.

Chakraborti, N. and Garland, J. (2016) *Hate Crime: Impact, Causes and Responses*. London: Sage.

A comprehensive book that gives a ready overview to the field of hate crime and debates about terminology. It looks at forms of victimisation that include homophobic attacks and gendered violence, and also discusses contemporary criminal justice system efforts to address these crimes and the media and societal responses to them.

Salter, M. (2013) *Organised Sexual Abuse*. London: Glasshouse/Routledge.

This book challenges the way that allegations of organised sexual abuse are often dismissed as examples of 'moral panic' or 'false memories'. It analyses discourse that invalidates testimony of severe trauma and presents interview data with 21 people describing organised sexual abuse in childhood to suggest that sexual exploitation occurs within common and everyday arrangements of social power.

REFERENCES

Brownmiller, S. (1975) *Against Our Will: Men, Women and Rape*. New York: Simon and Schuster.

Campbell, B. (1988) *Unofficial Secrets: Child Sexual Abuse – The Cleveland Case*. London: Virago.

Coker, D. (2004) 'Race, poverty, and the crime-centered response to domestic violence', *Violence Against Women*, 10(11): 1331–53.

Comstock, G. (1991) *Violence against Lesbians and Gay Men*. New York: Columbia.

Crossmaker, M. (1991) 'Behind locked doors – institutional sexual abuse', *Sexuality and Disability*, 9(3): 201–219.

Daly, K. and Bouhours, B. (2010) 'Rape and attrition in the legal process: a comparative analysis of five countries', *Crime and Justice*, 39(1): 565–650.

Doran, C. and Brannan, C. (1996) 'Institutional abuse', in P. Bibby (ed.), *Organised Abuse: The Current Debate*. London: Arena.

Finkelhor, D. (1979) *Sexually Victimized Children*. New York: Free Press.

Finkelhor, D. and Williams, L.M. (1988) *Nursery Crimes: Sexual Abuse in Day Care*. Newbury Park, CA: Sage.

Finkelhor, D. and Yllo, K. (1985) *License to Rape: Sexual Abuse of Wives*. New York: The Free Press.

Foucault, M. (1979) *The History of Sexuality: 1, the Will to Knowledge*. London: Allen Lane.

Frank, D.J., Hardinge, T. and Wosick-Correa, K. (2009) 'The global dimensions of rape-law reform: a cross-national study of policy outcomes', *American Sociological Review*, 74(2): 272–90.

Futter, S. and Mebane, W.R. (2001) 'Effects of rape law reform on rape case processing', *The Berkeley Women's Law Journal*, 16: 72.

Hechler, D. (1988) *The Battle and the Backlash: The Child Sexual Abuse War*. Lexington, MA: Lexington.

Herek, G. and Berrill, K. (eds) (1992) *Hate Crimes: Confronting Violence against Lesbians and Gay Men*. Newbury Park, CA: Sage.

Herek, G., Cogan, J. and Gillis, J. (2002) 'Victim experiences in hate crimes based on sexual orientation', *Journal of Social Issues*, 58: 319–39.

Jacobs, J. and Potter, K. (1998) *Hate Crimes: Criminal Law and Identity Politics*. New York: Oxford University Press.

Jenness, V. and Grattet, R. (2001) *Making Hate a Crime*. New York: Russell Sage Foundation.

Jordan, J. (2004) *The Word of a Woman? Police, Rape and Belief*. New York: Palgrave Macmillan.

Keenan, M. (2012) *Child Sexual Abuse and the Catholic Church*. Oxford: Oxford University Press.

Kelly, L. (1988) *Surviving Sexual Violence*. Oxford: Blackwell.

Kelly, L. (1998) 'Confronting an atrocity: the Dutroux case', *Trouble and Strife*, 36: 16–22.

Koss, M.P. (1987) 'The scope of rape: incidence and prevalence of sexual agression and victimization in a national sample of higher education students', *Journal of Consulting and Clinical Psychology*, 55(2): 162–70.

Koss, M.P. and Oros, C.J. (1982) 'Sexual experiences survey: a research instrument investigating sexual aggression and victimization', *Journal of Consulting and Clinical Psychology*, 50(3): 455–7.

Mason, A. and Palmer, A. (1996) *Queer Bashing: A National Survey of Hate Crimes against Lesbians and Gay Men*. London: Stonewall.

Mason, G. and Tomsen, S. (1997) (eds) *Homophobic Violence*. Sydney: Federation.

Mason, G. (2001) *The Spectacle of Violence: Homophobia, Gender and Knowledge*. London: Routledge.

Millett, K. (1971) *Sexual Politics*. London: Hart-Davis.

Moran, L. and Skeggs, B. with Tyrer, P. and Corteen, K. (2004) *Sexuality and the Politics of Violence and Safety*. London: Routledge.

Oates, K.R. (1996) *The Spectrum of Child Abuse: Assessment, Treatment and Prevention*. New York: Brunner/Mazel.

Rush, F. (1980) *The Best Kept Secret: Sexual Abuse of Children*. New York: McGraw Hill.

Russell, D.H. (1984) *Sexual Exploitation: Rape, Child Sexual Abuse, and Workplace Harassment*. Thousand Oaks, CA: Sage.

Salter, M. (2013) *Organised Sexual Abuse*. London: Glasshouse/Routledge.

Salter, M. and Richters, J. (2012) 'Organised abuse: a neglected category of sexual abuse with significant lifetime mental healthcare sequelae', *Journal of Mental Health*, 21(5): 499–508.

Scully, D. and Marolla, J. (1985) 'Convicted rapists' vocabulary of motive: excuses and motivations', *Social Problems*, 31(5): 530–44.

Smart, C. (1976) *Women, Crime and Criminology: A Critique*. London: Routledge.

Stanko, E. (1985) *Intimate Intrusions: Women's Experiences of Male Violence*. London: Routledge.

Stubbs, J. (2003) 'Sexual assault, criminal justice and law and order', *Women Against Violence: An Australian Feminist Journal*, 14: 14–26.

Tomsen, S. (2006) 'Homophobic violence, cultural essentialism and shifting sexual identities', *Social and Legal Studies*, 15(3): 389–407.

Tomsen, S. (2009) *Violence, Prejudice and Sexuality*. London: Routledge.

Walklate, S. (2008) 'What is to be done about violence against women?', *British Journal of Criminology*, 48(1): 39–54.

Weeks, J. (2012) *Sex, Politics and Society: The Regulation of Sexuality Since 1800*. Harlow: Pearson Education.

13 VICTIMS OF THE POWERFUL

Hazel Croall

It is generally agreed that victimisation from the crimes of the powerful vastly outstrips that from so called 'conventional crime'. Merely listing some of the harms involved, from genocide and torture through the destruction of people's economic security and health as a result of the neglect of financial, safety, health and environmental regulations to the myriad ways in which we are all charged more for or otherwise deceived about products and services, gives some idea of their massive impact. Yet much of this does not feature as 'crime' victimisation in criminological texts or the victim surveys, and the activities are not widely regarded as 'crime'. Corporate, along with white-collar crime, has always had a contested criminal status (Nelken, 2007), and 'war crimes' and 'crimes of humanity', albeit that they include violence and deliberate killing, tend to be regarded as the province of 'human rights' (Cohen, 1996). Since its very inception, the term 'crimes of the powerful' (Pearce, 1976; Tombs and Whyte, 2015) has served to expose these harms along with the ability of powerful offenders to conceal them and to resist their criminalisation. Before exploring dimensions of victimisation, therefore, it is important to look at how the term itself is defined and conceptualised.

CONCEPTUALISING CRIMINAL VICTIMISATION BY THE POWERFUL

Crimes of the powerful are normally taken to be crimes committed by large corporations and state agencies such as the police or army and include criminological categories of corporate, police, state and environmental crime, outlined in Box 13.1. A key feature of these crimes is a *relationship of power between offender and victim* (Whyte, 2009), and Ruggiero and Welch (2009) point to the *asymmetrical* relationships in what they describe as 'power crime'. Corporations, for example, have the power to exploit workers who need employment and a key element of state crime is the abuse of the power vested in the position of, for example, a soldier or police officer, who may use *legitimate 'force'*, but abuse their power to engage in *illegitimate violence* such as torture or genocide. Powerful actors can also 'cover up' their crimes.

BOX 13.1 DEFINITIONAL ISSUES – WHAT DO THE CRIMES OF THE POWERFUL INCLUDE?

Green and Ward (2000) define state crime as a form of 'organisational deviance involving human rights violations by state agencies'.

Their discussion in support of this definition can be used in relation to environmental crime and other crimes of the powerful (Green and Ward, 2000, 2004; Green et al., 2007). They argue that:

- Benchmarks for the inclusion of activities (as crime) should include human rights and international law which do define activities as war crimes or crimes against humanity.
- The UN has powers to impose economic and other *sanctions* and to use limited military intervention.
- Within states *respected* organisations ask questions which reflect widely accepted standards of acceptable and deviant behaviour.
- 'Crime' should be restricted to behaviour which is both *objectively illegitimate* and *subjectively deviant.*
- *Deviance* involves actors, rules, an audience and potentially significant sanctions.
- In respect of state crime, *actors* are state agencies and *rules* include international law, domestic law and widely accepted social morality.
- *Audiences* include international organisations, domestic and organisational civil society, other states and agencies within the offending state.
- These can impose *sanctions* which include legal punishments; censure or rebellion by the population; damage to a states' domestic and international reputation; economic and military sanctions.

Diverse though these crimes are, they share some key characteristics. Individuals commit offences as part of their occupational role – thus offences are *organisational* and originate in *legitimate organisations*. Responsibility is often diffused and denied as individuals claim that they 'were only following orders' or 'doing their job' (Punch, 2008). Offences are often *tolerated* within an organisational or *corporate culture* and justified by appeal to prioritising organisational goals of efficiency, profitability or the interests of 'justice' in the face of what are perceived as restrictive regulations. Thus profits may be prioritised over safety or health or the police officer may justify 'framing' a suspect assumed to be 'guilty'. Offences are also concealed within the legitimacy of the organisation.

The *victim–offender relationship* is also distinct. There may be no single 'event', but instead a series of offences, such as neglect of regulations, generating cumulative harm that builds over time (Tombs and Whyte, 2010a), and, as Sutherland (1949) observed, many offences have a 'rippling effect', causing a small loss to a large number of victims, but yielding large profits. In many cases, *victims* are *unaware* of any harm, such as being overcharged for substandard goods, and in others, such as pollution or tax evasion, the harm is so *diffuse* that there is no clear individual loss. Offenders' justifications may also involve *victim blaming*. Workers may be 'blamed' for working in unsafe environments, the doctrine of *caveat emptor* (let the buyer beware), crucial to consumer law, places the responsibility on consumers to be informed about products, and in cases of state violence a depersonalised 'enemy' is created (Cohen, 2001).

These examples also illustrate the very narrow borderline between legal and acceptable activities and from illegal and morally questionable ones, subtle distinctions which are reflected in the language used to describe them. How can, for example, a 'normal' sales 'pitch' be distinguished from 'mis-selling' or fraud? What distinguishes 'interrogation' from 'torture', or legitimate 'force' from illegitimate 'violence'? Many industrial or environmental 'accidents' are subsequently attributed to some form of managerial or corporate responsibility. These considerations, along with the ability of powerful actors to influence legal and social perceptions of 'crime', mean that the issue of what to include has always been contested. Some critical criminologists have suggested using the term 'harm' instead of crime (Hillyard and Tombs, 2004), whereas to others this is too subjective and allows criminologists to include activities which they themselves disapprove of and are unlikely to be accepted by criminology (Newburn, 2007). Nonetheless, many activities of the powerful *are* widely disapproved of and regarded as morally wrong, and are subject to a range of legal and other sanctions by reputable domestic and international organisations. Box 13.1 outlines suggested benchmarks for state and environmental crime, which can be applied to other forms of crimes of the powerful. Box 13.2 lists examples of the most commonly used categories of crimes of the powerful.

BOX 13.2 EXAMPLES OF CRIMES OF THE POWERFUL

Serious Corporate Frauds

Corporate tax evasion.

'Mis-selling' financial products and services.

Anti-competitive offences: price fixing, cartels.

(Continued)

(Continued)

Safety Crimes

Failure to comply with health and safety regulations covering industrial, commercial premises and transport: involves the safety of passengers, workers, consumers.

Economic exploitation of workers: for example, payment below minimum wage, neglect of employment legislation.

Crimes against Consumers

Misrepresenting the quality, safety, origins, contents or 'benefits' of consumer goods and foods.

Safety offences: use of dangerous and often inadequately tested chemicals and food additives.

Food frauds.

Environmental Crime

Pollution: breaches of regulations involving factory emissions, chemical pollution, farm waste, nuclear waste.

Illegal trades in toxic waste, timber, endangered species, biopiracy.

War related: use of depleted uranium, large-scale bombing, chemical weapons.

Animal abuse (non-human victims).

Other Corporate/Organisational Offences

Corporate corruption.

Crimes by 'professions': doctors, lawyers, pharmacists.

Crimes of world financial institutions.

State Crime

Political crime: bribery, corruption, election frauds.

State Violence

Crimes against humanity: genocide, genocidal rape. War crimes: crimes of aggression, torture, use of information obtained from torture, state-directed terror.

Disappearances.

Enslavement.

Use of child soldiers.

Human rights violations.

Institutional violence of state agencies: police, army.

Police crime and deviance.

State Corporate Crime

Bribery and corruption.

Awarding of contracts.

Failure to ensure adequate regulation of corporate activities.

Breaches of arms embargoes.

(Derived from Croall, 2011)

There are therefore strong arguments (Croall, 2015) for including not only activities which are quite unambiguously 'criminal' (e.g. fraud) and 'regulatory' crime (involving criminal breaches of official regulations), but also 'illegal but not criminal' breaches of, for example, competition laws which are subject to economic and other sanctions, and, perhaps most controversially, 'lawful but awful' activities (Passas, 2005) which are legal but widely condemned. An example of the latter are recurrent exposees of legal corporate tax avoidance (Farnsworth and Fooks, 2015) by banks and major companies such as Amazon and Google, which has now emerged as a major political issue. Much quoted is the then Chair of the House of Commons Public Accounts Committee's description of Google's activities as 'devious, calculated and, in my view, unethical', adding that 'you are a company that says you "do no evil" ... I think that you do do evil' (Bowers and Syal, 2013).

Should the victims of harmful but not criminal activities of the powerful be included in victimology? Provide some examples.

Look at national newspapers for one week. Using an inclusive definition, list cases of victimisation by the powerful. Are these cases described as 'crimes'? If not, how are they described and categorised?

RESEARCHING CRIMINAL VICTIMISATION BY THE POWERFUL

These characteristics of victimisation present many problems for the researcher (Croall, 2007; Whyte, 2007a) and render the victim survey largely inappropriate. Even where victims are aware of offences, they are often omitted from large-scale crime surveys because they are not regarded as victims of 'crime'. Official records of agencies, often a starting point for research, are also seriously limited. Many victims do not report offences, particularly when losses are regarded as 'trivial', and others blame themselves for being 'taken in'. An extremely wide range of regulatory bodies are involved and victims may not know which agency to approach. Many agencies, dealing for example with regulatory law, see themselves as being charged with maintaining standards, not 'prosecuting the guilty', and do not always record which 'complaints' or 'incidents' are due to 'offences'. Researchers aiming to 'count' offences must therefore deconstruct a range of different statistical sources (Tombs, 2000), as illustrated in Box 13.3.

BOX 13.3 WORKPLACE VICTIMS

In an attempt to 'count' victimisation from workplace safety crimes, Tombs (2000, 2010) analysed a variety of data including:

- Figures from Britain's Health and Safety Executive (HSE), combining deaths reported in the main occupational groups with those occurring in the course of sea fishing, transport and communications work and driving in the course of employment. This reveals total deaths far exceeding those from homicide.
- While not all can be attributed to crime, reliable research has attributed around 70 per cent of workplace fatalities to managerial responsibility (Tombs, 2010; Whyte, 2007a).
- Deaths from occupationally-caused lung diseases involving, for example, asbestos, used after its dangers were recognised, amount in Britain alone to around 4,000 per annum, peaking between 2011 and 2015 (Tombs, 2010).
- In any one year around 30,000 UK workers and 15,000 members of the public are seriously injured by so-called accidents associated with workplaces.
- Labour Force Surveys suggest 274,000 non-fatal but reportable injuries in 2006–07, which amounts to 1,000 per 100,000 workers. While these cannot be precisely compared to 'real crimes' such as assault, Tombs (2010) concludes that 'workplace violence' in Britain is more prevalent than the so-called 'real crimes' recorded by the Home Office.
- The 2006–07 Labour Force Survey further suggests that 2.2 million respondents suffered from an illness which they believe was caused or made worse by work.

These research problems are particularly severe for state crime. Governments can cover up their activities by, for example, classifying information as 'official secrets' and 'redacting' (blocking out) information. Access can be denied to academic and other researchers and researchers' legitimacy challenged (Hillyard, 2003). Government inquiries may have a restricted remit, take many years to complete and be criticised as partial, biased or as 'whitewashes'. The final reports in the case of Bloody Sunday and the Hillsborough disaster for example, both of which found state agencies to blame, were published 38 and 23 years respectively after the events. Similar issues arise with corporate activities with responsibility for financial 'scandals' or major environmental or industrial 'disasters' taking many years to be established.

Nevertheless, a range of useful information sources are available to the resourceful researcher. The harmful activities of the powerful are subject to criticism and investigation by, for example, relevant government departments, interest groups such as environmental, trade union, human rights, consumer and voluntary groups along with investigative journalism, all keen to disseminate findings. Some corporate offences are subject to victim-survey style research such as the Labour Force Survey (Tombs, 2010; and see Box 13.3), which asks about injuries and illnesses at work, or those carried out by consumer organisations such as *Which?* (2004) and the Office of Fair Trading (OFT) (Croall, 2010). A number of civil liberties and human rights organisations, both domestic and international, systematically gather information about abuses of state agencies and governments. Much of this is readily obtainable via the internet, although all information must be treated with caution and its reliability checked carefully.

PAUSE FOR REVIEW

Choose one form of crime outlined in Box 13.2 and consider what sources you would use to research victimisation through this type of offending.

DIMENSIONS OF VICTIMISATION

Box 13.2 outlines some of the main crimes of the powerful. These illustrate the direct and indirect ways in which different kinds of offences affect victims, and it should be borne in mind that behind total 'costs' lie 'real' experiences of individual victimisation.

SERIOUS FINANCIAL FRAUDS

Serious financial frauds are a good example of direct *and* diffuse forms of victimisation. Offences range from quite clearly 'criminal' frauds through breaches of financial regulations to the more legally ambiguous 'mis-selling' of financial products, anti-competitive practices such as price fixing, and so-called 'aggressive' tax planning where the line between the criminal and 'lawful but awful' is very narrow. Seemingly 'victimless' crimes such as tax evasion adversely affect the amounts governments have to spend on welfare or health, and while not always generally attributed to 'crime' or 'fraud', corporate collapses are often associated with morally questionable or outright fraudulent activities, as illustrated in Box 13.4 on the impact of the financial crisis of 2008.

BOX 13.4 VICTIMISATION AND THE FINANCIAL CRISIS OF 2008

McGurrin and Friedrichs (2010) explore the impact of the financial crisis of 2008. This, while leading to few prosecutions, they liken to a 'bank robbery' as it was associated with a range of fraudulent and widely condemned practices and led to considerable reputational damage being suffered by banks and other financial institutions. It had immeasurable consequences worldwide – in the US alone:

- millions of families experienced foreclosure on their homes;
- investors and savers suffered from stock market losses of $7trillion;
- hundreds of millions suffered devastating declines in retirement, college and other savings;
- older people had to return to work and others suffered a reduced standard of living in retirement and had to seek public assistance;
- many of these issues, at an individual level, contribute to stress, depression, domestic violence, marital and health problems.

Other examples include:

- *Serious frauds related to mortgages, savings and pensions*: Studies of victims of these kinds of fraud reveal a host of effects such as loss of retirement income, housing and financial security, which in turn can lead to depression, mental illness, marital problems and, in some cases, suicide (Shover et al., 1994; Spalek, 2001, 2007).
- *Losses from tax evasion and avoidance*: While difficult to count, conservative estimates suggest that in 2005, tax fraud in the UK, *excluding* income tax fraud, involved losses of nearly £2 billion to businesses; £2.75 billion in charity, consumer, investment and pension frauds; and £6.434 billion in frauds on public bodies such as the National Health Service (Levi and Burrows, 2008). Tax frauds take many different forms, and there are few accurate estimates – HMRC, for example, estimated the 'official' tax gap from non-payment and avoidance at £35 billion in 2013 (Syal, 2013), a figure which, however, was said by the Chair of the Public Accounts Committee to be the 'tip of the iceberg' with large numbers of wealthy individuals having money in tax havens and Swiss bank accounts. Government estimates of the 'corporate tax gap' involving the aforementioned avoidance schemes of Amazon and Google were £4.1 billion for 2010–11, but reliable independent estimates suggest a figure of as much as £12 billion (Farnsworth and Fooks, 2015).

WORKPLACE CRIME

Employees and members of the public are victims of deaths, injuries and ill health associated with a failure to comply with safety regulations in the workplace and both domestically and globally, workers are subject to exploitation by working for wages below the legal minima. A 'new slavery' has been identified, particularly in relation to agriculture, fishing and food, including, in South America, forced labour, punishment beatings and debt bondage in forest clearance and soya plantations (Lawrence, 2008). A recent case involves immigrant labourers, many Nepalese, being treated like slaves in Qatar on building sites for the 2022 football World Cup. So far 'dozens' are said to have died and investigations have revealed evidence of forced labour, the confiscation of passports and the denial of access to free drinking water in desert heat (Pattison, 2013).

Investigations following 'mass' deaths originally attributed to 'accidents' or 'disasters' have revealed many instances of corporate or managerial failings – although prosecutions may not result. These include:

- The 'world's worst' offshore oil disaster in 1988 when the Piper Alpha oil rig exploded killing 167 workers off the coast of Scotland (Ross and Croall, 2010).
- The spate of transport tragedies in Britain including the sinking of the ferry *MS Herald of Free Enterprise* near Zeebrugge in 1987, following a failure to close its bow doors, drowning 192 passengers, and a series of fatal rail crashes subsequently found to have been caused by routine failures to maintain signals or tracks (Slapper and Tombs,1999; Tombs and Whyte, 2007).
- The 'world's worst' industrial disaster in Bhopal, India, in December 1984, where an explosion released a poisonous gas killing over 20,000 and causing at least 200,000 injuries and illnesses (Pearce and Tombs, 1998).

The diffuse impact of workplace crime includes health and welfare costs and, where a company has to close, economic costs to the local community. Moreover, scores of individual workers suffer from deaths, injuries and ill health as outlined in Box 13.3.

CRIMES AGAINST CONSUMERS

The victimisation of consumers particularly illustrates the diffuse impact of offences involving relatively trivial individual losses but considerable gains to corporations. Routine selling and marketing practices systematically aim to deceive consumers about the benefits of goods and services and consumers pay more as a result of anti-competitive practices such as market rigging and price fixing. Consumers can also be killed, injured and made ill by contaminated food and dangerous goods and the use of often undeclared and untested 'chemical cocktails' in products such as cosmetics and food (Croall, 2009a, 2013). Consumer crimes also illustrate the power of the large manufacturers, supermarkets and food producers who dominate food production and other sectors to resist attempts to regulate their activities by, for example, providing fuller information about products and producing healthier products (Croall, 2013). Box 13.5 illustrates some of the crimes associated with the production, sale and marketing of food.

BOX 13.5 VARIETIES OF FOOD CRIME

Croall (2013) has looked at dimensions of crime involving the growing, production, marketing and selling of food, dominated by giant food producers, corporations and supermarkets. Examples include:

What's on the label? Food brands and wine can be easily faked by exchanging labels and revelations of food frauds have included falsely labelled 'free range' or 'organic' foods, 'basmati' rice and 'virgin' olive oil. Supermarkets have been fined for using excess amounts of water in meat products, and a very fine line divides 'fraudulent' or 'deceptive' descriptions from 'legal' but nonetheless misleading ones such as 'natural', and using pictorial images of, for example, farmyards or fruit on packaging for highly-processed foods. Fraud and organised crime were also implicated in the horsemeat 'scandal' of 2013 during which tests revealed up to 100 per cent horsemeat in frozen lasagne and spaghetti bolognese sold by Tesco, Aldi and Findus. Subsequent inquiries revealed a European-wide complex network of food suppliers with one giant firm, ABP, at the centre (Lawrence, 2013).

Unhealthy food: Food adulteration can be lethal, as, for example, in China in 2008, where six babies died and a further 300,000 became ill after consuming milk contaminated with melamine. Food poisoning, such as that involving e-coli 0157, linked to modern agricultural and food production processes and weak regulation, can kill. In 2011, 49 died in France and Germany in an outbreak attributed to Egyptian fenugreek seeds.

Food and exploitation: workers, indigenous populations, non-human animals and the environment are exploited in intensive food production. Agriculture has the highest global toll of occupationally associated deaths, 'sweat shops' have been reported in South Eastern England and food production is also involved in the so-called 'new slavery'(Croall, 2013; Lawrence, 2008). Chicken farms and intensive dairy and other agricultural units have been linked to appalling conditions, and globally, food production contributes to the destruction of rain forests, increasing greenhouse gases and airborne pollution (Lang et al. 2009).

Economic costs: Major food and drink corporations deprive producer countries of income through widespread tax avoidance utilising tax havens. They are also prime beneficiaries of agricultural subsidies, which, favouring crops such as grain and sugar, encourage the proliferation of unhealthy, fatty food (Lang et al., 2009). The notorious 'Buy one get one free' and other marketing practices not only contribute to food waste, but also have been related to the 'bullying' of suppliers by supermarkets who, along with milk companies, have been fined for price-fixing.

Other selective examples of crimes against consumers include:

- *Consumer 'detriment'* (which involves organisations accidentally or deliberately treating consumers unfairly) has been estimated, by a British OFT (2008) survey, to cost around £6.6 billion annually, with around one-third of respondents reporting at least one problem in 12 months. The majority of losses involved less than £5, but 4 per cent involved over £1,000, typically involving telecommunications, domestic fuel, personal banking, insurance and home maintenance. When losses were larger, consumers complained about having to spend personal time dealing with problems along with psychological effects.
- *Price fixing*. Several leading supermarket chains were found to have colluded to increase the retail prices of milk, butter and cheese, which, while involving little cost to individual consumers, involved a total gain of around £116 million (Minkes, 2010).
- *Deceptive marketing practices* such as the use of misleading packaging or failing to provide accurate information. In one recent case Tesco were fined £300,000 for mis-selling strawberries by offering them at 'half price' having only offered them at the 'full price' for seven days – making an excess profit of £2.3 million. Prosecutors argued that the average consumer could be deceived by thinking they were getting a good deal (Neville, 2013).
- *Consumer safety*. There are few reliable figures about how many consumers are harmed by unsafe consumer products, but one UK Government investigation estimated that a sample of unsafe goods, particularly toys and fireworks (Croall, 2010), caused or contributed to 95,000 injuries, 100 fires and 3 deaths per annum. Pharmaceutical products have also been associated with mass harms such as the drug Thalidomide which, marketed long after its dangers were known, affected thousands of babies, and the Dalkon Shield contraceptive, which was responsible for women's deaths, miscarriages and infections across the globe in the 1970s (Finley, 1996).

ENVIRONMENTAL CRIME

Environmental crime provides a good example of how, often indirectly and unknowingly, we are all victims, and green criminology also points to the victimisation of non-human animals (White, 2008; South et al., 2014; Lynch, 2013). Box 13.6 provides examples of pollution, including that associated with nuclear plants and military bases, raising issues about the involvement of government departments and the state.

BOX 13.6 POLLUTION

Pollution involves damage to land, air and water and its often invisible and undetectable impact includes:

- As many as 800,000 premature deaths globally, and at least 24,000 in the UK (Tombs and Whyte, 2010b) where life expectancy was said to be reduced by eight months as a direct result of air pollution (Walters, 2010). Chemical and other forms of air, water, soil and food pollutants may contribute to 'chronic and acute respiratory diseases, developmental diseases, reproductive effects and cancers' (Watterson, 2015: 13). A study of the impact of pollution in one local area, the North West of England (Whyte 2004), reveals that two plants between them annually released around four tons of cancer-causing chemicals, and the global corporation ICI was the worst environmental offender. The Sellafield nuclear reprocessing plant has been linked by Greenpeace with approximately 200 fatal cancers and 1,300 skin cancers (Whyte, 2004).
- The Dounreay nuclear plant in North East of Scotland was alleged to have 'recklessly' released radioactive particles for over 40 years before being convicted in 2007. A total of 250 safety failures were recorded in six years involving the radioactive contamination of whelks, winkles, rabbits, concrete, soil, water and beaches (Walters, 2007).
- The safety of nuclear weapons, some of which are transported in convoys across the country, has also raised many concerns, particularly where the involvement of major defence corporations has decreased the transparency of regulation (Edwards, 2014; Scottish Justice Matters, 2015; Croall, 2015).
- Herbicides and pesticides, widely used in agriculture, have been associated with increased risks of breast cancer among women, birth defects and a variety of diseases (Lynch and Stretesky, 2001).
- Lynch (2013) attempted to compare environmental and criminal victimisation incidents in the US, analysing official figures for air pollution, water pollution and proximity to hazardous waste sites. This revealed that around 90 million US citizens in any one day are exposed to air pollution levels violating federal air quality standards and, when the other offences were added, victimisation was estimated to be a staggering 32 million times more frequent than 'criminal' victimisation, with even this said to be an underestimate.

Other examples include:

- *Mass harms on a global scale*:
  - In the wake of the tsunami in 2005, hundreds of barrels containing radioactive waste disposed of by European companies were found on the shores of Somalia, causing infections, skin diseases and as yet un-measurable cancers (White, 2008) and in 2006, the ship *Probo Koala*, owned by Trafigura, carried toxic waste from

Amsterdam to Abidjan in the Ivory Coast (White, 2008; Amnesty International and Greenpeace Netherlands, 2012). As many as 16 people are said to have died and over 100,000 people sought medical attention. E-waste is 'dumped' on third-world countries with health and environmental dangers (White, 2011; Bisschop, 2015).
  - In less developed countries, individuals' ways of life and livelihoods are threatened by the 'corporate colonization of nature' and biopiracy in which, often in the name of 'development', international corporations and organisations such as the World Bank forcibly remove populations from their land and extract indigenous knowledge and resources for profit (South, 2007; White, 2008).

- *At a local level*: A host of offences such as illegal waste dumping, fly tipping, noise pollution from local businesses, and a general loss of amenities as a result of pollution affect residents. While often dismissed as 'low level', major corporations are involved – major high street chain stores in Glasgow were 'named and shamed' for dumping rubbish (Croall, 2009b). While seemingly trivial, the accumulated effect of these local pollution incidents can have 'modest to devastating changes in people's ... conditions of life' (South, 1998: 44).
- *The victimisation of non-human animals* is seen in the effect of major oil spills and illegal trades in endangered species, ivory, skins and traditional Asian medicines (Schneider, 2008). Intensive agriculture and illegal logging endanger habitats and intensive fishing threatens entire species. Food production involves cruelty to animals as in, for example, battery chicken farms (Croall, 2013), and so called wildlife crime such as the killing birds of prey (Thomson, 2015).

STATE CRIME

The main forms of state crime are outlined in Box 13.2. Agencies also neglect safety and other regulations, and, given the privatisation of many formerly state-owned or controlled industries including the use of private military contractors, *state corporate crime* is of rising concern. War itself can be criminal and criminogenic (Ruggiero, 2010). Box 13.7 illustrates some of the crime and victimisation associated with the Iraq war, widely perceived as an illegal war of aggression (Kramer and Michalowski, 2005).

BOX 13.7 VICTIMISATION AND THE IRAQ WAR

Kramer and Michalowski (2005) argue that the Iraq war can be regarded as a 'war of aggression' on the grounds that it involved clear violations of existing human rights standards and International Humanitarian Law (IHL) and there was significant censure within countries and internationally. Moreover, the US failed to obtain UN Security Council authorisation. Some of the crimes associated with this war include:

(Continued)

(Continued)

- The invasion itself was in breach of IHL, including the Hague and four Geneva conventions concerning failure to protect civilians and non-combatants – in itself a 'war crime'.
- Armed attacks on residential neighbourhoods; arrests and detention without probable cause; torture and abuse of prisoners.
- Routinised corruption, bribery and frauds (Whyte, 2007a). The Coalition Provisional Authority was intended to facilitate economic development for the people of Iraq, but instead firms were taken over, large sums were unaccounted for and Iraqi firms priced out of the market. Lax regulation led to few prosecutions.
- 'Lethal violence' associated with the 'contracting out' of security (Welch, 2009). In Baghdad's 'Bloody Sunday', Blackwater Security, a firm with close links to the Bush regime, fired on a crowd, killing between 8 and 20 civilians.
- The physical abuse, including being kept naked and in cruel positions, suffered by Iraqi detainees in the Abu Ghraib detention centre (Rothe, 2009).
- The death, in 2003, of Baha Mousa in British custody in Iraq. He had 93 separate injuries and was later found to have been subject to techniques of sleep deprivation, hooding and stress positions. At least eight prisoners died in British custody. While seven soldiers were acquitted in a court martial, one was imprisoned having admitted treating prisoners inhumanely – a war crime (Norton-Taylor, 2010a, 2010b, 2010c).

In total, the war involved the deaths of around 4,474 American, 179 British and 139 other coalition soldiers and 'hundreds of thousands' of Iraqi civilians, and economic losses have been estimated at US$100 billion in Baghdad and approximately US$329 for Iraq as a whole (Hagan et al., 2012). In Britain the war was also associated with the 'dodgy dossier', which contained misinformation about the threat posed by Saddam Hussein (Doig, 2010).

State violence is said to be increasing on a global level (Friedrichs, 2010), and Ruggiero (2007) comments that despite the 'civilization' process, the 20th century saw unprecedented state violence, including massacres, genocides and brutalities. These include:

- 11 million deaths, around 6 million of which were Jewish, associated with the holocaust in Germany from 1933–45;
- 100,000 executions associated with the attempt, in Cambodia in 1975–79, by the Khmer Rouge to 'totally restructure society';
- the deaths of 50–100,000 Tutsis in Rwanda in 1994;
- the estimated 200,000 Muslim victims of the 'ethnic cleansing' in Bosnia in 1992–95.

Many more suffer life-changing injuries and disease and the destruction of economic livelihoods, and wars also involve child soldiers, power rapes and other atrocities. Wars and genocide can also lead to environmental harms, the destruction of a country's social and economic fabric, and have a catastrophic effect on individual villages, towns and communities, adversely affecting hospitals, schools, water or electrical systems (Rothe, 2009).

State crime is often seen as happening in 'other' countries, although much has taken place in the UK (Croall, 2011; Doig, 2010), particularly involving the 'troubles' in Northern Ireland, torture during the Iraq war (see Box 13.7) and police corruption. UK cases, often only revealed after several inquiries, have included:

- The high-profile miscarriages of justice during the IRA terror campaign in England, involving the 'Birmingham 6', the 'Guildford 4', Judith Ward, who was accused of involvement in several explosions, and the Maguire 7. In all cases the defendants were subsequently released following appeals which exposed the use of physical and mental pressure, sleep deprivation and persistent questioning, the fabrication of confessions and the withholding of evidence (Punch, 2009).
- In Northern Ireland in 1982, the Royal Ulster Constabulary were involved in undercover 'revenge killings' involving collusion with paramilitaries and obstructing subsequent inquiries (Punch, 2009; Doig, 2010).
- In June 2010, the Savile Inquiry found that British Paratroopers were responsible for the deaths of 13 civil rights marchers in Londonderry in 1972, on 'Bloody Sunday', after a previous inquiry widely perceived as a 'whitewash' (Punch, 2011).
- In 1989, 96 people died in a crush at Hillsborough football stadium. Initially the drunken behavior of fans was 'blamed' but after a lengthy series of inquiries, the deaths were attributed, by an independent panel in 2012, to failings on the part of the South Yorkshire Police, the Hillsborough Football Club and the Local Council. Following a long-running campaign by the families of victims, evidence of tampering with witness statements has also been uncovered, manslaughter charges have been considered (Conn, 2013) and inquests conducted, at one of which the Police Commander in charge on the day has admitted that his actions in not closing a tunnel directly caused the deaths (Conn, 2015). In April 2016, a jury concluded that the fans were unlawfully killed and that the Senior Police officer involved was responsible for manslaughter by gross negligence (http://www.bbc.co.uk/news/uk-england-36138337).

State corporate crime, as outlined in Box 13.2, has also attracted attention, and Box 13.7 illustrates the role of private contractors in Iraq in both economic and violent crimes. The arms industry is particularly criminogenic and arms sales, vital to the economy, can be corruptly linked to overseas aid and breaching international rules covering arms embargoes. The arms corporations British Aerospace (BAE) and Lockheed, for example, were involved in arming the Indonesian occupation of East Timor, which involved mass deaths to the tune of 200,000, backed by governments and in clear breach of the New Labour Government's 'ethical foreign policy' instituted in 1997 (Green and Ward, 2004). BAE has also been involved in a series of cases involving corrupt arms deals in connection with the Tornado and Hawk aircraft, and making false statements to government investigations – with evidence of government interference with investigations (Doig, 2010). To the extent that governments fail to provide resources to implement tougher regulations in relation to health and safety, such as is the case in respect of the involvement of major defence corporations such as Lockheed in the transportation and storage of nuclear weapons (Edwards, 2011; Scottish Justice Matters, 2015), many other corporate crimes can be regarded as state corporate crimes.

THE UNEQUAL IMPACT OF VICTIMISATION

While we are all, directly or indirectly, affected by these offences whose impact is often seen as relatively indiscriminate (Croall, 2009a, 2010), some suffer more than others. Indeed the very phrase 'crimes of the powerful', involving as it does asymmetrical power relationships, is often accompanied by an assumption of the 'rich and powerful' victimising the 'poor and powerless'. The following sections illustrate a more complex picture by exploring the interrelated effects of inequalities of socio-economic status, race, age and gender.

Socio-economic status

The complexity of the relationship between socio-economic status and victimisation can be seen in relation to the many frauds involving investments and savings, which, as they require capital to invest or save, do not victimise the poorest. Irrespective of socio-economic status, all taxpayers are adversely affected by tax evasion, all citizens' health is endangered by pollution and safety crimes, and all citizens of countries laid waste by war crimes experience severe physical, economic and environmental harm.

Nonetheless, it can be argued that lower socio-economic groups are more at risk from many offences and suffer more severely. Tax fraud and evasion redistributes the tax burden away from large corporations elsewhere, including to those on low incomes, and undermines public policies towards, for example, education, health and pensions (Farnsworth and Fooks, 2015). Poorer consumers are more likely to have little choice but to purchase the cheapest and shoddiest consumer goods (Croall, 2009a). Non-unionised and casualised workers are more likely to be seriously and fatally injured at work (Tombs and Whyte, 2007; Whyte, 2007a). Pollution can affect us all, but often affects the most economically disadvantaged groups, neighbourhoods and communities (Tombs and Whyte, 2010b) already suffering from multiple deprivation through, for example, unemployment, low pay and ill health (Watterson, 2015). The lowest paid, often migrant workers, are most likely to be exploited. In contrast, the more affluent, who possess more 'cultural capital', can *avoid* victimisation (Croall, 2010). They have the knowledge and resources to seek legal and financial advice, avoid buying cheap goods or unhealthy foods, move away from polluted neighbourhoods, and escape from countries suffering from wars and conflict. Some of the worst forms of state crime are found in societies characterised by high amounts of poverty, linked to corruption and authoritarianism (Green and Ward, 2004).

Socio-economic status is strongly related to *race and ethnicity*. In respect of environmental crime, for example, more hazardous chemical plants in the US are sited closer to lower-class communities and communities of colour (Pinderhughes, 1996; Lynch et al., 2001). Race and ethnicity are of immense significance in state crime, which can involve 'ethnic cleansing' or genocide (an attempt to eliminate whole groups of the population) very often, as in the Holocaust, defined by race. Police and military violence can reflect discrimination against particular racial or ethnic groups, and the 'othering' or 'creation' of the 'enemy' very often involves racial characteristics. Rothe (2009: 147) argues that 'a central element in atrocity-producing environments is a set of intense ethnic rivalries and tensions.'

Global inequalities

Power asymmetries are particularly evident at the global level, where, in respect of corporate crime, corporations routinely exploit the less stringent financial, taxation, employment, safety, health and environmental regulations of countries who need inward investment (Croall, 2010). Cases of waste 'dumping' effectively involve the transfer of dangers from richer to poorer countries (White, 2008), and to the poorest within those countries. The 'new slavery' most adversely affects those from least-developed nations, as does 'biopiracy' which victimises indigenous populations (South, 2007). Wars, arms deals and other forms of state and state corporate crime are also strongly related to the desire of western nations to maximise profits at the expense of the developing world (Green and Ward, 2004).

Age

Victimisation also reflects age inequalities of domination and dependency. Consumer goods produced and marketed for specific age groups reflect cultural constructions of age, seen particularly in the prominence of pensions and investment frauds directed at the need to maximise financial security in old age. Nonetheless, this is related to socio economic status – despite stereotypes of elderly victims, affluent older people may be able to avoid victimisation (Croall, 2009a). In other offences, the greater physical vulnerability of the very old and young is a factor, as they may suffer more from some forms of food poisoning, pollution and the impact of war crimes. Other examples of age-related victimisation include:

- The sexual and physical abuse of children in care homes and other institutions (Muncie, 2009) and the elderly in institutional 'care' (Croall, 2007).
- Victimisation associated with products and services reflecting social constructions of age – the young, for example, may be more at risk from 'fake' fashion goods or misleading mobile phone contracts and from safety offences in relation to 'risky'

activities or night clubs (Croall, 2009a). A 'fear of ageing' can be used to sell products such as 'anti-wrinkle' creams which don't work or to use pressure-selling techniques for assistive devices and burglar alarms (Croall, 2009a).

- Muncie (2009) argues that a full 'youth victimology' would include many forms of victimisation from crimes of the powerful such as:
    - the use of techniques of physical restraint or solitary confinement in relation to young people in custody; 29 children died in penal institutions in England and Wales between 1990 and 2000, all from the most disadvantaged, damaged and distressed neighbourhoods.
    - global issues such as the exploitation of child labour and child slavery; around 218 million children between 5 and 17 worldwide are estimated to be child labourers, and many global and British-based companies rely on young people working in slavery to produce goods.
    - The impact of war on children and child soldiers.

Muncie's points underline the often concealed nature of youth victimisation, also a problem in relation to the elderly. To Brogden and Nijhar (2006), the victimisation of the elderly is often underplayed with the words 'elder abuse' masking the violence and power involved (see also Chapter 11). They further suggest that 'early deaths' of older people in institutions receive far less attention than other avoidable deaths.

Gender

Gendered power relationships and patriarchal power also affect victimisation and, although women are often seen as particularly vulnerable, it is important to explore the gendered victimisation of men *and* women (see Chapter 9; and Davies, 2007, 2011).

Women's victimisation can be related to products and services which aim to change women's bodies by, for example, controlling reproduction or conforming to dominant images of femininity (Simpson and Elis, 1996). Others are related to cultural stereotypes of the financially or technically less knowledgeable woman. Examples of women's victimisation include:

- 'Mass harms' associated with pharmaceutical products such as the Dalkon Shield contraceptive, silicone breast implants, cosmetic surgery and the use of botox (Croall, 2009a).
- The effects of, often inadequately regulated, 'chemical cocktails' in cosmetic, household and other products and cosmetic surgery (Croall, 2009a).
- Women are more likely to be the targets of frauds, car sales and service frauds and other forms of mis-selling.
- Patriarchal power is further reflected in global state crimes such as rape and sexual slavery arising out of conflicts (Davies, 2011).

Men are also victimised on a gendered basis. For example:

- So called 'man's work' is often 'risky' work, with higher rates of fatalities and injuries in the construction and fishing industries, and a 'macho' culture may act against compliance with safety requirements (Tombs and Whyte, 2007).
- Men can be targeted by fraudsters as they are assumed to be more likely to make high-risk investments.
- As for women, pharmaceutical and cosmetic products are targeted at men – and may be associated with harm.

Victimisation from crimes of the powerful therefore reflects wider social inequalities and it is important to recognise that these are interrelated – while the poor, women or the elderly might be seen as particularly vulnerable, more affluent older women may be less at risk (Croall 2010). Victimisation in the workplace reflects the gendered division of labour, and it is most often the poorest paid, often immigrant, workers who are most affected.

Provide examples of how victimisation from crimes of the powerful reflects a particular dimension of social inequality.

REFLECTIONS AND FUTURE RESEARCH: EXPOSING INVISIBLE VICTIMS

It is evident from what we have discussed that crimes of the powerful involve massive amounts of serious victimisation to which must be added considerable amounts of indirect and secondary victimisation, including:

- The loss of tax revenues and other forms of national income to fraud, corruption and tax evasion and avoidance which reduces resources for public expenditure.
- The 'delegitimation' effect (Shover et al., 1994) as public trust and confidence in major institutions such as banks, corporations, politicians, state agencies and governments is damaged.
- The often lengthy proceedings to establish culpability for major frauds, mass harms, serious environmental or safety 'disasters', and state violence can also be regarded as secondary victimisation as victims, families and survivors face a struggle to have their victimisation recognised and secure compensation. This can exacerbate economic hardship, emotional problems and feelings that justice is not being done.

Much of this victimisation is relatively invisible and is therefore what Walklate (2007) has described as victimisation that 'we cannot see', and exposing these harms has long been a theme in discussions of crimes of the powerful. Revealing further victimisation clearly requires more research, which might include:

- More victim surveys. While there are many problems in using victim surveys, they can be used for the many offences of which victims are aware and some, in particular safety, consumer and environmental offences, *could* be included in crime victim surveys, enabling better comparisons to other forms of crime.
- Local surveys, such as that on Merseyside (Whyte, 2004), could explore the combined effect of different offences at a local level, thus bringing their impact 'home' and demonstrating their importance, along with other crimes, to community safety (Croall, 2009b).
- Greater efforts could be made to establish the net 'costs' of different forms of fraud, tax evasion and avoidance, as is evident for example in the aforementioned work of the House of Commons Public Accounts Committee.

These would all depend on some reconceptualisation of these activities as crimes and there being a greater desire on the part of governments and the public to 'know' more about them. It might also be queried why more resources should be expended. It could be argued that outcomes of a greater exposure could lead to:

- a greater awareness of the crimes of the powerful, which could in turn contribute to greater political and public pressure to 'do something about them';
- a greater recognition of the plight of victims who so often have to struggle to have their victim status and right to compensation recognised.

As McGurrin and Friedrichs (2010) argue, exposing the harms and expanding the conceptualisation of crime victims by constructing harmful activities as 'criminal' can play a part in combating them.

SUMMARY

This chapter has sought to reveal the massive impact of the crimes of the powerful, albeit that it has only been able to provide highly selective examples of its many forms and effects on victims. It suggests that we are all victimised by these crimes more often than by so called 'conventional crimes', and that victimisation reflects wider structural inequalities of age, race, gender, class and global inequalities. Despite this, many remain relatively invisible and not regarded as crime, and there are strong arguments for challenging these perceptions, particularly by more research.

FURTHER READING

There is no main single source covering victimisation from crimes of the powerful but these all offer good introductions to its main forms:

Croall, H. (2009) 'White collar crime, consumers and victimization', *Crime, Law and Social Change*, 51: 127–46.

Croall, H. (2010) 'Economic crime and victimology: a critical appraisal', *International Journal of Victimology*, 8(2). Available at www.jidv.com/njidv/index.php/archives/150-jidv-23/425-economic-crime-and-victimology-a-critical-appraisal (accessed 14.10.16).

Whyte, D. (2007) 'Victims of corporate crime', in S. Walklate (ed.), *Handbook of Victims and Victimology*. Cullompton: Willan.

While not dealing specifically with victimisation, these three books provide good sources for state crime, particularly in the UK:

Doig, A. (2010) *State Crime*. Cullompton: Willan.

Green, P. and Ward, T. (eds) (2004) *State Crime: Governments, Violence and Corruption*. London: Pluto.

Punch, M. (2009) *Police Corruption: Deviance, Accountability and Reform in Policing*. Cullompton: Willan.

South, N. and Brisman, A. (eds) (2013) *International Handbook of Green Criminology*. London: Routledge.

REFERENCES

Amnesty International and Greenpeace Netherlands (2012) *The Toxic Truth: About a Company Called Trafigura, a Ship Called the Probo Koala, and the Dumping of Toxic Waste in Côte d'Ivoire*. London/Amsterdam: Amnesty International and Greenpeace Netherlands.

Bisschop, L. (2015) 'Governing the international trade in hazardous waste', *Scottish Justice Matters*, 3(1): 30–32.

Bowers, S. and Syal, R. (2013) 'MP on Google tax avoidance scheme: 'I think that you do do evil', *Guardian*. Available at www.theguardian.com/technology/2013/may/16/google-told-by-mp-you-do-do-evil (accessed 16.5.13).

Brogden, M. and Nijhar, P. (2006) 'Crime, abuse, and social harm: towards an integrated approach', in A. Wahidin and M. Cain (eds), *Age, Crime and Society*. Cullompton: Willan. pp. 35–52.

Cohen, S. (1996) 'Human rights and crimes of the state: the culture of denial', in J. Muncie, E. McLaughlin and M. Langan (eds), *Criminological Perspectives: Essential Readings*. London: Sage.

Cohen, S. (2001) *States of Denial*. Cambridge: Polity Press.

Conn, D. (2013) 'Hillsborough: police, FA, council and club could face manslaughter charges', *Guardian*, 12 September. Available at www.theguardian.com/football/2013/sep/12/hillsborough-manslaughter-police-fa-council-club (accessed 14.10.16).

Conn, D. (2015) 'Hillsborough: Duckenfield admits not closing tunnel directly caused 96 deaths', *Guardian*, 17 March. Available at www.theguardian.com/uk-news/2015/mar/17/hillsborough-duckenfield-admits-not-closing-tunnel-directly-caused-96-deaths (accessed 14.10.16).

Croall, H. (2007) 'Victims of white collar and corporate crime', in P. Davies, P. Francis and C. Greer (eds), *Victims, Crime and Society*. London: Sage.

Croall, H. (2009a) 'White collar crime, consumers and victimization', *Crime, Law and Social Change*, 51: 127–46.

Croall, H. (2009b) 'Community safety and economic crime', *Criminology and Criminal Justice*, 9(2): 965–85.

Croall, H. (2010) 'Economic crime and victimology: a critical appraisal', *International Journal of Victimology*, 8(2). Available at www.jidv.com/njidv/index.php/archives/150-jidv-23/425-economic-crime-and-victimology-a-critical-appraisal (accessed 14.10.16).

Croall, H. (2011) *Crime and Society in Britain* (2nd edn). Harlow: Pearson.

Croall, H. (2013) 'Food crime: a green criminology perspective', in N. South and A. Brisman (eds), *International Handbook of Green Criminology*. London: Routledge. pp. 167–83.

Croall, H. (2015) 'Crimes of the powerful in Scotland', in H. Croall, G. Mooney and M. Munro (eds), *Crime, Justice and Society in Scotland*. London: Routledge. pp. 131–148.

Davies, P. (2007) 'Lessons from the gender agenda', in S. Walklate (ed.), *Handbook of Victims and Victimology*. Cullompton: Willan. pp. 175–202.

Davies, P. (2011) *Gender, Crime and Victimisation*. London: Sage.

Doig, A. (2010) *State Crime*. Cullompton: Willan.

Edwards, R. (2011) 'Anger as US arms dealer takes over running of Scottish nuclear bomb base', *Sunday Herald*, 29 May. Available at www.heraldscotland.com/news/home-news/anger-as-us-arms-dealer-takes-over-running-of-scottish-nuclear-bomb-base.13864732 (accessed 14.10.16).

Edwards, R. (2014) 'Nuclear bomb convoys travelling across the UK suffer 70 safety lapses', *Sunday Herald*, 3 August, p. 30.

Farnsworth, K. and Fooks, G. (2015) 'Corporate taxation, corporate power and corporate harm', *Howard Journal*, 54(1): 25–41.

Finley, L.M. (1996) 'The pharmaceutical industry and women's reproductive health', in E. Szockyj and J.G. Fox (eds), *Corporate Victimization of Women*. Lebanon, NH: Northeastern University Press.

Friedrichs, D. (2010) 'Toward a prospective criminology of state crime', in W. Chambliss, R. Michalowski and R. Kramer (eds), *State Crime in the Global Age*. Cullompton: Willan. pp. 67–82.

Green, P. and Ward, T. (2000) 'State crime, human rights and the limits of criminology' *Social Justice*, 27:1.

Green, P. and Ward, T. (eds) (2004) *State Crime: Governments, Violence and Corruption*. London: Pluto Press.

Green, P., Ward, T. and McConnachie, K. (2007) 'Logging and legality: environmental crime, civil society, and the state', *Social Justice*, 34(2): 94–110.

Hagan, J., Kaiser J. and Rothenberg, D. (2012) 'Atrocity victimization and the costs of economic conflict crimes in the battle for Baghdad and Iraq', *European Journal of Criminology*, 9(5): 481–98.

Hillyard, P. (2003) 'Imaginative crimes or crimes of the imagination: researching the secret state', in S. Tombs and D. Whyte (eds), *Unmasking the Crimes of the Powerful*. New York: Lang.

Hillyard, P. and Tombs, S. (2004) 'Beyond criminology?', in P. Hillyard, C. Pantazis, S. Tombs and D. Gordon (eds), *Beyond Criminology: Taking Harm Seriously*. London: Pluto Press.

Kramer, R. and Michalowski, R. (2005) 'War aggression and state crime: a criminological analysis of the invasion and occupation of Iraq', *British Journal of Criminology*, 45(4): 446–69.

Lang, T., Barling, D. and Caraher, M. (2009) *Food Policy: Integrating Health, Environment and Society*. Oxford: Oxford University Press.

Lawrence, F. (2008) *Eat Your Heart Out: Why the Food Business is Bad for the Planet and Your Health*. London: Penguin.

Lawrence, F. (2013) 'Horsemeat scandal: the essential guide', *Guardian*, 15 February. Available at www.theguardian.com/uk/2013/feb/15/horsemeat-scandal-the-essential-guide (accessed 17.10.16).

Levi, M. and Burrows, J. (2008) 'Measuring the impact of fraud in the UK: a conceptual and empirical journey', *British Journal of Criminology*, 48(3): 293–318.

Lynch, M. (2013) 'Reflections on green criminology and its boundaries: comparing environmental and criminal victimization and considering crime from an eco-city perspective', in N. South and A. Brisman (eds), *International Handbook of Green Criminology*. London: Routledge. pp. 43–57.

Lynch, M.J. and Stretesky, P. (2001) 'Toxic crimes: examining corporate victimization of the general public employing medical and epidemiological evidence', *Critical Criminology*, 10(3): 153–72.

Lynch, M., Stretesky, P.J. and McGurrin, D. (2001) 'Toxic crimes and environmental justice', in G. Potter (ed.), *Controversies in White Collar Crime*. Cincinnati, OH: Anderson.

McGurrin, D. and Friedrichs, D.O. (2010) 'Victims of economic crime – on a grand scale', *International Journal of Victimology*, 8(2): 147–57.

Minkes, J. (2010) 'Corporate financial crimes', in F. Brookman, M. Maguire, H. Pierpoint and T. Bennett (eds), *Handbook on Crime*. Cullompton: Willan. pp. 653–73.

Muncie, J. (2009) *Youth Crime* (3rd edn). London: Sage.

Nelken, D. (2007) 'White collar crime', in M. Maguire, R. Morgan and R. Reiner (eds), *The Oxford Handbook of Criminology* (3rd edn). Oxford: Oxford University Press.

Neville, S. (2013) 'Tesco "half-price strawberries" deal prompts red faces and £300,000 fine', *Guardian*, 19 August. Available at www.theguardian.com/business/2013/aug/19/tesco-strawberry-deal-fine-birmingham (accessed 14.10.16).

Newburn, T. (2007) *Criminology*. Cullompton: Willan.

Norton-Taylor, R. (2010a) 'Baha Mousa inquiry: eight or more civilians died in British custody', *Guardian*, 16 March. Available at www.guardian.co.uk/world/2010/mar/16/baha-mousa-inquiry (accessed 14.10.16).

Norton-Taylor, R. (2010b) 'Soldiers viewed all Iraqis as "scum", Baha Mousa inquiry hears', *Guardian*, 27 April. Available at www.guardian.co.uk/world/2010/apr/27/baha-mousa-inquiry-soldiers (accessed 14.10.16).

Norton-Taylor, R. (2010c) 'Baha mousa death "a stain on army's character"', *Guardian*, 7 June. Available at www.guardian.co.uk/world/2010/jun/07/baha-mousa-death-stain-army-character (accessed 14.10.16).

Office of Fair Trading (2008) 'Consumer detriment: assessing the frequency and impact of consumer problems with goods and services'. Available at http://webarchive.nationalarchives.gov.uk/20140402142426/http:/www.oft.gov.uk/shared_oft/reports/consumer_protection/oft992.pdf (accessed 17.10.16).

Passas, N. (2005) 'Lawful but awful: "legal corporate crimes"', *Journal of Socio-Economics*, 34: 771–86.

Pattison, P. (2013) 'Revealed: Qatar's World Cup "slaves"', *Guardian*, 25 September. Available at www.theguardian.com/world/2013/sep/25/revealed-qatars-world-cup-slaves (accessed 14.10.16).

Pearce, F. (1976) *Crimes of the Powerful*. London: Pluto Press.

Pearce, F. and Tombs, S. (1998) *Toxic Capitalism: Corporate Crime and the Chemical Industry*. Aldershot: Ashgate.

Pinderhughes, R. (1996) 'The impact of race on environmental quality: an empirical and theoretical discussion', *Sociological Perspectives*, 39(2): 231–48.

Punch, M. (2008) 'The organization did it: individuals, corporations and crime', in J. Minkes and L. Minkes (eds), *Corporate and White Collar Crime*. London: Sage.

Punch, M. (2009) *Police Corruption: Deviance, Accountability and Reform in Policing*. Cullompton: Willan.

Punch, M. (2011) Shoot to Kill: Police Accountability, Firearms and Fatal Force. Bristol: Policy Press.

Ross, J. and Croall, H. (2010) 'Corporate crime in Scotland', in H. Croall, G. Mooney and M. Munro (eds), *Criminal Justice in Scotland*. Cullompton: Willan.

Rothe, D. (2009) *State Criminality: The Crime of All Crimes*. Lanham, MD: Lexington.

Ruggiero, V. (2007) 'War, crime, empire and cosmopolitanism', *Critical Criminology*, 15: 211–21.

Ruggiero, V. (2010) 'Privatising international conflict: war as corporate crime', in W. Chambliss, R. Michalowski and R. Kramer (eds), *State Crime in the Global Age*. Cullompton: Willan. pp. 103–117.

Ruggiero, V. and Welch, M. (2009) 'Power crime', *Crime Law and Social Change*, 51: 297–301.

Schneider, J. (2008) 'Reducing the illicit trade in endangered wildlife: the market reduction approach', *Journal of Contemporary Criminal Justice*, 24(3): 274–95.

Scottish Justice Matters (2015) 'Reporting on environmental crime and justice', *Scottish Justice Matters*, 3(1): 8–10.

Shover, N., Fox, G.L. and Mills, M. (1994) 'Consequences of victimization by white-collar crime', *Justice Quarterly*, 11: 75–98.

Simpson, S.S. and Elis, L. (1996) 'Theoretical perspectives on the corporate victimization of women', in E. Szockyj and J.G. Fox (eds), *Corporate Victimization of Women*. Boston, MA: Northeastern University Press.

Slapper, G. and Tombs, S. (1999) *Corporate Crime*. London: Longmans.

South, N. (1998) 'Corporate and state crimes against the environment: foundations for a green perspective in European criminology', in R. Ruggiero, N. South and I. Taylor (eds), *The New European Criminology: Crime and Social Order in Europe*. London: Routledge.

South, N. (2007) 'The "corporate colonization of nature": bio-prospecting, bio-piracy and the development of green criminology', in P. Beirne and N. South (eds), *Issues in Green Criminology*. Cullompton: Willan. pp. 230–47.

South, N., Brisman, A. and Beirne, P. (2014) 'A guide to a green criminology', in N. South and A. Brisman (eds), *International Handbook of Green Criminology*. London: Routledge. pp. 27–42.

Spalek, B. (2001) 'White-collar crime and secondary victimization: an analysis of the effects of the closure of BCCI', *Howard Journal of Criminal Justice*, 40: 166–79.

Spalek, B. (2007) *Knowledgeable Consumers? Corporate Fraud and Its Devastating Impacts*, Briefing 4. London: Centre for Crime and Justice Studies.

Sutherland, E. (1949) *White Collar Crime*. New York: Holt, Rinehart & Winston.

Syal, R. (2013) 'UK's tax gap rises by £1bn to £35 bn', *Guardian*, 11 October. Available at www.theguardian.com/politics/2013/oct/11/uk-tax-gap-rises-hmrc-avoidance-nonpayment (accessed 14.10.16).

Thomson, I. (2015) 'The illegal killing of birds of prey in Scotland', *Scottish Justice Matters*, 3(1): 19–21.

Tombs, S. (2000) 'Official statistics and hidden crimes: researching health and safety crimes', in V. Jupp, P. Davies and P. Francis (eds), *Doing Criminological Research*. London: Sage. pp. 64–81.

Tombs, S. (2010) 'Corporate violence and harm', in F. Brookman, M. Maguire, H. Pierpoint and T. Bennett (eds), *Handbook on Crime*. Cullompton: Willan.

Tombs, S. and Whyte, D. (2007) *Safety Crime*. Cullompton: Willan.

Tombs, S. and Whyte, D. (2010a) 'Reflections upon the limits of a concept: "victims" and corporate crime', *International Journal of Victimology*, 8: 184–99.

Tombs, S. and Whyte, D. (2010b) 'Crime, harm, and corporate power', in J. Muncie, D. Talbot and R. Walters (eds), *Crime: Local and Global*. Cullompton: Willan.

Tombs, S. and Whyte, D. (2015) 'Introduction to the Special Issue on "Crimes of the powerful"', *Howard Journal*, 54(1): 1–7.

Walklate, S. (2007) *Imagining the Victim of Crime*. Maidenhead: McGraw Hill/Open University Press.

Walters, R. (2007) 'Crime, regulation and radioactive waste in the United Kingdom', in P. Beirne and N. South (eds), *Issues in Green Criminology*. Cullompton: Willan. pp. 186–205.

Walters, R. (2010) 'Environmental crime', in H. Croall, G. Mooney and M. Munro (eds), *Crime and Criminal Justice in Scotland*. Cullompton: Willan. pp. 152–74.

Watterson, A. (2015) 'Pollution, "crime" and ill health impacts', *Scottish Justice Matters*, 3(1): 12–14.

Welch, M. (2009) 'Fragmented power and state-corporate killings: a critique of Blackwater in Iraq', *Crime, Law and Social Change*, 51: 351–64.

Which? (2004) 'Products recalls: a burning issue', *Which? Online*, March.

White, R. (2008) *Crimes Against Nature: Environmental Criminology and Ecological Justice*. Cullompton: Willan.

White, R. (2011) *Transnational Environmental Crime: Toward an Eco-global Criminology*. London: Routledge.

Whyte, D. (2004) 'All that glitters isn't gold: environmental crimes and the production of local criminological knowledge', *Crime Prevention and Community Safety*, 6(1): 53–63.

Whyte, D. (2007a) 'Victims of corporate crime', in S. Walklate (ed.), *Handbook of Victims and Victimology*. Cullompton: Willan.

Whyte, D. (2007b) 'The crimes of neo-liberal rule in occupied Iraq', *British Journal of Criminology*, 47(2): 177–95.

Whyte, D. (ed.) (2009) *Crimes of the Powerful: A Reader*. Maidenhead: Open University Press.

GLOSSARY

Administrative criminology refers to a group of criminological perspectives of the late 1970s and early 1980s onwards in the US and England and Wales which abandoned the search for the causes of crime in favour of the simpler task of prevention and regulation through deterrence and security measures. 'Administrative criminology' is often used as an umbrella term to capture the work of lifestyle theorists, routine activity theorists and rational choice theorists.

Adversarial criminal justice an adversarial system of justice refers to a legal system characterised by a trial where the prosecution and defence are in opposition to one another in the search for justice. An adversarial system is a feature of countries that follow the common law. See also **inquisitorial criminal justice.**

Attrition the process whereby cases and complainants 'drop out' of the legal process due to barriers and filtering mechanisms in the legal system from the initial report to the police to prosecution.

Backlash a reaction against a socio-cultural or political shift.

Bio-politics the regulation of subjects at the level of population – through risk management, public health initiatives and so on – that also influences the actions and activities of individuals. The term was popularised by Michael Foucault.

Black and Minority Ethnic (BME) refers to a person or group whose self-defined ethnicity is not 'White British'.

Bow Street Runners Magistrate Henry Fielding of Bow Street Court established a small force of six men in 1749. They were funded through the courts, but also took fees for private work detecting and bringing thieves to justice, for example. They were disbanded in 1839, ten years after the Metropolitan Police Force had been founded in London.

British Crime Survey see under **Crime Survey for England and Wales.**

Caregiver burden a broad term used in particular in healthcare and gerontology fields describing negative changes in a person's physical, psychological or social state as a result of caring for another person.

Central Criminal Court more popularly known as 'The Old Bailey', the court was originally built to deal with cases from London and Middlesex, but in 1834 it was renamed the Central Criminal Court and assumed responsibility for trying some of the most serious crimes committed anywhere in the country. It still has that role today.

Compounding this was a way of bypassing legal systems, whereby the 'offender' offered to recompense the 'victim' in financial terms for the harm that had been done. This was very common before the establishment of local lower-court systems. In magistrates' courts, the practice largely died out in the mid- to late-19th century.

Conservative criminology refers to a group of criminological perspectives whose core assumptions suggest that the causes of crime lie in an individuals' biosocial, physiological and psychological makeup, and that deterrence, incapacitation and intervention targeted at the individual are the best mechanisms through which crime and victimisation may be reduced, control and/or mitigated.

Contagious Diseases Acts due to fears about the spread of venereal disease through the armed forces, these acts were introduced from the 1860s to force women (prostitutes in the main) to have compulsory health checks, and be imprisoned in 'lock hospitals' until the disease was cured (or controlled at least). They subjected poor women to high levels of social control when they were in public spaces, and were repealed after vigorous lobbying by feminist/suffragette activists.

Crime science is a recent development in environmental criminology. There is no standard definition. Crime science is attributed to Nick Ross's creation of the Jill Dando Institute of Crime Science at UCL in 2001. It sits comfortably with victimologies of lifestyle, routine activities and rational choice perspectives. It draws upon a much wider and broader range of disciplines than many of these orthodox victimological perspectives, in an attempt to provide a holistic multi-disciplinary approach to crime reduction.

Crime Survey for England and Wales (CSEW) first compiled in 1982 under the name of the British Crime Survey. The new name took effect from the 2011/12 sweep onwards. It is a household survey which asks a representative sample of the population aged 16 and over about their experiences of crime in the last 12 months. From the 2011/12 sweep the survey has also interviewed children aged 10–15.

Criminalisation the social and legal processes by which a behaviour, individual or group is labelled as criminal.

Critical criminology/victimology an approach to the study of criminology/victimology which examines deficiencies and closures in existing theories and concepts, and which highlights the social origins of crime and its control. Critical victimology specifically is mostly associated with the work of Mawby and Walklate (1994, *Critical Victimology: International Perspectives*, SAGE) and draws upon critical social realism theory and some radical and feminist thinking to capture and understand the processes that go on behind our backs which can contribute to the victimisation that we experience.

Crown Prosecution Service (CPS) the state-funded agency established in 1985 (and operating from 1986) to carry out prosecutions deemed to be in the public interest.

Dark figure (of crime) unreported and unrecorded crime is often referred to by criminologists as the 'dark figure of crime'.

Deserving/undeserving victim terms use to designate the extent to which victims can or cannot be held responsible for what has happened to them.

Diffuse victimisation a type of victimisation that affects many people/vast areas. Examples include serious financial frauds, corporate and environmental forms of victimisation.

Elder Justice used variably in political and legal contexts, but defined in s.2011 the US Elder Just Act 2009 as 'from a societal perspective, efforts to (i) prevent, detect, treat, intervene in, and prosecute elder abuse, neglect, and exploitation; and (ii) protect elders with diminished capacity while maximizing their autonomy; and (B) from an individual perspective, the recognition of an elder's rights, including the right to be free of abuse, neglect, and exploitation.'

Ethnic group an ethnic group shares certain characteristics on the basis of common historical origin, close-knit patterns of interaction, and a sense of common identity. Members of an ethnic group are individuals who consider themselves, or are considered by others, to share common characteristics that differentiate them from other groups, and from which they develop their distinctive cultural behaviour such as religion, language, or politics. Members of an ethnic group may be identifiable in terms of racial attributes (Scott and Marshall, 2005, *Dictionary of Sociology*, Oxford University Press).

Ethnography a qualitative research methodology concerned with studying subjects within their own natural environment, frequently involving detailed observation and in-depth interviews, geared toward developing an appreciation and understanding of the social world as seen through the eyes of the researched population.

Extra-familial abuse the sexual abuse of children by perpetrators outside the family.

Feminism is concerned with advocating the claims of women and with bringing a woman-centred or feminist perspective to analyses.

Feminist victimology is concerned with advocating the claims of women and with bringing a woman-centred or feminist perspective to analyses to the study of victims and victimisation.

Gender-sensitive responses to victimisation measures or responses that meet victim's needs as gendered beings. Gender-relevant or gender-appropriate interventions.

General strain theory developed by the American criminologists Robert Agnew in response to the growing criticisms of older notions of 'strain' as a predictor and explanation for criminality, mainly espoused by Robert Merton in the late 1930s and early 1940s.

Agnew's general strain theory expands upon the factors that cause strain, and therefore crime. Key to Agnew's thought is that such factors are more than just financial and include failure to achieve positively valued stimuli, the loss of positively valued stimuli and the presentation of negative stimuli. The negative experiences of any of these, including mere emotional distress, can for Agnew result in criminality.

Geographic information systems (GIS) essentially a combination of hardware and software through which spatial relationships are identified following the capture, collation and analysis of a range of relevant data from different sources (e.g. police, crime surveys, business, A&E etc.) and presented, often in conjunction with grid-referenced crime data.

GLBTI Gay, lesbian, bisexual, transgender and intersex; 'queer' is a non-specific but similarly broad and inclusive term referring to an open and potentially shifting range of non-normative sexual identities stigmatised as inferior to procreative heterosexuality.

Hierarchy of victimisation describes a pecking order of sorts, representing the differential status of particular types and categories of crime victim in media and official discourses, including ideal victims (e.g. some child murder victims) at the top of the hierarchy, and non-deserving victims (e.g. youths injured in a drunken fight) near the bottom.

Ideal type Weber's term for an abstract statement or model of the essential characteristics of any social phenomenon.

Ideal victim A term coined by Christie (1986, 'The ideal victim', in E. Fattah (ed.), *From Crime Policy to Victim Policy*, Macmillan) to capture the key characteristics that make some people more readily recognised as victims. These characteristics draw particular attention to presumptions of weakness and innocence. Ideal victims are those persons or category of individual who, when hit by crime, most readily are given the complete and legitimate status of being a victim, including those who are perceived as vulnerable, defenceless, innocent and worthy of sympathy and compassion.

Immanent critique central to critical social science and theorising, with Hegelian and Marxist roots, it is a methodology aimed at identifying and understanding societies contradictions (historical and contemporary) in order to drive social and political change and transformation.

Indirect victimisation the impact that crime has on those people close to a primary victim such as friends, family and (sometimes) the wider community. Increasingly victimologists have examined the full impact of crime and criminal proceedings on these types of victims, with particular attention focused on the survivors of homicide. It is also used to refer to the more vicarious experience of victimisation when exposed to media coverage of traumatic events.

Inquisitorial criminal justice an inquisitorial system of justice refers to a legal system characterised by a trial where the method for exposing evidence in court is to discover the facts in the search for justice. An inquisitorial system is a typical feature in countries that base their legal systems on civil or Roman law.

Institutional racism defined by Macpherson (1999, *The Stephen Lawrence Inquiry*: 28 Para, 6.34, HMSO) as 'The collective failure of an organisation [such as the police] to provide an appropriate and professional service to people because of their colour, culture, or ethnic origin. It can be seen or detected in processes, attitudes and behaviour which amount to discrimination through unwitting prejudice, ignorance, thoughtlessness and racist stereotyping which disadvantage minority ethnic people.'

Islamophobia prejudice against, hatred towards, irrational fear of, or racism towards Muslims. In 1997, the British Runnymede Trust defined Islamophobia as the 'dread or hatred of Islam and therefore, [the] fear and dislike of all Muslims,' and the practice of discriminating against Muslims by excluding them from the economic, social, and public life of the nation. The implication of such opinions is that Islam has no values in common with other cultures, is inferior to the West, and is a violent political ideology rather than a religion (see Quraishi, 2005, *Muslims and Crime*, Ashgate).

Lifestyle theory developed by Hindelang et al. (1978, *Victims of Personal Crime*, Ballinger), lifestyle theory suggest that the risk and actual nature of victimisation is attributed to an an individual's lifestyle and their level of exposure to high-risk situations. In part this is a consequence of their structural position and their daily routines through work, leisure and play.

Multiculturalism or a multi-cultural society as in the case of the US and post-war Britain, is characterised by cultural pluralism. As an ideal, multi-culturalism celebrates cultural variety (e.g. linguistic and religious diversity), and may be contrasted with the 'assimilationist' ideal in which a cultural, immigrant or ethnic group becomes indistinguishably integrated into the host society (Scott and Marshall, 2005, *Dictionary of Sociology*, Oxford University Press).

New Police after the Metropolitan Police came into being in London in 1829, new borough forces were established across the country from 1835. The 'new police' were publically funded and uniformed, and for the first time established a preventative rather than reactive police agency. Derided and feared by many sections of the working classes, by the 20th century they had become the default agency dealing with the detection, arrest and prosecution of offenders.

News values those criteria that influence, often implicitly, the selection, production and prioritisation of events as news. Key news values include drama and action, immediacy, violence, celebrities and sex.

Normalisation refers to the process of making normal, to make conforming, to be so common a practice that it appears normal, such as in the normalisation of drug use.

Orthodox victimology is an umbrella term that captures the range of traditional or conventional victimological perspectives including positivist victimology, conservative victimology and liberal victimology, most associated with lifestyle, routine activity and rational choice approaches to understanding crime and victimisation.

Patriarchy a form of social order in which power and status differentially accrues to males at the expense of females.

Positivist victimology has roots in the mid-20th century positivist social science and is today recognisable through perspectives that focus on conventional crime types, analysis of the regular patterning and ordering of victimisation, public forms of victimisation, and assessment of victim's contribution to their own victimisation.

Primary victimisation used to refer to the direct impact that crime has on an individual.

Primary victims those who experience harm directly.

Procedural justice refers to the idea of fairness in the processes for achieving justice. Theorists such as Tom Tyler have argued that victims of crime often value procedural justice over the perception that the justice system has reached the 'correct' result instrumentally.

Race 'race' is sometimes placed in inverted commas to indicate that this way of categorising individuals and population groups is not based on any biologically valid distinctions between the genetic make-up of differently identified 'races'. Neither do phenotypically different physical looks correlate with genotypical differences (in genetic make-up). Therefore the causes and consequences of the socially constructed division of social groups according to their so-called race becomes the focus for proper study (Scott and Marshall, 2005, *Dictionary of Sociology*, Oxford University Press).

Racially/religiously aggravated an offence is racially/religiously aggravated if: a) at the time of committing the offence or immediately before or after doing so, the offender demonstrates towards the victim of the offence hostility based on the victim's membership (or presumed membership) of a racial or religious group; b) the offence is motivated (wholly or partly) by hostility towards members of a racial or religious group based on their membership of that group; c) 'Membership', in relation to a racial or religious group, includes association with members of that group. 'Presumed' means presumed by the offender.

Racist incident an 'incident which is perceived to be racist by the victim or any other person' (Macpherson, 1999, *The Stephen Lawrence Inquiry*, HMSO).

Radical criminology/victimology arising from the National Deviancy Conference of the 1960s, radical criminology/victimology draws upon Marxist, socialist and feminist thinking to explore the social construction of victimhood and victimisation through the lens of power, politics and representation. It is concerned with unearthing and exposing the voices of those often marginalised and excluded from mainstream victim narratives, such as victims of state crime.

Repeat victimisation refers to the patterning of criminal victimisation indicating that a small percentage of victims suffer from the majority of crime committed.

Restitution used in connection with community sanctions and refers to the notion of paying something back to the victim or the community.

Restorative justice a form of justice that concentrates on repairing the harm caused by criminal behaviour.

Revictimisation occurs when people are literally or metaphorically victimised again. Typically, someone who has suffered criminal victimisation suffers another similar incident (but this is more commonly called 'repeat victimisation'). Metaphorically, it refers to events or attitudes which make the victim feel as though they are undergoing another victimisation. See also **secondary victimisation.**

Revisionist perspectives in victimology Revisionism has a dual meaning in relation to revisionist victimology. First, it is used to refer to its revision of orthodox thinking about victims and victimisation. Second, it refers to the influence of radical, feminist and critical social science thinking in victimology.

Risk society a concept usually associated with the German sociologist Ulrich Beck that describes modern society as being predominantly concerned with the management of risk. The notion has been highly influential in criminological writings as a means of understanding how societies and criminal justice systems respond to (managing the risk of) crime, offending behaviours and reoffending behaviours as well as the risk of criminal (and broader) victimisations.

Routine activities theory developed by Lawrence Cohen and Marcus Felson, which turned attention away from more sociological causes of crime (poverty, relative deprivation etc.) and examines how social and economic conditions bring together the three elements needed for a crime to occur, which it holds as: a motivated offender with criminal intentions and the ability to act on these inclinations; a suitable victim or target; and the absence of a capable guardian who can prevent the crime from happening. These three elements must converge in time and space for a crime to occur.

Secondary victimisation used to refer to the harm (often emotional and/or psychological) caused to victims by the criminal justice system as a direct result of their participation in the Criminal Justice System. The concept has been particularly highlighted in relation to victims of rape and other sexual offences given the history of many adversarial criminal justice systems of defence lawyers using aggressive questioning in order to expose untruths in a victim's testimony and/or to call into question the victim's lack of consent to sex by reference to past sexual behaviours.

Sensationalist reporting from the 1870s, a new trend in sensational reporting spread across the British media. The so-called 'Yellow Press' gave lurid descriptions of crime, amongst other things, and can be identified as the main reason why some crimes (such as the 1888 Whitechapel murders, or crimes involving women and children) became notorious.

Sexual violence is a term used to signify any bodily harms or violation that have a sexual component and that may (or may not) be recognised in law or statute. Sexual violence is therefore a broader term than that of sexual offences.

Signal crimes a term coined by Martin Innes which refers to those particularly serious or high-profile crimes which impact not only on the immediate participants (victims, offenders, witnesses) but also on wider society, resulting in some reconfiguration of behaviours or beliefs (Innes, 2003, 'Signal crimes', in P. Mason (ed.), *Criminal Visions: Representations of Crime and Justice*, Willan).

Sub-legal non-illegal. A loophole in the law.

Survivor usually associated with the feminist movement as a way of capturing women's practices of resistance to their structural powerlessness. Feminists have long argued that the label 'victim' is itself disempowering and passive.

Tertiary victimisation this includes a wider circle of 'victims' who may have been affected by a particularly shocking event. For example, the rescue and medical personnel involved in some kind of traumatic incident (Spalek, 2006: 12, *Crime Victims Theory Policy and Practice*, Palgrave).

Trial by Media 'a market-driven form of populist justice in which individuals and institutions are accused, prosecuted, judged, sentenced and permanently stigmatised in the "court of public opinion"' (see Greer and McLaughlin, 2011 *Theoretical Criminology*, 15(1): 23–46; 2012 *Theoretical Criminology*, 16(4): 395–416; 2016 *Theoretical Criminology*, doi: 10.1177/1362480616645648.).

Unofficial victim movement victim action and support groups who campaign for a number of different issues including greater recognition as victims with specific needs arising from harms experienced.

Victim the label 'victim' is contingent, complex and dynamic. Rock (2002, 'On becoming a victim', *New Visions of Crime Victims*, Hart) suggests 'victim' is an identity and a social artefact that is constructed by different actors in different contexts. It is usually now associated with crime but also relates to someone suffering some kind of misfortune.

Victim blaming an emotively charged term closely associated with the phrase **victim-proneness** – this can result from attempts to understand how people become victims of crime. Early writers about victims created a tradition of victim blaming by putting the victims of particular types of crime into a variety of categories, partly according to how blameworthy they appeared to be. They focused on the individual victim's conduct and the victim's relationship with the offender (see e.g. the work of von Hentig and Mendelsohn).

Victim culpability closely associated with the concept of **victim precipitation**, victim culpability refers to the extent to which the victim can be held to be responsible for what has happened to them.

Victim focused in the policy context this refers to putting the victim 'centre-stage'. Sometimes policies claim to be victim-oriented rather than offender – or the smooth-running of the criminal justice system – focused. A real victim focus does not amount to political gimmicks aimed at wooing voters which are not necessarily in victims' interests, even if they are publicised as such.

Victim impact statement or victim personal statement is a written statement by a victim of crime to the courts and other criminal justice agencies. It can be a proforma or free-form victim-information statement where victims are invited to formally detail what physical, financial, psychological, social or emotional effects the offence had on them and the wider impact of the crime, including upon their family.

Victim lifestyle this refers to the connection and correlation between an individual's experience and risk of victimisation and their routine patterns of daily activities – thus their lifestyle (including vocational activities such as work, school and housework) and leisure and cultural activities.

Victim movement similar to the **unofficial victim movement** in its aspirations to support victims. The victim movement includes a range of well-known voluntary bodies and charities who engage in campaigns for a number of different issues including greater recognition of victims with specific needs.

Victim oriented see **victim focused.**

Victim perspectives refers to different ways of viewing the victim of crime. Sometimes called 'theoretical perspectives', these approaches differ as to how they approach the study of the victim of crime including who counts as a victim, how research is conducted and how policies might be developed. The main three are: positivist perspectives, radical perspectives and critical perspectives.

Victim precipitation closely associated with the concept of **victim culpability**, this concept draws attention to what it was that the victim did that resulted in their victimisation.

Victim proneness the notion that there are some people, by virtue of their structural characteristics, who are much more likely to be victims of crime than other people. It is a small step from victim proneness to victim blaming.

Victim provocation see **victim precipitation.**

Victim Support (VS) in the England and Wales context, this refers to a large number of locally based Victim Support schemes that operate according to the same guidelines and common principles as laid down nationally. The schemes provide sympathetic advice and support as well as practical assistance for victims. It is also a strong campaigning and lobbying group.

Victim typologies used in connection with the early scholars of the subject of victimology who were interested in victim–offender relationships and the extent to which victims of crime contributed to crime and their own victimisation. The classification schemes they devised are referred to as victim typologies and help show what different types of victims have in common and how they differ from others.

Victim/crime survey originally referred to as a crime survey but more latterly referred to as a victim survey – these terms are often used interchangeably. Such surveys are specifically designed to collect data about the incidence, patterning and experiences of victimisation. They typically take a representative sample from a general population and use structured interviews to gather information on individuals' experiences of a wide range of victimisation over a given period of time whether or not they reported it to the police and if not, why not. They therefore go some way to uncovering the so-called 'dark figure' of unreported or unrecorded crime.

Victimage can be distinguished from victimhood or victimisation in that it connotes the construction or identification of external threats that position the subject as victim or potential victim.

Victimhood the cultural assignation of the status of victim. See also **victim.**

Victimological other a phrase used to refer to the way in which victimology makes some groups of people more likely to be included as victims rather than others.

Victimology for some a sub-discipline of criminology, whilst for others a discipline it its own right, it has been referred to as an ugly neologism used as a general descriptor for the study of criminal victimisation, the advent of victim support mechanisms, the role of victims in the criminal justice system and the concept of victim rights. It is also concerned with exploring the causes, nature, extent and impact of victimisation in society and the dynamics of relationships between victims, offenders and the special and social structural environments in which they occur.

Victims' rights a term used in relation to the policy agenda for victims of crime. Some views of victims' rights are more like intentional commitments whilst others view victims' rights in a more legal manner.

Victim-witness the person who directly experienced the victimisation as a direct result of the crime. See also **witness.**

Violent racism is a phrase used by Bowling (1999: 13, *Violent Racism*, Clarendon Press) to describe 'racism in its various forms, especially its violent form' and 'as a form of racism rather than a form of violence'.

Visualisation of crime news the increasing prevalence and importance of visual representations of crime news, crime victims and criminal victimisation in the digital age, generally to enhance the immediate accessibility, human interest and overall communicative impact of the news product on media consumers.

Vulnerable victim the relationship between the risk from crime as compared with the harm done by crime. Policies often make the assumption that some people are by definition vulnerable (like children, the elderly, or people with mental health problems), though real-life experience might challenge such assumptions.

Vulnerable witness a witness who is entitled to 'special measures' as are intimidated witnesses. All child witnesses are defined as vulnerable, and in practice the special measures also apply to victims of sexual and violent offences and witnesses with a range of special needs. See also **vulnerable victim.**

White-collar crime originally defined by Edwin Sutherland in 1939 as 'a crime committed by a person of respectability and high social status in the course of his occupation' (*White Collar Crime*, Holt, Rinehart & Winston). It is often understood in terms of the type of crime involved (generally financial crime, fraud, economic and corporate crime) and/or the characteristics of the offender (generally offenders with a high socio-economic status, company managers, politicians and so on).

Witness a witness to crime is a person who might report a crime to the police or tell the police about what they know. They may stand up in court to state what they know about the crime after taking an oath to tell the truth.

Witness care/service/support witness support is usually provided by Victim Support volunteers in the courts. **Witness care units** provide a single point of contact for victims and witnesses, minimising the stress of attending court and keeping victims and witnesses up-to-date with any developments.

Zemiology the study of social harms which are not caused by activities officially labelled as criminal but can bring similar consequences for victims.

INDEX